The

Tuning In
The Great Gildersleeve

THE EPISODES AND CAST OF RADIO'S FIRST SPINOFF SHOW, 1941–1957

Clair Schulz

McFarland & Company, Inc., Publishers
Jefferson, North Carolina, and London

ISBN 978-0-7864-7336-6
softcover : acid free paper ∞

LIBRARY OF CONGRESS CATALOGUING DATA ARE AVAILABLE

BRITISH LIBRARY CATALOGUING DATA ARE AVAILABLE

Front cover photograph: *left to right* Walter Tetley as nephew Leroy
Forester, Harold Peary as Throckmorton Philharmonic Gildersleeve
and Louise Erickson as niece Marjorie Forester (author's collection);
radio tower (iStockphoto/Thinkstock)

Manufactured in the United States of America

*McFarland & Company, Inc., Publishers
Box 611, Jefferson, North Carolina 28640
www.mcfarlandpub.com*

Table of Contents

Preface

This book is a guide to one of radio's most enduring and best loved shows, *The Great Gildersleeve*, the medium's first major spinoff, a comedy that lasted from 1941 to 1957. Throckmorton P. Gildersleeve's short trip away from Wistful Vista and his friends Fibber McGee and Molly to look after the affairs of his niece and nephew in Summerfield turned into a home there and on radio receivers throughout the country.

Neither of the previous books on the subject, *The Great Gildersleeve* and *Gildy's Scrapbook*, surveyed the series in a format that allows readers to observe character progression, cast changes, and program development in a systematic fashion. The first unfolded the story of the program in a narrative style as if retelling the life of Gildersleeve before devoting the remaining 65 percent of its pages mainly to photographs and cast biographies. The 72-page *Scrapbook* is just what the name implies: photos, magazine clippings, and letters that capture moments in time but provide little insight into what made the product of those human efforts so special.

This study of *The Great Gildersleeve* examines the groundbreaking show from beginning to end by lighting the path ahead so each step along the way can be seen more distinctly. The episode entries, appearing in chronological order by broadcast date, are meant to be used by listeners to enrich their appreciation of the writers and performers. For decades fans of the show have been frustrated because recordings of numerous episodes, particularly those from 1942 to 1945, have not survived (e.g., only 26 of the 44 episodes aired during the 1943–1944 season are in circulation). No description of a Gildy escapade can deliver as much pleasure as hearing the frolic unfold in the show, but at least the mystery as to what happened on those silent nights is now over. Information for these broadcasts marked (Script) came from researching the microfilmed scripts of episodes for the years 1942–1954 at the Wisconsin State Historical Society Library.

Five appendices follow the episode guide. Appendix A contains short career overviews of the principal actors and actresses who had continuing roles in the radio series. Appendix B provides cast lists and brief summaries of the four Gildersleeve films released from 1942 to 1944 and the 39 episodes of the short-lived TV series from 1955 to 1956. To assist readers and listeners who may want to locate a particular show, Appendix C provides an alphabetical list of the radio episode titles. Appendix D is a list of first appearances by major cast members or characters and other notable occurrences. Appendix E summarizes the ratings and rankings of *The Great Gildersleeve* from 1941 to 1956.

Though never a ratings powerhouse like *The Bob Hope Show* or *The Jack Benny Program*, *The Great Gildersleeve* has staying power because of its enduring characters. The borders of Summerfield extend right to our front yard and the door of Gildy's house swings open at the right spot on our radio dial. Let's go in right now.

Introduction

The character of Throckmorton Philharmonic Gildersleeve, created by writer Don Quinn for *Fibber McGee and Molly*, was brought to life by Harold Peary. Peary, who had been assuming various characters on the program since 1937, stepped into the role for the first time on October 3, 1939. He became a sparring partner for Fibber nearly every week as the two traded insults; Peary's best parry was the adamant declaration that became his catch phrase: "You're a harrrrd man, McGee!" Quinn, who knew he had an ace in the hole with this volatile windbag who lived next door to the McGees, often saved Peary for the third act to set off the funny fireworks that closed the show with a bang.

By 1941 this larger-than-life character had outgrown the boundaries of Wistful Vista. On May 16 an audition of a new show starring Peary, sponsored by Johnson's Wax and written by Leonard Levinson, who had been assisting Quinn on scripts, was performed with the hope that it might become the summer replacement for *Fibber McGee and Molly*. Although Johnson's Wax decided to go with *Hap Hazard* starring Ransom Sherman that summer, Kraft bought the concept of Gildersleeve starting a new life in Summerfield as guardian of his nephew and niece, Leroy and Marjorie Forrester. On August 31, 1941, a new series, *The Great Gildersleeve*, radio's first spinoff, premiered. On that hot August night few listeners would have predicted that the program would outlast virtually every comedy show on the air.

Through all the years *The Great Gildersleeve* aired, everyone benefited from the program's consistency, built around Gildersleeve, Marjorie, and Leroy holding fast to the bedrock of NBC. From August 31, 1941, through June 9, 1946, the 30-minute show was heard on Sundays at 6:30 Eastern. It then moved to Wednesdays at 8:30 through June 2, 1954, when the Kraft sponsorship ended. A Sunday through Thursday 15-minute format with no studio audience, much like that of *Fibber McGee and Molly*, was tried from September 26, 1954, to June 27, 1955, airing at 10:15, right after Fibber and Molly closed the door at 79 Wistful Vista. Two shortened seasons of Thursday episodes with small casts followed: October 20, 1955, to March 29, 1956, at 8:00 or 8:05, and October 11, 1956, to March 14, 1957, at 8:00 or 8:35.

Regarding the handful of post–1954 recordings that exist, the quality of both the audio and the scripts can charitably be described as "less than great." The same three-word evaluation could have been applied to the hero of the program from first episode to last. One of the true ironies of *The Great Gildersleeve* is that the main character was a very flawed human being, about as far from great as the Great Barrier Reef is from Grass Lake. Besides being a washout as a water commissioner who was indolent, capricious, meddlesome, arbitrary, gullible, and argumentative, he also could be aptly described as a procrastinator, hypocritical malingerer, four-flusher, philanderer, and perpetual blunderer.

Somehow that combination of imperfections got rolled up into a portly package of moonstruck bungler with good intentions who managed to win everyone over. Eve Goodwin, one of his many sweethearts, told him on November 20, 1946, "I like you because you're human." The next year on October 8 girlfriend Ann Tuttle explained that it was his imperfections, including his clumsiness, that made him human and humane. On Christmas Eve in 1946 Eve spoke the unvarnished truth when she remarked, "You're the strangest combination of people." Leroy put it more bluntly when observing his uncle's contradictory behavior: "What a character!"

Peary knew that character, not complications, formed the heart of the program because he pointedly shunned the term "situation comedy" in favor of "character comedy." In *There's Laughter in the Air!* he attributed the success of the Gildersleeve character "to the fact that Gildy is a familiar person. There is one, if not in every family, at least one in every block. The familiar blowhard, an earnest, sincere man who fumbles a great deal in his enthusiasm to get ahead. Gildy realizes his errors, but is constantly trying. He's an 'average American.'"

The writers gave that average American plenty of above average unpredictability to keep millions of listeners laughing every week. A good five-minute sketch of Throckmorton was drawn on March 11, 1945, when he began the day at the office determined to clear his desk of old business, became disheartened after his secretary Bessie showed him a stack of unanswered correspondence, reverted to slacker form and impulsively wanted to dance with her instead of work, and then, after leaving city hall, rammed his car into another vehicle, excusing his erratic behavior with "You saw I was backing!"

On February 4, 1948, a tremulous Throcky grimly trudged to Mayor Terwilliger's office, fearing that his constant dilly-dallying was going to get him fired, then became so overjoyed after learning that he had been appointed temporary mayor during Terwilliger's brief absence that he capered off merrily to get a soda. Any sensible person would have responded to such a close call by buckling down immediately. Not mercurial Gildersleeve.

What would anyone expect a man to do after declaring "I have a great capacity for work" as Throckmorton did on December 2, 1947? Roll up his sleeves and toil for hours? Nope. Gildy takes a nap. This is Mr. Shirker who boldly states at the breakfast table on October 27, 1948, "I'll be at the office in a minute where I can get some sleep."

Gildersleeve did want to be alert when dating women, but even then it was not easy to tell if he was coming or going because he seemed to be incessantly entering into or retreating from love affairs. Announcer John Wald aptly described Throckmorton on November 10, 1948, as "the man with the ambidextrous heart" for if Gildy did not have a pair of women dangling on the line he was at least of two minds about the one he happened to be entertaining that evening. Gildersleeve only liked to kiss and run, using women when the urge hit him and feeling intense relief when he managed to back out of announced engagements. He wanted to play the field as a free agent and refused to commit to a long-term relationship. Sometimes his only motivation was to get in the game and go after a conquest solely to stymie a rival or, in Leroy's words from July 23, 1953, "He didn't want her till the other fellow got her." Gildy was a one-woman man — until the next woman came along.

What came along for Harold Peary in 1950 was an opportunity to leave NBC for a lucrative offer from CBS as other performers like Edgar Bergen and Jack Benny had done. Once under contract to CBS, Peary was obligated to bow out of *The Great Gildersleeve* when Kraft refused to move the program to the other network. Peary's new series on CBS, *Honest Harold*, lasted only one season. Willard Waterman, hired to replace Peary as the new Gildersleeve, played the role from September 6, 1950, through the end of the run in 1957.

Although a number of listeners and authors have commented on the similarity in voices of the two actors, Peary exhibited subtle nuances of delivery that are absent from the Waterman broadcasts. Peary's distinctive "dirty laugh" is an oft-cited difference, although the gimmick of opening broadcasts with that signature ended after June of 1948. A good gauge for measuring the distance between the two performers is to listen to Peary's inflections in the following scenes and imagine Waterman getting the same oomph and comic mileage out of them:

- To Horace Hooker after the judge explains how one stamp is worth more than another (February 24, 1946): "12 years for a stamp that's worth 35 cents in the sun? *I don't know, Judge.*"
- To Hooker after Horace brags about his friend's railroad line (August 29, 1943): "Tell him his railroad is a public disgrace."
- To the man outside a movie theater who has been telling people "Stepping to the side, please" and "Keeping the line moving, please" (October 31, 1943): "Shutting the mouth, please."
- To the two doctors who are talking about famous cases while he lies in bed nearby (January 9, 1944): "Do either of you remember Gildersleeve's case?"

- To Marjorie after hearing her excuse for burning the toast because her mind was somewhere else (January 20, 1946): "If you could just find where it is and move there."
- To Leroy to cease his endless jabbering (January 30, 1944): "Stop talking, Leroy. Nothing is coming out."
- To Leroy after hearing the boy's excuse that he was wiping his wet hands on his pants because he could not find any towels (April 7, 1946): "What if you had no pants?"
- To the world after becoming frustrated with the younger generation (May 13, 1945): "The judge was right. They ought to send them up for five years. Every one of them."
- To Peavey after getting little response to a witticism (January 17, 1943): "Telling a joke to you is like hollering it down a rain barrel."

Another point in Peary's favor is the arsenal of "drop-in" expressions he possessed which convey the situation better than a declaration or question. While others were chatting aimlessly as Marjorie and Marshall Bullard were doing on June 3, 1945, Peary inserted a "Yes, yes" to try to speed things along. When on a spot such as fearing the wrath of Bessie's boyfriend on May 27, 1945, his "Yes, indeed" followed by a nervous giggle told us he was in a real pickle. Another pet word when in a fix was "Heeee." Peary shifted between two gears on his Leroy call: into high on "LEEROY" when beckoning the boy or down into low for "Le-roy" in the presence of others when wanting his nephew to keep quiet or just to demonstrate impatience with the boy's behavior. The best evidence of Peary's irritation emerged as an "Oompf" followed by a spray of frustration which probably moistened the scripts of anyone nearby.

Listen to portions of several episodes in which Peary demonstrated physical comedy just by grunts, groans, exclamations, and moans and then imagine inserting Waterman into the same scenes: getting into breeches and boots in a tight booth (January 14, 1948); hitting his head, stepping in water, and getting an electric shock while in the basement (March 9, 1949); the lily pond scene near the porch (October 26, 1949). The two actors are in similar unsteady positions when Peary teeters on ice skates (December 31, 1944) and Waterman on roller skates (September 2, 1953). It is Peary's vocal tricks that allow listeners to see the great fall in sharper detail than the whip being cracked at Waterman's expense.

These observations are not meant to disparage Waterman's ability as an actor, for his radio work was more diversified than Peary's and his career on the stage and in movies eclipsed that of the man who originated the character of Throckmorton P. Gildersleeve. After being dressed in borrowed robes from 1950 to 1957, Waterman moved on and was accepted in other guises whereas Peary, like Arthur Lake who was Dagwood Bumstead in the public eye long after he stopped playing the part on *Blondie*, could never shake off completely the radio role that made him famous.

In Waterman's defense it should also be noted that he was playing a character that had undergone some significant changes after Peary left the program. Even though Gildersleeve remained a skirt-chasing layabout, the writers turned him into a somewhat egotistical man who seemed to be continually asking for trouble and usually getting it. He often talked to himself, especially when offering congratulations (e.g., "You're sly, Gildersleeve," "You have a way of making people happy," "What a diplomat!") or delivering sotto voce comments ("I wonder if she saw through me").

One positive outcome of having Gildy verbalize his inner feelings occurred at the end of certain shows such as on March 21, 1951, when, while surveying the sleeping babies, Waterman delivered a touching coda to the broadcast.

Whereas a number of episodes in the Peary period featured extended scenes at the office, during Waterman's reign as water commissioner he was rarely found at city hall. Beginning with the seventh episode of the first season (October 18, 1950) in which Gildersleeve is derided for being overweight and out of shape, the main character became more buffoon than blusterer, his primary function being to set himself up for a fall and then take it.

During this period Throckmorton grew more possessive of Leroy and envious of others who might take him away. He also became overtly obtrusive such as when he entered neighbor Bullard's home and created a mess among Rumson's fine furnishings. Occasionally he even obnoxiously intruded into the affairs of others like the evening he pried into the personal life of a girlfriend and engaged in deceitful behavior as he did on May 16, 1951.

Perhaps the most identifiable trait of the new Gildersleeve was a streak of hypocrisy. By the 1951–1952 season any categorical statement he made would be countermanded or violated by his own actions. The pattern became predictable: state a principle or resolution and then break it. Everyone could see trouble coming when they heard "I'll never speak to you or any member of your family again" (September 19, 1951), "I'll never look at another woman" (December 31, 1952), or "If there's one thing your uncle doesn't do, it's change his mind" (August 12, 1953). When Gildy scolds Leroy at the beginning of the August 26, 1953, show for not being self-reliant, it is just a matter of minutes before the chastiser is moping around the house at loose ends.

Instead of the plot complications that came from the title character's playfulness and adventuresome spirit during the Peary years, stubbornness and a flair for meddling often guided Gildersleeve's actions in the early 1950s. Being unreasonable and shortsighted became Gildy's MO such as on October 21, 1953, when he confronted a blameless Leroy about pranks at school with "Stop insisting you're innocent when I keep telling you you're guilty." When he eventually recanted his rash actions, it often came with a penitent admission such as "It was the worst mistake I ever made." And it was. Until the next one.

One mistake that writers inevitably encounter on long-running programs is the repetition of story lines. By 1952 the concept of continual conflicts between Gildersleeve and his various sweethearts had grown stale, yet the writers kept plugging in different combinations (e.g., Grace and Irene, Paula and Gloria, Grace and Paula, Grace and Marie) until the device of playful playboy was pretty much played out.

With the character of Marjorie the writers avoided stagnancy by moving her along the timeline from dreamy-eyed bobby soxer to college student to wife to mother of twins. Lurene Tuttle, who originated the role, stayed with the show through the completion of the third season. Louise Erickson took over for the next four years before being replaced by Mary Lee Robb.

As Tuttle repeatedly proved on *The Adventures of Sam Spade* and many other programs, she had a wonderful way of batting home a line with élan. As Marjorie, she could squeeze a tingle into the phrase "positively *handsome*" that no other actress could match and yet she could also deadpan a putdown such as "That bird hasn't got anything of his own except an appetite" in a way that would have pleased a master of the form like Joan Davis.

At 36 Tuttle was a bit mature to be acting like a 16-year-old so when she went on to other roles, Erickson, who just happened to be 16 and had already been playing the title character on *A Date with Judy*, seamlessly stepped in as Marjorie. The writers made her more a part of the teen scene, having her call Gildersleeve "Unkie, darling" and supplying her with slang expressions like "Drop dead" and "He's a mole."

Erickson imbued the role of Marjorie with the vivacity of adolescent anguish and ecstasy that never strikes a false note. Examples abound of the verisimilitude she brought to the show. These are from one year alone: the wistful longing in "Were you really in love with her?" and genuine excitement of "Your heart will be pounding" (March 28, 1945); this smarty-pants response to "When I need your help, I'll ask for it" spoken by her uncle: "Well, holler. I'll be up in my room" (November 4, 1945); priceless intonation on a throwaway line: "That couch isn't fit to sit on alone even" (May 20, 1945); indignation after being embarrassed by Gildersleeve in front of her boyfriend: "You're the stupidest man a girl ever had for an uncle. And you're fat, too" (September 16, 1945).

Marjorie's hesitant questions and answers while sitting with Marshall Bullard on the swing on May 6, 1945, cannot be bettered for rendering the authentic dialogue of youthful like before it turns into young love. After listening to the way Erickson plays out Marjorie's crush on singer Larry Lake in 1947 and a French teacher in 1948 and her delivery of lines like "How perfect can you be?" there is only response possible: "How perfect can she be?"

After Mary Lee Robb assumed the part of Marjorie, the writers moved the character rather quickly through courtship, engagement, and marriage the first two seasons, and pregnancy and motherhood the following one. The character lost some of her scintillating charm with maturity and became less involved in weekly plot entanglements once she and husband Bronco moved next door with the twins.

Leroy, however, still roamed the premises as the very unstill center of the Gildersleeve universe. Though his sister had moved from adolescence to adulthood, Leroy remained resolutely locked in the seventh grade, barely dabbling his toes into the teen years by the show's end. It did not matter if Walter Tetley had slipped into his 40s; Leroy found an age the writers liked and stuck with it.

The privileges of being a perpetual child include the right to read comics on the floor, peek at his sister's diary, cry on demand, and demand when he cried. But other boys could do that. How many of them could send semaphore signals by wiggling their ears? Very few.

Even fewer actors could load a line with the right amount of skepticism to invoke laughter like Tetley, unquestionably radio's wisest wise guy. On July 1, 1953, when Gildy asked his nephew to tell him how he was doing while trying to dance like a teen, Leroy supplied question and answer at the same time: "You wanna know?" Tetley could handle the long queries as well as shown on January 13, 1954: "He's putting on a blue serge suit so he can referee a fight between two parrots?" On May 27, 1945, Throckmorton said he would reward his nephew for doing chores at the office with an amount "equal to what you're worth." Leroy's immediate retort: "Is that all?"

Longtime writers for the program John Elliotte and Andy White milked Tetley's skill at increasing the humor potential of scenes by having Leroy come in late on conversations in progress so he could address a barrage of queries that were largely ignored until the frustration of either Throckmorton or Leroy broke through.

Although inquisitive Leroy had the "the soul of a train announcer" as Gildy claimed in 1945, cook Birdie also raised the rafters with her "I'll get it!" shout whenever the doorbell rang. Lillian Randolph played Birdie with jovial wisdom and wit which clearly demonstrated she did "get it" long before her boss caught on to most situations. To make matters clear to Gildersleeve, she frequently repeated one of her homemade maxims three times before punctuating her exit with a raucous laugh that clinched the conversation. Birdie provided the stabilizing maternal influence for Marjorie and Leroy and the corrective voice that Gildersleeve needed. Randolph had a way of driving home a critical comment with a wink in her eye and a lilt in her voice such as telling the putative head of the house on May 20, 1953, "It's human to make mistakes and you're the most human man I know."

Friend Horace Hooker also candidly admonished Gildy, though usually with an added cackle of derision to drive home the pungent counsel. Earle Ross played the judge as a cagey eccentric, a health-food devotee who kept coupons from fig bars locked in his safe. Hooker presided over the launch of the program as the magistrate in charge of Leroy and Marjorie's estate and remained an adviser and thorn in Throcky's side. After 1951 Ross was heard less frequently due to finding more work on *I Married Joan* and other television shows.

Conversely, Richard LeGrand's role on the series increased in the early 1950s when Richard Q. Peavey began appearing in both acts and sometimes even in the tag because Gildersleeve found himself confiding often with the friendly pharmacist. Of all people to ask for advice or an opinion on any matter, Throckmorton could not have made a worse choice than to ask the mealy-mouthed mossback, a man who, while standing behind a counter, would spend several minutes tracking his sales of hot chocolate through the four seasons when he could have summed up the matter in these few words: "I sell more when the weather is cold, none when it's hot." Mr. Roundabout got under the skin of Gildy on November 25, 1945, by answering if he likes football by way of Worcester, Massachusetts. On January 20, 1946, Throckmorton grew so tired of Peavey's flip-flopping that he stopped him after his last "On the other hand" with the blunt "On the other hand, she had warts!"

Never one to rush into matters, Peavey was engaged to his wife (whom he always addressed as Mrs. Peavey) for five years before marrying the woman he claimed had the gift of foresight. He informed Gildy, "She sees things that are coming." Gildy's topper: "Did she see you coming?"

But, deep inside, Gildersleeve valued the older man's wisdom. He openly expressed his admiration to his friend by telling him plainly "You're the only man who knows what it's all about" on January 27, 1946, and declaring at a public gathering on March 21, 1946, "Peavey is the only man in this town who's got any sense," to which all those assembled replied with Peavey's pet response: "Well, now, I wouldn't say that."

Joining Peavey, Gildersleeve, and Hooker as members of the Jolly Boys were barber Floyd Munson (Arthur Q. Bryan) and police chief Donald Gates (Ken Christy). Though arguments occasionally brought discord into the room above Floyd's shop and the five-part harmony sometimes came out less than harmonic, it was always fair weather when those good fellows got together.

Serving as both belle and bellwether, Leila Ransome bobbed into and out of Gildersleeve's life through most of show's run. Shirley Mitchell instilled the flighty flirt with so much seductive winsomeness that even Ransome's most obvious ploys proved nearly impossible for males to resist. A habitual fibber and schemer, she probably could have outfoxed Scarlett O'Hara but no doubt would have rebuffed Rhett Butler because, even though he might have been "the *hand*somest man," she, like Gildy, was constantly looking down the line for the one who might be a *little* more appealing. Fair of face and fickle of temperament, Leila always seemed out of place away from her southern comfort zone. But even when totally confused in money matters, some of her most empty-headed statements tinkled with down yonder charm, viz., "[The stock] doesn't amount to as much as I hoped it would, but, then again, I didn't think it would."

The up-tempo charms came from the inventive and distinctive musical patterns of the program. Unlike comedy programs such as *The Charlie McCarthy Show, The Jack Benny Program, Fibber McGee and Molly,* and *The Red Skelton Show* which featured instrumental and vocal selections by regular performers, *The Great Gildersleeve* usually confined its music to songs by the Jolly Boys and musical bridges. In lyrical Summerfield Birdie, Gildersleeve, Marjorie, Leroy, Peavey, or Hooker could also be counted on to deliver a refrain of a cappella joy at any moment.

Claude Sweeten, Jack Meakin, and Robert Armbruster served as musical directors at various times after 1943. For years reference sources have cited William Randolph and Billy Mills as two separate music directors of the program. At the conclusion of the final episode of the inaugural season on June 28, 1942, Peary saluted musical director "William Randolph Mills." On the May 22, 1945, episode of *Fibber McGee and Molly* Billy Mills was formally introduced by his full name, William Randolph Mills. In a 1979 letter published in *Gildy's Scrapbook*, Harold Peary confirmed that Mills supplied the music for the first year of *The Great Gildersleeve*. It is long past time to let William Randolph rest in peace for more than eight bars and to acknowledge that Mills ground out some exceedingly fine sounds simultaneously in Wistful Vista and Summerfield.

Upon taking charge of the program's music in September 1945, Meakin breathed new life into the theme song, composed a playful bridge that announced visits to Peavey's Pharmacy, and created inventive chords to match the show's action. In one episode alone (January 11, 1950) Meakin ingeniously wove five distinct melodies including "Yankee Doodle Dandy" and "Down by the Old Mill Stream" into the action which enhanced the total performance significantly. Jack's innovative work on the show did not go unnoticed. On May 7, 1947, noted columnist Jimmy Starr presented a plaque to Meakin for his "outstanding originality in composing, arranging, and conducting music for radio."

Also noted by attentive ears was the way the writers (particularly the teams of Elliotte and White and John Whedon and Sam Moore) wove literary allusions seamlessly into the fabric of *The Great Gildersleeve*. Many of the quotations were spoken without attribution because it really did not matter if the author cited happened to be Longfellow, Browning, Shakespeare, Scott, Masefield, Pope, Keats, or Whittier. The listeners recognized the citation as a pertinent notable quote worked unobtrusively into the narrative for the benefit of the characters and the audience.

Some measure of the size of that home audience is presented in the ratings and rankings summary tabulated in Appendix E which shows that *The Great Gildersleeve* did not approach the heights attained by *Lux Radio Theatre*, *The Bob Hope Show*, and other heavyweights. The show never broke into the top ten, and even during the five years it served as a gateway into *The Jack Benny Program* on Sundays it could not deliver numbers near the 24.1–31.0 share the Benny crew earned. However, as the companion chart demonstrates, *The Great Gildersleeve* outranked its CBS competitor in all but three of the 13 years tallied which meant that, more often than not, *The Great Gildersleeve* was the big cheese of its time slot.

No one could blame Kraft for jumping on the quiz show and "get rich" bandwagon of the late 1940s in hopes of raising ratings and increasing sales by promoting lucrative contests that could be worked into the plots, namely "Name the Baby," "Name Gildersleeve's Song," "Name the Twins," and "Name the Cake." The campaigns may have been financially successful, but it was not the Kraft product being presented or the promise of a shiny automobile or $500 cash that brought listeners to Summerfield. They came to be entertained by the flawed, funny folks who made them laugh at their foibles. Even now each time listeners tune in, it is like a visit to that place we call home and a chance to meet one more time those dear hearts and gentle people.

To air the show is human, to listen divine.

Format of Episode Entries

Date: Month, day, and year episode was broadcast. (Script) after a date indicates information was derived from a script because there is no extant recording of that episode.

Title: Theme of the episode in five words or less.

Cast: A list of the identifiable performers, each followed by the character's name in parentheses. The announcer's name is given after that of either Harold Peary or Willard Waterman.

Summary: A one-sentence synopsis of the plot that does not give away the ending.

Writers: The names of the credited authors of the scripts.

Allusion: The name of the character citing the quotation followed by the literary source, the author of the work, and the quotation.

Comments: Remarks on that particular episode indicating changes in characters, actors, announcers, and musical directors, notable first appearances and lines, bloopers and ad-libs, and character progression. Because residents of Summerfield are apt to break into song at any moment, titles of songs are listed with the singer even if that character only manages to carry the tune for one line.

EPISODE GUIDE

Date: May 16, 1941
Title: Leaving Wistful Vista for Summerfield (Audition)
Cast: Harold Peary (Throckmorton P. Gildersleeve), Harlow Wilcox, Lurene Tuttle (Evelyn), Walter Tetley (Leroy), Earle Ross (Horace Hooker), Frank Nelson (waiter, Ted Wills)
Summary: Gildersleeve travels by train to Summerfield to handle matters related to the estate of his nephew and niece.
Writer: Leonard (Len) Levinson
Comments: The connection between *Fibber McGee and Molly* and *The Great Gildersleeve* is apparent in this send-off show which is sponsored by Johnson's Wax and written by Levinson who had been assisting Don Quinn on a number of the 1940–1941 *McGee* scripts. Levinson's affection for puns is evident even in throwaway lines such as "I do hope that porter gives me a wide berth."

Date: August 31, 1941
Title: Leaving Wistful Vista for Summerfield
Cast: Harold Peary (Throckmorton P. Gildersleeve), Jim Bannon, Lurene Tuttle (Marjorie Forrester), Walter Tetley (Leroy Forrester), Earle Ross (Horace Hooker), Frank Nelson (waiter, Ted Wills)
Summary: Gildersleeve travels by train to Summerfield to handle matters related to the estate of his nephew and niece.
Writer: Leonard Levinson
Comments: Kraft is the show's longtime sponsor with Jim Bannon as the first announcer. Music is composed and conducted by William Randolph [Billy Mills]. Peary's dirty laugh becomes the show's calling card. The name of the niece has been changed from Evelyn to Marjorie. Gildersleeve stirs up old and new rivalries by calling McGee "a har-rrrd man" and referring to Hooker as an "old goat."

Date: September 7, 1941
Title: Marjorie's Cake
Cast: Harold Peary (Gildersleeve), Jim Bannon, Lurene Tuttle (Marjorie), Walter Tetley (Leroy), Earle Ross (Hooker), Lillian Randolph (Birdie Lee Coggins)
Summary: After eating a cake Marjorie prepared for a party, Gildy and Leroy try to replace it.
Writer: Leonard Levinson
Comments: Lillian Randolph appears for the first time. Gildersleeve

Throckmorton P. Gildersleeve (Harold Peary, center) stirred things up considerably on *Fibber McGee and Molly* with Jim and Marian Jordan before setting out on his own in Summerfield.

is already using flattery and charm to get what he wants from women. During the encounter with the girdle salesman, Peary unleashes one of his "Oompf!" double takes that will be used often in the coming years to generate laughs.

Date: September 14, 1941
Title: Leroy's Paper Route
   Cast: Harold Peary (Gildersleeve), Jim Bannon, Lurene Tuttle (Marjorie), Walter Tetley (Leroy), Earle Ross (Hooker), Lillian Randolph (Birdie), Frank Nelson (radio announcer)
   Summary: On a rainy day Gilder-sleeve drives Leroy around town to deliver newspapers.
   Writer: Leonard Levinson
   Comments: Summerfield's paper, the *Indicator-Vindicator*, is mentioned for the first time as is Leroy's pal, Piggy Banks. This is the first of the wild-goose chases that marked Levinson's only year as writer. The rather labored puns include "The Wright Brothers were wrong" and "He was my hobby, that little horse." The address of the Forrester home is given as 747 Parkside.

Date: September 21, 1941
Title: Marjorie's Girlfriend Visits

Cast: Harold Peary (Gildersleeve), Jim Bannon, Lurene Tuttle (Marjorie), Walter Tetley (Leroy), Lillian Randolph (Birdie), Frank Nelson (Ted Wills), Shirley Mitchell (Dorabelle Clayburn)

Summary: When a flirtatious friend upsets Marjorie, Leroy and his uncle develop a plot to switch the guest's affections to Gildersleeve.

Writer: Leonard Levinson

Comments: The show is dedicated to the residents of Gildersleeve, Connecticut. Shirley Mitchell makes her first appearance, vamping up for her later role of Leila Ransome. Lurene's skill as a fine screamer and crier on cue is displayed well in this outing.

Date: September 28, 1941
Title: Hiccups
Cast: Harold Peary (Gildersleeve), Jim Bannon, Lurene Tuttle (Marjorie), Walter Tetley (Leroy), Earle Ross (Hooker), Lillian Randolph (Birdie), Frank Nelson (Ted Wills), Ed Max (elevator operator, Lefty), Ken Christy (Red)

Summary: After Gildersleeve develops hiccups on the day of an important date in court, his friends and relatives suggest cures that prove to be ineffective.

Writer: Leonard Levinson

Comments: The reference to going back to Wistful Vista melds nicely into Peary's appearance on *Fibber McGee and Molly* on September 30th. Apparently in Summerfield hiccupping men get the same police escort to receive medical assistance as expectant mothers. Notable puns: "Little boys will always revert to type," "There's a big drip on the carpet." Ken Christy, who

will later take the part of Chief Gates, appears for the first time.

Date: October 5, 1941
Title: Investigating Jail Conditions
Cast: Harold Peary (Gildersleeve), Jim Bannon, Lurene Tuttle (Marjorie), Walter Tetley (Leroy), Earle Ross (Hooker), Lillian Randolph (Birdie), Frank Nelson (Ted Wills)

Summary: Gildersleeve purposely gets arrested so he can observe conditions at a local jail.

Writer: Leonard Levinson

Comments: Hooker's prediction that Throcky's participation in the undercover project could lead to a civic career foreshadows the great one's appointment as water commissioner. "You're a bright boy, Leroy" is the antipode of "You're a harrrrd man, McGee." Gildy's impromptu singing of "You and I" is the first of many times he will make merry melody in the coming years.

Date: October 12, 1941
No extant recording. No 1941 scripts at the Wisconsin State Historical Society.

Date: October 19, 1941
Title: School Pranks
Cast: Harold Peary (Gildersleeve), Jim Bannon, Lurene Tuttle (Marjorie), Walter Tetley (Leroy), Earle Ross (Hooker), Lillian Randolph (Birdie)

Summary: Leroy is suspected of an escapade that gets school canceled after overhearing his uncle and Judge Hooker reminiscing about practical jokes of their youth.

Writer: Leonard Levinson

Comments: Puns include "That's a heck of a note" and "A fellow starts out for a lark and ends up in a cage." This is the first time Gildersleeve and Hooker are bickering in a fashion reminiscent of the all-out battles of words between Throcky and McGee that nearly raised the roof at 79 Wistful Vista. Horace's confession "I was a baaad boy" mimics the pet expression of Lou Costello. Hooker invokes the name of Gutzon Borglum, sculptor of the figures on Mount Rushmore, and Gildy mentions Secretary Ickes in connection with gasoline, a reference to Interior Secretary Harold Ickes who closed gas stations during evening hours in 1941 in anticipation of an oil shortage.

Date: October 26, 1941
Title: Oliver Visits
    Cast: Harold Peary (Gildersleeve), Jim Bannon, Lurene Tuttle (Marjorie), Walter Tetley (Leroy), Lillian Randolph (Birdie), Verna Felton (Mrs. Beasley), Ken Christy (Grogan), Hans Conried (Oliver Honeywell)
    Summary: Hobbledehoy Oliver's overnight stay is interrupted by visits from firemen.
    Writer: Leonard Levinson
    Comments: Lurene Tuttle demonstrates her mastery of the intricacies of inflection by giving "That's all—Brother" and "That's wonderful!" the perfect delivery. Aesop, the pesky family cat, is mentioned for the first time. Notable puns: "I just love to go to blazes," "For a week knight, he finishes strong on Sunday." Jack Benny and Charlie McCarthy get a painless plug when Gildy mentions them as regulars

on the family listening schedule for Sundays.

Date: November 2, 1941
Title: Minding the Baby
    Cast: Harold Peary (Gildersleeve), Jim Bannon, Lurene Tuttle (Marjorie), Walter Tetley (Leroy), Lillian Randolph (Birdie), Paula Winslowe (Mrs. Dapple)
    Summary: Gildersleeve and Leroy have their hands full watching a baby while the mother runs errands.
    Writer: Leonard Levinson
    Comments: Birdie gets a few laughs just by naming grocery items at precisely the right moments in the dialogue. Puns include "the Venus de Milo Arms" and "If she drops the watch, you get the works." Uncle and nephew improvise their own lyrics to "Rock-a-Bye Baby."

Date: November 9, 1941
Title: Birdie Works for Judge Hooker
    Cast: Harold Peary (Gildersleeve), Jim Bannon, Lurene Tuttle (Marjorie), Walter Tetley (Leroy), Earle Ross (Hooker), Lillian Randolph (Birdie)
    Summary: After Hooker convinces Birdie to work for him, Leroy, Marjorie, and Gildersleeve devise a plan to win her back.
    Writer: Leonard Levinson
    Comments: In Summerfield ties come in three shades: loud, louder, and loudest. Puns include "morning serial," "You sneak in the grass." Horace Hooker resides at 2100 Burnside. Birdie proves she could be just as handy in a courtroom as in the kitchen when she throws legal jargon back at Hooker.

Date: November 16, 1941
Title: Servicemen for Thanksgiving
   Cast: Harold Peary (Gildersleeve), Jim Bannon, Lurene Tuttle (Marjorie), Walter Tetley (Leroy), Earle Ross (Hooker), Lillian Randolph (Birdie), Hans Conried (colonel)
   Summary: Gildersleeve finds slim pickings when he resolves to share Thanksgiving dinner with a serviceman.
   Writer: Leonard Levinson
   Comments: Leroy creates his own brand of discord on a musical instrument for the first time. Puns include "Barking dogs are cooled off in pup tents" and "convertible top."

Date: November 23, 1941
Title: Leroy Smokes Cigar
   Cast: Harold Peary (Gildersleeve), Jim Bannon, Lurene Tuttle (Marjorie), Walter Tetley (Leroy), Lillian Randolph (Birdie)
   Summary: Leroy and pal Piggy regret their decision to sample one of Gildersleeve's stogies.
   Writer: Leonard Levinson
   Comments: Gildy's garbled version of Piggy's account of the fire is a comic highlight of this misadventure. Puns include "Not as a little shaver," "all wool and a yard wide." Instead of a double take at the end, Peary and Tetley join in a double moan.

Date: November 30, 1941
Title: Canary Doesn't Sing
   Cast: Harold Peary (Gildersleeve), Jim Bannon, Lurene Tuttle (Marjorie), Walter Tetley (Leroy), Lillian Randolph (Birdie), Frank Nelson (officer)
   Summary: Gildersleeve and Leroy seek cures for a mute canary at the library and a doctor's office.
   Writer: Leonard Levinson
   Comments: The standard consulting fee for doctors in Summerfield appears to be $5.00 whether the matter is hiccupping humans or silent birds. Marjorie, Leroy, and Gildy warble a bit of "Let's All Sing Like the Birdies Sing."

Date: December 7, 1941
Title: Barbara Ann Visits
   Cast: Harold Peary (Gildersleeve), Jim Bannon, Lurene Tuttle (Marjorie), Walter Tetley (Leroy), Earle Ross (Hooker), Lillian Randolph (Birdie), Arthur Q. Bryan (Llewellyn)
   Summary: A mischievous cousin upsets the household with pranks and deceit.
   Writer: Leonard Levinson
   Comments: The show is interrupted numerous times with war bulletins resulting from the attack on Pearl Harbor. The mention of Topsy and Little Eva refers to characters in *Uncle Tom's Cabin*. Arthur Q. Bryan, who will later assume the role of Floyd Munson, is heard for the first time, speaking in his Elmer Fudd voice.

Date: December 14, 1941
Title: Iron Deer
   Cast: Harold Peary (Gildersleeve), Jim Bannon, Lurene Tuttle (Marjorie), Walter Tetley (Leroy), Lillian Randolph (Birdie), Arthur Q. Bryan (Llewellyn), Eddie Marr (Skinner)
   Summary: Complications arise when Birdie, Marjorie, and Leroy sell the same iron deer to different buyers.
   Writer: Leonard Levinson
   Comments: A war bulletin precedes

the beginning of the show. This episode resembles the misunderstandings that habitually infiltrated *The Aldrich Family*. Puns include "We can get a little dough out of that deer" and "That's the last time we'll ever try to pass that buck." The financial crisis is precipitated by buying defense stamps and bonds, an unselfish action that listeners will be encouraged to emulate in coming weeks.

Date: December 21, 1941
Title: Christmas Gift for McGee
  Cast: Harold Peary (Gildersleeve), Jim Bannon, Lurene Tuttle (Marjorie), Walter Tetley (Leroy), Earle Ross (Hooker), Lillian Randolph (Birdie), Arthur Q. Bryan (Llewellyn, Leo), Paula Winslowe (Fanny), Ed Max (Spike, clerk)
  Summary: After he receives a large box from Fibber McGee for a Christmas present, Gildersleeve shops for an expensive gift for his former neighbor in Wistful Vista.
  Writer: Leonard Levinson
  Comments: Among the Gildersleeve clan, it is the Christmas tie that binds the family together. The tasty stamps Llewellyn mentions are the Jell-O flavors. As she did on November 9th when telling off Judge Hooker, Birdie takes control of a situation by ordering her employer to stop snooping around his Christmas present. The tag sets up Gildersleeve's visit to Wistful Vista by plugging his December 23 appearance on *Fibber McGee and Molly*.

Date: December 28, 1941
Title: Leroy's Big Dog
  Cast: Harold Peary (Gildersleeve), Jim Bannon, Lurene Tuttle (Marjorie), Walter Tetley (Leroy), Earle Ross (Hooker), Lillian Randolph (Birdie),
  Summary: After Leroy's dog becomes a nuisance, uncle and nephew try to give the chowhound away.
  Writer: Leonard Levinson
  Comments: Saskatchewan moose hound will not be found in guides published by kennel clubs, although it sounds like an appropriate breed for this ravenous Rover. Puns include "enough to break the Banks" and "Tuxedo Unction."

Date: January 4, 1942
Title: Diet Bet
  Cast: Harold Peary (Gildersleeve), Jim Bannon, Lurene Tuttle (Marjorie), Walter Tetley (Leroy), Earle Ross (Hooker), Lillian Randolph (Birdie), Shirley Mitchell (waitress)
  Summary: Gildersleeve struggles to lose ten pounds in a week to win a $100 bet with Judge Hooker.
  Writer: Leonard Levinson
  Comments: Gildersleeve mimics Hooker's delivery for the first time when he echoes Horace's "sick." Hooker uses the "Gildy" nickname that will become his common way of referring to his friend and verbal sparring partner. Gildersleeve's weight is given as 213 pounds.

Date: January 11, 1942
Title: Driving to Fairview
  Cast: Harold Peary (Gildersleeve), Jim Bannon, Walter Tetley (Leroy), Lillian Randolph (Birdie), Frank Nelson (Franklin X. Tobey)
  Summary: Leroy and Gildersleeve encounter problems with rough roads,

car switches, and the police on their way to a rabbit breeder's show.

Writer: Leonard Levinson

Comments: Repetitive car confusion of this degree sounded believable in 1942 when most automobiles came in shades of black. The "horse around" joke could have been taken from Groucho Marx's gag file. Puns include "hares stood on end," "hold a little quiz, Kid." The plug for *Look Who's Laughing* in the tag gives a nod to all the stars of the film.

Date: January 18, 1942
Title: New Bed for Marjorie

Cast: Harold Peary (Gildersleeve), Jim Bannon, Walter Tetley (Leroy), Lillian Randolph (Birdie), Sam Hearn (Sam Schlepperman)

Summary: After Gildersleeve buys a new bed for Marjorie, he sets off a bidding war when he wants the old one back.

Writer: Leonard Levinson

Comments: This episode again sounds like the back-and-forth dilemmas Clifford Goldsmith had been creating for Henry Aldrich and Homer Brown. Schlepperman throws Gildy's "You're a harrrrd man" back at the great man. Puns include "Keen place for hiding," "Have me sleep on it."

Date: January 25, 1942
Title: Matchmaker

Cast: Harold Peary (Gildersleeve), Jim Bannon, Walter Tetley (Leroy), Earle Ross (Hooker), Lillian Randolph (Birdie), Paula Winslowe (Henrietta Banks)

Summary: Gildersleeve's efforts to match Hooker with Henrietta Banks misfire when the woman assumes it is Gildy who wants to marry her.

Writer: Leonard Levinson

Comments: Just as Fibber McGee actually regards Doctor Gamble, the man he often insults, as his best friend, so Gildy shows his affection for Judge Hooker: "Deep down I really like the little duffer." Throcky's plaintive "Oh, why was I ever born?" is his version of McGee's frequent lament of "Why does everything have to happen to me?" Puns include "drip of the first water," "organ recital."

Date: February 1, 1942
Title: Leroy Runs Away

Cast: Harold Peary (Gildersleeve), Jim Bannon, Lurene Tuttle (Marjorie), Walter Tetley (Leroy), Lillian Randolph (Birdie)

Summary: The efforts of Marjorie, Birdie, and Gildersleeve to track down a runaway Leroy are stymied by car problems.

Writer: Leonard Levinson

Comments: Beginning with this episode, the opening commercial is dropped in favor of one inserted in the middle of the action. Throckmorton gives Leroy's age as 13. Puns include "tell them our little boy blew," "moon came over this mountain," "highway rubbery." The allusion to Mrs. Uppington's window refers to the two-part adventure that created an air of mystery around Wistful Vista on January 13 and 20. The exchange between uncle and nephew in jail demonstrated how those too young or too old to serve in the military could still contribute to the war effort.

Date: February 8, 1942
Title: Teaching Auto Mechanics
   Cast: Harold Peary (Gildersleeve), Jim Bannon, Lurene Tuttle (Marjorie), Walter Tetley (Leroy), Earle Ross (Hooker), Lillian Randolph (Birdie), Shirley Mitchell (girl with drawl), Paula Winslowe (girl, Mrs. Salisbury Twitchell)
   Summary: Gildersleeve is on the spot when he agrees to demonstrate how automobiles operate for a group of Red Cross volunteers.
   Writer: Leonard Levinson
   Comments: Earle Ross unleashes his first genuine cackle of derision. Puns include "hear that Singer hum," "Were they giving me the needle?" As usual, it is the lure of pretty girls that induces the wolf in Gildersleeve to embark on this Miss Adventure. Peary uses his patented "You're a harrrrd man" in the tag to push the sale of defense bonds.

Date: February 15, 1942 (Script)
Title: Shirt at Chinese Laundry
   Cast: Harold Peary (Gildersleeve), Jim Bannon, Lurene Tuttle (Marjorie), Walter Tetley (Leroy), Earle Ross (Hooker), Lillian Randolph (Birdie)
   Summary: Gildersleeve searches for a missing laundry ticket so he can reclaim a dress shirt to wear to a formal party.
   Writer: Leonard Levinson
   Comments: The most notable pun takes the form of "four bad tiers" (of a bow tie). This is another of the "one mishap after another" stories. Levinson gives Peary leeway in delivering his sputtering double take of surprise by just putting "HAL: (Take)" in the script. Peary closes with a serious

appeal for donations to the American Red Cross.

Date: February 22, 1942
Title: Selling the Drugstore
   Cast: Harold Peary (Gildersleeve), Jim Bannon, Lurene Tuttle (Marjorie), Walter Tetley (Leroy), Earle Ross (Hooker), Lillian Randolph (Birdie), Paula Winslowe (Miss Capstock, Mrs. Salisbury Twitchell)
   Summary: After reprimanding Leroy for lying on George Washington's birthday, Gildersleeve finds it a struggle to tell the truth in the boy's presence while finding a buyer for an unprofitable business owned by the Forrester estate.
   Writer: Leonard Levinson
   Comments: Tetley generates humor just by repeating "Who, me?" in his inimitable fashion. Puns include "quite a whippersnapper" and "as a prophet, you're a total loss." Gildersleeve says, "This is one of my bad days" for the first time.

Date: March 1, 1942
Title: Fortune Teller
   Cast: Harold Peary (Gildersleeve), Jim Bannon, Lurene Tuttle (Marjorie), Walter Tetley (Leroy), Earle Ross (Hooker), Lillian Randolph (Birdie), Ken Christy (Lt. Quinn), Paula Winslowe (Mrs. Salisbury Twitchell)
   Summary: When Gildersleeve fills in for a delayed swami at a charity bazaar, he is hard-pressed to tell fortunes and is pressed hard by a policeman who thinks he is a crook.
   Writer: Leonard Levinson
   Comments: Peary makes the most of his opportunity to affect a foreign di-

alect. Gildy expresses his frustration in his "Oh, what's the use?" query for the first time. Puns include "tells you about your past and future for a present" and "in hot water since I put on this Turkish towel." The "I cannot bark" response to Hooker's question gets by the censor but not the audience. The language of the mystics may be colorful, but their crystal balls project future visions only in black-and-white.

Date: March 8, 1942 (Script)
Title: Defense Stamps in Book
   Cast: Harold Peary (Gildersleeve), Jim Bannon, Lurene Tuttle (Marjorie), Walter Tetley (Leroy), Earle Ross (Hooker), Lillian Randolph (Birdie), Paula Winslowe (Mrs. Salisbury Twitchell, girl)
   Summary: Throckmorton attempts to locate a book Marjorie donated to the Victory Book Drive which has $1,000 in Defense Stamps in it.
   Writer: Leonard Levinson
   Comments: The donated book is *Gone with the Wind* so Levinson trots out some appropriate puns (e.g., "the trouble Scarlett O'Hara had with her Butler"). The puns also fly as Marjorie, Leroy, and Gildy call off the titles of books they are searching through (e.g., feeling less miserable gets tied in with *Les Misérables*). Marjorie's reply to the fast-talking girl's question "Do things like this happen to your uncle every day?" is "No, just once a week." ("No, just on Sundays" was the original retort before part of it was crossed out.) Gildersleeve states that he served as a major in World War I, assigned to purchasing mules for the Army in 1918.

Date: March 15, 1942
Title: Best Dressed Racket
   Cast: Harold Peary (Gildersleeve), Jim Bannon, Lurene Tuttle (Marjorie), Walter Tetley (Leroy), Earle Ross (Hooker), Lillian Randolph (Birdie), Paula Winslowe (Mrs. Salisbury Twitchell)
   Summary: Gildersleeve and Hooker are lured by conmen who flatter them into buying tailored suits made from cheap material.
   Writer: Leonard Levinson
   Comments: Leroy and Gildersleeve improvise their own lyrics to "Deep in the Heart of Texas." Puns include "I hope you have a perfect fit" and "Make a little change whenever I can." Listeners then and now who picture cloth with a chocolate background and orange diagonal stripes set off by blue dots will recognize that twisted Orkney as a horse of a different color known as backstretch burlap.

Date: March 22, 1942
Title: New Neighbors
   Cast: Harold Peary (Gildersleeve), Jim Bannon, Lurene Tuttle (Marjorie), Walter Tetley (Leroy), Lillian Randolph (Birdie), Paula Winslowe (Dotty Dobson)
   Summary: Obnoxious neighbors drive Gildersleeve to a gym for training so he can confront the burly head of the family.
   Writer: Leonard Levinson
   Comments: This is one of the weakest shows of the first season with no memorable sequences. Puns include "both came in handy in a pinch," "dead on the level." Peary promotes his upcoming verbal fisticuffs with John

Barrymore on the March 26th *Rudy Vallee Show.*

Date: March 29, 1942
Title: Letters to Servicemen
   Cast: Harold Peary (Gildersleeve), Jim Bannon, Lurene Tuttle (Marjorie), Walter Tetley (Leroy), Earle Ross (Hooker), Lillian Randolph (Birdie), Paula Winslowe (Dotty)
   Summary: Confusion results when a serviceman receives a letter by mistake which suggests that Marjorie wants to marry him.
   Writer: Leonard Levinson
   Comments: *The Male Animal* reference is to the Broadway play and/or the new film that will be playing in theaters in April. Gildy's belief that his misery will be extended prompts him to alter his usual complaint to "This is going to be one of my bad weeks." The serious state of the world's condition at this time is evident in Peary's blunt choice at the end between bonds that can buy victory or the bonds of the Axis.

Date: April 5, 1942 (Script)
Title: Easter Egg Hunt
   Cast: Harold Peary (Gildersleeve), Jim Bannon, Lurene Tuttle (Marjorie), Walter Tetley (Leroy), Earle Ross (Hooker), Lillian Randolph (Birdie), Paula Winslowe (Mrs. Salisbury Twitchell, Dotty)
   Summary: When the Park Commissioner cancels the Easter egg hunt, Gildersleeve and Mrs. Twitchell go into the country to get eggs from farmers to hold their own hunt for the children of Summerfield.
   Writer: Leonard Levinson
   Comments: Notable puns include

"Lily Pons in lily ponds" and "Plymouth Rocks don't break." Things get messy when the eggs are not boiled before coloring and chaos reigns in the kitchen when some of the chicks hatch in the oven. The script indicates that J.L. Kraft delivers the first Easter greeting and that Peary reads Kraft's message on the rebroadcast.

Date: April 12, 1942 (Script)
Title: Cuts Elm Tree
   Cast: Harold Peary (Gildersleeve), Jim Bannon, Lurene Tuttle (Marjorie), Walter Tetley (Leroy), Earle Ross (Hooker), Lillian Randolph (Birdie), Paula Winslowe (Dotty)
   Summary: After consulting with various doctors, Gildersleeve decides to take down an elm tree himself.
   Writer: Leonard Levinson
   Allusion: Gildersleeve quotes from *Henry IV, Part II* by William Shakespeare: "It's an ill wind that blows no good."
   Comments: Notable puns include "I see you're sawing" and "Don't look a gift saw in the teeth." Marjorie tells an anecdote typical of that era, describing Birdie in the dark hall letting out a piercing scream after seeing a large white object without head or feet and then discovering it was a reflection in a mirror of her wearing a white nightgown. Peary inadvertently becomes a hero after bringing down a power line with the tree, thus causing his neighborhood to be the only one with 100% blackout during a test and giving him the title of Summerfield's Air Raid Warden. Peary closes with a reminder to save metals, paper, and rubber for scrap drives.

Date: April 19, 1942
Title: Selling and Planting Seeds
  Cast: Harold Peary (Gildersleeve), Jim Bannon, Lurene Tuttle (Marjorie), Walter Tetley (Leroy), Earle Ross (Hooker), Lillian Randolph (Birdie), Mel Blanc (salesman), Paula Winslowe (Dotty)
  Summary: Gildersleeve first talks himself into helping Leroy sell seeds and then into a growing contest with Judge Hooker.
  Writer: Leonard Levinson
  Comments: This escapade is to promote by (bad) example the importance of Victory Gardens. Puns include "Eight to the bar" and "Out in the country, I could sure go to town." Gildy indicates he is 5'10" tall which, coupled with his portly frame, only slightly disqualifies him as the inspiration for the top ten hit later that year, "Mister Five by Five."

Date: April 26, 1942
Title: Goat
  Cast: Harold Peary (Gildersleeve), Jim Bannon, Lurene Tuttle (Marjorie), Walter Tetley (Leroy), Earle Ross (Hooker), Lillian Randolph (Birdie), Mel Blanc (goat, Percy Bodkin), Richard LeGrand (McCorkle, farmer), Paula Winslowe (Dotty)
  Summary: Gildersleeve attempts to get rid of a ravenous goat that has taken residence on his property.
  Writer: Leonard Levinson
  Allusion: Gildersleeve quotes from *Locksley Hall* by Alfred, Lord Tennyson: "In the spring a young man's fancy lightly turns to thoughts of love."
  Comments: Blanc, who had been playing hiccupping characters on *Fibber McGee and Molly*, manages to put a hic into his bleats. Richard LeGrand, who will later assume the role of Richard Peavey, appears for the first time using his distinctive Swedish dialect. Puns include "very good bumper," "That's the last straw." Cheese products now become an integral part of the Kraft commercials. In the tag Lurene and Hal encourage listeners to support the Navy Relief Society.

Date: May 3, 1942
Title: Ship Christening
  Cast: Harold Peary (Gildersleeve), Jim Bannon, Lurene Tuttle (Marjorie), Walter Tetley (Leroy), Lillian Randolph (Birdie), Mel Blanc (George, Drizzlepuss, shipbuilder), Paula Winslowe (Dotty)
  Summary: Marjorie, Leroy, and Gildersleeve use trains, plane, jalopy, and taxicab to get them to San Francisco to christen the *SS Throckmorton P. Gildersleeve*.
  Writer: Leonard Levinson
  Allusion: Gildersleeve quotes Charles Cotesworth Pinckney: "Millions for defense, but not one cent for tribute." (Gildy attributes the saying to his great-grandfather.)
  Comments: The broadcast emanates from San Francisco. Gildy does a switch by saying "This is going to be one of my bad Wednesdays." Leroy says, "Oh, for corn's sake" for the first time. (In some scripts the wording is "Aw, for corn sake.") Puns include "Standing Pat," "pitch and toss."

Date: May 10, 1942
Title: Mystery Singer
  Cast: Harold Peary (Gildersleeve),

Jim Bannon, Lurene Tuttle (Marjorie), Walter Tetley (Leroy), Earle Ross (Hooker), Lillian Randolph (Birdie), Mel Blanc (Newbauer, Teddy), Frank Nelson (Pat Callahan, Wally), Shirley Mitchell (card player), Paula Winslowe (Dotty)

Summary: Gildersleeve assumes the guise of a Brazilian crooner on the radio to win a bet from Judge Hooker.

Writer: Leonard Levinson

Allusions: Hooker quotes from "The Hand That Rocks the Cradle" by William Ross Wallace: "The hand that rocks the cradle [is the hand that] rules the world." Hooker quotes from *Moral Essays* by Alexander Pope: "[Just] as the twig is bent the tree's inclined." Gildersleeve quotes from *Romeo and Juliet* by William Shakespeare: "Parting is such sweet sorrow."

Comments: Commercials are now at the beginning, middle, and end of the show. Gildy borrows Leroy's "Oh, for corn's sake." Gildy sings "My Rosita." Puns include "spot remover" and "out to lynch."

Date: May 17, 1942
Title: College Chum or Con Man?
Cast: Harold Peary (Gildersleeve), Jim Bannon, Lurene Tuttle (Marjorie), Walter Tetley (Leroy), Earle Ross (Hooker), Lillian Randolph (Birdie), Frank Nelson (Bob Brown), Mel Blanc (Sheehan, Conley)

Summary: Gildersleeve suspects that a man who professes to be an old classmate is selling shares in a fraudulent mining enterprise.

Writer: Leonard Levinson

Comments: If Gildersleeve was 22 when he graduated from Princeton in 1914, he would be about 50 in 1942. Puns include "fly by night," "get the lead out."

Date: May 24, 1942 (Script)
Title: Three Dates for Dance
Cast: Harold Peary (Gildersleeve), Jim Bannon, Lurene Tuttle (Marjorie), Walter Tetley (Leroy), Earle Ross (Hooker), Lillian Randolph (Birdie), Shirley Mitchell (Honey Tolliver), Paula Winslowe (Dotty)

Summary: Gildersleeve is on the spot when he is obligated to take Dotty, Honey, and Dolores to the USO Ball.

Writer: Leonard Levinson

Comments: Levinson reaps several punny jokes out of USO such as US-Owe. This is the first of many times when Throckmorton will have multiple dates for the same night, although this story takes the easy copout of making it seem like the whole misadventure was a dream Gildy had while asleep in a hammock. Hooker has the funniest line in the script when he claims the sight of Throckmorton in white flannel pants reminds him of the giant tooth that hangs outside his dentist's office.

Date: May 31, 1942
Title: Testimonial Dinner for Hooker
Cast: Harold Peary (Gildersleeve), Jim Bannon, Lurene Tuttle (Marjorie), Walter Tetley (Leroy), Earle Ross (Hooker), Lillian Randolph (Birdie), Mel Blanc (Duffy, Silsbey), Eddie Marr (Bear Barrel Bock)

Summary: Trying to keep a fete Gildy plans to commemorate the judge's 20 years on the bench a secret from Hooker frays the nerves of both the party-planner and the honoree.

Writer: Leonard Levinson

Comments: This episode contains several scenes that play funny on the stage of the theater of the mind including Throcky and Horace bumping heads as they reach for tickets on the floor and the moment when Gildersleeve inflates in anger like a balloon before releasing his pent-up frustration with a spritz that probably doused the microphone in saliva. Hooker appropriates Gildy's "one of my bad days" expression.

Date: June 7, 1942

Title: Sneezes

Cast: Harold Peary (Gildersleeve), Jim Bannon, Lurene Tuttle (Marjorie), Walter Tetley (Leroy), Earle Ross (Hooker), Lillian Randolph (Birdie), Frank Nelson (Dr. DePeyster), Mel Blanc (fireman), Paula Winslowe (Dotty, dental assistant)

Summary: Gildersleeve, after seeking relief for his sneezing fits from an allergist, gets stuck in a tree house.

Writer: Leonard Levinson

Comments: Levinson foreshadows the resolution to the story by introducing a pesky cat in the early dialogue. Puns include "blow a lot of money on my nose," "cat got your tongue," "bored with lodging here." Hooker teases his pal with creaky versions of "Rock-a-Bye Baby" and "Don't Sit Under the Apple Tree." In the tag Peary promotes patriotic summer shows replacing *The Jack Benny Program* on Sundays.

Date: June 14, 1942

Title: Summer Theater Play

Cast: Harold Peary (Gildersleeve), Jim Bannon, Lurene Tuttle (Marjorie), Walter Tetley (Leroy), Earle Ross (Hooker), Lillian Randolph (Birdie), Frank Nelson (Bruce Burdick), Mel Blanc (Charlie Robertson, Whalen), Elvia Allman (Mrs. Guernsey), Paula Winslowe (Dotty)

Summary: After Throckmorton convinces a theater group to perform the melodrama *Deep in the Heart of Maryland*, he finds himself playing multiple parts in the production.

Writer: Leonard Levinson

Comments: This episode, more than any other in the series, demonstrates Peary's skill with voices and characterization. The reference to Mr. Crosby's horses is an in-joke regarding Bing's stable of thoroughbreds. Puns include "my drama done told me" and "the Shingles."

Date: June 21, 1942

Title: Chair Mix-up

Cast: Harold Peary (Gildersleeve), Jim Bannon, Lurene Tuttle (Marjorie), Walter Tetley (Leroy), Earle Ross (Hooker), Lillian Randolph (Birdie), Sam Hearn (Sam Schlepperman), Frank Nelson (Lt. Miller), Mel Blanc (delivery man, Gus), Paula Winslowe (Dotty, Amelia Hooker)

Summary: Complications ensue when Leroy and Marjorie, Gildersleeve, and Hooker buy leather chairs for the Forrester living room.

Writer: Leonard Levinson

Comments: Hooker reveals Gildersleeve's birthday is July 21, which is quite close to Peary's actual birthday of July 25. The furniture follies on display resemble the action of stage farce. Puns include "putting blimps into shape again" and "You're hinting below the belt."

Date: June 28, 1942
Title: Courting Amelia Hooker
   Cast: Harold Peary (Gildersleeve), Jim Bannon, Lurene Tuttle (Marjorie), Walter Tetley (Leroy), Earle Ross (Hooker), Lillian Randolph (Birdie), Mel Blanc (park officer, musician), Paula Winslowe (Dotty, Amelia Hooker)
   Summary: Over the objections of Hooker, Gildy woos the judge's sister in town and country.
   Writer: Leonard Levinson
   Comments: On the phone Peary uses the Gooey Fooey voice he employed on *Fibber McGee and Molly*. Gildersleeve sings "Just a Little Love, a Little Kiss." In his last script for the program Levinson satirizes fraternal organizations by bestowing Horace with the title of Grand Screech of the local chapter of the International Order of Hoot Owls. Peary salutes the staff and cast at the end including producer Cecil Underwood. By mentioning musical director William Randolph Mills, Peary virtually admits that William Randolph had been a nom de baton for Billy Mills, music man for *Fibber McGee and Molly* since 1938. *Victory Parade* is the summer replacement series for *The Great Gildersleeve*.

Date: August 30, 1942
Title: Fishing Trip
   Cast: Harold Peary (Gildersleeve), Ben Alexander, Lurene Tuttle (Marjorie), Walter Tetley (Leroy), Earle Ross (Hooker), Lillian Randolph (Birdie)

   Summary: Acting upon his doctor's advice to get some rest, Gildersleeve takes the family to Lake Hackmatack for a vacation.
   Writer: John Whedon
   Comments: This is the first episode written by John Whedon. Whedon, who relied less on wordplay than Levinson did, could not resist the "bang out of this" clincher. Ben Alexander, who will later take the part of Marjorie's bashful beau Ben, appears for the first time. Tetley unleashes his underwater gargle that will become part of his comic repertoire on *The Phil Harris–Alice Faye Show*. The William Randolph guise is tossed aside in favor of direct credit to Billy Mills.

Date: September 6, 1942
Title: Golf Match
   Cast: Harold Peary (Gildersleeve), Frank Bingman, Lurene Tuttle (Marjorie), Walter Tetley (Leroy), Earle Ross (Hooker), Lillian Randolph (Birdie), Frank Nelson (Bill Ferris), Mel Blanc (announcer, waiter)
   Summary: Gildersleeve finds it difficult to concentrate on a golf match with Hooker when an egotistical bandleader becomes first an ill-mannered house guest and then a formidable opponent on the links.
   Writer: John Whedon
   Comments: Gildersleeve yells "Leroy!" for the first time, although he will stretch out the exclamation to greater comic effect on future occasions. Leroy descends the stairs in his rambunctious fashion for the first time. Whedon closes the show with a bang of a different sort than the one hinted at the previous week.

Date: September 13, 1942 (Script)
Title: Winning the War
   Cast: Harold Peary (Gildersleeve), Frank Bingman, Lurene Tuttle (Marjorie), Walter Tetley (Leroy), Earle Ross (Hooker), Lillian Randolph (Birdie), Richard LeGrand (Richard Q. Peavey)
   Summary: Gildersleeve, Leroy, and Marjorie spend the day collecting scrap and concentrating solely on efforts to win the war.
   Writer: John Whedon
   Allusion: Peavey quotes from Isaiah 21:11: "Watchman, what of the night?" Gildersleeve quotes from "The Village Blacksmith" by Henry Wadsworth Longfellow: "Something accomplished, something done / Has earned a night's repose."
   Comments: Gildersleeve sings "A Bicycle Built for Two." Richard LeGrand, in his first appearance as Richard Peavey, utters his catch phrase "Well, now, I wouldn't say that" three times. During their hunt for scrap, the family enters the attic for the first time. After putting his car up on blocks, resolving to put in a coal furnace, and looking for fires from atop the water tank, Gildy changes *his* catch phrase to "This has been one of my good days."

Date: September 20, 1942 (Script)
Title: Meets Leila Ransome
   Cast: Harold Peary (Gildersleeve), Frank Bingman, Lurene Tuttle (Marjorie), Walter Tetley (Leroy), Earle Ross (Hooker), Lillian Randolph (Birdie), Shirley Mitchell (Leila Ransome), Richard LeGrand (Peavey)
   Summary: Gildersleeve, curious about the widow who moves in next door, brings her candy, flowers, and also his heart on his sleeve.

Writer: John Whedon
   Comments: Gildersleeve sings "Speak to Me of Love" and "There Is a Tavern in the Town." Shirley Mitchell appears for the first time as Leila Ransome. Impetuous Gildy seeks Hooker's advice about marrying Leila on the same day he meets the southern charmer. Later in the series Throckmorton goes to the drugstore to select candy for his dates; this time Peavey brings two boxes of sweets to the house so Gildy can make the choice in the comfort of his living room.

Date: September 27, 1942 (Script)
Title: Competition from Hooker
   Cast: Harold Peary (Gildersleeve), Frank Bingham, Lurene Tuttle (Marjorie), Walter Tetley (Leroy), Earle Ross (Hooker), Lillian Randolph (Birdie), Shirley Mitchell (Leila), Richard LeGrand (Peavey), Mel Blanc (Floyd Munson)
   Summary: Gildersleeve, miffed because Hooker beat his time with Leila, resolves to give up pursuing the lady.
   Writer: John Whedon
   Comments: The character of Floyd the barber is heard for the first time. Again Peavey provides home delivery, this time bringing aspirin and ice cream. Leroy, who prefers cold cereal to the oatmeal that is pushed on him by adults, says he cannot get any more oatmeal down because it keeps sticking to his ribs. There is a funny scene in the barber shop in which feuding Gildy and Hooker talk through Floyd via the "Tell the judge" and "Tell Mr. Gildersleeve" routine, concluding with Throckmorton slapping Floyd and saying, "Give him that for me." Marjorie's

boyfriend Doug mentions her red hair, one of the very few times the color of her tresses is mentioned in the series. (An article in the July 1943 issue of *Tune In* referred to Tuttle as "copper-haired Lurene.")

Date: October 4, 1942
Title: Planting a Tree
 Cast: Harold Peary (Gildersleeve), Frank Bingman, Lurene Tuttle (Marjorie), Walter Tetley (Leroy), Earle Ross (Hooker), Lillian Randolph (Birdie), Shirley Mitchell (Leila Ransome), Richard LeGrand (Richard Peavey), Mel Blanc (delivery man, Floyd)
Summary: When Gildersleeve learns that the water pressure is inadequate to moisten dirt around a tree he has planted, he starts a petition of complaint to take to the city council.
Writer: John Whedon
Allusion: Gildersleeve quotes the title line from "When the Frost Is on the Punkin" by James Whitcomb Riley; Leroy corrupts the graveyard speech of *Hamlet* by complaining "Alas, poor Leroy, I knew him well."
Comments: Leroy utters his pet expression "Are you kiddin'?" for the first time. In the tag Leroy and Gildy plug Peary's appearance in the film *Here We Go Again*.

Date: October 11, 1942
Title: Early Snow
 Cast: Harold Peary (Gildersleeve), Frank Bingman, Lurene Tuttle (Marjorie), Walter Tetley (Leroy), Earle Ross (Hooker), Lillian Randolph (Birdie), Shirley Mitchell (Leila), Richard LeGrand (Peavey)
Summary: An unexpected snowfall

sends Gildersleeve in search of coal and female companionship.
Writer: John Whedon
Allusion: Gildy quotes/sings "Thanksgiving Day" by Lydia Maria Child: "Over the river and through the wood / To grandfather's house we'll go / The horse knows the way."
Comments: Peary manages to get shivers into his snores. A primary purpose of this episode was to emphasize the need to conserve oil resources, thereby using energy wisely.

Date: October 18, 1942
Title: Appointed Water Commissioner
 Cast: Harold Peary (Gildersleeve), Frank Bingman, Lurene Tuttle (Marjorie), Walter Tetley (Leroy), Earle Ross (Hooker), Lillian Randolph (Birdie), Shirley Mitchell (Leila, secretary), Richard LeGrand (Peavey, sergeant), Mel Blanc (Floyd, lieutenant)
Summary: After Hooker leads Gildersleeve to believe he will be the new water commissioner, the great man assumes it is a fait accompli and makes preparations to take office.
Writer: John Whedon
Comments: Leila's mention of Niagara Falls gets exactly the opposite reaction of the "Slowly I Turned" routine as Gildy "oompfs" into a "here I run." Gildersleeve seems to have shrunk 1½" from April 19 when he was 5'10" and gained about 17 pounds since January 4 when he weighed 213. Some years have been shaved off his age as well because if he was 44 in October 1942 and a member of the Princeton class of 1914 as noted on May 17, he would have graduated from college at the age of 16.

Date: October 25, 1942
Title: First Day as Commissioner
Cast: Harold Peary (Gildersleeve), Frank Bingman, Lurene Tuttle (Marjorie), Walter Tetley (Leroy), Earle Ross (Hooker), Lillian Randolph (Birdie), Shirley Mitchell (Leila, lady at city hall), Richard LeGrand (Peavey), Verna Felton (Miss Fitch), Ken Christy (Chief Gates)
Summary: Gildersleeve finds his way around the office in city hall and around the reservoir where he encounters a skinny-dipping Leroy.
Writer: John Whedon
Comments: Weather in Summerfield is truly mercurial, going from snowy on October 11 to warm enough to swim outdoors two weeks later. This is the first time Gildersleeve becomes frustrated at Peavey's equivocation, sputtering out a declaration that could have been the pharmacist's epitaph: "You'll die of moderation." Gildersleeve characteristically puts his foot in his mouth with his gaffe regarding the portrait and the slapstick scene with the painter. Ken Christy appears for the first time as chief of police Gates, although his first name will change from Charlie to Donald later.

Date: November 1, 1942
Title: Pal to Leroy
Cast: Harold Peary (Gildersleeve), Frank Bingman, Lurene Tuttle (Marjorie), Walter Tetley (Leroy), Earle Ross (Hooker), Lillian Randolph (Birdie), Shirley Mitchell (Leila), Richard LeGrand (Peavey)
Summary: After spending a strenuous morning hunting, Gildersleeve hopes to get out of his promise to spend the whole day with Leroy by pretending to be sick.
Writer: John Whedon
Allusion: Gildersleeve quotes from "The Face Upon the Floor" by Hugh Antoine d'Arcy: "It was a balmy summer evening / And a goodly crowd was there."
Comments: Crafty Gildersleeve knows which side his paycheck is buttered on by asking Birdie to bring him some cheese. Leroy's "Who does he think he's kidding?" is a precursor of his "What a character!" remark.

Date: November 8, 1942
Title: Quiet Evening at Home
Cast: Harold Peary (Gildersleeve), Ken Carpenter, Lurene Tuttle (Marjorie), Walter Tetley (Leroy), Earle Ross (Hooker), Lillian Randolph (Birdie), Shirley Mitchell (Leila), Richard LeGrand (Peavey), Verna Felton (Miss Fitch)
Summary: Gildersleeve resolves to save money by spending more evenings at home.
Writer: John Whedon
Comments: The distinctive voice of Ken Carpenter is heard for the first time as announcer. Donald Nelson, referred to in this episode and others in the coming months, served as director of the Office of Production Management and chairman of the War Production Board. Summerfield's department store, Hogan Brothers, is mentioned for the first time. Gildersleeve sings "Why Do I Love You?"

Date: November 15, 1942
Title: College Chum's Son Visits
Cast: Harold Peary (Gildersleeve),

Ken Carpenter, Lurene Tuttle (Marjorie), Walter Tetley (Leroy), Earle Ross (Hooker), Lillian Randolph (Birdie), Shirley Mitchell (woman by train, Leila), Richard LeGrand (Peavey), Verna Felton (Miss Fitch), Ben Alexander (Brink, Larry Brinkerhoff)

Summary: Gildersleeve welcomes the son of an old classmate who turns out to be an opportunistic Lothario like his father.

Writer: John Whedon

Comments: Peary does a credible job at playing a callow youth in the flashback. In this episode Hooker and Peavey show why they belong in the Geezer Hall of Fame, one ringing the gong with the purloined clapper, the other reveling in a crocheted watch fob.

Brooklyn's Dodgers were not in the same league with Summerfield's Codgers.

Date: November 22, 1942
Title: Thanksgiving Dinner
Cast: Harold Peary (Gildersleeve), Ken Carpenter, Lurene Tuttle (Marjorie), Walter Tetley (Leroy), Earle Ross (Hooker), Lillian Randolph (Birdie), Shirley Mitchell (woman in line, Leila), Richard LeGrand (man in line, Peavey), Frank Nelson (official), Verna Felton (Miss Fitch)

Summary: Gildersleeve has double trouble when his efforts to get a B ration book and a turkey seem to fail.

Writer: John Whedon

Allusions: Gildersleeve quotes from "Night Thoughts" by Edward Young: "Procrastination is the thief of time," *Poor Richard's Almanac* by Benjamin Franklin: "For want of a nail the shoe was lost," *Lord Chesterfield's Letters*:

"Never put off till tomorrow what you can do today," and *Don Quixote* by Miguel de Cervantes: "Strike while the iron is hot."

Comments: Leroy can be excused for muffing "Prithee, Miss Priscilla," a natural tongue twister. Gildersleeve behaves in a typically hypocritical way, mouthing aphorisms about procrastination before finding himself in a bind because of delayed actions.

Date: November 29, 1942
Title: Operetta Star in Town
Cast: Harold Peary (Gildersleeve), Frank Bingman, Lurene Tuttle (Marjorie), Walter Tetley (Leroy), Earle Ross (Hooker), Lillian Randolph (Birdie), Shirley Mitchell (Leila), Richard LeGrand (Peavey), Mel Blanc (Floyd), Elvia Allman (Vera LaValle)

Summary: Gildersleeve is on the spot after promising to bring a singer he does not know personally to a social gathering after the star performs at the opera house.

Writer: John Whedon

Comments: Gildersleeve sings "Deep in My Heart." Separately Leroy, Birdie, and Vera sing "Mister Five by Five." Whedon invents a wonderful name for a bandleader, Toots Malarkey, who would be right at home waving a baton in front of Ziggy Elman, Wingy Manone, and Dizzy Gillespie.

Date: December 6, 1942
Title: Toothache
Cast: Harold Peary (Gildersleeve), Ken Carpenter, Lurene Tuttle (Marjorie), Walter Tetley (Leroy), Earle Ross (Hooker), Lillian Randolph (Birdie), Shirley Mitchell (Leila, Miss Mitchell),

Richard LeGrand (Peavey), Verna Felton (Miss Fitch), Mel Blanc (Floyd), Arthur Q. Bryan (Doctor Shanks)

Summary: Gildersleeve puts off attending to a sore tooth until Marjorie forces him to go to a dentist.

Writer: John Whedon

Comments: The ride downtown is a delight to the eye and ear as listeners envision driver Horace pointing to the inside of his mouth while passenger Throckmorton hangs on for dear life. Marjorie boldly states her assertion that Leroy does not have a nerve in his entire body for a logical reason: "If he did, he couldn't stand the noises he makes." The purpose of the stop at the barbershop is to stress the importance of conserving rubber and gasoline. Gildy gives Floyd's last name as *Munyon* which will later be changed to *Munson*.

Date: December 13, 1942 (Script)
Title: Birdie Visits Relatives
   Cast: Harold Peary (Gildersleeve), Ken Carpenter, Lurene Tuttle (Marjorie), Walter Tetley (Leroy), Earle Ross (Hooker), Lillian Randolph (Birdie), Shirley Mitchell (Leila), Richard LeGrand (Peavey)

Summary: Gildersleeve and the children suffer hunger pains when Birdie goes away for two weeks.

Writer: John Whedon

Comments: Leila and Gildersleeve sing "Speak to Me of Love." When the famished threesome visit the drugstore in search of nourishment, Peavey runs through a list of items he *doesn't* have before admitting that all he can offer outside of the soda fountain treats are fig newtons. (Gildy and the youngsters settle for banana splits.) Throckmorton

shows he places his stomach above his heart by leaving Leila in the lurch the moment Leroy brings news that Birdie has returned.

Date: December 20, 1942
Title: Christmas Shopping for Hooker
   Cast: Harold Peary (Gildersleeve), Ken Carpenter, Lurene Tuttle (Marjorie), Walter Tetley (Leroy), Earle Ross (Hooker), Lillian Randolph (Birdie), Shirley Mitchell (Leila), Richard LeGrand (Peavey), Verna Felton (Miss Fitch), Arthur Q. Bryan (Floyd, man at airport)

Summary: After accompanying Hooker to the airport to see Leila off, Throckmorton shops for a present for the judge.

Writer: John Whedon

Allusion: Gildersleeve quotes from "To a Mouse" by Robert Burns: "The best-laid plans of mice and men / Gang aft agley."

Comments: Gildy is in typical form, asleep on the job and behind on his shopping due to procrastination. Leila also behaves in her usual self-centered manner, taking offense easily, crying crocodile tears, and making eyes at a handsome man at the airport. Arthur Q. Bryan appears for the first time as Floyd. Peavey sings a bit of "White Christmas." Birdie's method of correcting electrical problems by unplugging the cord and trying again is akin to rebooting computers.

Date: December 27, 1942
Title: Leroy Makes Nitroglycerin
   Cast: Harold Peary (Gildersleeve), Ken Carpenter, Lurene Tuttle (Marjorie), Walter Tetley (Leroy), Earle Ross

(Hooker), Lillian Randolph (Birdie), Richard LeGrand (Peavey), Verna Felton (Miss Fitch), Arthur Q. Bryan (gruff man on street, Floyd), Ken Christy (Leonard P. Brody)

Summary: Leroy accidentally creates a touchy situation when he uses the chemistry set he got for Christmas to concoct a possible explosive.

Writer: John Whedon

Comments: Leroy's take on SWAK is unromantic but typical of his attitude toward females: Some Women Are Krazy [sic]. Gildy's order to Birdie that passes without notice is humorous in reflection: "Don't let it go off till I get there." In the tag Gildersleeve sings a couple lines from "Auld Lang Syne" and promotes his appearance on *Fibber McGee and Molly* on December 29th. Ken Carpenter plugs Peary's new film *The Great Gildersleeve*.

Date: January 3, 1943
Title: Engaged to Leila
  Cast: Harold Peary (Gildersleeve), Ken Carpenter, Lurene Tuttle (Marjorie), Walter Tetley (Leroy), Earle Ross (Hooker), Lillian Randolph (Birdie), Shirley Mitchell (Leila), Richard LeGrand (Peavey)

Summary: Hooker and Gildersleeve intend to ask for Leila's hand in marriage upon her return to Summerfield.

Writer: John Whedon

Comments: In his usual way of leaping before looking, Gildersleeve announces his engagement to others before proposing to his future bride. Gildersleeve sings "A Little Love, a Little Kiss." The importance of women in the workforce is the focus of this broadcast just as it was on the December 8,

1942 episode of *Fibber McGee and Molly*.

Date: January 10, 1943
Title: McGees Visit Summerfield
  Cast: Harold Peary (Gildersleeve), Ken Carpenter, Lurene Tuttle (Marjorie), Walter Tetley (Leroy), Earle Ross (Hooker), Lillian Randolph (Birdie), Shirley Mitchell (Leila), Richard LeGrand (Peavey), Jim Jordan (Fibber McGee), Marian Jordan (Molly McGee)

Summary: Gildersleeve is somewhat apprehensive about entertaining the McGees because he fears Fibber will make insulting remarks if he learns about Gildy's engagement.

Writer: John Whedon

Comments: Listeners get a clear view of the Forrester property (100 feet wide, 170 feet deep) and its distance from Peavey's Pharmacy (three blocks). Molly shows Fibber what happens when closets are opened in the homes of other people: nothing. Gildy borrows Fibber's "clavicle" line and Fibber tries on Leroy's "Are you kiddin'?" query.

Date: January 17, 1943
Title: Women's Club Speech
  Cast: Harold Peary (Gildersleeve), Ken Carpenter, Lurene Tuttle (Marjorie), Walter Tetley (Leroy), Earle Ross (Hooker), Lillian Randolph (Birdie), Shirley Mitchell (Leila), Richard LeGrand (Peavey), Arthur Q. Bryan (Floyd), Elvia Allman (Irene, Mrs. Pettibone), Pauline Drake (Bessie)

Summary: Gildersleeve, tardy in preparing a speech, takes out his frustration on those he encounters at home and downtown.

Writers: John Whedon, Sam Moore

Comments: Sam Moore, who also penned jokes for Eddie Cantor, joins Whedon as co-writer. Pauline Drake appears for the first time as Bessie. A little-known fact is that Pauline played an uncredited character named Bessie in the 1940 Mr. Wong film, *The Fatal Hour.* Mrs. Peavey and husband, with their silent variety of laughter, would have made the ideal audience for a Charlie Chaplin film festival.

Date: January 24, 1943
Title: Sabotage Rumors
   Cast: Harold Peary (Gildersleeve), Ken Carpenter, Lurene Tuttle (Marjorie), Walter Tetley (Leroy), Earle Ross (Hooker), Lillian Randolph (Birdie), Shirley Mitchell (Leila), Richard LeGrand (Peavey), Arthur Q. Bryan (Jackson), Pauline Drake (Bessie), Ken Christy (Gates)
   Summary: Gildersleeve, who begins to see spies around every corner, finds himself spending the night guarding the reservoir.
   Writers: John Whedon, Sam Moore
   Comments: Even before listeners know Gildersleeve has officially hired Bessie as his new secretary, he utters the threat he will make often in the coming months: "I'm going to have to let her go." Cussing Charlie Anderson, gosh-darned superintendent of the dad-busted waterworks, appears for the first time. Charlie popped up irregularly through the years, making each cantankerous visit a highlight of the episodes in which he appeared, although the actor playing the part was not mentioned in the scripts or in the closing credits until the 1950s when Cliff Ar-

quette and Jack Moyles assumed the role.

Date: January 31, 1943
Title: Fire Engine Committee
   Cast: Harold Peary (Gildersleeve), Ken Carpenter, Lurene Tuttle (Marjorie), Walter Tetley (Leroy), Earle Ross (Hooker), Lillian Randolph (Birdie), Shirley Mitchell (Leila), Richard LeGrand (Peavey), Elvia Allman (Mrs. Pettibone)
   Summary: Tempers flare among members of a committee over the best way to raise funds for a new fire engine.
   Writers: John Whedon, Sam Moore
   Allusion: Hooker quotes from *A Tale of Two Cities* by Charles Dickens: "It is a far, far better thing I do, than I have ever done before. It is a far, far better rest I go to than I have ever known."
   Comments: Gildersleeve sings "Drink to Me Only with Thine Eyes." Peary covers Shirley's small fluff by saying, "Don't get nervous." The purpose of the cans clattering out of the closet was not to borrow a bit from *Fibber McGee and Molly* but to deliver a practical lesson about hoarding. Marjorie courageously speaks up for her uncle as she did on October 18, 1942 when seeking an appointment for him as water commissioner.

Date: February 7, 1943
Title: Leila's Sister Visits
   Cast: Harold Peary (Gildersleeve), Ken Carpenter, Lurene Tuttle (Marjorie), Walter Tetley (Leroy), Earle Ross (Hooker), Lillian Randolph (Birdie), Shirley Mitchell (Leila), Richard LeGrand (Peavey), Arthur Q. Brya (Floyd), Pauline Drake (Bessie)

Summary: Gildersleeve finds that a visit from Leila's sister and nephew keeps him from romancing his fiancée.

Writers: John Whedon, Sam Moore

Comments: Gildersleeve's advice to Leroy ("Stay out of sight") is one he wishes he could give to Michael. Bing Crosby gets another plug as the star of a film playing in Summerfield. Peary delivers a timely message about shoe rationing.

Date: February 14, 1943 (Script)
Title: Valentine Prank
  Cast: Harold Peary (Gildersleeve), Ken Carpenter, Lurene Tuttle (Marjorie), Walter Tetley (Leroy), Earle Ross (Hooker), Lillian Randolph (Birdie), Shirley Mitchell (Leila), Richard LeGrand (Peavey), Ben Alexander (Ben Waterford)
  Summary: Throckmorton thinks a valentine sent as a prank by Leroy is actually from Leila.
  Writers: John Whedon, Sam Moore
  Comments: Birdie sings "Sometimes I Feel Like a Motherless Child." Ben Alexander appears for the first time as Ben Waterford. Leroy gripes about a valentine sent by the classmate he will not be able to shed for years, Ethel Hammerschlag. Peavey tells about the same comic valentine with pine needles on it that he gives to his wife every year with this sentiment inside: "For you I pine — For you I balsam."

Date: February 21, 1943 (Script)
Title: Keystone Club
  Cast: Harold Peary (Gildersleeve), Ken Carpenter, Lurene Tuttle (Marjorie), Walter Tetley (Leroy), Earle Ross

(Hooker), Lillian Randolph (Birdie), Shirley Mitchell (Leila), Richard LeGrand (Peavey), Ben Alexander (Ben), Pauline Drake (Bessie)
  Summary: Gildersleeve considers going into politics after being invited to join the prestigious Keystone Club.
  Writers: John Whedon, Sam Moore
  Allusion: Gildersleeve quotes from *Poor Richard's Almanac* by Benjamin Franklin: "For want of a nail the shoe was lost."
  Comments: Leroy selects a dandy title for his essay on the first president: "If George Washington Was Alive, He'd Be an Outfielder." Twice in this episode Peavey states he is 63 years old. Gildy nearly proposes to Leila in the drugstore.

Date: February 28, 1943 (Script)
Title: Birthday Dance for Hooker
  Cast: Harold Peary (Gildersleeve), Ken Carpenter, Lurene Tuttle (Marjorie), Walter Tetley (Leroy), Earle Ross (Hooker), Lillian Randolph (Birdie), Shirley Mitchell (Leila), Richard LeGrand (Peavey), Ben Alexander (Ben)
  Summary: A party for Judge Hooker is dampened by Birdie's disappearance.
  Writers: John Whedon, Sam Moore
  Comments: Leroy sings "When the Lights Go On Again." Birdie sings "Can't Help Lovin' That Man" to win a $50 prize at the dinner dance, allowing her to pay off the finance company from whom she was hiding. The birthday being celebrated is the judge's 60th. The writers pack considerable information about ration stamps into almost three pages of dialogue between Throckmorton and Birdie.

Date: March 7, 1943 (Script)
Title: Dieting Again
Cast: Harold Peary (Gildersleeve), Ken Carpenter, Lurene Tuttle (Marjorie), Walter Tetley (Leroy), Earle Ross (Hooker), Lillian Randolph (Birdie), Shirley Mitchell (Leila), Richard LeGrand (Peavey), Ben Alexander (Ben), Pauline Drake (Bessie)
Summary: Gildersleeve begins to think of himself as being old and out-of-shape.
Writers: John Whedon, Sam Moore
Allusion: Carpenter quotes from *Locksley Hall* by Alfred, Lord Tennyson: "In the spring a young man's fancy lightly turns to thoughts of love." Gildersleeve quotes from *The Rubáiyát of Omar Khayyám*: "A loaf of bread, a jug of wine, and thou."
Comments: Throckmorton is upset when Leroy orders an exercise kit from a pulp magazine but then tries it, giving forth with his usual grunts and moans. For the first and only time both Peavey and Gildersleeve leave the pharmacy to stand on the sidewalk and view the druggist's window display.

Date: March 14, 1943
Title: Income Tax
Cast: Harold Peary (Gildersleeve), Ken Carpenter, Lurene Tuttle (Marjorie), Walter Tetley (Leroy), Earle Ross (Hooker), Lillian Randolph (Birdie), Shirley Mitchell (Leila), Richard LeGrand (Peavey), Ben Alexander (Ben), Frank Nelson (voice of conscience), Arthur Q. Bryan (Floyd)
Summary: Throckmorton frets over his taxes as he hastens to get the forms completed before the deadline.
Writers: John Whedon, Sam Moore

Comments: Claude Sweeten is now musical director of the program. Gildy, as usual, has waited until the last weekend to prepare his taxes. The electric eye in the drugstore serves another purpose in addition to awaking the slumbering pharmacist: it signals Gildersleeve's weekly visit with Peavey.

Date: March 21, 1943 (Script)
Title: Community Victory Garden
Cast: Harold Peary (Gildersleeve), Ken Carpenter, Lurene Tuttle (Marjorie), Walter Tetley (Leroy), Earle Ross (Hooker), Lillian Randolph (Birdie), Shirley Mitchell (Leila), Richard LeGrand (Peavey)
Summary: Gildersleeve convinces his friends to join forces to plant a communal vegetable garden.
Writers: John Whedon, Sam Moore
Comments: Baseball is in the air because Gildy wants Birdie to come to the garden "to throw out the first potato." Throckmorton gets the last laugh when the governor commends him and not the mayor, who was a Terwilliger-come-lately in the garden process.

Date: March 28, 1943
Title: Springtime in Summerfield
Cast: Harold Peary (Gildersleeve), Ken Carpenter, Lurene Tuttle (Marjorie), Walter Tetley (Leroy), Earle Ross (Hooker), Lillian Randolph (Birdie), Shirley Mitchell (Leila), Richard LeGrand (Peavey), Pauline Drake (Bessie), Ben Alexander (Ben)
Summary: Gildersleeve's enthusiasm over the arrival of spring is dampened by the cool reception his romantic overtures get from Leila.
Writers: John Whedon, Sam Moore

Leroy (Walter Tetley), Gildersleeve (Peary), and Marjorie (Lurene Tuttle) demonstrate the soggy way to plant a victory garden in 1943.

Comments: Goldbricker Gildersleeve dawdles two hours after breakfast and takes a two-hour lunch break. Gildersleeve sings "Moonlight Becomes You."

Date: April 4, 1943
Title: Repairing the Car
Cast: Harold Peary (Gildersleeve), Ken Carpenter, Lurene Tuttle (Marjorie), Walter Tetley (Leroy), Earle Ross (Hooker), Lillian Randolph (Birdie), Richard LeGrand (Peavey), Ben Alexander (Ben)

Summary: When Gildersleeve's efforts to fix the car fail, he cajoles Ben into doing the job, much to the displeasure of Marjorie.
Writers: John Whedon, Sam Moore
Allusions: Hooker quotes from the Mathew's Henry's *Commentary* on Jeremiah: "[There are] none so blind as those that will not see." Gildersleeve quotes from "The Village Blacksmith" by Henry Wadsworth Longfellow: "Something accomplished, something done to earn a night's repose."
Comments: Peary's exclamations

and grunts add much to the slapstick of the scene under the hood. Peavey uses the word *Lucifer*, a rarely-heard term for a match.

Date: April 11, 1943
Title: Car Accident with Hooker
   Cast: Harold Peary (Gildersleeve), Ken Carpenter, Lurene Tuttle (Marjorie), Walter Tetley (Leroy), Earle Ross (Hooker), Lillian Randolph (Birdie), Shirley Mitchell (Leila), Richard LeGrand (Peavey)
   Summary: A fender-bender threatens to break up the friendship between Hooker and Gildersleeve.
   Writers: John Whedon, Sam Moore
   Allusion: Hooker quotes from "Alexander's Feast" by John Dryden: "None but the quick [brave] deserves the fair."
   Comments: A member of the audience with a distinctive laugh makes his presence felt throughout this broadcast. Leila, Gildy, and Hooker demonstrate how they can change their moods in a minute.

Date: April 18, 1943
Title: Nature Hike
   Cast: Harold Peary (Gildersleeve), Ken Carpenter, Lurene Tuttle (Marjorie), Walter Tetley (Leroy), Earle Ross (Hooker), Lillian Randolph (Birdie), Shirley Mitchell (Leila), Richard LeGrand (Peavey)
   Summary: Gildersleeve finds going on a hike with three boys wearing on his nerves and his arches.
   Writers: John Whedon, Sam Moore
   Allusion: Gildersleeve quotes Napoleon Bonaparte: "An army marches [travels] on its stomach."

   Comments: Captain Wonderman seems to be a blend of Superman and Captain Marvel. There is irony in the uncle's warning the nephew about the dangers of hanging around drugstores and Gildersleeve's later flight of fantasy after visiting with Peavey. The writers unapologetically devote two minutes for a visit with *Little Women* in order to touch the hearts of listeners and to show the closeness of families.

Date: April 25, 1943
Title: Easter Rabbits
   Cast: Harold Peary (Gildersleeve), Ken Carpenter, Lurene Tuttle (Marjorie), Walter Tetley (Leroy), Earle Ross (Hooker), Lillian Randolph (Birdie), Shirley Mitchell (Leila), Richard LeGrand (Peavey), Ben Alexander (Ben), Kay Francis
   Summary: Leroy's purchase of rabbits leads Gildersleeve to believe that Leroy needs a mother, thus prompting him to pressure Leila to set a date for their marriage.
   Writers: John Whedon, Sam Moore
   Comments: Kay Francis delivers an inspirational war message. When Lurene named two of the rabbits, she had no idea that in 1949 she would be part of another rabbit caper with Flopsy, Mopsy (and Cottontail) while serving as secretary to Sam Spade. Peavey reveals his first name is Richard. Company President J.L. Kraft delivers an Easter message that is uplifting and unabashedly Christian.

Date: May 2, 1943 (Script)
Title: Hard Water
   Cast: Harold Peary (Gildersleeve), Ken Carpenter, Lurene Tuttle (Mar-

jorie), Walter Tetley (Leroy), Earle Ross (Hooker), Lillian Randolph (Birdie), Shirley Mitchell (Leila), Richard Le-Grand (Peavey), Pauline Drake (Bessie)

Summary: Throckmorton considers resigning when a plan to soften the city's water is not approved by the finance department.

Writers: John Whedon, Sam Moore

Comments: Peavey, who claims to drink eight to ten glasses of water a day, pauses in his conversation with Gildy to drink a glass of water in the commissioner's presence. Throckmorton gets a close look at the ever-malfunctioning snifter valve at the pump house. Leroy saves the day by not mailing his uncle's resignation which was rashly written in the midst of one of Gildy's snits.

Date: May 9, 1943
Title: Wedding List
   Cast: Harold Peary (Gildersleeve), Ken Carpenter, Lurene Tuttle (Marjorie), Walter Tetley (Leroy), Earle Ross (Hooker), Lillian Randolph (Birdie), Shirley Mitchell (Leila), Richard Le-Grand (Peavey)

Summary: After going over the roster of wedding guests with Leila, Gildersleeve goes golfing with his buddies.

Writers: John Whedon, Sam Moore

Allusion: Gildersleeve quotes from "He Fell Among Thieves" by Henry Newbolt: "Fell among thieves."

Comments: Leroy says, "What a character!" for the first time. Gildersleeve, Hooker, Powers, and Pettibone sing "On Moonlight Bay."

Date: May 16, 1943
Title: Burton House
   Cast: Harold Peary (Gildersleeve),

Ken Carpenter, Lurene Tuttle (Marjorie), Walter Tetley (Leroy), Earle Ross (Hooker), Lillian Randolph (Birdie), Shirley Mitchell (Leila), Richard Le-Grand (Peavey), Arthur Q. Bryan (Floyd)

Summary: Throckmorton is reluctant to give in to pressure from Hooker and Leila to purchase the spacious but spooky Burton house.

Writers: John Whedon, Sam Moore

Comments: The movie Leroy saw, *The Mummy's Claw*, is Whedon and Moore's takeoff on the Universal creature feature *The Mummy's Hand*. Leila comes across more Delilah than Dixie belle, right down to the way she wants some hair removed from her Samson.

Date: May 23, 1943
Title: Leroy's Job at Peavey's
   Cast: Harold Peary (Gildersleeve), Ken Carpenter, Lurene Tuttle (Marjorie), Walter Tetley (Leroy), Earle Ross (Hooker), Lillian Randolph (Birdie), Shirley Mitchell (Leila), Richard Le-Grand (Peavey), Ben Alexander (Ben)

Summary: After Peavey hires Leroy to work at the drugstore, Gildersleeve is confronted with the job of mowing the lawn himself.

Writers: John Whedon, Sam Moore

Comments: One can be certain this was only show on the air using the word *collywobbles* during this week in 1943. Whedon and Moore accurately capture the banter of boys in the "Who says so?" "I say so." exchange between Leroy and Piggy.

Date: May 30, 1943
Title: Making a Will
   Cast: Harold Peary (Gildersleeve), Ken Carpenter, Lurene Tuttle (Mar-

jorie), Walter Tetley (Leroy), Earle Ross (Hooker), Lillian Randolph (Birdie), Shirley Mitchell (Leila), Richard Le-Grand (Peavey), Ben Alexander (Ben)

Summary: Memorial Day festivities interrupt Gildersleeve as he prepares his will and considers his legacy.

Writers: John Whedon, Sam Moore

Comments: Peavey's information about his wife suggests he has known her for 30 years. Leila punctuates her double take with an emphatic bang on the piano keys. Gildersleeve sings "Soon."

Date: June 6, 1943
Title: Wedding Shower for Leila

Cast: Harold Peary (Gildersleeve), Ken Carpenter, Lurene Tuttle (Marjorie), Walter Tetley (Leroy), Lillian Randolph (Birdie), Shirley Mitchell (Leila), Richard LeGrand (Peavey), Ben Alexander (Ben), Elvia Allman (Mrs. Pettibone)

Summary: Gildersleeve, feeling left out of wedding shower plans, teaches Leroy the art of self-defense with boxing gloves.

Writers: John Whedon, Sam Moore

Allusion: Ken Carpenter quotes from *The Vision of Sir Launfal* by James Russell Lowell: "What is so rare as a day in June? / Then, if ever, come perfect days."

Comments: Leila is not speedy about picking up Gildy's hints about the shower but is lightning-quick at sensing imagined slights. Peary's blooper of *chickenware* gets little reaction from the audience. Leroy cries twice: once after receiving a punch, once after delivering one. Products like Alkazeeno that have a pleasant taste but do little good or

harm can still be found lining the shelves of drugstores.

Date: June 13, 1943
Title: Honeymoon Preparations

Cast: Harold Peary (Gildersleeve), Ken Carpenter, Lurene Tuttle (Marjorie), Walter Tetley (Leroy), Earle Ross (Hooker), Lillian Randolph (Birdie), Shirley Mitchell (Leila), Richard Le-Grand (Peavey), Ben Alexander (Ben), Pauline Drake (Bessie)

Summary: Gildersleeve prepares staff and family for his absence when he takes his honeymoon with Leila.

Writers: John Whedon, Sam Moore

Comments: Gildy's idea of a wedding trip resembles a hunting or fishing expedition. Peavey indicates he has been married 23 years. Gildersleeve sings a bit of "The Night Was Made for Love."

Date: June 20, 1943 (Script)
Title: Bachelor Dinner

Cast: Harold Peary (Gildersleeve), Ken Carpenter, Lurene Tuttle (Marjorie), Walter Tetley (Leroy), Earle Ross (Hooker), Lillian Randolph (Birdie), Shirley Mitchell (Leila), Richard Le-Grand (Peavey), Ben Alexander (Ben)

Summary: Throckmorton attends a dinner party after which he has a falling out with Leila that threatens to cancel his wedding.

Writers: John Whedon, Sam Moore

Comments: Gildersleeve sings "Time on My Hands." After observing the henpecked and dull lives Pettibone and Peavey have lived, Gildersleeve has reservations about getting married. At the end Throckmorton is so panic-stricken he asks Ben, who is going overseas, to let him know if he hears of a spot in the navy for him.

Date: June 27, 1943
Title: Wedding Day
  Cast: Harold Peary (Gildersleeve), Ken Carpenter, Lurene Tuttle (Marjorie), Walter Tetley (Leroy), Earle Ross (Hooker), Lillian Randolph (Birdie), Shirley Mitchell (Leila), Richard LeGrand (Peavey)
  Summary: As the time for his marriage approaches, Gildersleeve gets cold feet and seeks a way to get the wedding cancelled.
  Writers: John Whedon, Sam Moore
  Comments: Birdie sings "Nobody Knows the Trouble I've Seen." Leroy squeaks out a bit of "Oh Promise Me" and "I Love You Truly." Gildersleeve sings "Am I Blue?" Gildersleeve comes to realize that the ghost of Beauregard would haunt his union with Leila like that of the spirit of Rebecca towering over Manderley. Throcky's last-minute suggestion to Leroy that they run off to the Burton house clearly indicates he is no more ready for marriage than his adolescent nephew. *Men at Sea* is the summer replacement series.

Date: August 29, 1943
Title: Vacation at Grass Lake
  Cast: Harold Peary (Gildersleeve), Ken Carpenter, Lurene Tuttle (Marjorie), Walter Tetley (Leroy), Earle Ross (Hooker), Lillian Randolph (Birdie), Richard LeGrand (Peavey), Arthur Q. Bryan (assistant manager), Bea Benaderet (Miss Foltz, woman by lake)
  Summary: Gildersleeve fends off the advances of women at the Idlewood

Hotel before returning to Summerfield with family and Judge Hooker.
  Writers: John Whedon, Sam Moore
  Allusion: Gildersleeve quotes from "Sea-Fever" by John Masefield: "I must go down to the sea again, to the lonely sea and sky."
  Comments: Gildersleeve and Hooker sing "Home! Sweet Home!" Bea Benaderet appears for the first time. The eligible manpower shortage on the home front makes Gildy a much-wanted party at the resort. The information Peavey provides suggests he has been married since 1913 after being engaged for five years prior to the wedding.

Date: September 5, 1943 (Script)
Title: New School Principal
  Cast: Harold Peary (Gildersleeve), Ken Carpenter, Lurene Tuttle (Marjorie), Walter Tetley (Leroy), Earle Ross (Hooker), Lillian Randolph (Birdie), Richard LeGrand (Peavey), Bea Benaderet (Eve Goodwin)
  Summary: After several mothers complain to Gildersleeve about increasing juvenile delinquency in town, Throckmorton takes the matter up with the new principal.
  Writers: John Whedon, Sam Moore
  Allusion: Gildersleeve quotes from "The Children's Hour" by Henry Wadsworth Longfellow: "Between the dark and the daylight, / When night is beginning to lower, / Comes pause in the day's occupation, / That is known as the children's hour."
  Comments: Bea Benaderet appears for the first time as Eve Goodwin. The petty problems of Summerfield residents are put in perspective when Eve

describes her relief after learning that her brother, presumed lost in the South Pacific, is alive and well. In the tag Leroy gains his uncle's confidence that he has learned his lesson and is maturing — until he asks for a quarter to see *I Walked with a Zombie*.

Date: September 12, 1943
Title: War Bond Drive
   Cast: Harold Peary (Gildersleeve), Ken Carpenter, Lurene Tuttle (Marjorie), Walter Tetley (Leroy), Earle Ross (Hooker), Lillian Randolph (Birdie), Shirley Mitchell (Leila), Richard LeGrand (Peavey), Pauline Drake (Bessie), Arthur Q. Bryan (man in hall, mayor), Bea Benaderet (Eve), Paula Winslowe (Mrs. Kirk)
   Summary: A dispute with the chairman of a committee causes Gildersleeve to strike out on his own campaign to sell bonds.
   Writers: John Whedon, Sam Moore
   Comments: Kraft turns its commercial time over to the Third War Loan Drive. Peavey hits upon Gildersleeve's Achilles heel: "You just like women." Gildy's stubborn behavior shows listeners how obstinate loners can let their pride blind them to seeing the big picture.

Date: September 19, 1943
Title: Preparing for Leila's Return
   Cast: Harold Peary (Gildersleeve), Ken Carpenter, Lurene Tuttle (Marjorie), Walter Tetley (Leroy), Earle Ross (Hooker), Lillian Randolph (Birdie), Shirley Mitchell (Leila), Richard LeGrand (Peavey)
   Summary: Restricting Marjorie and Leroy to stay close to home frays Gil-

dersleeve's nerves as he anticipates the return of Leila Ransome and plans for his next meeting with Eve Goodwin.
   Writers: John Whedon, Sam Moore
   Comments: Gildersleeve sings "Speak to Me of Love." After Gildersleeve's bust-out performance in the drugstore, it seems obvious he would be the last person chosen in a phone booth stuffing contest.

Date: September 26, 1943
Title: Leila Returns
   Cast: Harold Peary (Gildersleeve), Ken Carpenter, Lurene Tuttle (Marjorie), Walter Tetley (Leroy), Earle Ross (Hooker), Lillian Randolph (Birdie), Shirley Mitchell (Leila), Richard LeGrand (Peavey), Bea Benaderet (Eve)
   Summary: Throckmorton entertains thoughts of culture and education in the presence of Eve while simultaneously contemplating the return of his former fiancée Leila.
   Writers: John Whedon, Sam Moore
   Comments: Leroy jumps from boogie woogie to Bach and back in a minuet. In the tag Gildersleeve characteristically leaps from impartial exemplar to wounded warrior when his own ox is being gored.

Date: October 3, 1943 (Script)
Title: After School Activities
   Cast: Harold Peary (Gildersleeve), Ken Carpenter, Lurene Tuttle (Marjorie), Walter Tetley (Leroy), Earle Ross (Hooker), Lillian Randolph (Birdie), Richard LeGrand (Peavey), Bea Benaderet (Eve)
   Summary: Hooker and Gildersleeve have differing opinions on unsupervised play for children.

Writers: John Whedon, Sam Moore
Allusion: Gildersleeve quotes from "Barefoot Boy" by John Greenleaf Whittier: "Blessings on thee, little man, / Barefoot boy with cheek of tan."
Comments: The writers give Peavey a great scene in which he tells a story about a dark secret in his past, the time he snuck up behind a girl and — grabbed a handful of berries from her basket without her knowledge. Gildy and Hooker fight and make up several times. Leroy gets spanked at the conclusion of this entry, the only time he actually is paddled before the ears of the listeners.

Date: October 10, 1943
Title: Royal Visit
   Cast: Harold Peary (Gildersleeve), Ken Carpenter, Lurene Tuttle (Marjorie), Walter Tetley (Leroy), Earle Ross (Hooker), Lillian Randolph (Birdie), Shirley Mitchell (Leila), Richard Le-Grand (Peavey)
   Summary: When Cyrus Brinkerhoff and his countess wife plan to visit Summerfield, Gildersleeve scrambles around to get the house ready to entertain them.
   Writers: John Whedon, Sam Moore
   Comments: This AFRS rebroadcast introduced by Howard Duff includes musical interludes by Kay Kyser and vocalists in place of Kraft commercials. Leila characteristically has used her feminine wiles to get what she wants by luring a painter from Gildersleeve's house into her lair. Even Peavey is upset by the bad news at the end, causing him to deliver his strongest oath: "He's an old foof!"

Date: October 17, 1943 (Script)
Title: Heart Troubles
   Cast: Harold Peary (Gildersleeve), Ken Carpenter, Lurene Tuttle (Marjorie), Walter Tetley (Leroy), Earle Ross (Hooker) Lillian Randolph (Birdie), Shirley Mitchell (Leila), Richard Le-Grand (Peavey), Bea Benaderet (Eve)
   Summary: Gildersleeve wonders if he should switch doctors after Pettibone treats his palpitations rather lightly.
   Writers: John Whedon, Sam Moore
   Comments: Gildersleeve sings "In the Gloaming." Gildy reacts rather melodramatically to heartburn caused by eating too many cupcakes, looking for sympathy with soulful comments like "I may not be around much longer." A sign of those times: Throckmorton complains about the high price of a prescription Peavey fills which costs the great man all of 78 cents.

Date: October 24, 1943
Title: Waterworks Breaks Down
   Cast: Harold Peary (Gildersleeve), Ken Carpenter (WSUM announcer), Lurene Tuttle (Marjorie), Walter Tetley (Leroy), Earle Ross (Hooker), Lillian Randolph (Birdie), Richard LeGrand (Peavey), Pauline Drake (Bessie), Ken Christy (mayor)
   Summary: When the water pressure drops considerably, Gildersleeve is under pressure from citizenry and the mayor to remedy the situation.
   Writers: John Whedon, Sam Moore
   Allusion: Ken Carpenter quotes from "Elegy Written in a Country Churchyard" by Thomas Gray: "[The commissioner] homeward plods his weary way."
   Comments: Marjorie and Leroy sing

"Sunday, Monday, or Always." Gildersleeve mimics Hooker's cackle wonderfully. In the tag Gildy and Leroy demonstrate a practical way to make cash and help the war effort at the same time.

Date: October 31, 1943
Title: Halloween Party
  Cast: Harold Peary (Gildersleeve), Ken Carpenter, Lurene Tuttle (Marjorie), Walter Tetley (Leroy), Earle Ross (Hooker), Lillian Randolph (Birdie), Shirley Mitchell (Leila), Richard LeGrand (man in line, Peavey), Bea Benaderet (cashier, Eve)
  Summary: At Leila's urging, Throckmorton hosts a Halloween party that produces more tricks than treats.
  Writers: John Whedon, Sam Moore
  Allusion: Wally Hoff quotes from *Childe Harold's Pilgrimage* by Lord Byron: "On with the dance! Let joy be unconfined."
  Comments: This is one of the best episodes in the entire series, filled with high jinks and pleasant seasonal festivities for both youth and adults. Even Peavey reveals a mild prank from his languid past. *The Undying Monster* and *I Walked with a Zombie* were contemporary movies, but *The Living Dead* was a product of Leroy's fevered imagination.

Date: November 7, 1943
Title: Pot Roast
  Cast: Harold Peary (Gildersleeve), Ken Carpenter, Lurene Tuttle (Marjorie), Walter Tetley (Leroy), Earle Ross (Hooker), Lillian Randolph (Birdie), Shirley Mitchell (Leila), Richard LeGrand (Peavey), Bea Benaderet (customer, Eve), Arthur Q. Bryan (Floyd)

  Summary: Gildersleeve contends with a weeping Marjorie as she laments her love life and a scheming Leila who appropriates his pot roast.
  Writers: John Whedon, Sam Moore
  Comments: As on the December 6, 1942 show, Floyd becomes the scapegoat for the complainers who grumble about shortages. Birdie sings her version of "Get on Board, Little Children." Leila uses quarter-truths and beguiling language to get what she wants.

Date: November 14, 1943
Title: Rebuffed by Eve
  Cast: Harold Peary (Gildersleeve), Ken Carpenter, Lurene Tuttle (Marjorie), Walter Tetley (Leroy), Earle Ross (Hooker), Lillian Randolph (Birdie), Shirley Mitchell (Leila), Richard LeGrand (Peavey), Bea Benaderet (Eve), Pauline Drake (Bessie)
  Summary: After rejecting a romantic overture from Leila, Gildersleeve finds his advances repulsed by Eve.
  Writers: John Whedon, Sam Moore
  Allusion: Gildersleeve quotes from "Home" by Edgar Guest: "It takes a heap o' livin' [in a house to make a home]"
  Comments: Gildersleeve sings "People Will Say We're in Love." Leila and Gildersleeve sing "Speak to Me of Love." Kraft's middle commercial is replaced by a reminder to conserve food resources. A clue to the size of Summerfield is revealed when Hooker cites its 1913 population as 14,967.

Date: November 21, 1943 (Script)
Title: Moose Hunting
  Cast: Harold Peary (Gildersleeve), Ken Carpenter, Lurene Tuttle (Mar-

Judge Hooker (Earle Ross), Gildersleeve (Harold Peary), Marjorie (Lurene Tuttle), and Leroy (Walter Tetley) about to enjoy a meal prepared and served by Birdie (Lillian Randolph).

jorie), Walter Tetley (Leroy), Earle Ross (Hooker), Lillian Randolph (Birdie), Richard LeGrand (Peavey), Arthur Q. Bryan (Floyd)

Summary: A moose spotted in the area leads Floyd, Hooker, Gildy, Peavey, and Leroy out on a hunting trip to Green Lake.

Writers: John Whedon, Sam Moore

Comments: The four men (long before they become Jolly Boys) sing "When Good Fellows Get Together" and "D'ye ken John Peel." This is a rare episode in which both acts open away from home or city hall. Act one begins in the drugstore, all of act two takes place at the lake. The climax finds Gildy and Leroy face-to-face with the moose, but Throckmorton cannot pull the trig-

ger because, he tells his nephew, the beast looks too much like Hooker.

Date: November 28, 1943 (Script)
Title: Concert Pianist
Cast: Harold Peary (Gildersleeve), Ken Carpenter, Lurene Tuttle (Marjorie), Walter Tetley (Leroy), Earle Ross (Hooker), Lillian Randolph (Birdie), Richard LeGrand (Peavey)

Summary: Leroy and Gildersleeve befriend a concert pianist.

Writers: John Whedon, Sam Moore

Comments: Birdie sings "Deacon Jones." This episode, which opens at Peavey's Pharmacy, gives Peavey a chance to divulge another secret from his past: the only time he stayed home from working at a chain drugstore was the day he decided to go into business for himself.

Date: December 5, 1943 (Script)
Title: Unpaid Water Bill
   Cast: Harold Peary (Gildersleeve), Ken Carpenter, Lurene Tuttle (Marjorie), Walter Tetley (Leroy), Earle Ross (Hooker), Lillian Randolph (Birdie), Richard LeGrand (Peavey), Shirley Mitchell (Leila), Pauline Drake (Bessie)
   Summary: Throckmorton finds it a real challenge to collect Leila's long overdue water bill.
   Writers: John Whedon, Sam Moore
   Comments: Leila boldly declares she will pay her water bill "when television comes in." Peavey's window advertisement will not win any awards for creativity from Madison Avenue: "This Christmas—Why not give a mustard plaster?"

Date: December 12, 1943 (Script)
Title: Marjorie Runs Away
   Cast: Harold Peary (Gildersleeve), Ken Carpenter, Lurene Tuttle (Marjorie), Walter Tetley (Leroy), Earle Ross (Hooker), Lillian Randolph (Birdie), Richard LeGrand (Peavey)
   Summary: Bad news from Ben and an argument with her uncle causes Marjorie to leave home.
   Writers: John Whedon, Sam Moore
   Allusion: Gildersleeve quotes from "Night Thoughts" by Edward Young: "Procrastination is the thief of time."
   Comments: Ben's "Dear Jane" letter to Marjorie describes his engagement to another girl. Several pages of dialogue are devoted to Gildersleeve and Leroy reading parts of *A Christmas Carol*, an adaptation of which is being presented as a school play. Leroy strongly objects to being required to kiss Ethel Hammerschlag in the production.

Date: December 19, 1943 (Script)
Title: Marjorie Returns for Christmas
   Cast: Harold Peary, Ken Carpenter, Lurene Tuttle (Marjorie), Walter Tetley (Leroy), Earle Ross (Hooker), Lillian Randolph (Birdie), Shirley Mitchell (Leila), Richard LeGrand (Peavey), Bea Benaderet (Eve), Arthur Q. Bryan (Floyd)
   Summary: After an argument with her uncle, Marjorie stays away all night, prompting Gildersleeve to organize a searching party that is called off when his niece returns in time to see Leroy's Christmas play and celebrate the holiday at home.
   Writers: John Whedon, Sam Moore
   Comments: The script reveals an episode filled with much jumping to conclusions regarding Marjorie's whereabouts and the plan to scour the countryside with Floyd and Gildy acting as deputies. It turns out Marjorie was right next door with Leila. After the middle commercial, the scene shifts to the school where Leroy narrates the last portion of *A Christmas Carol* and Gildy sneaks a backstage kiss from Eve. Later, back at home the children finish trimming the tree, Peavey drops in for a visit and exchange of gifts, Gildy plants another yuletide kiss (this time on Leila) before joining the other members of the family on "Jingle Bells" and revealing to Leroy a surprise present (a puppy) in the basement. There is little humor in the script but the strong message of affection and good will makes the season bright.

Date: December 26, 1943 (Script)
Title: Chaos after Christmas
  Cast: Harold Peary (Gildersleeve), Ken Carpenter, Lurene Tuttle (Marjorie), Walter Tetley (Leroy), Earle Ross (Hooker), Lillian Randolph (Birdie), Richard LeGrand (Peavey), Shirley Mitchell (Leila)
  Summary: Chemistry experiments gone awry and a lit cigar disrupt the household considerably right after Christmas.
  Writers: John Whedon, Sam Moore
  Comments: The fire department is called upon to put out the fire caused by Gildy's negligence with a cigar. 271 Lakeside Avenue is given as the house address.

Date: January 2, 1944 (Script)
Title: New Year, New Man
  Cast: Harold Peary (Gildersleeve), Ken Carpenter, Lurene Tuttle (Marjorie), Walter Tetley (Leroy), Earle Ross (Hooker), Lillian Randolph (Birdie), Richard LeGrand (Peavey), Bea Benaderet (Eve), Pauline Drake (Bessie)
  Summary: Throckmorton resolves to attend to business at the office *and* in his personal affairs at home.
  Writers: John Whedon, Sam Moore
  Comments: Gildersleeve and Eve sing "Auld Lang Syne." Gildersleeve admits to being 42. Gildy posts bond for Charlie Anderson after the engineer celebrates too vociferously upon hearing that his son in the Navy, presumed missing in action, has been found safe. Peary and Carpenter issue separate pleas for more young women to consider nursing as a career.

Date: January 9, 1944
Title: Hospitalized
  Cast: Harold Peary (Gildersleeve), Ken Carpenter, Lurene Tuttle (Marjorie), Walter Tetley (Leroy), Earle Ross (Hooker), Lillian Randolph (Birdie), Shirley Mitchell (Leila), Richard LeGrand (Peavey), Mary Wickes (Miss Riley)
  Summary: After being examined by two physicians, malingering Gildersleeve finds himself in a hospital wondering if he really has some malady.
  Writers: John Whedon, Sam Moore
  Comments: Gildy acts more juvenile than usual throughout, from the shirking of his daily duties at the beginning to his cringing from the needle at the end.

Date: January 16, 1944
Title: Income Tax Forms
  Cast: Harold Peary (Gildersleeve), Ken Carpenter, Lurene Tuttle (Marjorie), Walter Tetley (Leroy), Earle Ross (Hooker), Lillian Randolph (Birdie), Shirley Mitchell (Leila), Richard LeGrand (Peavey)
  Summary: Gildersleeve struggles with income tax forms and with building a doghouse for Leroy's puppy.
  Writers: John Whedon, Sam Moore
  Allusion: Gildersleeve quotes from *Lord Chesterfield's Letters:* "Whatever is worth doing, is worth doing well." Gildersleeve quotes the proverb "Many hands make light work."
  Comments: Leila spins a sugary web of flattery around Gildy before pouncing on him. Gildersleeve sings "Why Do I Love You?" Hooker sings "Put on Your Old Grey Bonnet."

Date: January 23, 1944
Title: Seeking Mother for Leroy
   Cast: Harold Peary (Gildersleeve), Ken Carpenter, Lurene Tuttle (Marjorie), Walter Tetley (Leroy), Earle Ross (Hooker), Lillian Randolph (Birdie), Shirley Mitchell (Leila), Richard LeGrand (Peavey), Bea Benaderet (Eve)
   Summary: Acting upon a suggestion from Eve Goodwin that Leroy needs a maternal influence, Gildersleeve decides to rekindle the blaze with old flame Leila Ransome.
   Writers: John Whedon, Sam Moore
   Comments: The $21.86 figure Gildersleeve cringes from for dressing a boy from head in toe in 1944 would not even purchase a decent pair of dress shoes today. The few notes that Leroy sneaks in on the piano after his Bach bit are from one of the big hits of the day, "Pistol Packin' Mama." Gildersleeve obtusely overlooks the willing Eve in his own backyard and instead pursues the fickle temptress next door.

Date: January 30, 1944
Title: Marjorie the Actress
   Cast: Harold Peary (Gildersleeve), Ken Carpenter, Lurene Tuttle (Marjorie), Walter Tetley (Leroy), Earle Ross (Hooker), Lillian Randolph (Birdie), Richard LeGrand (Peavey)
   Summary: Gildersleeve and family entertain a pilot who helps to sell bonds and also to cure a star-truck Marjorie.
   Writers: John Whedon, Sam Moore
   Comments: Lurene puts the perfect bloom in the calla lilies with her Hepburnesque mimicry. The age game Peavey and Gildy play is a weak offshoot of the "You're 40, she's 10" routine Abbott and Costello trotted out often in the 1940s. The musical cue "Any Bonds Today?" leads into Birdie's no-nonsense appeal to invest in the most sensible way to end the war sooner.

Date: February 6, 1944
Title: Sleigh Ride
   Cast: Harold Peary (Gildersleeve), Ken Carpenter, Lurene Tuttle (Marjorie), Walter Tetley (Leroy), Earle Ross (Hooker), Lillian Randolph (Birdie), Shirley Mitchell (Leila), Richard LeGrand (Peavey), Bea Benaderet (Eve), Arthur Q. Bryan (Floyd)
   Summary: Hooker and Gildersleeve take advantage of a fresh snowfall by organizing a sleigh ride.
   Writers: John Whedon, Sam Moore
   Comments: Floyd's last name, Munson, is given for the first time. Hooker sings "On Moonlight Bay." In a preview of how the Jolly Boys will be harmonizing later, Hooker, Gildy, Munson, and Peavey sing "Jingle Bells" and "There Is a Tavern in the Town." In customary fashion Gildy shows up at the last minute, expecting the women to join the party at a moment's notice.

Date: February 13, 1944 (Script)
Title: Anonymous Valentine
   Cast: Harold Peary (Gildersleeve), Ken Carpenter, Lurene Tuttle (Marjorie), Walter Tetley (Leroy), Earle Ross (Hooker), Lillian Randolph (Birdie), Richard LeGrand (Peavey), Shirley Mitchell (Leila), Bea Benaderet (Eve), Pauline Drake (Bessie)
   Summary: Gildersleeve wonders if the unsigned valentine he received is from Leila or Eve.
   Writers: John Whedon, Sam Moore
   Comments: Leila and Gildersleeve

sing "Speak to Me of Love." Leroy sings "Mairzy Oats." Gildersleeve sings "Chloe." Long scenes with Leila and Eve make up most of the script. Bessie confesses at the end she sent the valentine. Throckmorton makes a mistake when he asks Peavey "Is this good candy?" because the pharmacist then proceeds to read aloud all the ingredients on the box to prove the wholesomeness of the sugary treats.

Date: February 20, 1944 (Script)
Title: Self-Improvement
   Cast: Harold Peary (Gildersleeve), Ken Carpenter, Lurene Tuttle (Marjorie), Walter Tetley (Leroy), Earle Ross (Hooker), Lillian Randolph (Birdie), Richard LeGrand (Peavey), Bea Benaderet (Eve)
   Summary: Throckmorton, encouraged by Eve, attempts to become more cultured by reading good books and getting involved in theatrical productions.
   Writers: John Whedon, Sam Moore
   Comments: Unlike his uncle who wants to reach upward and attend films such as *Jane Eyre*, Leroy yearns to see *Frankenstein Marries a Zombie*, Whedon and Moore's takeoff on *Frankenstein Meets the Wolf Man*. The writers also parody experimental theater with the fictitious play *Six Who Pass While the Lentils Boil.*

Date: February 27, 1944 (Script)
Title: Plays Cyrano
   Cast: Harold Peary (Gildersleeve), Ken Carpenter, Lurene Tuttle (Marjorie), Walter Tetley (Leroy), Earle Ross (Hooker), Lillian Randolph (Birdie), Shirley Mitchell (Leila), Richard Le-

Grand (Peavey), Bea Benaderet (Eve), Arthur Q. Bryan (Floyd), Pauline Drake (Bessie)
   Summary: Gildersleeve is encouraged by Eve to take part in an amateur production of *Cyrano de Bergerac.*
   Writers: John Whedon, Sam Moore
   Comments: Gildersleeve sings "I Kiss Your Hand, Madame." A revised version of this script will be used on the June 2, 1946 broadcast. The tag in this episode is an extended two-page conversation between Floyd and Gildersleeve in which the latter chastises the former for buying black market meat.

Date: March 5, 1944 (Script)
Title: Balancing Checkbook
   Cast: Harold Peary (Gildersleeve), Ken Carpenter, Lurene Tuttle (Marjorie), Walter Tetley (Leroy), Earle Ross (Hooker), Lillian Randolph (Birdie), Richard LeGrand (Peavey), Shirley Mitchell (Leila)
   Summary: Gildersleeve struggles to make an accounting of his finances while simultaneously giving Leroy lessons on getting along with his friends.
   Writers: John Whedon, Sam Moore
   Comments: Throckmorton is having such financial difficulties when Peavey drops in to present him with an overdue bill for 37 cents the distraught commissioner says, "Peavey, you're a hard man."

Date: March 12, 1944 (Script)
Title: Testing Political Waters
   Cast: Harold Peary (Gildersleeve), Ken Carpenter, Lurene Tuttle (Marjorie), Walter Tetley (Leroy), Earle Ross (Hooker), Lillian Randolph

(Birdie), Richard LeGrand (Peavey), Bea Benaderet (Eve), Pauline Drake (Bessie)

Summary: Eve encourages Throckmorton to abandon his usual complacency and challenges him to run for mayor

Writers: John Whedon, Sam Moore

Comments: This is the episode in which Gildy virtually gets Eve to agree to marry him if he wins the election. Gildersleeve provides a good citizenship lesson to Marjorie and Leroy by instilling in them the importance of voting. Even Whedon and Moore seem uncertain about the street the family lives on: 271 Lakeside Avenue is typed in the script, but *Lake* is crossed out and *Park* is written above those four letters in pencil.

Date: March 19, 1944
Title: Running for Mayor
  Cast: Harold Peary (Gildersleeve), Ken Carpenter, Lurene Tuttle (Marjorie), Walter Tetley (Leroy), Earle Ross (Hooker), Lillian Randolph (Birdie), Shirley Mitchell (Leila), Richard LeGrand (Peavey), Bea Benaderet (Eve)

Summary: Gildersleeve's decision to run for mayor takes a back seat to Leila's birthday party.

Writers: John Whedon, Sam Moore

Comments: Peavey reveals that his wife's favorite perfume is My Sin, although after seven years of being open it might smell like My Booboo. Gildy might have mentioned that the problem with the obstinate lid might have been avoided if Leila had purchased Kraft's Miracle Whip instead of a jar of mayonnaise.

Date: March 26, 1944
Title: Campaign Photo
  Cast: Harold Peary (Gildersleeve), Ken Carpenter, Lurene Tuttle (Marjorie), Walter Tetley (Leroy), Lillian Randolph (Birdie), Earle Ross (Hooker), Bea Benaderet (Eve), Arthur Q. Bryan (Floyd), Joseph Kearns (Hofstadter)

Summary: Gildersleeve primps for a photograph to be used in his campaign for mayor.

Writers: John Whedon, Sam Moore

Comments: Gildersleeve sings "I Kiss Your Hand, Madame." From the AFRS musical interludes which replace the Kraft commercials Kay Kyser and singers offer "My Heart Tells Me" and "If You Please." Howard Duff is heard as the AFRS announcer. Leroy's aversion to taking baths is reiterated in stereo by Marjorie and Throckmorton.

Date: April 2, 1944 (Script)
Title: Planning Political Platform
  Cast: Harold Peary (Gildersleeve), Ken Carpenter, Lurene Tuttle (Marjorie), Walter Tetley (Leroy), Earle Ross (Hooker), Lillian Randolph (Birdie), Richard LeGrand (Peavey), Shirley Mitchell (Leila), Arthur Q. Bryan (Floyd)

Summary: Throckmorton endeavors to find some policies he can include in his platform for the office of mayor.

Writers: John Whedon, Sam Moore

Comments: Gildy is more qualified for dogcatcher than for mayor as he spends more time looking for Leroy's stray mutt than in forming any meaningful plans for the city's future.

Date: April 9, 1944
Title: Political Crony a Phony

Cast: Harold Peary (Gildersleeve), Ken Carpenter, Lurene Tuttle (Marjorie), Walter Tetley (Leroy), Earle Ross (Hooker), Lillian Randolph (Birdie), Shirley Mitchell (Leila), Richard LeGrand (St. Peter, Peavey), Bea Benaderet (Eve), Arthur Q. Bryan (Floyd)

Summary: After Gildersleeve makes an oral agreement with a shady wheeler dealer, Eve gives him reason to suspect he has made a bad decision.

Writers: John Whedon, Sam Moore

Comments: Gildersleeve sings "Hello Central, Give Me Heaven." The dialogue harks back to the March 12 script in which Eve pledged her love to Gildy if he became mayor. J.L. Kraft delivers another inspirational Easter message.

Date: April 16, 1944 (Script)
Title: Quits the Race

Cast: Harold Peary (Gildersleeve), Ken Carpenter, Lurene Tuttle (Marjorie), Walter Tetley (Leroy), Earle Ross (Hooker), Lillian Randolph (Birdie), Richard LeGrand (Peavey), Shirley Mitchell (Leila), Bea Benaderet (Eve), Pauline Drake (Bessie)

Summary: Fed up with the deceitful tactics of the political machine, Gildersleeve decides to give up his campaign for mayor.

Writers: John Whedon, Sam Moore

Comments: Gildersleeve sings "Oh, What a Beautiful Morning" and "The Best Things in Life Are Free." Gildy is overjoyed after pulling out of the race because it relieves him of responsibilities just as he is giddy beyond belief when his close calls at the altar fall through. But, being mercurial Throcky,

when Eve pumps his courage up, he's back on the campaign trail.

Date: April 23, 1944 (Script)
Title: Speaker

Cast: Harold Peary (Gildersleeve), Ken Carpenter, Lurene Tuttle (Marjorie), Walter Tetley (Leroy), Earle Ross (Hooker), Lillian Randolph (Birdie), Richard LeGrand (Peavey), Bea Benaderet (Eve)

Summary: Eve and Horace encourage Throckmorton to present a speech at the Arbor Day Festivities.

Writers: John Whedon, Sam Moore

Comments: Eve calls Gildersleeve "Darling" for the first time. Giddy Gildy then goes too far by blurting out details of their impending wedding plans to the crowd hearing his speech, embarrassing Eve and almost ruining their engagement.

Date: April 30, 1944
Title: Engaged to Eve

Cast: Harold Peary (Gildersleeve), Ken Carpenter, Lurene Tuttle (Marjorie), Walter Tetley (Leroy), Earle Ross (Hooker), Lillian Randolph (Birdie), Shirley Mitchell (Leila), Richard LeGrand (Peavey), Arthur Q. Bryan (Floyd), Bea Benaderet (Eve)

Summary: After Gildersleeve announces his engagement to friends and family, he and Eve attend a party hosted by Leila Ransome.

Writers: John Whedon, Sam Moore

Comments: Gildersleeve sings "Love Is the Sweetest Thing." Hooker sings "Speak to Me of Love." Gildersleeve uses reason with Leroy before resorting to threats of punishment. The men in the drugstore summarize love and marriage in one word: Hooker, habit; Munson, accident; Peavey, miracle. With Gildersleeve, his habit of falling in love leads to accidents of hurt feelings and it is a miracle he does not learn from his mistakes.

Date: May 7, 1944
Title: Campaign Heats Up
Cast: Harold Peary (Gildersleeve), Ken Carpenter, Lurene Tuttle (Marjorie), Walter Tetley (Leroy), Earle Ross (Hooker), Lillian Randolph (Birdie), Richard LeGrand (Peavey), Bea Benaderet (Eve), Pauline Drake (Bessie), Joseph Kearns (Carl Crowfoot)
Summary: After hearing an inflammatory speech by his opponent, Gildersleeve prepares a give a rebuttal on station WSUM.
Writers: John Whedon, Sam Moore
Comments: Gildersleeve sings "Tea for Two." The writers finally give the mayor a full name, Cyrus Terwilliger, an appropriate moniker for a pompous politico. Gildy has good reason to wonder if he is an uncle or an umpire because he is rarely safe at home and is always put out about something.

Date: May 14, 1944
Title: Torn Between Leila and Eve
Cast: Harold Peary (Gildersleeve), Ken Carpenter, Lurene Tuttle (Marjorie), Walter Tetley (Leroy), Earle Ross (Hooker), Lillian Randolph (Birdie), Shirley Mitchell (Leila), Richard LeGrand (Peavey), Bea Benaderet (Eve)
Summary: Gildersleeve, overflowing with the spirit of spring, pours out his heart to both his former and current fiancées.
Writers: John Whedon, Sam Moore

Allusions: Dr. Needham quotes Matthew 22:21: "Render unto Caesar the things that are Caesar's." Hooker quotes the proverb "There's many a slip 'twixt the cup and the lip."
Comments: Gildersleeve provides another reason for Hooker's regular visits besides friendship: the judge lives just three blocks away. Procrastinating Uncle Mort asks Marjorie to remind him to oil the porch swing — next spring. At the end gleeful Gildy foolishly leaves his mouth in gear, starts to coast, and puts on the brakes too late to avoid a mishap.

Date: May 21, 1944
Title: City Employees Picnic
Cast: Harold Peary (Gildersleeve), Ken Carpenter, Lurene Tuttle (Marjorie), Walter Tetley (Leroy), Earle Ross (Hooker), Lillian Randolph (Birdie), Richard LeGrand (Peavey), Bea Benaderet (Eve)
Summary: Gildersleeve reluctantly goes to the big picnic in hopes of mending fences with Eve.
Writers: John Whedon, Sam Moore
Comments: Gildersleeve sings "Shine On, Harvest Moon," "Without a Song," "I Want a Girl (Just Like the Girl)," "Love Is Just a Game." Leroy is again matched with the girl he courted in the Thanksgiving play on November 22, 1942, the ever-popular Ethel Hammerschlag. Peary's ear for mimicry is again tuned in on the right frequency as he matches Hooker's munching mouthfuls exquisitely.

Date: May 28, 1944
Title: Campaign Headquarters
Cast: Harold Peary (Gildersleeve),

Ken Carpenter, Lurene Tuttle (Marjorie), Walter Tetley (Leroy), Earle Ross (Hooker), Lillian Randolph (Birdie), Richard LeGrand (Peavey), Arthur Q. Bryan (Floyd), Ken Christy (Gates)

Summary: Hooker and Throckmorton cajole Floyd Munson into allowing them to use the room above the barbershop as headquarters for Gildy's mayoral campaign.

Writers: John Whedon, Sam Moore

Comments: Gildersleeve, Hooker, Peavey, Munson, and Gates sing "Mother." The action sets the stage for the formation of the Jolly Boys in October by establishing the place (the vacant room) and purpose (playing cards, harmonizing). This episode has somewhat of a "men's club" atmosphere as Gildy's amours are ignored completely.

Date: June 4, 1944
Title: Eve's Mother Arrives
   Cast: Harold Peary (Gildersleeve), Ken Carpenter, Lurene Tuttle (Marjorie), Walter Tetley (Leroy), Earle Ross (Hooker), Lillian Randolph (Birdie), Shirley Mitchell (Leila), Richard Le-Grand (vocal fan, Peavey), Bea Benaderet (Eve), Verna Felton (Mrs. Goodwin)

Summary: Gildersleeve gets a welcome reception at a ballpark before encountering car problems while driving to pick up Eve's mother.

Writers: John Whedon, Sam Moore

Comments: The baseball crowd sings "Take Me Out to the Ball Game." Bea does a credible impression of Peavey's twang. The catalog of the contents of Leroy's pockets reveals nothing surprising to those who know him: knife,

skate key, pebbles, rusty nail, old hinge, rubber band, eraser, marbles, and a Willkie button. Gildy's childish behavior should also not shock regular listeners: he talks silly like a bad boy, skips on the street, walks on the cracks in the sidewalk, runs a stick along a picket fence, splashes people with a hose, and impetuously stops the car for a selfish kiss that results in being late to the station.

Date: June 11, 1944
Title: Dinner for Eve's Mother
   Cast: Harold Peary (Gildersleeve), Ken Carpenter, Lurene Tuttle (Marjorie), Walter Tetley (Leroy), Earle Ross (Hooker), Lillian Randolph (Birdie), Richard LeGrand (Peavey), Bea Benaderet (Eve), Verna Felton (Mrs. Goodwin)

Summary: Gildersleeve is displeased when entertaining Mrs. Goodwin takes time away from being alone with Eve.

Writers: John Whedon, Sam Moore

Comments: Gildersleeve sings "Deep in My Heart, Dear" and "Polly Wolly Doodle." Why Gildersleeve takes pride in having a greater lead in the local poll than Alf Landon did in 1936 is a mystery considering that the Republicans lost that election by more than 11 million votes and carried only two states. Eve apparently considers kissing in the same family of sweets as desserts because she turns down Gildy's request for a buss with the excuse that "it's too soon after dinner."

Date: June 18, 1944
Title: Eve's Mother Stays On
   Cast: Harold Peary (Gildersleeve), Ken Carpenter, Lurene Tuttle (Mar-

jorie), Walter Tetley (Leroy), Earle Ross (Hooker), Lillian Randolph (Birdie), Shirley Mitchell (Leila), Richard Le-Grand (supporter, Peavey), Arthur Q. Bryan (Floyd), Verna Felton (Mrs. Goodwin), Bea Benaderet (Eve)

Summary: Throckmorton uses his influence to get a train ticket for Mrs. Goodwin in an effort to spend more time canoodling with Eve.

Writers: John Whedon, Sam Moore

Comments: Gildersleeve sings "The Best Things in Life Are Free" and "School Days." Birdie sings "Oh, What a Beautiful Morning." Marjorie sings "It's Love, Love, Love." Birdie says she is 21, going on 34, both favorable figures considering Lillian Randolph's actual age of 45. Gildersleeve's explanation about Progressive Fusionists and Independent Progressives is the 1944 version of being politically correct so as to not offend any Democrats or Republicans. In the tag the writers use Peavey's timidity and Gildersleeve's bravado to emphasize the importance of buying war bonds.

Date: June 25, 1944
Title: Election Day

Cast: Harold Peary (Gildersleeve), Ken Carpenter, Lurene Tuttle (Marjorie), Walter Tetley (Leroy), Earle Ross (Hooker), Lillian Randolph (Birdie), Shirley Mitchell (Leila), Richard Le-Grand (Peavey), Bea Benaderet (Eve), Verna Felton (Mrs. Goodwin), Joseph Kearns (WSUM announcer)

Summary: Gildersleeve, fearing victory in the mayoral primary will force him into a sudden wedding, does all he can to get citizens to vote for the incumbent.

Writers: John Whedon, Sam Moore

Allusions: Peavey quotes from "The Milkmaid and Her Pail" fable of Aesop: "Don't count your chickens before they're hatched." Gildersleeve quotes the "There's many a slip 'twixt the cup and the lip" proverb. Peavey misquotes from *Don Quixote* by Miguel de Cervantes, turning "Many a little makes a mickle" into "Many a mickle makes a muckle."

Comments: Just as in the final episode of the previous season, Gildersleeve wants to back out of a marriage because he regrets losing his freedom and is reluctant to make a permanent commitment with one woman. Eve's declaration that she wouldn't marry Gildy if he was the last man on earth seems more than a bit harsh, suggesting that she is not the marrying kind either. Lurene Tuttle appears for the last time. Frank Pittman is credited as director in the closing comments by Peary, who ends the season with a plug for his most recent picture, *Gildersleeve's Ghost*. Again *Men at Sea* replaces *The Great Gildersleeve* in the 6:30 pm spot on Sundays during the summer of 1944.

Date: September 3, 1944 (Script)
Title: Family Together Again

Cast: Harold Peary (Gildersleeve), Ken Carpenter, Louise Erickson (Marjorie), Walter Tetley (Leroy), Earle Ross Hooker), Lillian Randolph (Birdie), Shirley Mitchell (Leila), Richard Le-Grand (Peavey)

Summary: After moping about the house alone at the end of summer, Gildersleeve is happy to welcome back Birdie from her vacation, Leroy from

One small happy family: nephew Leroy (Walter Tetley), uncle Mort (Harold Peary), niece Marjorie (Louise Erickson).

two weeks at camp, and Marjorie from visiting friends.

Writers: John Whedon, Sam Moore

Comments: Leroy returns from camp with an arsenal of slang which he exercises at the table, asking for the axle grease (butter), blood (ketchup), and a glass of cow (milk). The first words Louise Erickson speaks in her first appearance as Marjorie are "Oh, Unkie," indicative of the "younger" Marjorie the writers and Louise will bring to this part in the coming months. For a change Gildersleeve gets a ginger ale at the drugstore instead of his usual Coke. Volatile Gildy is in mid-season form, overjoyed to see the children again at the beginning of act two, working himself into such a state of peevishness over trifles in the next few scenes that he sends both Marjorie and Leroy to bed, yet closing the action with "It's great to have them home again."

Date: September 10, 1944
Title: Rainmaker Hired
   Cast: Harold Peary (Gildersleeve), Ken Carpenter, Louise Erickson (Marjorie), Walter Tetley (Leroy), Earle Ross (Hooker), Lillian Randolph (Birdie), Richard LeGrand (Peavey), Pauline Drake (Bessie)
   Summary: Concerned about the declining supply of water in the reservoir, Gildersleeve authorizes $500 for the services of a rainmaker without consulting his superior.
   Writers: John Whedon, Sam Moore
   Allusions: Peavey quotes the aphorism attributed to Mark Twain: "Everybody talks about the weather, but nobody does anything about it." Teaberry quotes Admiral George Dewey: "Fire when ready Gridley." Teaberry quotes from *King Henry V* by William Shakespeare: "Once more into the breach." Teaberry quotes Commander James Lawrence: "[I won't] give up the ship." Gildersleeve quotes from "Elegy Written in a Country Churchyard" by Thomas Gray: "The paths of glory lead but to the grave."
   Comments: Short musical selections are played this season into and out of the opening commercial. The first selection is "Of Thee I Sing." Gildersleeve's self-pity after his dismissal is as amusing as anything else in this episode as he grumbles about ingratitude after giving "the best years of my life to the water department" (he had been on the job for less than 23 months) and hoping that his staff will "carry on in the Gildersleeve tradition" which so far has meant goldbricking, lollygagging, and four-flushing.

Date: September 17, 1944
Title: McGee's Invention
   Cast: Harold Peary (Gildersleeve), Ken Carpenter, Louise Erickson (Marjorie), Walter Tetley (Leroy), Earle Ross (Hooker), Lillian Randolph (Birdie), Shirley Mitchell (Leila) Richard LeGrand (Peavey)
   Summary: Gildersleeve is enthusiastic about his partnership with Fibber McGee until he learns what McGee's invention is.
   Writers: John Whedon, Sam Moore
   Allusion: Peavey quotes the saying attributed to Ralph Waldo Emerson: "Build a better mousetrap [and the world will beat a path to your door]"
   Comments: The music for "I'll Get By" leads into the theme of the show nicely. Gildersleeve sings "Someday I'll Find You." More mercurial than ever, Gildy is soaring amid the clouds, then in the depths of despair, and back building castles in the air without a shred of evidence to support his feelings of euphoria or depression. In the tag Peary delivers a practical message regarding inflation.

Date: September 24, 1944
Title: Wooing Banker's Son

Cast: Harold Peary (Gildersleeve), Ken Carpenter, Louise Erickson (Marjorie), Walter Tetley (Leroy), Earle Ross (Hooker), Lillian Randolph (Birdie), Richard LeGrand (Peavey), Ken Christy (Ainsworth Todd)

Summary: Gildersleeve encourages Marjorie to be friendly with a banker's son to enhance the chances of getting a loan for his mousetrap factory.

Writers: John Whedon, Sam Moore

Comments: The opening musical excerpt is "I'll Be Seeing You." Leroy sings "Is You Is or Is You Ain't My Baby?" Peavey sings "There'll Be a Hot Time in the Old Town Tonight." Gildy unleashes a "Whoooa," a device he first used on *Fibber McGee and Molly* when he detects the presence of a party he has been talking about with another person. Peary adeptly copies Everett's adolescent squeak.

Date: October 1, 1944
Title: Selling the House

Cast: Harold Peary (Gildersleeve), Ken Carpenter, Louise Erickson (Marjorie), Walter Tetley (Leroy), Earle Ross (Hooker), Lillian Randolph (Birdie), Shirley Mitchell (Leila), Richard LeGrand (Peavey), Arthur Q. Bryan (Floyd), Bea Benaderet (Gladys Wheeler)

Summary: After Throckmorton sells the house for a quick profit, he scrambles around almost as quickly trying to find a replacement home for his family.

Writers: John Whedon, Sam Moore

Allusion: Gildersleeve refers to one of Aesop's fables by stating "Don't be a dog in the manger."

Comments: The introductory musical selection, "The Best Things in Life Are Free," points to the subject of the show. Hooker and Gildersleeve sing "Home! Sweet Home!" Dreamer Gildersleeve again pictures himself as a millionaire before he even becomes a thousandaire. Even though Throcky will refer to their abode as Gildersleeve Manor the following week, this episode reemphasizes the point that the home technically belongs to Leroy and Marjorie. The judge mentions his favorite beverage, Kalak Water, for the first time.

Date: October 8, 1944
Title: Jolly Boys Formed

Cast: Harold Peary (Gildersleeve), Ken Carpenter, Louise Erickson (Marjorie), Walter Tetley (Leroy), Earle Ross (Hooker), Lillian Randolph (Birdie), Richard LeGrand (Peavey), Arthur Q. Bryan (Floyd), Ken Christy (Gates)

Summary: Hoping to emulate Bing Crosby's character in *Going My Way*, Gildersleeve organizes a singing and recreational club for boys that eventually turns into a glee club for men.

Writers: John Whedon, Sam Moore

Comments: The opening musical selection is "When You're Smiling." Birdie sings "Swingin' on a Star." Hooker, Gildersleeve, Munson, Peavey, and Gates (hereafter known as the Jolly Boys) sing "Dear Old Girl" and "There Is a Tavern in the Town." As often happens among teens whose affections change more frequently than wind direction, Everett has advanced in Marjorie's estimation from the status of a mole on September 24 to a very nice boy two weeks later. Leroy's mention of 7B suggests he is in the seventh grade. Peary neatly ties the show's theme of finding worthwhile pursuits for youth into a plea for support of the National War Fund.

Date: October 15, 1944
Title: Job Hunting
   Cast: Harold Peary (Gildersleeve), Ken Carpenter, Louise Erickson (Marjorie), Walter Tetley (Leroy), Earle Ross (Hooker), Lillian Randolph (Birdie), Shirley Mitchell (Leila), Richard LeGrand (Peavey), Virginia Gordon (interviewer)
   Summary: Discouraged by the failure of McGee's invention, Gildersleeve turns to his friends for employment leads.
   Writers: John Whedon, Sam Moore
   Allusion: Peavey quotes from "To a Mouse" by Robert Burns: "The best-laid plans of mice and men / Gang aft agley."
   Comments: The show opens asking the musical question "Who?" Gildy alludes to Hull, a reference to Secretary of State Cordell Hull, who, coincidentally, would also be vacating his position in 1944. Virginia Gordon, who appeared in 37 episodes of *Fibber McGee and Molly* from 1942 to 1949, was the wife of Gale Gordon, who will in 1948 assume the role of Rumson Bullard, Gildy's neighbor. Leila's rapid rejection of Throckmorton's invitation recalls a time when no "respectable" woman entered a barbershop or poolroom. It should come as no surprise that a mouse finds the trap appetizing considering it is constructed of soybeans and rhubarb.

Date: October 22, 1944
Title: Phone Problems

   Cast: Harold Peary (Gildersleeve), Ken Carpenter, Louise Erickson (Marjorie), Walter Tetley (Leroy), Earle Ross (Hooker), Lillian Randolph (Birdie), Shirley Mitchell (Leila), Richard LeGrand (Peavey)
   Summary: Gildersleeve gets upset over unwanted phone calls and not being able to get a call from the one party he does want to speak with.
   Writers: John Whedon, Sam Moore
   Comments: The opening musical number is "A Pretty Girl Is Like a Melody." Stubborn Gildy refuses to learn from earlier mistakes (trying to get into Peavey's phone booth) and present blunders (tearing the phone cord from the wall). The request he makes to the phone company might be hard to honor: "If you sent anybody to fix it, don't bother." Peary imitates Peavey using the number system.

Date: October 29, 1944
Title: Water Commissioner Again
   Cast: Harold Peary (Gildersleeve), Ken Carpenter, Louise Erickson (Marjorie), Walter Tetley (Leroy), Earle Ross (Hooker, library patron), Lillian Randolph (Birdie), Richard LeGrand (Peavey), Bea Benaderet (Eve), Pauline Drake (Bessie), Joseph Kearns (McCarthy)
   Summary: Gildersleeve considers his options when he is offered a position in industry and his old job in the water department.
   Writers: John Whedon, Sam Moore
   Allusion: Ken Carpenter cites the newspaper headline which quotes from Isaiah 21:11: "Watchman, what of the night?"
   Comments: The musical selection is "I Cried for You." Gildersleeve's admo-

nition to Leroy not to act until getting all the facts is one he often forgets. Peavey has a cagey idea for enhancing the perceived quality of the cigars in this store: don't improve the stock, just raise the price.

Date: November 5, 1944
Title: Election Bet
   Cast: Harold Peary (Gildersleeve), Ken Carpenter, Louise Erickson (Marjorie), Walter Tetley (Leroy), Earle Ross (Hooker), Lillian Randolph (Birdie), Richard LeGrand (Peavey), Bea Benaderet (Eve, Miss Farquhar), Arthur Q. Bryan (Floyd), Leon Belasco (Leo Morgan)
   Summary: After Gildersleeve and Hooker wager on the mayoral election, Gildy becomes so tired of political talk that he considers not voting for either candidate.
   Writers: John Whedon, Sam Moore
   Allusion: Gildersleeve quotes from "Elegy Written in a Country Churchyard" by Thomas Gray: "Far from the madding crowd ['s ignoble strife.]"
   Comments: The warm-up amuses Ken Carpenter so much his laughter precedes his introduction. The musical number is "Blue Skies." Floyd sings "On the Banks of the Wabash." Gildersleeve, Floyd, and Peavey sing "Put on Your Old Grey Bonnet." An odd part of the bet is that there is no consequence Hooker has to pay if his candidate loses. A sound effect earns the longest laugh of the night when Leroy hits a nail. The November 22, 1949 episode of *Fibber McGee and Molly* also contains the plot element of a grateful new citizen shaming a complacent native-born American.

Date: November 12, 1944
Title: Spanish Dancing Teacher
   Cast: Harold Peary (Gildersleeve), Ken Carpenter, Louise Erickson (Marjorie), Walter Tetley (Leroy), Earle Ross (Hooker), Lillian Randolph (Birdie), Richard LeGrand (Peavey), Arthur Q. Bryan (Floyd), Ken Christy (Gates)
   Summary: Love-struck Horace asks Gildersleeve to help him find a way to approach a Spanish dancing teacher on his behalf.
   Writers: John Whedon, Sam Moore
   Comments: On this AFRS rebroadcast musical interludes replace the Kraft commercials. Leroy sings "The Trolley Song." Peavey, Gates, and Munson sing "Down by the Old Mill Stream. The Jolly Boys sing "There Is a Tavern in the Town." Gildersleeve and Dolores sing "Bésame Mucho." Veola Vonn might be the woman playing Dolores Del Rey, although the actress is not identified in the scripts. Gates gives Hooker's age as 60.

Date: November 19, 1944
Title: Reception for Del Rey
   Cast: Harold Peary (Gildersleeve), Ken Carpenter, Walter Tetley (Leroy), Earle Ross (Hooker), Lillian Randolph (Birdie), Shirley Mitchell (Leila), Richard LeGrand (Peavey), Bea Benaderet (Eve), Arthur Q. Bryan (Floyd)
   Summary: The reception Hooker and Gildersleeve host for the new dancing instructor is sparsely attended.
   Writers: John Whedon, Sam Moore
   Comments: The opening musical selection is "I Know That You Know." Gildersleeve sings "Duna." Dolores and Gildersleeve sing "Bésame Mucho." Louise Erickson may have been ill be-

cause Marjorie's absence is attributed to a sore throat. Gildy's remark to Hooker that "This is going to take finesse" drips with irony all over his ill-advised comments to Leila and Eve. Mrs. Peavey appears long enough to utter one word ("Richard!"), which listeners can assume is usually the final word in conversations with her husband.

Date: November 26, 1944
Title: Reception Aftermath
   Cast: Harold Peary (Gildersleeve), Ken Carpenter, Louise Erickson (Marjorie), Walter Tetley (Leroy), Earle Ross (Hooker), Richard LeGrand (Peavey), Bea Benaderet (Eve), Arthur Q. Bryan (Floyd), Pauline Drake (Bessie)
   Summary: After mending fences with Floyd and Eve regarding the Del Rey reception, Gildersleeve treats Marjorie and Leroy to luncheon downtown.
   Writers: John Whedon, Sam Moore
   Comments: The opening musical selection is "Oh, Lady Be Good." Gildersleeve sings "Bésame Mucho." Peavey's revelation that seven people tested the thermometer at the factory makes one wonder how hygienic the instruments are when sent to stores. How Leroy has progressed from D student to a straight-A scholar with no change of behavior or study habits is not explained.

Date: December 3, 1944
Title: Date with Dolores
   Cast: Harold Peary (Gildersleeve), Ken Carpenter, Louise Erickson (Marjorie), Walter Tetley (Leroy), Earle Ross (Hooker), Lillian Randolph (Birdie), Shirley Mitchell (Leila), Richard Le-Grand (Peavey)

Summary: Gildersleeve enlists Leila's help to disrupt the romance between Hooker and Dolores, thereby giving him a clear shot at the Spanish charmer.
   Writers: John Whedon, Sam Moore
   Allusion: Hooker paraphrases Psalm 90:10 "The years allotted to man are threescore and ten."
   Comments: This AFRS rebroadcast has a musical interlude in place of the Kraft commercials. Gildersleeve sings "Dolores." The cast performed at Navy Pier in Chicago on behalf of the Sixth War Loan Drive. Birdie's much ado about nothing snit over a missing chicken wing includes a nod to the host city when she confesses she could "work for a lady in Chicago." When a few musical notes are heard at the wrong time (perhaps a piano was being moved into position for Peary's vocal), Hal ad-libs "I supply my own sound effects, too."

Date: December 10, 1944
Title: Breaking Up with Dolores
   Cast: Harold Peary (Gildersleeve), Ken Carpenter, Louise Erickson (Marjorie), Walter Tetley (Leroy), Earle Ross (Hooker), Lillian Randolph (Birdie), Richard LeGrand (Peavey), Ken Christy (Gates)
   Summary: Feeling guilty about his amorous longings toward Dolores, Gildersleeve resolves to end the affair.
   Writers: John Whedon, Sam Moore
   Allusions: Gildersleeve cribs from "A Red, Red Rose" by Robert Burns: "O my love's like a red, red rose, / That's newly sprung in June; / O my love's like the melody / That's sweetly played in tune." Peavey adds the second stanza of the poem: "As fair art thou, my bonnie lass, / So deep in love am I; / And I will

love thee still, my dear, / Till all the seas gang dry."

Comments: The opening musical number is "Liza." The Jolly Boys sing "On Moonlight Bay." Gildy, ever a slave of the flesh, greets the good news of Birdie's improved condition with the thought that he will again be eating hotcakes. Judging from the records in the house, Spike Jones is tops of the pops, Frank Sinatra a distant second.

Date: December 17, 1944
Title: Hiding Out
   Cast: Harold Peary (Gildersleeve), Ken Carpenter, Louise Erickson (Marjorie), Walter Tetley (Leroy), Earle Ross (Hooker), Lillian Randolph (Birdie), Richard LeGrand (Peavey), Arthur Q. Bryan (Floyd)
Summary: Throckmorton resorts to hiding and to donning disguises because he expects to be served a subpoena.
Writers: John Whedon, Sam Moore
Comments: The writers have Gildersleeve running from shadows and little men who aren't there in this contrived offering for, as he admits in the early going, he doesn't even know if he is being sued at all. Vacillating Gildy goes from calling Peavey the "worst detective I ever saw" to declaring the druggist "a genius" in 19 seconds. Peary flubs the closing: "Go tonight. Go to bed. Goodnight. Hello." He might have added, with Groucho's leer, "I must be going."

Date: December 24, 1944
Title: Christmas Eve Party
   Cast: Harold Peary (Gildersleeve), Ken Carpenter, Louise Erickson (Marjorie), Walter Tetley (Leroy), Earle Ross

(Hooker), Lillian Randolph (Birdie), Shirley Mitchell (Leila), Richard LeGrand (Peavey), Bea Benaderet (Eve), Arthur Q. Bryan (Floyd)
Summary: Gildersleeve snaps out of his depression over his last romance and his unwarranted fear of being sued in time to get in the spirit of the season by buying gifts and inviting friends to stop in for some holiday cheer.
Writers: John Whedon, Sam Moore
Comments: The opening musical number is "Of Thee I Sing." The Jolly Boys sing "Deck the Halls." Everyone joins in singing "Joy to the World." It should come as no surprise that Dolores has no case because the only person who has even suggested that a breach of promise suit might be filed is Gildersleeve. It is probably best that Hooker and Del Rey also go their separate ways for Horace and Dolores would be too corny a pairing even for the tunesmiths along Tin Pan Alley.

Date: December 31, 1944
Title: New Year's Eve
   Cast: Harold Peary (Gildersleeve), Ken Carpenter, Louise Erickson (Marjorie), Walter Tetley (Leroy), Earle Ross (Hooker), Lillian Randolph (Birdie), Shirley Mitchell (Leila), Richard LeGrand (Peavey), Arthur Q. Bryan (Floyd)
Summary: After skating with the children, Gildersleeve plans to welcome in 1945 alone with Leila at home.
Writers: John Whedon, Sam Moore
Comments: Gildersleeve sings "Speak to Me of Love." Peary adroitly uses vocal teetering so listeners can "see" him wobbling for his balance before taking a fall on the ice. The two "need"

lines get well-deserved laughs when Peavey tells Gildy "For that area, you'll need the larger bottle" and Throckmorton suggests to Leila "You need something there." In the tag Hal sends out an alert regarding the shortage of army nurses.

Date: January 7, 1945 (Script)
Title: Dreams of Trial
   Cast: Harold Peary (Gildersleeve), Ken Carpenter, Louise Erickson (Marjorie), Walter Tetley (Leroy), Earle Ross (Hooker), Lillian Randolph (Birdie), Shirley Mitchell (Leila), Richard LeGrand (Peavey), Bea Benaderet (Eve)
   Summary: After Gildersleeve refuses to pay a settlement of $5,000 offered by Dolores Del Rey's lawyer, he suffers through a disconcerting nightmare in which he defends himself in a breach of promise suit.
   Writers: John Whedon, Sam Moore
   Allusion: Gildersleeve quotes from Matthew 5:45: "The rain falls on the just, and on the unjust."
   Comments: Dolores sings "Bésame Mucho." Groundwork is laid for Hattie's extended visit with a lengthy opening scene concerning the gifts she sent Leroy, Marjorie, and Throckmorton for Christmas. (Leroy is none too thrilled with his present, a book entitled *How to Make Things with Raffia*.) Ross's distinctive rat-tat-tat way of laughing derisively is written right into the script: "JUDGE: You're being sued. (Cackle)" Peary's mutterings upon being awakened are also spelled out: "HAL: Heef? Hoomph? Whatchafaw?" Three times on the witness stand Peavey pleads his version of the Fifth Amendment: "Well, now, I wouldn't say that."

Date: January 14, 1945
Title: Engagement Strategy
   Cast: Harold Peary (Gildersleeve), Ken Carpenter, Louise Erickson (Marjorie), Walter Tetley (Leroy), Earle Ross (Hooker), Lillian Randolph (Birdie), Shirley Mitchell (Leila), Richard LeGrand (Peavey), Bea Benaderet (Eve)
   Summary: Gildersleeve frantically tries to become engaged to Eve or Leila in order to thwart a potential lawsuit.
   Writers: John Whedon, Sam Moore
   Comments: Shifty Throckmorton declares bold-facedly that he has always been engaged to Eve Goodwin mere minutes after averring that he had never been involved with any woman. Only Gildy would expect one woman to be receptive to his romantic request by arriving at her home as if in cardiac arrest and then appear on the doorstep of another woman he plans to woo wearing a malodorous helmet while proffering a nickel peanut bar as a love token.

Date: January 21, 1945
Title: Hockey Player
   Cast: Harold Peary (Gildersleeve), Ken Carpenter, Louise Erickson (Marjorie), Walter Tetley (Leroy), Lillian Randolph (Birdie), Richard LeGrand (Peavey), Richard Crenna (Keith Kelsey)
   Summary: After Gildersleeve upsets Marjorie by forbidding her to go out with a new boy, he hopes to make amends by holding a surprise party for her.
   Writers: John Whedon, Sam Moore
   Allusion: Marjorie quotes from *Macbeth* by William Shakespeare: "Tomorrow, and tomorrow, and to-

morrow / Creeps in this petty pace from day to day."

Comments: The musical number is "Look for the Silver Lining." Richard Crenna, who will later assume the role of Bronco Thompson, appears for the first time. Decades before the concept of fast food became popular, Peavey delivers a lightning-quick treat by producing a chocolate malt for a customer before he even asks for it.

Date: January 28, 1945 (Script)
Title: Aunt Hattie Arrives
  Cast: Harold Peary (Gildersleeve), Ken Carpenter, Louise Erickson (Marjorie), Walter Tetley (Leroy), Lillian Randolph (Birdie), Shirley Mitchell (Leila), Arthur Q. Bryan (Floyd)
  Summary: Hattie immediately makes her presence felt by supervising Birdie's cooking and guiding the actions of Marjorie and Leroy.
  Writers: John Whedon, Sam Moore
  Comments: Marjorie sings "Don't Fence Me In." After Gildersleeve shifts cleaning duties he promised to do off to Marjorie, Birdie mutters Leroy's line of confused amazement: "What a character!" Before Hattie makes her entrance, a parenthetical comment by the writers indicates she is a pleasant woman of about 45, although her actions suggest she fits more in the meddlesome old biddy category. Hattie refers to Marjorie's blonde hair, a change from the September 27, 1942, script when her hair was red. With both Ross and LeGrand absent from the cast, Floyd becomes the sounding board for Gildy's complaints about Hattie. In the tag that runs to almost two full pages Peary delivers a stern message about the

war not being over and presents a handful of reasons why the conflict with Japan could be a long one.

Date: February 4, 1945
Title: Aunt Hattie Becomes Stubborn
  Cast: Harold Peary (Gildersleeve), Ken Carpenter, Louise Erickson (Marjorie), Walter Tetley (Leroy), Earle Ross (Hooker), Lillian Randolph (Birdie), Shirley Mitchell (Leila), Richard Le-Grand (Peavey)
  Summary: Gildersleeve finds himself in strong disagreement with his sister-in-law regarding childrearing and managing a household.
  Writers: John Whedon, Sam Moore
  Allusion: Marjorie quotes from "Annabel Lee" by Edgar Allan Poe: "It was many and many a year ago, / In a kingdom by the sea."
  Comments: During this rehearsal Peary provides an extra mention of Kraft at the beginning and the end as well as supplying the "pong" of Peavey's electric eye device. The script was still a work in progress at the time of recording for the tag had not yet been written.

Date: February 11, 1945 (Script)
Title: Hattie Plays Matchmaker
  Cast: Harold Peary (Gildersleeve), Ken Carpenter, Louise Erickson (Marjorie), Walter Tetley (Leroy), Earle Ross (Hooker), Lillian Randolph (Birdie), Shirley Mitchell (Leila), Richard Le-Grand (Peavey), Bea Benaderet (Eve)
  Summary: Hattie invites Eve to dinner in hopes of rekindling the flame between her and Throckmorton, but complications arise when Leila also drops in that evening.

Writers: John Whedon, Sam Moore

Comments: Gildersleeve sings "They Didn't Believe Me." After finding out that Gildersleeve had been engaged to both Eve and Leila, Hattie poses the question that listeners have been asking since 1941: "What kind of man are you?" An implicit message that the war effort supersedes petty jealousies is evident in the cooperation Leila and Eve engage in at the local Red Cross center.

Date: February 18, 1945
Title: Aunt Hattie Stays On

Cast: Harold Peary (Gildersleeve), Ken Carpenter, Louise Erickson (Marjorie), Walter Tetley (Leroy), Earle Ross (Hooker), Lillian Randolph (Birdie), Richard LeGrand (Peavey), Arthur Q. Bryan (Floyd), Ken Christy (Gates)

Summary: Gildersleeve devises a scheme so Hooker will entertain Hattie while he enjoys an evening with the Jolly Boys.

Writers: John Whedon, Sam Moore

Comments: Gildersleeve sings "Accentuate the Positive." Gates sings "The Prisoner's Song." The Jolly Boys sing "On the Banks of the Wabash." Hooker and Hattie sing "Oh, Promise Me." Gildy's penchant for talking out of both sides of his mouth at the same time draws a comment from Carpenter ("That Kraft-y fellow") and prompts Marjorie to borrow Leroy's "What a character!"

Date: February 25, 1945
Title: Hattie-Hooker Romance

Cast: Harold Peary (Gildersleeve), Ken Carpenter, Louise Erickson (Marjorie), Walter Tetley (Leroy), Earle Ross

(Hooker), Lillian Randolph (Birdie), Richard LeGrand (Peavey)

Summary: Throckmorton attempts to disrupt a romance between Hooker and Hattie so his sister-in-law will leave Summerfield and return home.

Writers: John Whedon, Sam Moore

Comments: The musical number is "Oh, Lady Be Good." Some recordings from this date have several minutes of patter from Peary and Tetley while waiting for a war bulletin from Guam to end. Throckmorton may have been the only reader in the country who had trouble concentrating on the provocative novel *Forever Amber*. Gildy utters "I just pay the bills around here," his moan of self-pity, for the first time. The mention of the typewriter belonging to the water department might remind listeners that Gildersleeve has not been heard actively on the job since becoming commissioner again in the fall, his occupation having given way to romantic entanglements and resolving domestic matters.

Date: March 4, 1945 (Script)
Title: Hiding from Hattie

Cast: Harold Peary (Gildersleeve), Ken Carpenter, Louise Erickson (Marjorie), Walter Tetley (Leroy), Earl Ross (Hooker), Lillian Randolph (Birdie), Shirley Mitchell (Leila), Richard LeGrand (Peavey)

Summary: Leila and Hattie have a falling out that leaves Gildersleeve in the middle.

Writers: John Whedon, Sam Moore

Comments: The show opens with Leroy sending various Morse code messages in the living room to his sister and uncle, one of which is "Aunt Hattie is a big —" which Gildy interrupts with "I can guess the rest." A rare instance of a character using the title of the program in the dialogue is heard when Horace greets his friend with "Well, if it isn't the Great Gildersleeve." Leila, who speaks the truth only under oath, tells Hattie she is 32.

Date: March 11, 1945
Title: Chairman of Red Cross Drive
   Cast: Harold Peary (Gildersleeve), Ken Carpenter, Louise Erickson (Marjorie), Earle Ross (Hooker), Lillian Randolph (Birdie), Shirley Mitchell (Leila), Richard LeGrand (Peavey), Bea Benaderet (Eve), Pauline Drake (Bessie)
   Summary: Gildersleeve takes over as head of the women's Red Cross committee, not realizing that he will be more referee than chairman due to bickering among members of the group.
   Writers: John Whedon, Sam Moore
   Comments: Marjorie's mention of an age difference between her and Charlie Pettibone suggests that she is 16. Over the phone Gildy states that his residence is 219 Lakeside, a change from the 747 Parkside address mentioned on September 14, 1941. This is the first episode without Walter Tetley in the cast.

Date: March 18, 1945 (Script)
Title: Leila Hears a Prowler
   Cast: Harold Peary (Gildersleeve), Ken Carpenter, Louise Erickson (Marjorie), Earle Ross (Hooker), Lillian Randolph (Birdie), Shirley Mitchell (Leila), Richard LeGrand (Peavey), Arthur Q. Bryan (Floyd), Ken Christy (Gates)

   Summary: After Leila suspects a burglar has broken into her house, she calls Throckmorton and just about every man she knows to come to her aid.
   Writers: John Whedon, Sam Moore
   Comments: The Jolly Boys sing "A Little Bit of Heaven." Of all the missing episodes for which no recording exists, this one seems to be the greatest loss because the script abounds in comical scenes such as Gildy finding his air raid warden helmet filled with mothballs ("How can I catch any burglars? They'll smell me a mile away") and riotous slapstick as Leila and Gildersleeve stumble around in the dark. Shirley has some wonderful lines in the second act, apologizing for being in a roomful of men in her negligee ("I have a better one, but it's at the cleaners") and taking Peavey's suggestion that the alleged intruder had been a Peeping Tom as a compliment ("Mr. Peavey, aren't you nice!") In the tag Peary assured listeners that Tetley, who had been absent from the last two shows due to illness, would be back the following week.

Date: March 25, 1945
Title: Old Flame Violet
   Cast: Harold Peary (Gildersleeve), Ken Carpenter, Louise Erickson (Marjorie), Walter Tetley (Leroy), Earle Ross (Hooker), Lillian Randolph (Birdie), Shirley Mitchell (Leila), Richard LeGrand (Peavey, man on the street)
   Summary: Gildersleeve is smitten all over again when he receives a letter from a woman he loved in his youth and eagerly looks forward to a reunion with her.
   Writers: John Whedon, Sam Moore

Comments: When Peavey recalls his past, it's a matter of magnesia, not nostalgia. Marjorie's response to Gildersleeve's admission that he is old and fat ("You're not old") earns nary a snicker from the audience.

Date: April 1, 1945
Title: Pig in the House
   Cast: Harold Peary (Gildersleeve), Ken Carpenter, Louise Erickson (Marjorie), Walter Tetley (Leroy), Earle Ross (Hooker), Lillian Randolph (Birdie), Richard LeGrand (Peavey), Arthur Q. Bryan (Floyd)
   Summary: Gildersleeve purchases a piglet as a way to combat the meat shortage.
   Writers: John Whedon, Sam Moore
   Comments: Musical interludes replace the Kraft commercials on this AFRS rebroadcast. The sanitation department in Summerfield is decades ahead of many communities in not accepting in the trash such items as bottles and tin cans which could be reused.

Date: April 8, 1945
Title: Pig for a Pet
   Cast: Harold Peary (Gildersleeve), Ken Carpenter, Louise Erickson (Marjorie), Walter Tetley (Leroy), Earle Ross (Hooker), Lillian Randolph (Birdie), Shirley Mitchell (Leila), Richard Le-Grand (Peavey), Ken Christy (Gates)
   Summary: Informed that he cannot keep a pig on his property, Throckmorton resolves to either sell or slay the porker.
   Writers: John Whedon, Sam Moore
   Comments: Birdie sings "Summertime." In one week the pig moves from

bacon on the hoof to the object of everyone's affection. The rent-an-animal resolution will be used again on April 28, 1946 with a horse.

Date: April 15, 1945
   (Preempted by memorial program for Franklin D. Roosevelt)

Date: April 22, 1945
Title: Leila's Party
   Cast: Harold Peary (Gildersleeve), Ken Carpenter, Louise Erickson (Marjorie), Walter Tetley (Leroy), Earle Ross (Hooker), Lillian Randolph (Birdie), Shirley Mitchell (Leila), Richard Le-Grand (Peavey), Bea Benaderet (Eve)
   Summary: After deciding to wear his tuxedo to a soiree hosted by Leila rather than donating the garment to a clothing drive, Throckmorton discovers he is the only one so formally dressed.
   Writers: John Whedon, Sam Moore
   Allusion: Hooker quotes from the *Essay on Man* by Alexander Pope: "The proper study of mankind is man."
   Comments: Gildersleeve sings "Chloe." Just as on January 21st when Gildersleeve showed prejudice against Marjorie's friend Keith because he disliked an old acquaintance with that name, so Gildy brands James Eustace Calhoun a gigolo merely because Leila is attracted to the man. The society column of the newspaper cited at the beginning of the show could have included this note which would have accurately described Throckmorton's contribution to the affair: "Things were really popping at the Leila Ransome party."

Date: April 29, 1945
Title: Rumson Bullard Moves In

Cast: Harold Peary (Gildersleeve), Ken Carpenter, Louise Erickson (Marjorie), Walter Tetley (Leroy), Earle Ross (Hooker), Lillian Randolph (Birdie), Shirley Mitchell (Leila), Richard LeGrand (Peavey), Arthur Q. Bryan (Floyd), Ken Christy (Gates)

Summary: Gildersleeve's opinion of his new neighbor causes some confusion at home and also creates harsh feelings among the Jolly Boys.

Writers: John Whedon, Sam Moore

Allusion: Marjorie quotes from *Pippa Passes* by Robert Browning: "The year's at the spring / And day's at the morn; / Morning's at seven; / The hillside's dew-pearled: / "The lark's on the wing; / The snail's on the thorn."

Comments: The Jolly Boys sing "For He's a Jolly Good Fellow." The usual suspects behave totally in character: impetuous Gildy, ready to sue someone over damage to a lawn he has not even inspected; man-hungry Leila muttering under her breath "He *would* have to be married;" and impassive Peavey perched sturdily on the fence so as to not lean toward either side of a dispute.

Date: May 6, 1945
Title: Marjorie Meets Marshall Bullard
Cast: Harold Peary (Gildersleeve), Ken Carpenter, Louise Erickson (Marjorie), Walter Tetley (Leroy), Lillian Randolph (Birdie), Shirley Mitchell (Leila), Richard LeGrand (Peavey)

Summary: After Gildersleeve gets better acquainted with Rumson Bullard, he clumsily tries to see that Marjorie and Bullard's son do the same.

Writers: John Whedon, Sam Moore

Comments: Carpenter indicates that Gildersleeve is going to the drugstore

"to consult the oracle," an apt remark for Gildy is frequently seeking Peavey's opinion more than his notions or potions. Even though he is blundering right up to the end of the show, cocky Throcky proudly declares "Don't tell me I don't know how to handle kids."

Date: May 13, 1945
Title: Meets Craig Bullard
Cast: Harold Peary (Gildersleeve), Ken Carpenter, Louise Erickson (Marjorie), Walter Tetley (Leroy), Earle Ross (Hooker), Lillian Randolph (Birdie), Richard LeGrand (Peavey), Bea Benaderet (Eve), Tommy Bernard (Craig Bullard)

Summary: Gildersleeve suffers a trying day minding the neighbor's boy while preparing a speech on child-rearing.

Writers: John Whedon, Sam Moore

Comments: Gildersleeve and Hooker sing "Darktown Strutters' Ball." Gildersleeve's repeated cry of "Ye Gods!" gets the censor's approval probably because Peary makes the exclamation sound like a plea for divine intervention. Peavey's muttered "spoiled little devil" suggests that Craig is powered by an infernal engine.

Date: May 20, 1945
Title: Windfall
Cast: Harold Peary (Gildersleeve), Ken Carpenter, Louise Erickson (Marjorie), Walter Tetley (Leroy), Earle Ross (Hooker), Lillian Randolph (Birdie), Shirley Mitchell (Leila), Richard LeGrand (Peavey), Bea Benaderet (Miss Conrad), Tommy Bernard (Craig)

Summary: After Gildersleeve purchases over $200 worth of stocks, he second-guesses himself into a nervous state, fearful that he might lose his entire investment.

Writers: John Whedon, Sam Moore

Comments: Birdie sings "Nobody Knows the Trouble I've Seen." The First National Bank of Wistful Vista cuts no ice on *Fibber McGee and Molly* for McGee's financial ire was always directed at The Third National Bank and its president. Once again the dull but wise Peavey is the lodestone Gildy is drawn back to when he comes to his senses.

Date: May 27, 1945
Title: Secretary Trouble
Cast: Harold Peary (Gildersleeve), Ken Carpenter, Louise Erickson (Marjorie), Walter Tetley (Leroy), Earle Ross (Hooker), Lillian Randolph (Birdie), Richard LeGrand (Peavey), Arthur Q. Bryan (Floyd)

Summary: After Gildersleeve rashly lets his secretary go, he recruits handy but unsatisfactory replacements in Marjorie and Leroy.

Writers: John Whedon, Sam Moore

Comments: Leroy warbles "O Solo Mio." Inconsistent Gildy, who shows up one day for work at 10:00 AM and eats lunch at 3:45 on another, at least stays the course with his motto for the week: "Fire away."

Date: June 3, 1945
Title: Leila as New Secretary
Cast: Harold Peary (Gildersleeve), Verne Smith, Louise Erickson (Marjorie), Walter Tetley (Leroy), Earle Ross (Hooker), Lillian Randolph (Birdie), Shirley Mitchell (Leila), Richard LeGrand (Peavey), Tommy Bernard (Craig)

Summary: After being unable to find a capable secretary, Gildersleeve hires inexperienced Leila who turns out to be more of a hindrance than a help.

Writers: John Whedon, Sam Moore

Comments: Verne Smith is the new announcer, taking over from Ken Carpenter for the remainder of the season. Gildersleeve gives his phone number as Summerfield 2371. *R* sounds in adjoining words cause Hal to stumble twice, saying "They've crumbed for Craig" and "Strike nigh." At the end Gildy gives Birdie an order which will be countermanded at his earliest convenience: "Don't pay attention to anything I say."

Date: June 10, 1945
Title: Reading a Good Book
Cast: Harold Peary (Gildersleeve), Verne Smith, Louise Erickson (Marjorie), Walter Tetley (Leroy), Earle Ross (Hooker), Lillian Randolph (Birdie), Richard LeGrand (Peavey), Bea Benaderet (Eve), Arthur Q. Bryan (Floyd), Ken Christy (Gates), Joseph Kearns (Griswold)

Summary: Gildersleeve, finding it hard to stay awake and concentrate on a new book, leaves the house in search of companionship.

Writers: John Whedon, Sam Moore

Allusions: Smith quotes from "Elegy Written in a Country Churchyard" by Thomas Gray: "The curfew tolls the knell of parting day, / The lowing herd wind slowly o'er the lea, / The ploughman [water commissioner] homeward plods his way, / And leaves the world to darkness and to me." Griswold quotes from "Sleep and Poetry" by John Keats: "What is more gentle than a wind in summer? / What is more soothing than the pretty hummer...."

Comments: The Jolly Boys sing "Old Kentucky Home" and "Silver Threads among the Gold." The middle commercial is inserted less obtrusively than usual with Smith tiptoeing in and out of Gildersleeve's slumber. The dream flashback reveals that Gildy was a slacker even in college. When Throcky dozes off, he falls asleep from head to foot.

Date: June 17, 1945
Title: Marshall Bullard's Party
  Cast: Harold Peary (Gildersleeve), Verne Smith, Louise Erickson (Marjorie), Walter Tetley (Leroy), Earle Ross (Hooker), Lillian Randolph (Birdie), Shirley Mitchell (Leila), Richard LeGrand (Peavey), Tommy Bernard (Craig Bullard)
  Summary: After Marjorie cheers up and decides to go to the party across the street, Gildersleeve plans to have some time alone with Leila.
  Writers: John Whedon, Sam Moore
  Comments: Gildersleeve sings "Goodnight, Sweetheart" with a coda by Leroy. Leroy accepts the "contemptible" accusation by his sister but resents being called "nosey" even though he has snooped repeatedly into her belongings. Tetley delivers his scoffing "Ha!" for the first time, although it is rather subdued and not as sassy as it will become in future shows. The elders know that children obey the dollar sign: Craig is bought off with five bucks and Leroy with two dollars. Leroy's resolve to use his money for war stamps is reinforced by Peary's more direct appeal to buy bonds in the tag.

Date: June 24, 1945 (Script)
Title: Marjorie Ashamed of House
  Cast: Harold Peary (Gildersleeve), Verne Smith, Louise Erickson (Marjorie), Walter Tetley (Leroy), Earle Ross (Hooker), Lillian Randolph (Birdie), Shirley Mitchell (Leila), Richard LeGrand (Peavey)
  Summary: Gildersleeve and the family spruce up the house in preparation for inviting the Bullards for dinner.
  Writers: John Whedon, Sam Moore
  Comments: Gildersleeve manages to get both Leila and Marjorie angry with him when he bungles the invitation to his neighbors over the phone. As it turns out, it is much ado about nothing because the Bullards are going to be out of town for a week.

Date: July 1, 1945 (Script)
Title: Jolly Boys Picnic
  Cast: Harold Peary (Gildersleeve), Verne Smith, Louise Erickson (Marjorie), Walter Tetley (Leroy), Earle Ross (Hooker), Lillian Randolph (Birdie), Shirley Mitchell (Leila), Richard LeGrand (Peavey), Bea Benaderet (Eve), Arthur Q. Bryan (Floyd), Ken Christy (Gates), Tommy Bernard (Craig)
  Summary: Gildersleeve, friends, and family spend a wonderful Fourth of July, highlighted by a hayride and picnic.
  Writers: John Whedon, Sam Moore
  Allusion: Leila quotes from "Barbara Frietchie" by John Greenleaf Whittier: "'Shoot if you must this old grey head, / But spare your country's flag,' she said."
  Comments: The Jolly Boys sing "Take Me Out to the Ball Game" and "In the Good Old Summertime." This

episode is a wonderful piece of Americana, capturing a bygone time of a patriotic holiday in Anytown, U.S.A. *Men at Sea* is the summer replacement series.

Date: September 2, 1945
Title: Labor Day at Grass Lake
   Cast: Harold Peary (Gildersleeve), John Laing, Louise Erickson (Marjorie), Walter Tetley (Leroy), Earle Ross (Hooker), Lillian Randolph (Birdie), Richard LeGrand (Peavey), Tommy Bernard (Craig)
   Summary: After resisting entreaties to spend the holiday at Grass Lake, Gildersleeve finally agrees to drive there with Hooker and Leroy but cuts his stay short and returns home.
   Writers: John Whedon, Sam Moore
   Comments: John Laing is the new announcer. Jack Meakin takes over as musical director. This recording is a rehearsal with no studio audience but with full sound effects. As a test for two shows a plot-teaser plays out before the first commercial.

Date: September 9, 1945
Title: Leroy's New Teacher
   Cast: Harold Peary (Gildersleeve), John Laing, Louise Erickson (Marjorie), Walter Tetley (Leroy), Earle Ross (Hooker), Lillian Randolph (Birdie), Richard LeGrand (Peavey), Bea Benaderet (Eve), Tommy Bernard (Craig)
   Summary: Leroy's improved attitude at the start of the school year causes Gildersleeve to buy a set of encyclopedias and to consider sending the boy to college.
   Writers: John Whedon, Sam Moore
   Comments: Again no audience is

present for this recording. A tick-tock musical introduction now precedes visits to Peavey's Pharmacy. Meakin's music also helps listeners follow Gildy up the stairs. Gildy's statement that Leroy will not be going to college for five years suggests the boy is in the seventh grade. Throcky tells Hooker that he graduated from the state university which conflicts with the information given on May 17, 1942 that he was a member of the Princeton class of 1914.

Date: September 16, 1945
Title: Leroy Suspended from School
   Cast: Harold Peary (Gildersleeve), John Laing, Louise Erickson (Marjorie), Walter Tetley (Leroy), Earle Ross (Hooker), Lillian Randolph (Birdie), Richard LeGrand (Peavey), Tommy Bernard (Craig)
   Summary: Leroy discovers that the worst part of his one-week suspension is being ostracized by his schoolmates.
   Writers: John Whedon, Sam Moore
   Comments: For the first time a character steps into one of the commercials when Leroy calls John Laing "What a character!" Meakin leads out of the classroom scene with "School Days." Listeners are left with the amusing image of Gildy fleeing for his life with a hose-wielding teacher in hot pursuit.

Date: September 23, 1945
Title: Leila Returns Again
   Cast: Harold Peary (Gildersleeve), John Laing, Louise Erickson (Marjorie), Walter Tetley (Leroy), Earle Ross (Hooker), Lillian Randolph (Birdie), Shirley Mitchell (Leila), Richard LeGrand (Peavey), Arthur Q. Bryan (Floyd), Ken Christy (Gates)

Summary: Leila returns in style to resume her dalliance with Gildersleeve.

Writers: John Whedon, Sam Moore

Comments: Kraft Cheese now becomes Kraft Foods. Gildersleeve sings "I Love Life." The Jolly Boys sing "I Love You Truly," "I Dream of Jeannie," and "The Sweetheart of Sigma Chi." Meakin's "hot stuff" and back-and-forth pacing music sets the tempo for the Leila and Gildy love match. Although Summerfield certainly isn't a one-horse town, it appears to be home to a one-person airport whose sole employee is more omnipresent than Kilroy.

Date: September 30, 1945
Title: Marjorie the Ballerina
  Cast: Harold Peary (Gildersleeve), John Laing, Louise Erickson (Marjorie), Walter Tetley (Leroy), Earle Ross (Hooker), Lillian Randolph (Birdie), Shirley Mitchell (Leila), Richard LeGrand (Peavey)
  Summary: Encouraged by her uncle and Leila, Marjorie is determined to pursue a career as a dancer.

Writers: John Whedon, Sam Moore

Comments: Hooker's math is off by two years for in 25 years Marjorie would be 41, not 43. Peavey slips in a sly witticism with his "The cost of liver is going up" remark. Marjorie, a typical teen, swings quickly on her pendulum, contemplating the pit of an early death and envisioning an upward swing to the heights of fame on the same day.

Date: October 7, 1945
Title: Raking Leaves
  Cast: Harold Peary (Gildersleeve), John Laing, Louise Erickson (Mar-

jorie), Walter Tetley (Leroy), Earle Ross (Hooker), Lillian Randolph (Birdie), Shirley Mitchell (Leila), Richard LeGrand (Peavey), Tommy Bernard (Craig)
  Summary: Raking and burning leaves in the front yard leads to an encounter with the Bullards that jeopardizes Leroy's invitation to Craig's party.

Writers: John Whedon, Sam Moore

Allusion: Gildersleeve quotes from Luke 10:7: "The laborer is worthy of his hire."

Comments: Gildersleeve is one of the very first to throw a handful of ice cubes on the Cold War as the war is hardly over and he is already spying Communists under the leaves. Meakin blows up some autumn gales of music to simulate the raking of leaves as well as a wind effect. Peary is so eager to burst into the tag he muffs Laing's name.

Date: October 14, 1945
Title: Leroy Breaks a Vase
  Cast: Harold Peary (Gildersleeve), John Laing, Louise Erickson (Marjorie), Walter Tetley (Leroy), Earle Ross (Hooker), Lillian Randolph (Birdie), Richard LeGrand (Peavey), Bea Benaderet (Eve), Arthur Q. Bryan (Floyd)
  Summary: When Leroy breaks a vase with a football, his uncle demands that he pay for it out of his allowance.

Writers: John Whedon, Sam Moore

Allusions: Gildersleeve quotes from *Tom Brown's School-Days* by Thomas Hughes: "Life isn't all beer and skittles." Gildersleeve paraphrases from *Virginibus Puerisque* by Robert Louis Stevenson: "Life isn't a bed of roses."

Comments: Birdie sings "Home!

Sweet Home!" Laing uses atomic energy to take listeners on a bird's eye view of the house. The name Gildy jokingly gives to Hooker is a nod to football innovator Amos Alonzo Stagg. The barbershop palaver is a wonderful time capsule of that notable year when Mr. Inside and Mr. Outside made Army a gridiron powerhouse, the plight of Dick Tracy could push front page headlines into second-hand news, and the Cubs (despite being nudged out of the conversation by the Tigers) played in a World Series. For those marking time, it is five seconds between Gildy's declaration that "If he'd only come back, I'll never speak harshly to him again" and his stern demand "Leroy, where the devil have you been?" Meakin punctuates Leroy's new-found wealth with a few bars of "We're in the Money."

Date: October 21, 1945
Title: Lightfoot Visits Leila
  Cast: Harold Peary (Gildersleeve), John Laing, Louise Erickson (Marjorie), Walter Tetley (Leroy), Earle Ross (Hooker), Lillian Randolph (Birdie), Shirley Mitchell (Leila), Richard Le-Grand (Peavey)
  Summary: Gildersleeve is irritated at the prospect of meeting an old flame of Leila's.
  Writers: John Whedon, Sam Moore
  Allusion: Hooker quotes from one of Aesop's fables: "Dog in the manger."
  Comments: Gildersleeve sings "Auld Lang Syne" and "Speak to Me of Love" Leila's house number is given as 269, although no street is given. Gildersleeve provides a measure of the size of Summerfield when he indicates the water department services 10,000 residences.

Peary fluffs Dupree's first name in the tag by calling him "Littlefoot."

Date: October 28, 1945
Title: Rumor about Mrs. Peavey
  Cast: Harold Peary (Gildersleeve), John Laing, Louise Erickson (Marjorie), Walter Tetley (Leroy), Earle Ross (Hooker), Lillian Randolph (Birdie), Shirley Mitchell (Leila), Richard Le-Grand (Peavey), ? (Floyd), Ken Christy (Gates)
  Summary: When a story is spread that Peavey's wife is ill, the Jolly Boys solicit customers for the drugstore so Peavey will have enough money for her operation.
  Writers: John Whedon, Sam Moore
  Comments: The Jolly Boys sing "There Is a Tavern in the Town" and "Dear Old Pal of Mine." Another actor substitutes for Arthur Q. Bryan in the role of Floyd. Gildy indicates that the monthly dues for the Jolly Boys Social Club is 50 cents. In the tag Peary gives an incidental plug to *The Jack Benny Program* which, of course, followed *The Great Gildersleeve* on Sundays.

Date: November 4, 1945
Title: Helping Leroy with Homework
  Cast: Harold Peary (Gildersleeve), John Laing, Louise Erickson (Marjorie), Walter Tetley (Leroy), Earle Ross (Hooker), Lillian Randolph (Birdie), Shirley Mitchell (Leila), Richard Le-Grand (Peavey), ? (Bessie)
  Summary: Gildersleeve finds it hard to deliver on his promise to tutor Leroy so the boy's grades will improve.
  Writers: John Whedon, Sam Moore
  Allusions: Hooker quotes from "Night Thoughts" by Edward Young:

"Procrastination is the thief of time." Peavey paraphrases from *Invictus* by William Ernest Henley: "I am the captain of my fate and my unconquerable soul."

Comments: Birdie sings "Nobody Knows the Trouble I've Seen." Gloria Holliday will soon be assuming the role of Bessie, but she is not playing the part in this episode nor is Pauline Drake. The reference to B7 made by Marjorie again suggests that Leroy is in the seventh grade. *Romance in the Rain* is a fictitious film title. In the gag Louise delivers a teen-to-teen message promoting the Junior Red Cross.

Date: November 11, 1945
Title: Marjorie Tries Homemaking
Cast: Harold Peary (Gildersleeve), John Laing, Louise Erickson (Marjorie), Walter Tetley (Leroy), Earle Ross (Hooker), Lillian Randolph (Birdie), Shirley Mitchell (Leila), Richard Le-Grand (Peavey)
Summary: Gildersleeve attempts to get Marjorie to abandon her dreams of a career and learn the domestic arts instead.
Writers: John Whedon, Sam Moore
Comments: Peavey sings "Tell Me Pretty Maiden." Meakin employs appropriate music to simulate Marjorie's descent down the stairs. Famous Jones is a fictitious drummer in the mold of Chick Webb or Cozy Cole.

Date: November 18, 1945
Title: Jolly Boys Fall Out
Cast: Harold Peary (Gildersleeve), John Laing, Louise Erickson (Marjorie), Walter Tetley (Leroy), Earle Ross (Hooker), Lillian Randolph (Birdie),

Shirley Mitchell (Leila), Richard LeGrand (Peavey), Arthur Q. Bryan (Floyd), Ken Christy (Gates), Tommy Bernard (Craig)
Summary: Harsh words and hurt feelings threaten to break up the Jolly Boys when Gildersleeve's visit with Rumson Bullard convinces him that his neighbor is too refined for their club.
Writers: John Whedon, Sam Moore
Comments: The Jolly Boys sing "Down by the Old Mill Stream" and "There Is a Tavern in the Town." Gildersleeve sings "I Hear You Calling Me." Peary's "gold tip" ad-lib breaks up the cast even more than the audience.

Date: November 25, 1945
Title: Football Game
Cast: Harold Peary (Gildersleeve), John Laing, Louise Erickson (Marjorie), Walter Tetley (Leroy), Earle Ross (Hooker), Lillian Randolph (Birdie), Shirley Mitchell (Leila), Richard Le-Grand (Peavey)
Summary: Gildersleeve takes Leila to the state university football game where there is more action in the stands than on the field.
Writers: John Whedon, Sam Moore
Comments: Leroy sings the University of Michigan fight song, "The Victors." When Leila yearns "to be 16 instead of pushing 30," she is pushing her own clock back a decade. The writers create a hilarious picture of Gildy on his hands and knees amid peanut shells while people tromp on his fingers as the only touchdown of the game is being scored. Just a sampling of "Home! Sweet Home!" by Meakin is enough to get Throcky from the stadium to his living room.

Date: December 2, 1945
Title: Opera Sponsor
 Cast: Harold Peary (Gildersleeve), John Laing, Louise Erickson (Marjorie), Walter Tetley (Leroy), Earle Ross (Hooker), Lillian Randolph (Birdie), Richard LeGrand (Peavey), Arthur Q. Bryan (Floyd), Ken Christy (Gates)
 Summary: Gildersleeve finds it challenging to sell his allotment of 15 opera tickets until he turns to the Jolly Boys.
 Writers: John Whedon, Sam Moore
 Allusion: Gildersleeve invokes "Liberty Hall" from *She Stoops to Conquer* by Oliver Goldsmith.
 Comments: Gildersleeve sings "O Solo Mio." The Jolly Boys sing "The Toreador Song" and "Funiculi, Funicula." Peary says "starts make loving" instead of "starts making love." Much about Gildy's behavior can be summed up in the exchange between his friend and his niece when Hooker asks, "How long has he been like this?" and Marjorie replies, "Since birth, I guess." In the tag Hal promotes the purchase of Victory Bonds.

Date: December 9, 1945
Title: Opera Committee Chairman
 Cast: Harold Peary (Gildersleeve), John Laing, Louise Erickson (Marjorie), Walter Tetley (Leroy), Earle Ross (Hooker), Lillian Randolph (Birdie), Shirley Mitchell (Leila), Richard LeGrand (Peavey), Bea Benaderet (Eve)
 Summary: Women drive Gildersleeve to distraction at the dressmaker and later drive him to cover after he promises four women the same honorary title at the opera.
 Writers: John Whedon, Sam Moore
 Comments: Peary covers his fluff of

"The poor women [*sic*] is running a madhouse" with "It's beginning to get me." In the tag Peary promotes his first set of recordings for children in which he retells the stories of "Jack and the Beanstalk," "Puss in Boots," and "Rumpelstiltskin."

Date: December 16, 1945
Title: Night of the Opera
 Cast: Harold Peary (Gildersleeve), John Laing, Louise Erickson (Marjorie), Walter Tetley (Leroy), Earle Ross (Hooker), Lillian Randolph (Birdie), Richard LeGrand (Peavey), Bea Benaderet (Eve), Arthur Q. Bryan (Floyd), Ken Christy (Gates), John Wald (WSUM announcer)
 Summary: Gildersleeve, inspired by attending an opera, resolves to amend his dilatory ways and use his talents wisely.
 Writers: John Whedon, Sam Moore
 Comments: Gildersleeve sings "Song of the Evening Star." John Wald, who will later assume the role of Kraft announcer on the program, appears for the first time. Gildy predictably backslides on his resolution, becoming a slugabed who passes on his good intentions regarding a musical career to a mystified Leroy. Except for the appeal to buy Christmas Seals in the tag, the upcoming holiday has been shoved out of sight, out of mind by the three-week opera adventure.

Date: December 23, 1945
Title: Wrapping Christmas Presents
 Cast: Harold Peary (Gildersleeve), John Laing, ? (Marjorie), Walter Tetley (Leroy), Earle Ross (Hooker), Lillian Randolph (Birdie), Shirley Mitchell

(Leila), Richard LeGrand (Peavey), Tommy Bernard (Craig)

Summary: Gildersleeve and his family prepare gifts and exchange them with friends who drop in for some holiday cheer.

Writers: John Whedon, Sam Moore

Allusions: Several references are made to "A Visit from St. Nicholas" by Clement Clarke Moore: Laing quotes "His eyes, how they twinkle, his dimples, how merry." Hooker quotes "Merry Christmas to all, and to all a good night." Gildersleeve quotes "'Twas the night before Christmas, when all through the house / Not a creature was stirring...."

Comments: Birdie sings "Coventry Carol." The family sings "Joy to the World." Another actress, possibly Gloria Holliday, fills in for Louise Erickson. It is appropriate that this episode, basking in the radiance of a family Christmas, is one of the few in the series with all the action taking place right at home.

Date: December 30, 1945
Title: New Year's Eve at Home
Cast: Harold Peary (Gildersleeve), John Laing, ? (Marjorie), Walter Tetley (Leroy), Earle Ross (Hooker), Lillian Randolph (Birdie), Richard LeGrand (Peavey), John Wald (radio announcer)

Summary: Gildersleeve, full of self-pity, spends the last evening of the year alone until Hooker joins him at the last moment.

Writers: John Whedon, Sam Moore

Allusion: Gildersleeve quotes from *The American Crisis* by Thomas Paine: "These are the times that try men's souls."

Comments: Leroy sings "My Melan-choly Baby." Gildersleeve and Hooker sing "Auld Lang Syne." The part of Marjorie is again played by another actress, not Louise Erickson. This episode, like the previous one, is housebound. Hooker divulges to Gildy that his age is 62. Throcky asks the rhetorical question millions still ask when they press the "off" button: "How can they put that drivel on the air?"

Date: January 6, 1946
Title: Ben Returns from the Navy
Cast: Harold Peary (Gildersleeve), John Laing, Louise Erickson (Marjorie), Walter Tetley (Leroy), Earle Ross (Hooker), Lillian Randolph (Birdie), Richard LeGrand (Peavey), Ben Alexander (Ben)

Summary: Gildersleeve's efforts to rekindle the romance between Marjorie and Ben seem to stall until he steps aside and leaves the two youngsters alone.

Writers: John Whedon, Sam Moore

Comments: Marjorie sings "It Might As Well Be Spring," later to be joined by Gildersleeve. Meakin's "Anchor's Away" brings Ben back in high style. Lillian has her smallest part with just a few words to say. Leroy finally delivers a "Ha!" with the full gusto of a natural-born scoffer. *The Mummy's Revenge* is a fictitious film title. For once Gildersleeve confesses openly to Peavey that he seeks out the druggist for advice, not conversation.

Date: January 13, 1946
Title: Ben Sells Insurance
Cast: Harold Peary (Gildersleeve), John Laing, Louise Erickson (Marjorie), Walter Tetley (Leroy), Earle Ross

(Hooker), Lillian Randolph (Birdie), Richard LeGrand (Peavey), Ben Alexander (Ben), Gloria Holliday (Bessie)

Summary: After getting timid Ben a job selling insurance, Gildersleeve tries to bolster the young man's confidence by finding prospects for him.

Writers: John Whedon, Sam Moore

Comments: Gloria Holliday appears for the first time as Bessie. Gildersleeve's proposed solution for the overflowing piles of letters and papers in his office is typical: get a bigger desk. Hooker tells Ben he is 55, shaving seven years off the figure he gave two weeks before. Throcky impatiently leaps all over Peavey, accusing him of being greedy just for attending to business by answering the phone.

Date: January 20, 1946
Title: Palm Reader a Fraud?

Cast: Harold Peary (Gildersleeve), John Laing, Louise Erickson (Marjorie), Walter Tetley (Leroy), Earle Ross (Hooker), Lillian Randolph (Birdie), Shirley Mitchell (Leila), Richard LeGrand (Peavey), Arthur Q. Bryan (Floyd), Ken Christy (Gates), Joseph Kearns (Sartorius)

Summary: Gildersleeve's distrust of a palm reader leads him and Floyd as undercover deputies to investigate the fortune teller.

Writers: John Whedon, Sam Moore

Allusions: Gildersleeve quotes from Ecclesiastes and Luke: "Eat, drink, and be merry." Gildersleeve quotes from *The Rubáiyát of Omar Khayyám*: "A loaf of bread, a jug of wine, and thou."

Comments: Peavey sings "White Christmas," an odd choice for late January. A clever remark about the burnt toast deserves a second look: "It would turn to ashes in my mouth — if not before." Bryan earns the big laugh of the night with matchless delivery of just two words: "Oh, well."

Date: January 27, 1946
Title: Facing Old Age

Cast: Harold Peary (Gildersleeve), John Laing, Louise Erickson (Marjorie), Walter Tetley (Leroy), Earle Ross (Hooker), Lillian Randolph (Birdie), Shirley Mitchell (Leila), Richard LeGrand (Peavey), Ben Alexander (Ben)

Summary: Leila and Throckmorton feel the pangs of the advancing years as they contemplate their lost youth and the uncertainty of their futures.

Writers: John Whedon, Sam Moore

Comments: Gildersleeve sings "Just a Little Love, a Little Kiss." Leila climbs the age ladder from 32 to 36 to 37, and even then she may be trimming a couple years off the top. Gildersleeve gives his age as 42, a reasonable figure except when one considers that he also claims to have served in World War I, which would mean he was only 14 at the end of hostilities in 1918. Whedon and Moore create just enough insipid dialogue for the sappy onscreen romance so listeners will agree with the rating of 0 stars on the Gildy / Peavey scale, i.e., "It was no good at all."

Date: February 3, 1946
Title: Diplomat

Cast: Harold Peary (Gildersleeve), John Laing, Louise Erickson (Marjorie), Walter Tetley (Leroy), Earle Ross (Hooker), Lillian Randolph (Birdie), Shirley Mitchell (Leila), Richard LeGrand (Peavey), Tommy Bernard (Craig)

Summary: Gildersleeve's efforts to teach diplomacy to Leroy are put to the test after a squabble breaks out with the Bullards.

Writers: John Whedon, Sam Moore

Comments: Gildy's boast, "Tell me I don't know how to handle kids," turns out to be ironic when the two boys give a lesson to their elders about resolving disputes. Leroy's selection as the tenth most popular boy in 7B is about as prestigious as being voted fourth alternate to the prom court. The conciliatory tone of the resolution is capped by Meakin's "When Good Fellows Get Together."

John Whedon and Sam Moore wrote scripts for the show from 1942 to 1947.

Date: February 10, 1946
Title: New Car or College?

Cast: Harold Peary (Gildersleeve), John Laing, Louise Erickson (Marjorie), Walter Tetley (Leroy), Earle Ross (Hooker), Lillian Randolph (Birdie), Shirley Mitchell (Leila), Ken Christy (Bank Guard Gates), Ben Alexander (Ben), Jim Backus (Larry Ganz)

Summary: The poor condition of his car and the attention paid to Rumson Bullard's new automobile prompt Throckmorton to consider using savings bonds reserved for Leroy's college education to purchase a sleek convertible.

Writers: John Whedon, Sam Moore

Comments: Ganz lures Gildy with the carrot salesmen have been dangling before bachelors for decades: hot cars attract hot women. The questionable endorsement that Gildy gives to Cords ("They're so good they don't make them anymore") could be applied to a multitude of makes: Imperial, Kaiser, DeSoto, Jordan, Oldsmobile, Studebaker, Hudson....

Date: February 17, 1946
Title: Leroy Is Sick

Cast: Harold Peary (Gildersleeve), John Laing, Louise Erickson (Marjorie), Walter Tetley (Leroy), Lillian Randolph (Birdie), Richard LeGrand (Peavey), Bea Benaderet (Eve), John Wald (radio announcer)

Summary: Gildersleeve spends the day taking care of his ill nephew.

Writers: John Whedon, Sam Moore

Comments: Louise shows a pro's patience by waiting to deliver her "We'll wait" line. Meakin's musical scales lend just the right touch so listeners can follow Gildy's arduous ups and downs. Gildersleeve gives his phone number as 2413, a change from the number of 2371 given on June 3, 1945. The scene of Gildy under Leroy's bed is a gem, capped by the typical boy's explanation for how a bizarre object like a bird's nest ended up in his room: "Must've got lost."

Date: February 24, 1946
Title: Hobby
Cast: Harold Peary (Gildersleeve), John Laing, Louise Erickson (Marjorie), Walter Tetley (Leroy), Earle Ross (Hooker), Lillian Randolph (Birdie), Shirley Mitchell (Leila), Richard Le-Grand (Peavey)
Summary: When Hooker suggests Gildersleeve take up a hobby, Throcky briefly considers stamp collecting before attempting to build model ships.
Writers: John Whedon, Sam Moore
Comments: Gildersleeve sings "Only Make Believe." The song is an appropriate one for Gildy is only making believe he is interested in putting ships in bottles until the next unattached woman comes along. Philandering, not philately, is Throckmorton's avocation.

Date: March 3, 1946
Title: State Water Inspector
Cast: Harold Peary (Gildersleeve), John Laing, Louise Erickson (Marjorie), Walter Tetley (Leroy), Earle Ross

(Hooker), Lillian Randolph (Birdie), Shirley Mitchell (Leila), Richard LeGrand (Peavey), Arthur Q. Bryan (Floyd), Gloria Holliday (Bessie)
Summary: Gildersleeve frets up a storm trying to make certain everything in the water department will pass muster when a state official visits Summerfield.
Writers: John Whedon, Sam Moore
Allusion: Gildersleeve paraphrases the proverb that can be traced back to Euripides: "The darkest hour is just before the dawn."
Comments: After Peary reads Bryan's line, he blames it on the hot towel. Gildy tries the phone booth at the drugstore for the third time, getting in with Peavey's help and getting out when the writers cut to the next scene. A worm gear has replaced the snifter valve as the loose cog in the waterworks. The reference to Burton Holmes, a mostly-forgotten man today, is to the lecturer who made travelogues a way for his audiences to see the world without leaving town.

Date: March 10, 1946
Title: Marjorie's Dance Date
Cast: Harold Peary (Gildersleeve), John Laing, Louise Erickson (Marjorie), Walter Tetley (Leroy), Earle Ross (Hooker), Lillian Randolph (Birdie), Shirley Mitchell (Leila), Ben Alexander (Ben)
Summary: When Marjorie cannot get shy Ben to take her to the country club dance, her uncle escorts her to the function.
Writers: John Whedon, Sam Moore
Allusion: Gildersleeve quotes from *Childe Harold's Pilgrimage* by Lord

Byron: "On with the dance! Let joy be unrefined [unconfined]."

Comments: Gildersleeve sings "The Sweetheart of Sigma Chi." The writers capture well the vagaries of teen social life, and Louise realistically portrays the ups and downs of adolescent girlhood. Gildersleeve drives his Cinderella to the ball in more of a lemon than a pumpkin, his 1938 Studebaker that a month ago had been called a jalopy by an auto dealer. The audience can scarcely control a scoffing "Ha!" a la Leroy when Gildy scolds Marjorie: "You've got a temper, my dear. I don't know where you got it from." Although totally sober at the dance, Throcky behaves boorishly like the drunk who keeps calling for the band to play "Melancholy Baby."

Date: March 17, 1946
Title: Leroy Arrested
  Cast: Harold Peary (Gildersleeve), John Laing, Louise Erickson (Marjorie), Walter Tetley (Leroy), Earle Ross (Hooker), Lillian Randolph (Birdie), Richard LeGrand (Peavey), Arthur Q. Bryan (Floyd), Ken Christy (Gates), Tommy Bernard (Craig)
  Summary: After Leroy and Craig are accused of taking lumber from a construction site, Gildersleeve tries to get the charge dropped by appealing to Chief Gates.
  Writers: John Whedon, Sam Moore
  Allusions: Gildersleeve quotes from "Barefoot Boy" by John Greenleaf Whittier: "Blessings on thee, little man, / Barefoot boy with cheek of tan." Hooker quotes from *The Merchant of Venice* by William Shakespeare: "The quality of mercy is not strained, / It

droppeth [falleth] as the gentle rain from heaven."

Comments: The Jolly Boys sing "A Little Bit of Heaven." For the first time Gildersleeve releases his "bridge of sighs" as he sits down to relax. This is the first time someone mentions a moose head in the sparsely-furnished room above the barbershop.

Date: March 24, 1946
Title: Ancestry
  Cast: Harold Peary (Gildersleeve), John Laing, Louise Erickson (Marjorie), Walter Tetley (Leroy), Earle Ross (Hooker), Lillian Randolph (Bosun Coggins), Shirley Mitchell (Leila, native girl, Josie, Amber), Richard LeGrand (Snodgrass)
  Summary: Gildersleeve, wanting to get a suitable costume so he can portray an ancestor at an upcoming social affair with an historical theme, researches his genealogy at the public library.
  Writers: John Whedon, Sam Moore
  Comments: This episode has the flavor of "The Secret Life of Walter Mitty" as staid Gildersleeve daydreams his way into exotic adventures. The audience catches on to the innuendo of "Take off your things and make yourself comfortable." The writers add to the fun with an in-joke making one of Throcky's ancestors a taxidermist named John Whedon Gildersleeve. The regular cast receives credit at the end.

Date: March 31, 1946
Title: Spring Picnic
  Cast: Harold Peary (Gildersleeve), John Laing, Louise Erickson (Marjorie), Walter Tetley (Leroy), Earle Ross (Hooker), Lillian Randolph (Birdie),

Shirley Mitchell (Leila), Richard Le-Grand (Peavey), John Wald (radio announcer, landowner)

Summary: As a way of escaping all the doomsday talk on the news, Throckmorton takes the children and Leila on a picnic in the country.

Writers: John Whedon, Sam Moore

Comments: Leila, Gildersleeve, Marjorie, and Leroy sing "Put on Your Old Grey Bonnet." Peary puts his own special brand of sportive lechery into his reaction to Leila's admission that her wet playsuit will shrink: "I'd like to see that." Lazy Throcky lets the others go about their tasks at the picnic site while he takes it easy. There is more than a bit of truth in Gildersleeve's story about the Leila who "found all Yankees make her heart go pit-a-pat."

Date: April 7, 1946
Title: Estate Report

Cast: Harold Peary (Gildersleeve), John Laing, Louise Erickson (Marjorie), Walter Tetley (Leroy), Earle Ross (Hooker), Lillian Randolph (Birdie), Richard LeGrand (Peavey), Bea Benaderet (Eve)

Summary: Gildersleeve and the children, who have misgivings about spending an evening with Hooker, are pleasantly surprised by the judge's generosity.

Writers: John Whedon, Sam Moore

Allusion: Hooker paraphrases Psalm 90:10: "The allotted span of man is threescore years and ten."

Comments: Although the audio quality of this episode is less than desirable, it is a splendid example of how the show mingled humanity and hilarity. Ross dons the role of avuncular

benefactor as easily as that of experienced jurist. LeGrand shows how riotous underplaying a part can be when he uses the Swedish dialect he will later employ when portraying Ole on *Fibber McGee and Molly.*

Date: April 14, 1946
Title: Bank Robber

Cast: Harold Peary (Gildersleeve), John Laing, Louise Erickson (Marjorie), Walter Tetley (Leroy), Earle Ross (Hooker), Lillian Randolph (Birdie), Shirley Mitchell (Leila), Richard LeGrand (Peavey), Arthur Q. Bryan (Floyd), Ken Christy (Gates)

Summary: A breakout at the county jail causes Gildersleeve to panic until he is reassured the escapee is harmless.

Writers: John Whedon, Sam Moore

Comments: The Captain O'Benny reference is to the role Jack took on the police skits that were performed occasionally on *The Jack Benny Program.* Gildersleeve is more two-faced than usual, declaring to Leroy that he but not his nephew can read newspapers at the table because "I'm different," switching from scared stiff to "I'll save you" mode in the blink of an eye, and doing a complete turnabout on the sheriff's capabilities at the end.

Date: April 21, 1946
Title: Petition

Cast: Harold Peary (Gildersleeve), John Laing, Louise Erickson (Marjorie), Walter Tetley (Leroy), Lillian Randolph (Birdie), Richard LeGrand (Peavey), Ben Alexander (Ben)

Summary: Gildersleeve circulates a petition to restrict makeshift housing which might decrease property values after a streetcar is moved on a nearby lot.

Writers: John Whedon, Sam Moore

Comments: The writers bring home the problem of the housing shortage for returning servicemen in a very practical manner, and Meakin's music sets the pace nicely with the "The Trolley Song" leading into the second act and the hoof beat bridges between house visits. Ben, who rarely gets upset, is judiciously interrupted by Gildersleeve before delivering a vulgarity but still gets his point across with "Well, they can." Peary reads J.L. Kraft's Easter message when technical difficulties prevent the president of the company from delivering it himself.

Date: April 28, 1946
Title: Leroy Wants a Horse

Cast: Harold Peary (Gildersleeve), John Laing, Louise Erickson (Marjorie), Walter Tetley (Leroy), Earle Ross (Hooker), Lillian Randolph (Birdie), Richard LeGrand (Peavey), Tommy Bernard (Craig)

Summary: Gildersleeve tries to appease Leroy, who has his heart set on a pony, by taking his nephew to a farm where the boy can see a horse up close.

Writers: John Whedon, Sam Moore

Comments: Though Leroy is at least five years older than Craig, he acts just as childishly as his neighbor by crying and behaving selfishly. For the second consecutive week, Peavey demonstrates more common sense than Gildersleeve. After watching his blowhard uncle spend barely ten seconds on the horse and justifying his retreat with "No

sense in overdoing it," Leroy tries to take a chip off the old block by trotting out an excuse of his own that also fails miserably.

Date: May 5, 1946
Title: In a Rut

Cast: Harold Peary (Gildersleeve), John Laing, Louise Erickson (Marjorie), Earle Ross (Hooker), Shirley Mitchell (Leila), Richard LeGrand (Peavey), Arthur Q. Bryan (Floyd)

Summary: When Leila takes up with a younger man, Gildersleeve is determined to break out of his usual pattern and do something unpredictable.

Writers: John Whedon, Sam Moore

Allusion: Hooker quotes from "Song" by Sir John Suckling: "Why so pale and wan, fond lover?" Floyd quotes from *Don Quixote* by Miguel de Cervantes: "Faint heart never won fair lady."

Comments: Gildersleeve sings "Yours Is My Heart Alone" and "When Day Is Done." Both Walter Tetley and Lillian Randolph are absent so most of the action takes place away from the house. The tonics Peavey stocks (e.g., Dr. Fagin's Nature Compound, Bilbo's Beef, Iron, and Wine, and Slug's Liver Extract) sound like nostrums that might be peddled by Eustace McGargle out of the back of a wagon.

Date: May 12, 1946
Title: Leila's New Suitor

Cast: Harold Peary (Gildersleeve), John Laing, Louise Erickson (Marjorie), Walter Tetley (Leroy), Earle Ross (Hooker), Lillian Randolph (Birdie), Shirley Mitchell (Leila), Richard LeGrand (Peavey), Arthur Q. Bryan (Floyd), Jim Backus (Mark Ward)

Summary: A jealous Gildersleeve seeks a way to drive a wedge between Leila and her friend Mark, even to the point of considering marrying his ex-fiancée.

Writers: John Whedon, Sam Moore

Allusion: Mark quotes from *As You Like It* by William Shakespeare: "All the world's a stage, / And all the men and women merely players." Mark quotes from *Twelfth Night* by William Shakespeare: "If music be the food of love, play on."

Comments: Mark sings "Penthouse Serenade." Meakin creatively plays on the Pagliacci theme by employing different tempos to indicate Gildy's changing moods. Mark behaves more admirably than Leila and Gildy for he at least faces his present and future honestly.

Date: May 19, 1946
Title: Leroy Hosts Ethel
    Cast: Harold Peary (Gildersleeve), John Laing, Louise Erickson (Marjorie), Walter Tetley (Leroy), Lillian Randolph (Birdie), Richard LeGrand (Peavey), Bea Benaderet (Eve)
    Summary: In order to impress upon his nephew the importance of getting along with girls, Gildersleeve invites Ethel Hammerschlag to spend her birthday with Leroy.
    Writers: John Whedon, Sam Moore
    Comments: Two tugging matches make for comic highlights in this outing: Leroy's grabbing of his uncle's leg and Peavey and Gildy pulling on a snapper. Peary does a fair job of playing both stern father and sheepish son, misfiring only at the end when he steps back into the present.

Date: May 26, 1946
Title: Memories of Leila
    Cast: Harold Peary (Gildersleeve), John Laing, Louise Erickson (Marjorie), Walter Tetley (Leroy), Earle Ross (Hooker), Lillian Randolph (Birdie), Shirley Mitchell (Leila), Richard LeGrand (Peavey), Ben Alexander (Ben)
    Summary: Gildersleeve recalls the early days after meeting Leila in 1942.
    Writers: John Whedon, Sam Moore
    Allusions: Gildersleeve quotes from *Lord Chesterfield's Letters*: "Whatever is worth doing at all, is worth doing well." Gildersleeve quotes from *Midsummer Night's Dream* by William Shakespeare: "The course of true love never did run smooth."
    Comments: Many of the events in this flashback were reported in the September 20 and 27, 1942 episodes. Ben appears in this broadcast, although his character was not introduced until 1943.

Date: June 2, 1946
Title: Plays Cyrano (Repeat)
    Cast: Harold Peary (Gildersleeve), John Laing, Louise Erickson (Marjorie), Walter Tetley (Leroy), Earle Ross (Hooker), Lillian Randolph (Birdie), Shirley Mitchell (Leila), Richard LeGrand (Peavey), Bea Benaderet (Eve), Arthur Q. Bryan (Floyd), Gloria Holliday (Bessie)
    Summary: Gildersleeve recalls the time he prepared to take the role of Cyrano de Bergerac in a little theater production.
    Writers: John Whedon, Sam Moore
    Comments: Gildersleeve sings "I Kiss Your Hand, Madame." This episode borrows elements from the script

of February 27, 1944. Switching productions 24 hours before opening night is improbable, almost impossible, except in the world of make-believe. Bessie's timetable for celebrating her boss's fourth anniversary as water commissioner is off because Gildersleeve's first day on the job was October 25, 1942.

Date: June 9, 1946
Title: Jolly Boys Picnic (Repeat)
    Cast: Harold Peary (Gildersleeve), John Laing, Louise Erickson (Marjorie), Walter Tetley (Leroy), Earle Ross (Hooker), Lillian Randolph (Birdie), Shirley Mitchell (Leila), Richard LeGrand (Peavey), Bea Benaderet (Eve), Arthur Q. Bryan (Floyd), Ken Christy (Gates), Tommy Bernard (Craig)
    Summary: Gildersleeve's recollections of the previous Fourth of July are highlighted by a hayride and picnic.
    Writers: John Whedon, Sam Moore
    Allusion: Leila quotes from "Barbara Frietchie" by John Greenleaf Whittier: "'Shoot if you must this old grey head, / But spare your country's flag,' she said."
    Comments: This is a slightly revised version of the script used on July 1, 1945. The Jolly Boys sing "Take Me Out to the Ball Game" and "In the Good Old Summertime." Peary's "extra step" ad-lib draws a big laugh from Shirley Mitchell. This episode is a wonderful piece of Americana, capturing a bygone time of a patriotic holiday in Anytown, U.S.A., aided by Meakin's melodies of "Yankee Doodle Dandy" and "Down by the Old Mill Stream." Peary informs the audience that when the program returns in September it will be heard on Wednesday evenings. The summer

replacement series is the quiz program *Ask Me Another* with *The Bob Burns Show* taking over the 6:30 Sunday slot in the fall of 1946.

Date: September 11, 1946 (Script)
Title: More Discipline
    Cast: Harold Peary (Gildersleeve), John Laing, Louise Erickson (Marjorie), Walter Tetley (Leroy), Earle Ross (Hooker), Lillian Randolph (Birdie), Shirley Mitchell (Leila), Richard LeGrand (Peavey)
    Summary: Disturbed that the lackadaisical habits of summer are lingering into the fall, Gildersleeve sets down more stringent requirements regarding dress, neatness, and mealtimes.
    Writers: John Whedon, Sam Moore
    Comments: The show is now heard on Wednesdays over NBC at 8:30 Eastern. Laing's introduction gives a bird's eye view of downtown Summerfield by placing the bus station across the street from Peavey's Pharmacy. Leroy's pet of the moment in a garter snake that causes panic in the kitchen when it gets loose. When Gildy discovers Leroy's bed filled with sneakers, comic books, baseball mitt, scissors, boxes of candy, and a toy gun he issues an amusing but confusing edict: "I will not have the house filled with sneaks and snakers."

Date: September 18, 1946
Title: Turns Off Water
    Cast: Harold Peary (Gildersleeve), John Laing, ? (Marjorie), Walter Tetley (Leroy), Earle Ross (Hooker), Lillian Randolph (Birdie), Shirley Mitchell (Leila), Richard LeGrand (Peavey), Gloria Holliday (Bessie)
    Summary: After reading about a

Shirley Mitchell (who played Leila Ransome), Louise Erickson, and Hal Peary pose to promote the program's move from Sundays to Wednesdays in September 1946.

water commissioner charged with malfeasance, Gildersleeve cracks down on delinquent subscribers by having their water cut off.

Writers: Frank Moore, Bill Kelsay

Comments: Gildersleeve sings "Heigh Ho" and "Speak to Me of Love." This is the first episode penned by Frank Moore and Bill Kelsay. Another actress other than Louise Erickson takes the small part given to Marjorie as evidenced by no credit given for that role at the end of the show. Gildersleeve says a mouthful when he admits "I'm not tough—I'm just lovable," although "I'm just gullible" would be more accurate as Leila gets him to do her bidding just by appealing to his vanity. Gildy utters several self-incriminating remarks including a complaint that Bessie is "out of the office so much I'd get lonesome if I was here very often myself."

Date: September 25, 1946
Title: Leila Instead of P.T.A.
Cast: Harold Peary (Gildersleeve), John Laing, Louise Erickson (Marjorie), Walter Tetley (Leroy), Earle Ross (Hooker), Lillian Randolph (Birdie), Shirley Mitchell (Leila), Richard Le-Grand (Peavey), Bea Benaderet (Eve)
Summary: Gildersleeve gets Hooker to take his place at a P.T.A. meeting so he can spend the evening with Leila, who has some startling news for him.
Writers: John Whedon, Sam Moore
Comments: Gildersleeve sings "When I Was a Young Man," "Duna," and "Speak to Me of Love." Gildy again reveals he is passion's slave by nibbling on Leila's ear when caught up on the wings of rapture and then munching on candy when gripped by the pangs of hunger. Laing plugs the article about *The Great Gildersleeve* in the October *Radio Mirror*.

Date: October 2, 1946
Title: Leila's Wedding Invitation
Cast: Harold Peary (Gildersleeve), John Laing, John Wald, ? (Marjorie), Walter Tetley (Leroy), Earle Ross

(Hooker), Lillian Randolph (Birdie), Shirley Mitchell (Leila), Richard LeGrand (Peavey), Arthur Q. Bryan (Floyd), Ken Christy (Gates), Gloria Holliday (Bessie)
Summary: Everyone assumes Gildersleeve is heartbroken over Leila's impending marriage, much to the irritation of Throcky.
Writers: John Whedon, Sam Moore
Comments: The Jolly Boys sing "On the Banks of the Wabash" and "I Wonder Who's Kissing Her Now." John Laing handles the Kraft messages, but John Wald takes the part of narrator. An unidentified actress again plays Marjorie. Liberties in compressing time are a necessity of half-hour weekly shows, but even announcements of shotgun weddings are blasted into mailboxes more than seven days before the ceremony. Time also means nothing to Gildy who declares his affair with Leila "was all over years ago" scarcely a week after necking with her. The writers give listeners a whiff of the forbidden when Throckmorton suggests Leila must have kept the fragrant letters "among her … things." *The Great Gildersleeve*, which led into a powerhouse with *The Jack Benny Program* on Sundays, is now in less favorable surroundings so Peary is asked to plug the Wednesday night lineup of *Mr. District Attorney, Duffy's Tavern,* and *The Fabulous Dr. Tweedy.*

Date: October 9, 1946
Title: Leila Leaves Summerfield
Cast: Harold Peary (Gildersleeve), John Laing, Walter Tetley (Leroy), Earle Ross (Hooker), Lillian Randolph (Birdie), Shirley Mitchell (Leila),

Richard LeGrand (Peavey), Arthur Q. Bryan (Floyd), Ken Christy (Gates)

Summary: Gildersleeve is remorseful and given to wishful thinking on Leila's last day in town before leaving to be married.

Writers: John Whedon, Sam Moore

Comments: Leila and Throckmorton again behave like immature teens instead of middle-aged adults, breaking out with emotional entreaties and tearful recriminations over past mistakes. Gildy's comment about Leila's deep side is ironical for she is still a shallow, fibbing, self-centered schemer whose farewell to her "beloved" is a curse. Peary's promotion of his appearance on *Kay Kyser's Kollege of Musical Knowledge* that evening also includes a boost for NBC, "the senior network."

Date: October 16, 1946
Title: Retirement Plans

Cast: Harold Peary (Gildersleeve), John Laing, Louise Erickson (Marjorie), Walter Tetley (Leroy), Earle Ross (Hooker), Lillian Randolph (Birdie), Richard LeGrand (Peavey), Arthur Q. Bryan (Floyd), Jim Backus (Clifford Bradley)

Summary: Gildersleeve starts looking ahead to living well in the future until he realizes that he is just getting by in the present.

Writers: John Whedon, Sam Moore

Comments: Meakin contributes "We're in the Money" bridges to fit the occasion. Gildy again plays the four-flusher, spouting off about being willing to pay a buck to a manicurist when he can barely scrape up 50 cents for a shave. Peary tries to save his fluff of the "You're a fool" line by adding "Fuel for thought," and muffs his indignant response to the salesman the end.

Date: October 23, 1946
Title: Money Woes

Cast: Harold Peary (Gildersleeve), John Laing, Louise Erickson (Marjorie), Walter Tetley (Leroy), Earle Ross (Hooker), Lillian Randolph (Birdie), Richard LeGrand (Peavey), Ken Christy (Gates), Tommy Bernard (Craig)

Summary: Gildersleeve implements an austerity program at home to cut expenses and seeks a raise at work to increase income.

Writers: John Whedon, Sam Moore

Comments: Meakin adds to the mood with kazoo, a cavalry charge, tick-tock notes to reflect plodding footsteps, and "Brother, Can You Spare a Dime?" Gildersleeve again behaves true to form, putting his perceived humiliation ahead of Leroy's unselfish act and calling Gates chicken-hearted when he himself is afraid to face the mayor alone. Gildy redeems himself somewhat by writing a check to the Community Chest to demonstrate that charity begins at home.

Date: October 30, 1946
Title: Hooker a Possible Boarder

Cast: Harold Peary (Gildersleeve), John Laing, Louise Erickson (Marjorie), Walter Tetley (Leroy), Earle Ross (Hooker), Lillian Randolph (Birdie), Richard LeGrand (Peavey)

Summary: Gildersleeve invites Hooker to supper to see if the judge would make a suitable boarder if he decides to sell his home.

Writers: John Whedon, Sam Moore

Allusion: Gildersleeve invokes "Liberty Hall" from *She Stoops to Conquer* by Oliver Goldsmith.

Comments: A stunned Leroy says that Hooker's suit purchased in 1932 is older than he is, implying that he is 13 or younger, a reasonable age for a seventh-grader. (Tetley was 31 at this time.) Marjorie indicates her uncle has acted impulsively three times in the last year when sensing a whiff of easy money in real estate. This time Gildy pulls a figure of $40,000 out of the same airspace reserved for his other castles in the sky.

Date: November 6, 1946
Title: Slumber Party
Cast: Harold Peary (Gildersleeve), John Laing, Louise Erickson (Marjorie), Walter Tetley (Leroy), Earle Ross (Hooker), Lillian Randolph (Birdie), Richard LeGrand (Peavey), Ben Alexander (Ben)
Summary: After hosting a pajama party at which boys were the main topic, Marjorie decides to pursue the topic of engagement with boyfriend Ben, much to the displeasure of her uncle.
Writers: John Whedon, Sam Moore
Comments: Gildersleeve sings "If You Were the Only Girl in the World." The girls sing "South America, Take It Away." Meakin escorts Marjorie down the stairs with "A Pretty Girl Is Like a Melody." The conflict portrayed in this outing, always old, always new, is best expressed by Gildy's complaint "I don't understand this younger generation." The title of the movie Mrs. Peavey wants to see, *To Each His Own*, describes the dialogue in the drugstore as each man goes down his own chosen path.

Date: November 13, 1946
Title: Pretty Woman
Cast: Harold Peary (Gildersleeve), John Laing, Louise Erickson (Marjorie), Walter Tetley (Leroy), Earle Ross (Hooker), Richard LeGrand (Peavey), Arthur Q. Bryan (Floyd)
Summary: After falling for an attractive woman he sees at the Summerfield Grill, Gildersleeve uses Hooker to get invited to a country club dinner at which his heartthrob will be the guest of honor.
Writers: John Whedon, Sam Moore
Allusion: Gildersleeve quotes form "I Wandered Lonely as a Cloud" by William Wordsworth: "And then my heart with pleasure [rapture] fills, / And dances with the daffodils."
Comments: Gildersleeve sings "The Darktown Strutter's Ball" and "People Will Say We're in Love." Meakin's "When You're Smiling" leads into Gildy's sour grapes tag. Throckmorton, the hopeless romantic, is in full bloom in this broadcast, acting like a schoolboy as he gushes "This is the real thing" about a woman he has not even met. His Dr. Jekyll/Mr. Hyde behavior in the living room merits a stereo version of "What a character!" from Marjorie and Leroy. An in-joke is inserted in the script when Gildersleeve greets Mrs. Van Hartesveldt. (Fran Van Hartesveldt directed the show at this time.)

Date: November 20, 1946
Title: Study Habits
Cast: Harold Peary (Gildersleeve), John Laing, Louise Erickson (Marjorie), Walter Tetley (Leroy), Earle Ross (Hooker), Lillian Randolph (Birdie), Frances Robinson (Eve Goodwin)

Summary: Gildersleeve, determined to improve Leroy's methods of learning, also attempts to add to his own knowledge by reading Plato's *Republic*.

Writers: John Whedon, Sam Moore

Comments: A male chorus gives out with "Hey-Ba-Ba-Re-Bop" which, to Gildy's sensitive ears, sounds like "Hooray for Bob." Frances Robinson temporarily takes over the part of Eve Goodwin from Bea Benaderet. Marjorie's view on platonic love may be the best two-word definition on the planet: "Holding hands." Gildy's double standard regarding concentration and tasks started is patently glaring in this episode. The exchange of chortles between Throckmorton and Horace is a wordless duel that ends in a draw. The reference to Louise as "the girl who doesn't want to go to Memphis" looks ahead to the January 8, 1947 broadcast.

Date: November 27, 1946
Title: Birdie's Vacation
  Cast: Harold Peary (Gildersleeve), John Laing, Louise Erickson (Marjorie), Walter Tetley (Leroy), Earle Ross (Hooker), Lillian Randolph (Birdie), Richard LeGrand (Peavey), Arthur Q. Bryan (Floyd), Tommy Bernard (Craig), Amanda Randolph (Lily Bee)
  Summary: After the Bullards' cook quits, Gildersleeve fears Birdie might do the same so he gives her an at-home vacation.
  Writers: John Whedon, Sam Moore
  Allusion: Floyd quotes from one of Aesop's fables: "Don't be a dog in the manger."
  Comments: Birdie sings "Summertime." For the second consecutive week a conversation with Rumson Bullard

triggers Gildersleeve's actions. Throckmorton exclaims "Holy Jumpin' Jehoshaphat!" in spite of there being no evidence in scripture the king ever left the ground. Gildy is not only responsible for the embarrassing shortage of funds at the restaurant but also for the ruined supper. Attentive listeners who hear the electric eye chime three times know for whom the bell tolls even before the trio get to the drugstore counter. Hooker usually appears earlier in the action, but on this occasion does not enter until the tag. Peary (with mock humility and an assist from Laing) promotes his second album of stories for children, this one featuring his versions of "The Brave Little Tailor" and "Hansel and Gretel."

Date: December 4, 1946
Title: Adopting an Orphan
  Cast: Harold Peary (Gildersleeve), John Laing, Louise Erickson (Marjorie), Walter Tetley (Leroy), Earle Ross (Hooker), Lillian Randolph (Birdie), Richard LeGrand (Peavey), Arthur Q. Bryan (Floyd), Ken Christy (Gates)
  Summary: Acting upon an appeal from a clergyman, the Jolly Boys visit an orphanage to consider sponsoring a baby girl.
  Writers: John Whedon, Sam Moore
  Allusion: Dr. Needham paraphrases Romans 8:13: "Mortify the flesh and improve the spirit."
  Comments: The Jolly Boys and Needham sing "Love Me and the World Is Mine." Meakin bookends the visit to the orphanage with "Rock-a-bye Baby." Gildersleeve's timetable for the Jolly Boys is more accurate than that provided by Hooker, who claims the group

organized in the fall of 1943. (The actual date of the club's formation was October 8, 1944.) Peavey's "No facilities" comment suggests that the men probably go downstairs to the barbershop when nature calls. In addition to the warm message of humanity in this episode, its structure is precisely symmetrical as Throckmorton and Horace assume the same positions in the upper room at the beginning and end of the action.

Date: December 11, 1946
Title: Leroy Intimidated by Bully
  Cast: Harold Peary (Gildersleeve), John Laing, Louise Erickson (Marjorie), Walter Tetley (Leroy), Earle Ross (Hooker), Lillian Randolph (Birdie), Richard LeGrand (Peavey), Frances Robinson (Eve), Tommy Bernard (Craig)
  Summary: Gildersleeve encourages Leroy to be more aggressive after the boy confesses his fear of a school rowdy.
  Writers: John Whedon, Sam Moore
  Comments: Meakin contributes "Who's Afraid of the Big Bad Wolf?" to the weaving and bobbing of the pugilistic posers. Bullard and Gildersleeve have a hard time drawing a line in the sand with their feet of clay. Throckmorton even carries his combative mood into the arena of love by taking a long-distance swing at Miss Fenwick after being turned down for a date.

Date: December 18, 1946
Title: Leroy Wants a Scooter
  Cast: Harold Peary (Gildersleeve), John Laing, Louise Erickson (Marjorie), Walter Tetley (Leroy), Lillian Randolph (Birdie), Richard LeGrand (Peavey), Frances Robinson (Eve)

Summary: Acting upon a suggestion by Eve Goodwin, Throckmorton tries to interest his nephew in a different present other than the expensive motor scooter the boy has been coveting for weeks.
  Writers: John Whedon, Sam Moore
  Allusion: Gildersleeve invokes "Liberty Hall" from *She Stoops to Conquer* by Oliver Goldsmith.
  Comments: Meakin adds a lush version of "Toyland" to set a mood of yuletide tranquility. It is just like impulsive Gildy to jump on a passing train of thought without considering how much the cars and other accessories cost and then attempt to pull a switch to throw Leroy off the track.

Date: December 25, 1946
Title: Playing Santa for Craig
  Cast: Harold Peary (Gildersleeve), John Laing, Louise Erickson (Marjorie), Walter Tetley (Leroy), Earle Ross (Hooker), Lillian Randolph (Birdie), Richard LeGrand (Peavey), Frances Robinson (Eve), Arthur Q. Bryan (Floyd), Ken Christy (Gates), Tommy Bernard (Craig)
  Summary: While Mr. and Mrs. Bullard are away, Throckmorton dons a Santa Claus suit and shares some of the family's gifts with Craig.
  Writers: John Whedon, Sam Moore
  Comments: All sing "Jingle Bells" and "Joy to the World." Birdie sings "Coventry Carol." Meakin's "Santa Claus Is Coming to Town" leads Santa Gildersleeve across the street. Gildy gives his address as 738 Lakeside Avenue, a change from the 737 Parkside address given on September 14, 1941, and 219 Lakeside on March 11, 1945.

The self-portrait on the driver's license shows him to be stocky at 5'8" and 230 pounds, but, Throcky might add with a wink and a line Chuck Berry would make famous a decade later, still a "brown-eyed handsome man."

Date: January 1, 1947
Title: New Year's Eve Ball
   Cast: Harold Peary (Gildersleeve), John Laing, Louise Erickson (Marjorie), Walter Tetley (Leroy), Earle Ross (Hooker), Lillian Randolph (Birdie), Richard LeGrand (Peavey), Frances Robinson (Eve), Arthur Q. Bryan (Floyd), Ken Christy (Gates)
   Summary: Gildersleeve goes stag to a costume ball where he is attracted to a lady bareback rider.
   Writers: John Whedon, Sam Moore
   Comments: Gildersleeve (later joined by all) sings "Auld Lang Syne." That Gildersleeve would not recognize his niece is pretty far-fetched for, even if Marjorie wore a wig and a full-faced mask, stature and carriage should be a sure giveaway. It is also rather unseemly that Gildy is casting his usual amorous gleam toward his next of kin. Throckmorton is still harboring irrational stereotypes (e.g., "All basketball players are wild") and behaving childishly by pouting when he doesn't get his way. While listening to the radio, Throcky gives a nod to two Tuesday NBC programs he missed, *A Date with Judy* (Louise Erickson's show) and *Fibber McGee and Molly*, the launching pad for *The Great Gildersleeve.*

Date: January 8, 1947
Title: Leila Back Again
   Cast: Harold Peary (Gildersleeve),

John Laing, Walter Tetley (Leroy), Earle Ross (Hooker), Shirley Mitchell (Leila), Richard LeGrand (Peavey)
   Summary: Gildersleeve has conflicting feelings about meeting Leila when she returns to Summerfield.
   Writers: John Whedon, Sam Moore
   Comments: This broadcast from Memphis which commemorates the new Kraft branch distribution center has a small cast of just five regulars. Louise Erickson, described on the November 20th broadcast as "the girl who doesn't want to go to Memphis," probably was tied up with her work on *A Date with Judy.* Mrs. Pettibone puts out a weary version of "Just Awearyin' for You." This episode represents a low point for both Throckmorton who behaves so irrationally that when he says, "Gildersleeve, you're a nincompoop," no one would disagree with him, and for Leila who spins such a lengthy skein of lies she even traps herself in her silken web of deceit.

Date: January 15, 1947
Title: Hooker Is Sick
   Cast: Harold Peary (Gildersleeve), John Laing, Louise Erickson (Marjorie), Walter Tetley (Leroy), Earle Ross (Hooker), Lillian Randolph (Birdie), Richard LeGrand (Peavey), Frances Robinson (Eve), Arthur Q. Bryan (Floyd), Ken Christy (Gates)
   Summary: The plans of the Jolly Boys to enjoy a sleigh ride are threatened by reports that Horace is gravely ill.
   Writers: John Whedon, Sam Moore
   Allusion: Gildersleeve quotes from "Crossing the Bar" by Alfred, Lord Tennyson: Let "there be no moaning

at [of] the bar, / When I put out to sea."

Comments: The Jolly Boys sing "Down by the Old Mill Stream" and "Aunt Dinah's Quilting Party." This broadcast from Chicago is tied to the Parkay distribution plant in that city. Just like the Christmas show three weeks earlier when he fueled the flames of rumor about the Bullards breaking up, so Gildy again churns away on the gossip mill by making the judge's condition seem much worse than it actually is.

Date: January 22, 1947
Title: Dancing Class
　　Cast: Harold Peary (Gildersleeve), John Laing, Louise Erickson (Marjorie), Walter Tetley (Leroy), Earle Ross (Hooker), Lillian Randolph (Birdie), Richard LeGrand (Peavey), Frances Robinson (Eve), Tommy Bernard (Craig)
　　Summary: Gildersleeve, who wants Leroy to take a dancing class to learn how to behave with girls, searches for insights in dealing with the opposite sex himself.
　　Writers: John Whedon, Sam Moore
　　Comments: Skirt-chasing Throcky does not see the irony in calling Marjorie boy crazy. Eve's suggestion to build a relationship with a woman and Peavey's description of his lengthy courtship do not connect very solidly with a man who thrives on instant gratification. Marjorie and Leroy again give their uncle a double-barreled "What a character!" when he does a quick turnabout. After Gildy gloats "Tell me I don't know how to handle women" and then his crass approach

with Miss Fenwick gets him ejected from her residence, everyone in the audience would have been entitled to say, "OK, you asked for it: you don't know how to handle women."

Date: January 29, 1947
Title: Marjorie's New Boyfriend
　　Cast: Harold Peary (Gildersleeve), John Laing, Louise Erickson (Marjorie), Walter Tetley (Leroy), Earle Ross (Hooker), Lillian Randolph (Birdie), Richard LeGrand (Peavey), Arthur Q. Bryan (Floyd), Ben Alexander (Ben)
　　Summary: Following Floyd's advice, Gildersleeve uses reverse psychology on his niece, hoping that by urging her to elope with her boyfriend she will break off with him.
　　Writers: John Whedon, Sam Moore
　　Comments: Marjorie and friends sing "Open the Door, Richard." Gildy's hypocritical prejudices sometimes bump right into each other such as his claim to be open-minded followed immediately by "I just don't like the fellow, that's all." The calling of bluffs near the end is somewhat forced, but the making up is quite believable and constitutes one of the more touching scenes in the entire series. Like the November 27, 1946 broadcast, Hooker does not appear until the tag.

Date: February 5, 1947
Title: Magazine Salesman
　　Cast: Harold Peary (Gildersleeve), John Laing, Louise Erickson (Marjorie), Walter Tetley (Leroy), Earle Ross (Hooker), Lillian Randolph (Birdie), Richard LeGrand (Peavey), Arthur Q. Bryan (Floyd), Tommy Bernard (Craig)
　　Summary: Gildersleeve, helping Le-

roy sell subscriptions to *The Postwar Barn and Home Magazine* by going door-to-door, becomes frustrated when many of those doors are slammed in his face.

Writers: Bill Kelsay, Frank Moore

Comments: Gildersleeve, the child at heart, attacks the parcel like a tyke tugging at the corners of Christmas presents hidden in the closet and, according to Marjorie, also causes an acid spill on the carpet when playing with Leroy's chemistry set. Whenever Throckmorton announces "This ought to be a cinch," listeners are prepared for him to wind up in a pinch.

Date: February 12, 1947
Title: Old High School Friend
Cast: Harold Peary (Gildersleeve), John Laing, Louise Erickson (Marjorie), Walter Tetley (Leroy), Earle Ross (Hooker), Lillian Randolph (Birdie), Richard LeGrand (Peavey), Arthur Q. Bryan (Floyd), Ken Christy (Gates), Gloria Holliday (Bessie)

Summary: Gildersleeve, after inviting an old classmate for supper, is chagrined to learn that the man is more successful than he is.

Writer: Paul West

Comments: This is the first script by Paul West who also wrote for both the radio and television versions of *Father Knows Best*. Meakin sends Gildy off to slumberland with "Sleep" and on his way about town with "When Good Fellows Get Together." Gildersleeve characteristically dreams big, envisioning a syndicated newspaper column for himself even before he has typed one paragraph of his first article. By making Gildersleeve a high school graduate in

1921, this episode shaves a full decade off his age from May 17, 1942 when he claimed to be a member of the Princeton class of 1914. Living up to "false face must hide what the false heart doth know," Throckmorton, seconds after pronouncing his former classmate a big phony, warmly declares him to be "Good old Eddie" in the presence of his current colleagues.

Date: February 19, 1947
Title: Substitute Secretary
Cast: Harold Peary (Gildersleeve), John Laing, Louise Erickson (Marjorie), Walter Tetley (Leroy), Earle Ross (Hooker), Lillian Randolph (Birdie), Richard LeGrand (Peavey), Arthur Q. Bryan (Floyd), Gloria Holliday (Bessie)

Summary: Throckmorton, pleasantly surprised by the beauty and efficiency of Bessie's cousin who is acting as temporary secretary, attempts to beat Hooker to the punch in dating pretty Prudence.

Writers: Bill Kelsay, Sam Moore

Comments: Gildersleeve sings "Zip-a-Dee-Doo-Dah" and "The Whole World Is Singing My Song." Gildersleeve must have found the business motto he quotes to Peavey from a Whitman sampler: "Candy is the first perquisite of a well-organized office." Several lines in the script are loaded with significance, including Throcky's complaint to Bessie over the phone when he learns she will be absent that day ("Somebody has to do some work down there") and Hooker's cutting remark about the self-centered commissioner, that he had just dictated the most important thought he ever had: "Throckmorton P. Gildersleeve."

Date: February 26, 1947

Title: Dismissing Bessie

    Cast: Harold Peary (Gildersleeve), John Laing, Louise Erickson (Marjorie), Walter Tetley (Leroy), Earle Ross (Hooker), Lillian Randolph (Birdie), Richard LeGrand (Peavey), Arthur Q. Bryan (Floyd), Gloria Holliday (Bessie)

    Summary: After Gildersleeve tries unsuccessfully to discharge his secretary, Bessie unwittingly presents him with a possible solution to the situation.

    Writers: John Whedon, Sam Moore

    Comments: Not only does Gildy mishandle the firing, he fumbles the *telling* about that mishap so badly Birdie misinterprets the object of his dissatisfaction. Although the ride with Hooker is shorter than the one taken on December 6, 1942, it is almost as hilarious.

Date: March 5, 1947

Title: Marjorie Loves Larry Lake

    Cast: Harold Peary (Gildersleeve), John Laing, Louise Erickson (Marjorie), Walter Tetley (Leroy), Earle Ross (Hooker), Lillian Randolph (Birdie), Richard LeGrand (Peavey), Frances Robinson (Eve), Ken Carson (Larry Lake)

    Summary: Gildersleeve, weary of Marjorie's infatuation with a singer, follows Eve's advice by taking his niece to a symphony concert in hopes of improving her appreciation for classical music.

    Writer: Phil Leslie

    Comments: Larry Lake sings "You Broke the Only Heart" and "On the Road to Mandalay." Gildersleeve sings "On the Road to Mandalay." Phil Leslie was also writing scripts for *Fibber McGee and Molly* at this time. Mrs. Van Hartesveldt gets another salute, and Leslie also squeezes in a mention of his daughter Anne. Meakin lulls the audience and Throcky into a serene mood four times before playing Clancy by lowering the boom. Louise gives a totally credible performance as a teenager who changes musical idols as frequently as bobby socks. This is perhaps the best of the "generation gap" episodes, culminating with Gildy's question that he might be addressing to himself: "How mixed up can you be?" Ken Carson will be the featured vocalist on the replacement series that summer, *Summerfield Bandstand*.

Date: March 12, 1947

Title: Leroy Arrested (Revised Version)

    Cast: Harold Peary (Gildersleeve), John Laing, Walter Tetley (Leroy), Earle Ross (Hooker), Lillian Randolph (Birdie), Richard LeGrand (Peavey), Arthur Q. Bryan (Floyd), Ken Christy (Gates), Tommy Bernard (Craig)

    Summary: When Leroy and Craig are accused of taking lumber from a construction site, Gildersleeve tries to get the charges dropped by appealing to Chief Gates.

    Writers: John Whedon, Sam Moore

    Allusions: Gildersleeve quotes from "Barefoot Boy" by John Greenleaf Whittier: "Blessings on thee, little man, / Barefoot boy with cheek of tan." Hooker quotes from *The Merchant of Venice* by William Shakespeare: "The quality of mercy is not strained, / It droppeth [falleth] as the gentle rain from heaven."

    Comments: The Jolly Boys sing "A Little Bit of Heaven." This is a slightly revised version of the March 17, 1946 episode. The main difference is that the opening scene on this evening takes place at the construction site to recreate the theft whereas the 1946 show opened at home with a part for Louise, who is absent on this occasion. For the first time Peavey's appearance is greeted with applause.

Date: March 19, 1947
Title: Guarding Money at Home
   Cast: Harold Peary (Gildersleeve), John Laing, Louise Erickson (Marjorie), Walter Tetley (Leroy), Earle Ross (Hooker), Lillian Randolph (Birdie), Richard LeGrand (Peavey), Arthur Q. Bryan (Floyd)
   Summary: Throckmorton, forced to take $2,200 in water collection funds home overnight, becomes a suspicious worrywart who sees potential robbers lurking everywhere.
   Writers: John Whedon, Sam Moore
   Comments: As usual, Gildersleeve is responsible for his predicament because it is his visit to Peavey's to brag about the cash stash that makes him too late to deposit the funds in the bank. Gildy twice holds up a $20 bill as a rarely-seen object of reverence, and perhaps for him it was because he does not even know which president's portrait can be found on a double sawbuck.

Date: March 26, 1947
Title: New Piano Teacher
   Cast: Harold Peary (Gildersleeve), John Laing, Louise Erickson (Marjorie), Walter Tetley (Leroy), Earle Ross (Hooker), Lillian Randolph (Birdie), Richard LeGrand (Peavey), Janet Waldo (Joanne Piper)

   Summary: Frustrated by Leroy's lack of progress at the piano, Gildersleeve is determined to end his lessons until he falls for the attractive replacement teacher.
   Writers: John Whedon, Sam Moore
   Allusion: Marjorie quotes from "The Old Vicarage, Grantchester" by Rupert Brooke: "Ah God! To see the branches stir / Across the moon at Grantchester!" "Say, is there Beauty yet to find? / And Certainty? And Quiet kind?" "Stands the Church clock at ten to three? / Is there honey still for tea?"
   Comments: For the second consecutive week cold tongue, a food abhorrent to many people today, is offered as if it constituted a rare delicacy. Gildy's fourth attempt to call from Peavey's phone booth is less laborious than the others, perhaps because the call is so short he never allows his avoirdupois to fully flatten out. Throcky's cocky comment to himself, "Nobody plays Gildersleeve for a sucker," invites the logical comeback from the listener: "No one needs to because you do such a great job of it yourself." Janet and Louise should have hit it right off away from the microphones for, as Corliss Archer and Judy Foster, they were the two best-known teenage girls on the air.

Date: April 2, 1947
Title: Dinner with Miss Piper
   Cast: Harold Peary (Gildersleeve), John Laing, Louise Erickson (Marjorie), Walter Tetley (Leroy), Lillian Randolph (Birdie), Richard LeGrand (Peavey), Arthur Q. Bryan (Floyd), Janet Waldo (Joanne Piper)
   Summary: Captivated by Leroy's new piano teacher, Gildersleeve invites

her to stay for a meal and then accompanies her home.

Writers: John Whedon, Sam Moore

Allusions: Dr. Needham quotes scripture three times: Matthew 26:41: "The spirit is willing but the flesh is weak," Matthew 22:21: "Render unto Caesar the things that are Caesar's," and Luke 10:7: "The laborer is worthy of his hire."

Comments: Gildersleeve sings a bit of "I'm Always Chasing Rainbows," a most appropriate choice for the man with an incurable yen for every pretty woman he sees. Just as Marjorie opened the action on March 26, so Floyd serves as narrator of the first scene this week. When Gildy gives his weight as 197, he may be shaving quite a bit off the bottom because his driver's license on the December 25, 1946, show indicated a heftier figure of 230. President James L. Kraft again presents an inspirational Easter message.

Date: April 9, 1947
Title: Picnic with Joanne
   Cast: Harold Peary (Gildersleeve), John Laing, Louise Erickson (Marjorie), Walter Tetley (Leroy), Earle Ross (Hooker), Lillian Randolph (Birdie), Janet Waldo (Joanne Piper)
   Summary: Finding it difficult to be alone with Joanne at home, Gildersleeve arranges for an impromptu picnic in the country.
   Writers: John Whedon, Sam Moore
   Allusions: Dr. Needham quotes from Matthew 9:37: "The harvest truly is plenteous, but the laborers are few" and paraphrases Matthew 25:35: "She was a stranger and ye took her in."
   Comments: Gildersleeve sings "Yours Is My Heart Alone." Although

Throckmorton's request to Leroy and Marjorie is "Go find" your sibling, what he really means is "Get lost." When Gildy is caught in the throes of love, he stops at nothing to achieve his goal including telling falsehoods on the threshold of a clergyman's house and lying to an innocent girl, claiming to be "crazy about birds" just so she might be more receptive to his advances. Throcky does not even reveal his "penny thought" for, while Joanne is contemplating the noble concept of world peace, he is considering what Hamlet called "country matters."

Date: April 16, 1947
Title: Whole Town Is Talking
   Cast: Harold Peary (Gildersleeve), John Laing, Louise Erickson (Marjorie), Walter Tetley (Leroy), Earle Ross (Hooker), Lillian Randolph (Birdie), Shirley Mitchell (Leila), Janet Waldo (Joanne Piper)
   Summary: Gildersleeve, concerned about the age difference between him and Joanne and also about the gossip around town, turns to Leila for her opinion on older men courting younger women.
   Writers: John Whedon, Sam Moore
   Allusion: Gildersleeve quotes from *A Tale of Two Cities* by Charles Dickens: "It is a far, far better thing I do, than I have ever done before."
   Comments: Gildersleeve sings "Speak to Me of Love." A bouncy jingle and the "P-A-R-K-A-Why, it's wonderful" slogan are used for the first time. Gildersleeve rides a jet-propelled pendulum of emotions this week, acting like a despondent Sidney Carton peering into the murky waters of the reservoir and

the next minute like a devil-may-care Lothario declaring "I'm irresistible" to Leila. Gildersleeve's age is given as 44, Joanne's as 20. (Peary was actually 38 at the time, Waldo 23.)

Date: April 23, 1947
Title: Joanne Meets Leila
Cast: Harold Peary (Gildersleeve), John Laing, John Wald, Louise Erickson (Marjorie), Walter Tetley (Leroy), Earle Ross (Hooker), Lillian Randolph (Birdie), Shirley Mitchell (Leila), Janet Waldo (Joanne Piper), Ken Carson (Leonard Albright)
Summary: Gildersleeve is pleased with the progress of a dinner Leila is giving for Joanne until another male guest makes his presence felt.
Writers: John Whedon, Sam Moore
Comments: Gildersleeve sings "Just a Little Love, a Little Kiss." Albright sings "For Sentimental Reasons." In solitude Gildy asks the $64 question concerning women he will never be able to answer: "How can I be wrong about them every single time?" John Wald steps in at the end to deliver a listening reminder about Daylight Saving Time.

Date: April 30, 1947
Title: Tchaikovsky Love Story
Cast: Harold Peary (Gildersleeve), John Laing, Louise Erickson (Marjorie), Walter Tetley (Leroy), Earle Ross (Hooker), Lillian Randolph (Birdie), Shirley Mitchell (Leila), Bea Benaderet (Eve Goodwin), Janet Waldo (Joanne Piper)
Summary: Joanne convinces Throckmorton their relationship should emulate that of Tchaikovsky and Nadezhda von Meck.

Writers: John Whedon, Sam Moore
Allusions: Leila quotes from *Don Quixote* by Miguel de Cervantes: "Faint heart never won fair lady." Joanne quotes from "Ode on a Grecian Urn" by John Keats: "For ever will thou love, and she be fair."
Comments: Gildersleeve sings "Tonight We Love." Bea Benaderet returns after recovering from an accident which also kept her off *Fibber McGee and Molly*. The parting dialogue between uncle and nephew ("Where are you going?" "Out.") was probably followed up upon Leroy's return with lines that formed the basis of Robert Paul Smith's best-seller ten years later: *Where Did You Go? Out. What Did You Do? Nothing*. Nothing could be farther from the truth than Throckmorton's statement concerning his work: "My mind is seldom off it," for there is little room in his consciousness for anything other than his current love interest(s).

Date: May 7, 1947
Title: Craig's Birthday Party
Cast: Harold Peary (Gildersleeve), John Laing, Louise Erickson (Marjorie), Walter Tetley (Leroy), Earle Ross (Hooker), Lillian Randolph (Birdie), Shirley Mitchell (Leila), Richard LeGrand (Peavey), Tommy Bernard (Craig), Jimmy Starr
Summary: When Leroy mopes about the house because he is not invited to Craig's birthday party, Gildersleeve tries to cheer the boy up by playing with him in the backyard hut.
Writers: John Whedon, Sam Moore
Comments: Birdie sings "Easy Street." The central commercial, like those in the last several episodes, in-

volves dialogue between two people so listeners keep tuning in on the message instead of tuning out until the plot thickens again. Richard LeGrand returns after an absence of four weeks. Leroy again behaves like his uncle by giving in to the pleasures of life, shunning Craig from adolescent activities because the neighbor boy is too young and yet eager to get in on the food and pony rides accompanying a child's birthday celebration. Noted columnist Starr presents the Jimmy Starr Plaque to Jack Meakin for his "outstanding originality in composing, arranging, and conducting music for radio."

Date: May 14, 1947
Title: Peavey Missing
   Cast: Harold Peary (Gildersleeve), John Laing, Louise Erickson (Marjorie), Walter Tetley (Leroy), Earle Ross (Hooker), Lillian Randolph (Birdie), Shirley Mitchell (Leila), Richard LeGrand (Peavey), Arthur Q. Bryan (Floyd), Ken Christy (Gates)
   Summary: When Peavey disappears after a meeting of the Jolly Boys, his friends set out to find him and to lend comfort to his wife.
   Writers: John Whedon, Sam Moore
   Comments: The Jolly Boys sing "When You Were Sweet Sixteen." Peavey sings "There Is a Tavern in the Town." Floyd sings "Dear Old Pal of Mine." Gildersleeve's phone number is given as 8126, a change from 2413 mentioned on February 17, 1946, and 2371 given on June 3, 1945. The scene of the household awakening is both funny and true-to-life. Leila's repeated declaration of "I just this minute got here" is her attempt to assume a virtue,

though she has it not. Sending a special delivery postcard to a recipient who lives in a small town is tantamount to having its written message broadcast over the local radio station.

Date: May 21, 1947
Title: Confronting Leroy's Teacher
   Cast: Harold Peary (Gildersleeve), John Laing, Louise Erickson (Marjorie), Walter Tetley (Leroy), Earle Ross (Hooker), Lillian Randolph (Birdie), Shirley Mitchell (Leila), Richard LeGrand (Peavey), Bea Benaderet (Eve)
   Summary: Upset over Leroy's apparent lack of progress in his schoolwork, Gildersleeve takes the matter up with his nephew's teacher and principal who open his eyes to the plight of education locally and nationally.
   Writers: John Whedon, Sam Moore
   Comments: It could well be that Leroy's lack of concentration comes from observing his uncle who finds the cartoons in magazines more stimulating than the articles. Bea makes the most of her chance to shine, sounding just like a seasoned but frustrated administrator who sees little hope for meaningful change in the system. Hal's direct message to the audience is a powerful and poignant appeal to the brain, capped by Meakin's uplifting rendition of "America the Beautiful" which leaves a lump in the throat.

Date: May 28, 1947
Title: Gives Up Cigars
   Cast: Harold Peary (Gildersleeve), John Laing, Earle Ross (Hooker), Lillian Randolph (Birdie), Shirley Mitchell (Leila), Richard LeGrand (Peavey), Willard Waterman (Purvis)

Summary: Upon the advice of a physician, Gildersleeve stops smoking.

Writers: John Whedon, Sam Moore

Allusion: Purvis quotes from *The Lady of the Lake* by Sir Walter Scott: "Foeman worthy of my steel."

Comments: Willard Waterman, who will take over the role of Throckmorton P. Gildersleeve in 1950, appears for the first time. Peavey makes a sale with the first flavor of gum he mentions, then continues reciting every variety in the store including horehound, which would likely not appeal to hound or … human.

Date: June 4, 1947
Title: Income Tax Audit
Cast: Harold Peary (Gildersleeve), John Laing, Louise Erickson (Marjorie), Walter Tetley (Leroy), Earle Ross (Hooker), Lillian Randolph (Birdie), Shirley Mitchell (Leila), Richard LeGrand (Peavey), Arthur Q. Bryan (priest), Ken Christy (guard)

Summary: After attending a movie with the children, Gildersleeve receives news of an impending visit with the IRS that haunts him in his sleep.

Writers: John Whedon, Sam Moore

Comments: Tetley does a fine job of conveying the joy of the current moment for the adolescent boy as Leroy is ecstatic over the prospect of a double treat: dessert downtown *and* a picture show. In less than three minutes Meakin uses fanfares and bits of "The Sidewalks of New York" and "The Prisoner's Song" to wonderfully complement the actors and sound effects team in encapsulating a crime melodrama. When the guard says, "OK, Jack let her go," Meakin's crew lets loose with a 2,000-volt

sting that awakens the self-condemned man from his nightmare. Hal promotes *Summerfield Bandstand*, the summer replacement series featuring Meakin's music, Ken Carson's songs, and visits from some of the members of *The Great Gildersleeve* cast.

Date: September 10, 1947
Title: Behaving Badly, Making Up
Cast: Harold Peary (Gildersleeve), John Wald, Louise Erickson (Marjorie), Walter Tetley (Leroy), Earle Ross (Hooker), Lillian Randolph (Birdie), Richard LeGrand (Peavey), Bea Benaderet (Eve), Tommy Bernard (Craig)

Summary: After Gildersleeve treats the children unjustly, he makes up for it by offering to spend an evening with them and makes up for lost time by pursuing his passion for Eve Goodwin.

Writers: Jack Robinson, Gene Stone

Comments: This is the first script by the team of Robinson and Stone who will also write for Peary's CBS show, *Honest Harold*. John Wald takes over as announcer. To begin the season, members of the cast interact with Wald in the central commercial. Gildersleeve sings "Why Do I Love You?" When Throckmorton tells Eve that number is "our song," he must have been thinking of Leila for she is the person he sang it to on other occasions. When Hooker tells Gildy he would enjoy *Mother Wore Tights* more than the children, Horace is referring to the glamour and gams of the film's star, Betty Grable. Gildersleeve's fifth foray against the phone booth is a stalemate as he is in and out in a few seconds. Eve wisely counsels Throcky on the differences between them for she is interested in culture, he in cuddling. In the tag Peary promotes Jack Carson's taking over *The Sealtest Village Store* (Sealtest was a division of Kraft Foods) for what turned out to be the program's final season.

Date: September 17, 1947
Title: Organizing Work
    Cast: Harold Peary (Gildersleeve), John Wald, Louise Erickson (Marjorie), Walter Tetley (Leroy), Earle Ross (Hooker), Lillian Randolph (Birdie), Richard LeGrand (Peavey), Gloria Holliday (Bessie)
Summary: Throckmorton returns home after a brief stay at the office to orchestrate a cleanup of the house.
    Writers: John Elliotte, Andy White
    Comments: This is the first script by the team of Elliotte and White. When Gildersleeve tells Hooker "I wasn't myself," he is mistaken for he has been acting like the usual shirking, fibbing, blustery blunderer all day: he half-heartedly puts in five minutes at city hall pawing over correspondence dating back to 1946, tells the children he has been slaving "like a dog at the office," shifts responsibility to others for duties he should do himself, does more harm than good on the roof, gets involved in an accident partially caused by allowing hedges near the driveway to become overgrown, and leaves the children to clean up a mess he created by citing a flimsy excuse to get out of the house.

Date: September 24, 1947
Title: Rival for Bessie
    Cast: Harold Peary (Gildersleeve), John Wald, Louise Erickson (Marjorie), Walter Tetley (Leroy), Earle Ross (Hooker), Lillian Randolph (Birdie),

Richard LeGrand (Peavey), Arthur Q. Bryan (Floyd), Ken Christy (Gates), Gloria Holliday (Bessie)
Summary: After accompanying Bessie on a shopping trip, Gildersleeve fears his actions have been misinterpreted by her boyfriend.
    Writers: Jack Robinson, Gene Stone
    Comments: Peavey sings "Daisy, Daisy." The Jolly Boys sing "When You Wore a Tulip." Floyd calls Gildersleeve Commish for the first time. Gildy's rhetorical question to himself, "How do I get into these silly things?," and how he gets himself out of them is what keeps *The Great Gildersleeve* on the air. Throckmorton's run for the door is reminiscent of a child rushing home from watching a scary movie with visions of Karloff or Lugosi being only two leaps and a pounce behind. Arthur Q. Bryan, Ken Christy, and Gloria Holliday are named in the credits for the first time.

Date: October 1, 1947
Title: Loan Request
    Cast: Harold Peary (Gildersleeve), John Wald, Louise Erickson (Marjorie), Walter Tetley (Leroy), Earle Ross (Hooker), Lillian Randolph (Birdie), Richard LeGrand (Peavey), Bea Benaderet (Eve), Arthur Q. Bryan (Floyd), Stan Farrar (Terwilliger)
Summary: After Gildersleeve tries to prove a point to Leroy by asking for $100 from several friends, he is dismayed when people assume he is in dire need of money.
    Writers: John Elliotte, Andy White
    Comments: Stan Farrar makes his first appearance as Mayor Terwilliger. Impulsive Gildy wants to end his phone

service rather than ride out this temporary storm.

Date: October 8, 1947
Title: Meets Miss Tuttle
   Cast: Harold Peary (Gildersleeve), John Wald, Walter Tetley (Leroy), Earle Ross (Hooker), Lillian Randolph (Birdie), Richard LeGrand (Peavey), Arthur Q. Bryan (Floyd), Tommy Bernard (Craig)
   Summary: Attracted by a guest of the Bullards, Gildersleeve finds her to be as self-reliant as she is beautiful.
   Writers: John Elliotte, Andy White
   Allusions: John Wald quotes from "To Autumn" by John Keats: "Season of mists and mellow fruitfulness." Wald quotes from "Hymn to Intellectual Beauty" by Percy Bysshe Shelley: "There is a harmony in autumn and a luster in its sky."
   Comments: Craig's age (six) and hair color (red) are given for the first time. Meakin contributes some clip-clop music to complement Gildy's accelerated pace in pursuit of his quarry. Louise Erickson is mentioned in the credits but does not appear. This is one time when a woman actually tells the blundering klutz that it is his clumsiness, his impetuousness, which makes him human and therefore endearing.

Date: October 15, 1947
Title: Meets Doris Dalrymple
   Cast: Harold Peary (Gildersleeve), John Wald, Louise Erickson (Marjorie), Walter Tetley (Leroy), Earle Ross (Hooker), Lillian Randolph (Birdie), Richard LeGrand (Peavey), Arthur Q. Bryan (Floyd), Ben Alexander (Ben)

   Summary: Gildersleeve takes over from Marjorie as babysitter when he learns that the mother is a babe herself.
   Writers: John Elliotte, Andy White
   Comments: Leroy sings "Rock-a-Bye Baby." Perhaps there never was a time in real life when a parent would leave an infant in the care of a person who just showed up at the door, especially one who cries "wolf" with every suggestive remark he makes, but in radio life listeners will go along even if the situation "isn't that cute." Rather than join the Book-of-the-Month Club, Throcky seems content with his personal woman-of-the-week setup.

Date: October 22, 1947
Title: Studying for Advancement
   Cast: Harold Peary (Gildersleeve), John Wald, Louise Erickson (Marjorie), Walter Tetley (Leroy), Earle Ross (Hooker), Lillian Randolph (Birdie), Richard LeGrand (Peavey), Arthur Q. Bryan (Floyd), Gloria Holliday (Bessie), Stan Farrar (Terwilliger)
   Summary: Spurred by Hooker's challenge to make something of his life, Gildersleeve considers applying himself so he can someday embark upon a political career.
   Writers: John Elliotte, Andy White
   Comments: F.A. Pittman, the fictitious author of *Hydraulics and Water Supply*, is an in-joke referring to director Frank Pittman. Meakin's rendition of "The William Tell Overture" and the "Thataway" dialogue offer a capsule parody of westerns. Melodramatic Gildy goes from the lofty heights of exalting himself into the halls of Congress to the depths of living a dissolute life as a vagabond. The final commercial is

dropped in lieu of an in-character message about food conservation.

Date: October 29, 1947
Title: Halloween Party with Doris
  Cast: Harold Peary (Gildersleeve), John Wald, Louise Erickson (Marjorie), Walter Tetley (Leroy), Earle Ross (Hooker), Lillian Randolph (Birdie), Richard LeGrand (Peavey), Arthur Q. Bryan (Floyd), Ken Christy (Gates), Gloria Holliday (Bessie)
  Summary: Gildersleeve, not enthused about attending a party at Mrs. Dalrymple's house because the Jolly Boys will be there, hatches a plan so he and Doris can be by themselves.
  Writers: John Elliotte, Andy White
  Comments: Gildersleeve sings "Tea for Two." Peavey sings "There Is a Tavern in the Town." The Jolly Boys sing "When Good Fellows Get Together." No more needs to be said about his wife's visage than Peavey's comment that he is going to take a mask home for her that covers the whole face. El Lobos are the perfect cigar for Summerfield's leading wolf. For the second consecutive week the PSA is inserted right into the tag's dialogue.

Date: November 5, 1947
Title: Two Dates for Hayride
  Cast: Harold Peary (Gildersleeve), John Wald, Louise Erickson (Marjorie), Walter Tetley (Leroy), Earle Ross (Hooker), Lillian Randolph (Birdie), Richard LeGrand (Peavey), Bea Benaderet (Eve), Arthur Q. Bryan (Floyd), Tommy Bernard (Craig)
  Summary: When Doris accepts an invitation to go on a hayride she had earlier cancelled, Gildersleeve is in a predicament because he has already asked Eve Goodwin to accompany him.
  Writers: John Elliotte, Andy White
  Allusions: Floyd quotes from "The Female of the Species" by Rudyard Kipling: "The female of the species is more deadly than the male." Floyd quotes "The Law of the Jungle," also by Kipling.
  Comments: Gildersleeve sings "Shine On Harvest Moon," later reprised by all on the hayride. Peavey sings "There Is a Tavern in the Town." Meakin plays "Louisiana Hayride" to lead into the fun event. For the first time Throckmorton compliments himself with "You're sly, Gildersleeve," which will serve as a precursor to his being outwitted by someone or else being caught by his own stratagems. Marjorie's question addressed to her uncle, "Aren't you ever going to grow up?," is certainly answered by his actions on this occasion because Throcky's solutions to his dilemma are first to offer a bribe of hunting knife like a urchin reaching into his pocket for something to swap and then to run away from the situation by trying to hide in a child's clubhouse.

Date: November 12, 1947
Title: Buys Coat from Swindler
  Cast: Harold Peary (Gildersleeve), John Wald, Louise Erickson (Marjorie), Walter Tetley (Leroy), Earle Ross (Hooker), Lillian Randolph (Birdie), Richard LeGrand (Peavey), Arthur Q. Bryan (Floyd), Ken Christy (Gates), Stan Farrar (officer), Gale Gordon (W.R. Fowler)
  Summary: Gildersleeve runs afoul of the law when he buys suspicious coats and rings from a con man.

Writers: John Elliotte, Andy White

Comments: Marjorie sings "Civilization." Gale Gordon, who will later take the role of Rumson Bullard, appears for the first time. Floyd's roguish suggestion that the commissioner cut the water two to one brings up the question "What does one dilute water with? Air?" Like the March 12, 1947 story dealing with juvenile theft presented at the request of the Boys Clubs of America, this episode in association with the Better Business Bureau also has a social message, that of alerting listeners to the dangers of consumer fraud.

Date: November 19, 1947
Title: School Play

Cast: Harold Peary (Gildersleeve), John Wald, Louise Erickson (Marjorie), Walter Tetley (Leroy), Earle Ross (Hooker), Lillian Randolph (Birdie), Richard LeGrand (Peavey), Bea Benaderet (Eve), Arthur Q. Bryan (Floyd)

Summary: Leroy is relieved when released from his part in the school play, but Throckmorton, upset because he sold tickets on the basis of his nephew's prominent role, takes the matter up with the director of the production.

Writers: Jack Robinson, Gene Stone

Allusion: Hooker paraphrases a line from *Childe Harold's Pilgrimage* by Lord Byron: "Let the play begin: Let joy be unconfined."

Comments: Gildersleeve again behaves childishly, willing to turn back and go home rather than face his friends at the auditorium. Throckmorton has not learned from his last bumptious visit to school on May 27, 1947, when Eve also had to step in to provide the voice of reason.

Date: November 26, 1947
Title: Tom Sawyer Raft

Cast: Harold Peary (Gildersleeve), John Wald, Louise Erickson (Marjorie), Walter Tetley (Leroy), Earle Ross (Hooker), Lillian Randolph (Birdie), Richard LeGrand (Peavey), Arthur Q. Bryan (Floyd), Tommy Bernard (Craig)

Summary: Gildersleeve, after suggesting that Leroy and Craig emulate the actions of Tom Sawyer, becomes frantic when he believes the boys have run away from home.

Writers: John Elliotte, Andy White

Comments: Marjorie acts more mature than her uncle, refusing to panic while Gildersleeve imagines all sorts of calamities have befallen the youngsters and shirks his duty by wanting Hooker to inform Rumson that his son is missing. Gildy would have made quite a fashion statement in his open-toed hip boots. Meakin delivers a bit of the "Sailor's Hornpipe."

Date: December 3, 1947
Title: Fiscal Report Due

Cast: Harold Peary (Gildersleeve), John Wald, Walter Tetley (Leroy), Earle Ross (Hooker), Lillian Randolph (Birdie), Richard LeGrand (Peavey), Gloria Holliday (Bessie), Eleanor Audley (secretary)

Summary: Gildersleeve is under the gun with double-barreled pressure as he needs to finish an important report and help Leroy pass a geography test on the same night.

Writers: John Elliotte, Andy White

Comments: Gildersleeve sings "Just a Little Love, a Little Kiss," which he tells Doris is their song, "yours and mine." And Leila's. Meakin contributes

"Whistle While You Work" to the show's theme. Eleanor Audley, who will later take the part of Mrs. Pettibone, appears for the first time. The name of the water commissioner Gildy replaced on October 29, 1944, was McCarthy; for the sake of this episode the name is given as Robbins. Throckmorton's self-assessment, "I have a great capacity for work," omits the important word *avoiding* before *work* for no sooner are the words out of his mouth than he is on a fast boat to dreamland. The script is short so there is more fill music at the end than usual.

Date: December 10, 1947
Title: Christmas Shopping for Airplane
  Cast: Harold Peary (Gildersleeve), John Wald, Louise Erickson (Marjorie), Walter Tetley (Leroy), Earle Ross (Hooker), Lillian Randolph (Birdie), Richard LeGrand (Peavey), Arthur Q. Bryan (Floyd, vocal customer)
  Summary: Throckmorton dilly-dallies at Hogan Brothers instead of purchasing the model airplane Leroy wants for Christmas.
  Writers: Jack Robinson, Gene Stone
  Allusion: John Wald paraphrases from "To a Mouse" by Robert Burns: "The best-laid plans of mice and men and the Great Gildersleeve often go astray."
  Comments: Hooker sings "Toyland." Gildersleeve sings "You Do" and "My Wild Irish Rose." Peavey sings "Come Josephine in My Flying Machine." Meakin contributes much to the shopping experience with "Jingle Bells," "Santa Claus Is Coming to Town," and rhythmic rides on the elevator and escalator. Hooker's admonitions of

"You're not a kid any more" and "Why don't you grow up?" could be applied to the uncle transfixed by toy trains and to the nephew who is still crying at the age of 12 when disappointed.

Date: December 17, 1947
Title: Sulking in Room
  Cast: John Wald, Louise Erickson (Marjorie), Walter Tetley (Leroy), Earle Ross (Hooker), Lillian Randolph (Birdie), Richard LeGrand (Peavey), Arthur Q. Bryan (Floyd), Ken Christy (Gates), Eleanor Audley (customer)
  Summary: Friends and family attempt to convince Gildersleeve, who is pouting in his bedroom after reading that the mayor is cracking down on lackadaisical city officials, to come out and go to work so he does not lose his job.
  Writers: John Whedon, Sam Moore
  Comments: The immediate tip-off that Peary would not be in the cast is the absence of both his trademark laugh and his star billing at the beginning of the broadcast. This is the only episode Hal missed in his nine years on the program. Just as when Jim Jordan was ill for the March 27, 1951 *Fibber McGee and Molly*, the other cast members carry on valiantly, but each program suffers significantly without its driving force even if the bullheaded behavior of Gildy and Fibber can sometimes drive everyone up the wall.

Date: December 24, 1947
Title: Christmas Puppy
  Cast: Harold Peary (Gildersleeve), John Wald, Louise Erickson (Marjorie), Walter Tetley (Leroy), Earle Ross (Hooker), Lillian Randolph (Birdie),

Richard LeGrand (Peavey), Arthur Q. Bryan (Floyd), Ken Christy (Gates), Willard Waterman (Santa Claus)

Summary: Leroy learns the true spirit of Christmas when he finds a boy who needs a gift from the heart more than he does.

Writers: Jack Robinson, Gene Stone

Comments: Birdie sings "Coventry Carol." Everyone sings "Joy to the World." In addition to the usual Christmas tunes, Meakin adds a bit of "Chloe" to the search for the dog. The gladsome sight of the current Gildersleeve (Peary) sitting on the lap of the future Gildersleeve (Waterman) is a present that can be appreciated every time this episode is played.

Date: December 31, 1947
Title: New Year's Eve with Hooker

Cast: Harold Peary (Gildersleeve), John Wald, Louise Erickson (Marjorie), Walter Tetley (Leroy), Earle Ross (Hooker), Lillian Randolph (Birdie), Richard LeGrand (Peavey), Arthur Q. Bryan (Floyd), Ken Christy (Gates), Gloria Holliday (Bessie)

Summary: Munson and Peavey convince Gildersleeve to celebrate New Year's Eve at home with Hooker.

Writers: John Elliotte, Andy White

Comments: Gildersleeve sings "When It's Springtime in the Rockies." The Jolly Boys sing "Put on Your Old Grey Bonnet" and "Auld Lang Syne." Horace, after reflecting back on the time six years ago when as judge he turned 12-year-old Leroy and late teen Marjorie over to Gildy, may ponder even more deeply over how Leroy remains stuck on 12 and Marjorie is now a sweet 16. Floyd should have passed some of that

cough syrup he intended to get for Lovey on to Birdie as Lillian Randolph gamely carries on despite her cold.

Date: January 7, 1948
Title: Ann Tuttle Returns

Cast: Harold Peary (Gildersleeve), John Wald, Louise Erickson (Marjorie), Walter Tetley (Leroy), Earle Ross (Hooker), Lillian Randolph (Birdie), Richard LeGrand (Peavey), Arthur Q. Bryan (Floyd)

Summary: Gildersleeve goes the formal route in courting Ann Tuttle by sending her a personalized invitation, purchasing flowers, and dressing in tuxedo for a special dance.

Writers: Jack Robinson, Gene Stone

Allusion: Gildersleeve quotes from "To Electra" by Robert Herrick: "I dare not ask a kiss, / I dare not beg a smile, / Lest having that, or this, / I might grow proud the while."

Comments: Gildersleeve sings "One Dozen Roses." Meakin arranges some fluttering notes to simulate the tossing out of cards and the plopping down of Gildersleeve. Floyd appears only in the middle commercial, not in the action of the script itself.

Date: January 14, 1948
Title: Riding Outfit

Cast: Harold Peary (Gildersleeve), John Wald, Louise Erickson (Marjorie), Walter Tetley (Leroy), Earle Ross (Hooker), Lillian Randolph (Birdie), Richard LeGrand (Peavey), Bea Benaderet (Eve), Arthur Q. Bryan (Floyd), Eleanor Audley (saleslady)

Summary: To better teach Marjorie equestrienne skills, Gildersleeve purchases riding breeches and boots that pinch his limbs more than his wallet.

Writers: John Elliotte, Andy White

Allusion: John Wald quotes the maxim "The outside of a horse is good for the inside of a man."

Comments: Gildersleeve sings "Take Me Back to My Boots and Saddles." Meakin manages to simulate a wakeup call that combines a rooster's crow and "Reveille." It was about a year ago (February 29, 1947) that Floyd gave Throckmorton similar advice regarding Marjorie to the suggestion Eve dispenses on this occasion. Stretch, captain of the basketball team who could be a star athlete like dull-witted Stretch Snodgrass soon to be heard on *Our Miss Brooks*, must be a seven-footer if he is two feet taller than Marjorie.

Date: January 21, 1948
Title: School Board Election

Cast: Harold Peary (Gildersleeve), John Wald, Louise Erickson (Marjorie), Walter Tetley (Leroy), Earle Ross (Hooker), Lillian Randolph (Birdie), Richard LeGrand (Peavey), Bea Benaderet (Eve), Arthur Q. Bryan (Floyd)

Summary: Hooker and Gildersleeve, the two nominees for chairman of the school board, try to capture the swing vote held by Chester Pettibone by currying favor with the doctor and his wife.

Writers: Jack Robinson, Gene Stone

Comments: Meakin's "A Hot Time in the Old Town Tonight" sets the tone for the heated contest between the two rivals. For the first time Birdie unwinds her shtick of repeating some piece of information three or four times before unleashing a hearty laugh. When Mrs. Pettibone expresses her admira-

tion for Throckmorton's dignity, the audience is alerted that somehow in the next few minutes the great man is going to be caught in a most undignified situation. Peary's start in radio over KZM when he was only 15 is celebrated on this occasion of his 25th year on the air.

Date: January 28, 1948
Title: License Plates

Cast: Harold Peary (Gildersleeve), John Wald, Louise Erickson (Marjorie), Walter Tetley (Leroy), Earle Ross (Hooker), Lillian Randolph (Birdie), Richard LeGrand (Peavey), Arthur Q. Bryan (Floyd), Ken Christy (Gates), Gale Gordon (desk sergeant)

Summary: Gildersleeve puts off getting his 1948 license plates while he curries favor with Chief Gates so he can be part of a traveling barbershop quartet.

Writers: John Elliotte, Andy White

Allusions: John Wald quotes from *The Lay of the Last Minstrel* by Sir Walter Scott: "Breathes there a man with soul so dead / Who never to himself hath said...." Gildersleeve quotes from "Night Thoughts" by Edward Young: "Procrastination is the thief of time."

Comments: Birdie puts the blame for the dirty windows where it belongs, on the procrastinator who promised to clean them last fall. Gildy acts in his usual fashion of misplaced priorities: distracted from his primary goal of purchasing new plates when he is next in line, he runs off in pursuit of a friend he could see later that day at his own convenience. The Acmeodo cigars Peavey offers sound like the brand that might explode in the face of Wile E.

Walter **"Leroy"** Tetley · Hal **"Gildy"** Peary · Louise **"Marjorie"** Erickson

Earle **"Hooker"** Ross · Lil **"Birdie"** Randolph · Dick **"Peavey"** LeGrand

Arthur **"Floyd"** Q. Bryan · Gloria **"Bessie"** Holliday · Jack **"Music"** Meakin

FOR KRAFT FOODS CO.

The cast in 1948.

Coyote, who was always ordering specious merchandise from the Acme Corporation.

Date: February 4, 1948
Title: Acting Mayor
  Cast: Harold Peary (Gildersleeve), John Wald, Louise Erickson (Marjorie), Walter Tetley (Leroy), Earle Ross (Hooker), Lillian Randolph (Birdie), Richard LeGrand (Peavey), Arthur Q. Bryan (Floyd, Scoutmaster Plack), Ken Christy (Gates), Gloria Holliday (Bessie), Stan Farrar (Terwilliger)
  Summary: Gildersleeve takes it easy and also takes liberties when Terwilliger appoints him to take over during the mayor's temporary absence.
  Writers: Jack Robinson, Gene Stone
  Comments: Gildersleeve sings "On the Sunny Side of the Street." Peavey sings "Tell Me Pretty Maiden" and "Ta-Ra-Ra-Boom-De-Ay." Meakin inserts some appropriate "day of doom" chords to accompany Gildersleeve's walk to Terwilliger's office. As he frequently does, Floyd plays the scamp, whispering Machiavellian thoughts in Throcky's eager ears. Gates appears only in the central commercial.

Date: February 11, 1948
Title: Gets Glasses
  Cast: Harold Peary (Gildersleeve), John Wald, Louise Erickson (Marjorie), Walter Tetley (Leroy), Earle Ross (Hooker), Lillian Randolph (Birdie), Richard LeGrand (Peavey), Bea Benaderet (Eve), Gloria Holliday (Bessie)
  Summary: Throckmorton is not pleased to learn that he needs glasses because he fears it is a sign of old age.
  Writers: John Elliotte, Andy White

  Comments: Less than two minutes after asking "Why does Eve have the idea I'm flirtatious?" Gildy the wolf is pouncing on his next victim. The two plugs for *The Jolson Story* are natural tie-ins for the star of *The Kraft Music Hall.*

Date: February 18, 1948
Title: Adeline Fairchild Arrives
  Cast: Harold Peary (Gildersleeve), John Wald, Louise Erickson (Marjorie), Walter Tetley (Leroy), Earle Ross (Hooker), Lillian Randolph (Birdie), Richard LeGrand (Peavey), Una Merkel (Adeline Fairchild), Arthur Q. Bryan (Floyd)
  Summary: After resolving half-heartedly not to give in to the charms of new neighbor Adeline Fairchild, Gildersleeve finds himself irresistibly attracted to her when she asks for help with repairs.
  Writers: Jack Robinson, Gene Stone
  Allusion: Gildersleeve quotes from *Othello* by William Shakespeare: "Loved not wisely but too well."
  Comments: Gildersleeve sings "Contented" and "Speak to Me of Love." Floyd sings "Swanee River." Meakin's music captures the seesaw nature of Gildy's soliloquy about women. Una Merkel makes her first appearance and gets co-star billing. Throckmorton's declaration that "no woman is ever going to make a fool of me again" is probably true because he always beats any woman to it. When Floyd, ever the provocateur, parades a handful of calendar girls before the commissioner, he unleashes a scent that sends the hound in pursuit of the fox.

Date: February 25, 1948
Title: Treats Birdie with Kindness
 Cast: Harold Peary (Gildersleeve), John Wald, Louise Erickson (Marjorie), Walter Tetley (Leroy), Earle Ross (Hooker), Lillian Randolph (Birdie), Richard LeGrand (Peavey), Una Merkel (Adeline)
 Summary: Gildersleeve, concerned that Adeline is trying to lure Birdie away, strives to make the cook's life easier.
 Writers: John Elliotte, Andy White
 Comments: Gildersleeve sings "Sweet Adeline" and "I Kiss Your Hand, Madame." The flashback snapshot that starts the action is a recap technique used for the first time on this program. When Gildy's heart is wounded, he gets moody; when his meal ticket it threatened, he gets even.

Date: March 3, 1948
Title: Leroy Shy with Girls
 Cast: Harold Peary (Gildersleeve), John Wald, Louise Erickson (Marjorie), Walter Tetley (Leroy), Lillian Randolph (Birdie), Richard LeGrand (Peavey), Arthur Q. Bryan (Floyd, Cactus)
 Summary: Gildersleeve makes Leroy play host to a girl so the boy will overcome his discomfort with the opposite sex.
 Writers: Jack Robinson, Gene Stone
 Allusion: Floyd quotes from "Barefoot Boy" by John Greenleaf Whittier: "Blessings on thee, little man, / Barefoot boy, with cheek of tan."
 Comments: As he did on May 19, 1946, in a similar "Leroy and girl" episode, Peary plays both autocratic father and weak-willed son in a bittersweet flashback. The door knob Leroy

carries with him may be part of the boy's magic act for, no matter how involved the trick, he always has a way out.

Date: May 10, 1948
Title: Considers Virtues of Marriage
 Cast: Harold Peary (Gildersleeve), John Wald, Louise Erickson (Marjorie), Walter Tetley (Leroy), Earle Ross (Hooker), Lillian Randolph (Birdie), Richard LeGrand (Peavey), Una Merkel (Adeline), Arthur Q. Bryan (Floyd), Ken Christy (Gates)
 Summary: The Jolly Boys do a fair job of selling Throckmorton on the merits of marriage until the light of day reveals some of its drawbacks.
 Writers: John Elliotte, Andy White
 Allusion: Peavey quotes from "The Shooting of Dan McGrew" by Robert W. Service: "So cramful of cozy joy, and crowned with a woman's love."
 Comments: The Jolly Boys sing "Asleep in the Deep" and "Dear Old Girl." Peavey sings "There Is a Tavern in the Town." Gildersleeve sings "Indian Love Call." Meakin contributes a discordant version of the "Wedding March." Gildersleeve, as usual, jumps back and forth on the matter of marriage, but when push comes to shove he backs off because he will always have the wandering eye in search of the next pretty face that comes along.

Date: March 17, 1948
Title: Worried about Duel
 Cast: Harold Peary (Gildersleeve), John Wald, Louise Erickson (Marjorie), Walter Tetley (Leroy), Earle Ross (Hooker), Lillian Randolph (Birdie), Richard LeGrand (Peavey), Una Merkel

(Adeline), Gloria Holliday (Bessie), Arthur Q. Bryan (Floyd)

Summary: Gildersleeve is upset over the prospect of a jealous former beau of Adeline's coming up from the south to challenge him to a duel with pistols.

Writers: Jack Robinson, Gene Stone

Allusions: Marjorie alludes to the title of Thomas Moore's poem "Love's Young Dream." Gildersleeve paraphrases from "The Ballad of East and West" by Rudyard Kipling: "South is South and North is North and never the twain shall meet."

Comments: Meakin music simulates March winds and also delivers a call to arms with "Dixie." Gildy never learns that lying is the worst policy for it is the untruth "Kissing you is the farthest thing from my mind" that sets Adeline off on the first of her snits. Adeline and Throckmorton behave so capriciously their relationship resembles a ping pong match more than a courtship.

Date: March 24, 1948
Title: Jolly Boys Invaded

Cast: Harold Peary (Gildersleeve), John Wald, Louise Erickson (Marjorie), Walter Tetley (Leroy), Earle Ross (Hooker), Lillian Randolph (Birdie), Richard LeGrand (Peavey), Arthur Q. Bryan (Floyd), Ken Christy (Gates), Una Merkel (Adeline)

Summary: Acting under pressure from Adeline, Gildersleeve asks the Jolly Boys if she can join them for one night.

Writers: John Elliotte, Andy White

Allusion: John Wald quotes from *Doctor Faustus* by Christopher Marlowe: "Helen of Troy had the face to launch a thousand ships."

Comments: Birdie sings "Hallelujah." The Jolly Boys sing "On the Banks of the Wabash." Gildersleeve sings "Every Day Is Ladies' Day with Me." Marjorie, Adeline, and Leroy sing "The Big Brass Band from Brazil." Meakin adds "Good Night, Sweetheart." *King of the Palominos* is a fictitious title. A minute after Gildy confesses "This is the worst idea I ever had" he comes up with another loser, then accuses women of being fickle when fate's finger is pointing directly at him. Peary as Gildersleeve receives the honorary appointment of being named water commissioner of Arcadia, California.

Date: March 31, 1948
Title: Marjorie Loves French Teacher

Cast: Harold Peary (Gildersleeve), John Wald, Louise Erickson (Marjorie), Walter Tetley (Leroy), Earle Ross (Hooker), Lillian Randolph (Birdie), Richard LeGrand (Peavey), Una Merkel (Adeline), Ben Alexander (Ben)

Summary: After Marjorie falls in love with a teacher, Throckmorton attempts to shift her affection back to Ben, her former boyfriend.

Writers: Jack Robinson, Gene Stone

Comments: Meakin contributes "The Last Time I Saw Paris" to the French theme, and also includes a bit of "I Hear a Rhapsody' and "Wedding March." Although Leroy remains a 12-year-old, at least Marjorie has progressed to 17. Ben's age is given as 23 or 24 so it is puzzling why Gildy is fussing over the possibility of Marjorie going with a man who is just a few years older at 27. On this occasion Marjorie is as flighty as her uncle, falling in love with someone based on looks when not a word of affection has been passed between them.

Date: April 7, 1948
Title: Baseball Field
    Cast: Harold Peary (Gildersleeve), John Wald, Louise Erickson (Marjorie), Walter Tetley (Leroy), Earle Ross (Hooker), Lillian Randolph (Birdie), Richard LeGrand (Peavey), Arthur Q. Bryan (Floyd), Una Merkel (Adeline), Tommy Bernard (Craig), Stan Farrar (Terwilliger)
    Summary: Gildersleeve spearheads a campaign to find a vacant lot where boys can play baseball and to raise funds for bats, gloves, and balls.
    Writers: John Elliotte, Andy White
    Comments: Gildersleeve sings "Take Me Out to the Ball Game." Like the March 12, 1947 episode that was requested by the Boys Clubs of America, this script was specially written to coincide with National Boys Club Week. Mr. Peavey behind the plate and Mrs. Peavey in the store doorway are a study in contrasts: one calls them the way he sees them, the other appalls them when they see her.

Date: April 14, 1948
Title: Radio Speech
    Cast: Harold Peary (Gildersleeve), John Wald, Louise Erickson (Marjorie), Walter Tetley (Leroy), Earle Ross (Hooker), Lillian Randolph (Birdie), Richard LeGrand (Peavey), Gloria Holliday (Bessie), Arthur Q. Bryan (Floyd)
    Summary: Throckmorton, thrilled when asked to appear on a radio show to talk about his department until he realizes he knows 0 about H_2O, approaches Hooker to write the speech for him.
    Writers: Jack Robinson, Gene Stone
    Comments: It is no surprise that Floyd says, "I'll take *Fibber McGee and Molly*" as Bryan was playing Doctor Gamble on that program. Jack Benny also gets a mention because he was still part of the NBC family at this time, but *Inner Sanctum Mysteries* has to be hidden under the fictitious *Squeaking Door Mystery Theater* because it was heard over CBS.

Date: April 21, 1948
Title: Pretends Adeline Is Secretary
    Cast: Harold Peary (Gildersleeve), John Wald, Louise Erickson (Marjorie), Walter Tetley (Leroy), Earle Ross (Hooker), Lillian Randolph (Birdie), Richard LeGrand (Peavey), Una Merkel (Adeline), Stan Farrar (Terwilliger), Arthur Q. Bryan (Floyd)
    Summary: When Gildersleeve is caught with Adeline in his office by Mayor Terwilliger at night, he passes her off as his secretary which leads to embarrassing and amusing complications.
    Writers: John Elliotte, Andy White
    Allusion: Hooker quotes from *Marmion* by Sir Walter Scott: "Beard the lion in his den."
    Comments: Leroy's capsule summary of comics is far from complete, but "Wow! Zip! Zowie! Take that! Rat-tat-tat-tat! To be continued!" appropriately epitomizes the colorful brand of action he craves. Elliotte and White borrow several elements from farce including misunderstandings, improvised explanations, and even hiding someone in the closet. They also trans-

fer the "pocketa, pocketa" noise that Floyd finds radiating off Gildy's noggin from the surgery daydream of Walter Mitty.

Date: April 28, 1948
Title: Kitchenware Salesman
   Cast: Harold Peary (Gildersleeve), John Wald, Louise Erickson (Marjorie), Walter Tetley (Leroy), Earle Ross (Hooker), Lillian Randolph (Birdie), Richard LeGrand (Peavey), Una Merkel (Adeline), Arthur Q. Bryan (Floyd), John McIntire (Wright)
   Summary: With Birdie out of town, Gildersleeve makes plans for a salesman to provide a meal for the children and Adeline.
   Writers: Jack Robinson, Gene Stone
   Comments: Gildersleeve sings "By the Light of the Silvery Moon." Gildersleeve's retort to Leroy's "What a character!" line is not original or witty but true: "Well, so are you." The comparison to Ingrid Bergman, considered a high compliment at this time, would not have been considered for scripts just two years later when she was regarded as persona non grata.

Date: May 5, 1948
Title: Fishing with Leroy
   Cast: Harold Peary (Gildersleeve), John Wald, Louise Erickson (Marjorie), Walter Tetley (Leroy), Earle Ross (Hooker), Lillian Randolph (Birdie), Richard LeGrand (Peavey), Arthur Q. Bryan (Floyd), Ken Christy (Gates), Una Merkel (Adeline)
   Summary: After Leroy hauls in eight bass at Grass Lake, Gildersleeve leads friends to believe he caught them even though he does not have a fishing license.

Writers: John Elliotte, Andy White
Comments: Gildersleeve sings "Sonny Boy." The Jolly Boys sing "For He's a Jolly Good Fellow." This show has a similar theme to the broadcast of February 22, 1942, in that both times Gildersleeve chastises his nephew for fibbing and later is guilty of stretching the truth himself. Leroy is still tied to the ball and chain of age 12.

Date: May 12, 1948
Title: Malingers at Home
   Cast: Harold Peary (Gildersleeve), John Wald, Louise Erickson (Marjorie), Walter Tetley (Leroy), Earle Ross (Hooker), Lillian Randolph (Birdie), Richard LeGrand (Peavey), Arthur Q. Bryan (radio announcer), Ken Christy (Gates), Una Merkel (Adeline), Tommy Bernard (Craig)
   Summary: Gildersleeve, pretending to be sick, gets very little rest and sustenance in or out of the house.
   Writers: Jack Robinson, Gene Stone
   Allusion: Hooker quotes from "Address to a Nightingale" by Richard Barnfield: "Every one that flatters thee / Is no friend in misery. / Words are easy, like the wind; / Faithful friends are hard to find."
   Comments: Gildersleeve sings "The Sunny Side of the Street." Sound effects man Monty Fraser receives credit for the first time. When Throckmorton tells the children "I'm not going to work today," he is telling the truth, regardless of whether he is at the office or at home.

Date: May 19, 1948
Title: Green Thumb Club
   Cast: Harold Peary (Gildersleeve), John Wald, Louise Erickson (Marjorie),

Walter Tetley (Leroy), Earle Ross (Hooker), Lillian Randolph (Birdie), Richard LeGrand (Peavey), Arthur Q. Bryan (Floyd), Gloria Holliday (Bessie), Una Merkel (Adeline), Eleanor Audley (Mrs. Pettibone)

Summary: Gildersleeve is anxious to get his paycheck back after his secretary mistakenly gives it to a garden club.

Writers: John Elliotte, Andy White

Allusion: John Wald paraphrases from the Song of Solomon 2:12: "And the voice of the turtle is no longer heard throughout the land."

Comments: Another sign of Throckmorton's immaturity is his admission to Adeline that he "was about to ask you to go steady," a phrase and a phase of life usually reserved for adolescents. Gildy's take home salary of $80.67 gives listeners a hint that he probably grossed about $100 a week or about $5,000 a year which was above average income for 1948. Floyd's admonition about "taking this nature boy seriously" refers to the top ten record of the day, "Nature Boy."

Date: May 26, 1948
Title: Drives a Mercedes
   Cast: Harold Peary (Gildersleeve), John Wald, Louise Erickson (Marjorie), Walter Tetley (Leroy), Earle Ross (Hooker), Lillian Randolph (Birdie), Richard LeGrand (Peavey), Arthur Q. Bryan (Floyd), Gale Gordon (Rumson Bullard), Eddie Marr (Smiling Sam)
   Summary: Gildersleeve's driving a Mercedes around town gives his friends the impression he is now wealthy.
   Writers: Jack Robinson, Gene Stone
   Comments: The Jolly Boys sing "When You Wore a Tulip" and "When Good Fellows Get Together." Gale Gordon makes his first appearance in the role of Rumson Bullard. Just as the car salesman on February 10, 1946, enticed Gildy with the promise of women looking his way, Smiling Sam uses the lure of "every girl will want your phone number" to convince Throckmorton to give the Mercedes a try.

Date: June 2, 1948
Title: Fired
   Cast: Harold Peary (Gildersleeve), John Wald, Louise Erickson (Marjorie), Walter Tetley (Leroy), Earle Ross (Hooker), Lillian Randolph (Birdie), Richard LeGrand (Peavey), Arthur Q. Bryan (Floyd), Ken Christy (Gates), Una Merkel (Adeline), Gloria Holliday (Bessie), Stan Farrar (Terwilliger)
   Summary: After Throckmorton is fired for loafing on the job, the Jolly Boys attempt to get him restored as water commissioner.
   Writers: John Elliotte, Andy White
   Comments: The Jolly Boys sing "Smiles." Meakin music includes "Summertime," "In the Good Old Summertime," and a raindrop melody. Gildersleeve reacts to bad news in the same way his nephew does, with tears and a whimper. Louise Erickson appears for the last time as Marjorie. The summer replacement series is *Jack and Cliff* starring Jack Pearl and Cliff Hall.

Date: September 8, 1948
Title: Mystery Baby
   Cast: Harold Peary (Gildersleeve), John Wald, Mary Lee Robb (Marjorie), Walter Tetley (Leroy), Earle Ross (Hooker), Lillian Randolph (Birdie),

Richard LeGrand (Peavey), Ken Christy (Gates), Una Merkel (Adeline)

Summary: Gildersleeve discovers that he is becoming attracted to the abandoned baby he found in his car.

Writers: Jack Robinson, Gene Stone

Comments: Leroy sings "That's Where My Money Goes." Peary's laugh at the beginning of the program is dropped. Mary Lee Robb appears for the first time in a credited role as Marjorie. Meakin adds a little more lilt to the opening theme and drops in "Brahms's Lullaby" several times. Birdie will be featured in numerous exchanges with Wald in the central commercial this season.

Date: September 15, 1948
Title: Sitting with Baby
   Cast: Harold Peary (Gildersleeve), John Wald, Mary Lee Robb (Marjorie), Walter Tetley (Leroy), Earle Ross (Hooker), Lillian Randolph (Birdie), Richard LeGrand (Peavey), Una Merkel (Adeline)

Summary: Gildersleeve, unsuccessful at getting his friends to help him mind the baby for a night, resorts to singing to the baby.

Writers: John Elliotte, Andy White

Comments: Gildersleeve sings "Little Buckaroo." Birdie may not be exaggerating when she gives her weight as 160 because she has always made her formidable presence felt. Hooker refers to the Schmoo, a creature appearing in Li'l Abner who resembled a bottom-heavy version of Casper the friendly ghost.

Date: September 22, 1948
Title: Leroy Jealous of Baby
   Cast: Harold Peary (Gildersleeve),

John Wald, Mary Lee Robb (Marjorie), Walter Tetley (Leroy), Earle Ross (Hooker), Lillian Randolph (Birdie), Richard LeGrand (Peavey), Tommy Bernard (Craig), Eleanor Audley (Mrs. Pinckney)

Summary: Leroy takes up residence in his clubhouse in protest of the lack of attention he is receiving since the baby has been brought into the home.

Writers: Jack Robinson, Gene Stone

Comments: Gildersleeve sings "The Sunny Side of the Street." Meakin sets the tone with "Twinkle, Twinkle, Little Star," "Feudin' and Fightin'" after the uncle/nephew quarrel, newsreel music during the photo session, and "to the rescue" chords when Throcky has a change of heart.

Date: September 29, 1948
Title: Naming the Baby
   Cast: Harold Peary (Gildersleeve), John Wald, Mary Lee Robb (Marjorie), Walter Tetley (Leroy), Earle Ross (Hooker), Lillian Randolph (Birdie), Richard LeGrand (Peavey), Arthur Q. Bryan (Floyd), Ken Christy (Gates), Una Merkel (Adeline), Gloria Holliday (Bessie)

Summary: Gildersleeve solicits names for the foundling from family and friends.

Writers: John Elliotte, Andy White

Allusion: Hooker quotes from *Hints Toward Reform* by Horace Greeley: "Go West, young man, and grow up with the country."

Comments: The Jolly Boys sing "Mighty Like a Rose." Gildersleeve gives his address as 217 Elm Street, a change from earlier addresses of 738 Lakeside, 737 Parkside, and 219 Lakeside. Wald announces the beginning of the "Name the Baby" contest.

Date: October 6, 1948
Title: Welfare Investigator
   Cast: Harold Peary (Gildersleeve), John Wald, Mary Lee Robb (Marjorie), Walter Tetley (Leroy), Earle Ross (Hooker), Lillian Randolph (Birdie), Richard LeGrand (Peavey), Arthur Q. Bryan (Floyd), Gloria Holliday (Bessie), Una Merkel (Adeline), Eleanor Audley (Mrs. Pettibone)
   Summary: Throckmorton works hard to get a character reference from Mrs. Pettibone in order to impress a representative from the welfare department.
   Writers: Jack Robinson, Gene Stone
   Comments: Gildersleeve jumps to unfounded conclusions and, imagining that things will go bad, makes matters worse by offending his friends.

Date: October 13, 1948
Title: Aunt Hattie Visits Again
   Cast: Harold Peary (Gildersleeve), John Wald, Mary Lee Robb (Marjorie), Walter Tetley (Leroy), Earle Ross (Hooker), Lillian Randolph (Birdie), Richard LeGrand (Peavey), Una Merkel (Adeline)
   Summary: Anxious to get Aunt Hattie to leave, Gildersleeve and the children take Peavey's advice to be kind to her.
   Writers: John Elliotte, Andy White
   Allusion: Peavey quotes from *The Taming of the Shrew* by William Shakespeare: "To kill a wife with kindness."
   Comments: Gildersleeve and Leroy sing "Heigh Ho." Meakin's melodies include "Oh, What a Beautiful Morning."

Gildy is on the verge of tears after Hattie's decision to stay and Birdie is almost tearing her hair out. The reference to Dewey appointing a federal water commissioner indicates how favorable the public regarded his chances to defeat Truman in November.

Date: October 20, 1948
Title: Marjorie Pursues Ben
   Cast: Harold Peary (Gildersleeve), John Wald, Mary Lee Robb (Marjorie), Walter Tetley (Leroy), Earle Ross (Hooker), Lillian Randolph (Birdie), Richard LeGrand (Peavey), Ben Alexander (Ben)
   Summary: Marjorie attempts to persuade Ben to marry her so they can adopt the baby.
   Writers: Jack Robinson, Gene Stone
   Comments: Marjorie has slipped back from being 17 on March 31, 1948, to the old reliable 16. Marjorie's assessment of Wally as being "irresponsible, lazy, and will never amount to anything" could also apply to her uncle.

Date: October 27, 1948
Title: Proposes to Adeline
   Cast: Harold Peary (Gildersleeve), John Wald, Mary Lee Robb (Marjorie), Walter Tetley (Leroy), Earle Ross (Hooker), Lillian Randolph (Birdie), Richard LeGrand (Peavey), Una Merkel (Adeline), Gale Gordon (Rumson Bullard), Tommy Bernard (Craig)
   Summary: Fearful that Bullard might beat him to adopting the baby, Throckmorton prepares to ask Adeline to be his wife.
   Writers: John Elliotte, Andy White
   Allusion: Adeline quotes from "The Spider and the Fly" by Mary Howitt:

"'Won't you come into my parlor?' said the spider to the fly."

Comments: Meakin contributes "Pretty Baby" and a discordant "Wedding March" to the proceedings. Dr. Needham may have gone to greener pastures because Dr. Prescott is now delivering the sermons at Throckmorton's church. For the first time filtered voices are used to indicate the thoughts of the speakers. The actions of Gildersleeve are pretty silly, running around saying "I've got to get married," willing to spend the rest of his life with a woman he is mildly attracted to for the sake of a foundling he has known for seven weeks.

Date: November 3, 1948
Title: Announcing Engagement
   Cast: Harold Peary (Gildersleeve), John Wald, Mary Lee Robb (Marjorie), Walter Tetley (Leroy), Earle Ross (Hooker), Lillian Randolph (Birdie), Richard LeGrand (Peavey), Una Merkel (Adeline), Arthur Q. Bryan (Floyd), Ken Christy (Gates)
   Summary: Gildersleeve's wishes to keep his engagement a secret are not honored by Adeline who spreads the word promiscuously.
   Writers: Jack Robinson, Gene Stone
   Comments: Adeline, Gildersleeve, Hooker, Floyd, and Gates each sing the start of "Oh, Promise Me." The Jolly Boys sing "Wedding Bells Are Breaking Up that Old Gang of Mine." Meakin adds "The Prisoner's Song" and "Memories" as bridges. The usual sex roles are reversed with Adeline being the assertive person attentive to detail while Throcky is the faint-hearted, foolhardy fainter.

Date: November 10, 1948
Title: Engaged to Two Women
   Cast: Harold Peary (Gildersleeve), John Wald, Mary Lee Robb (Marjorie), Walter Tetley (Leroy), Earle Ross (Hooker), Lillian Randolph (Birdie), Shirley Mitchell (Leila), Richard LeGrand (Peavey), Una Merkel (Adeline), Arthur Q. Bryan (Floyd), Gloria Holliday (Bessie)
   Summary: After Leila leads Throckmorton into a proposal of sorts, he looks for a way out of one or both of his engagements.
   Writers: John Elliotte, Andy White
   Comments: Gildersleeve sings "Speak to Me of Love." "He's lovely! He's engaged!" is a parody of the slogan used by a cold cream product: "She's lovely! She's engaged! She uses Pond's!" Hooker's appraisal of Leila ("The grace of Diana, the charm of Helen of Troy, the allure of Cleopatra") judiciously omits "the deceitfulness of Delilah." The film Floyd refers to is *Mr. Peabody and the Mermaid.*

Date: November 17, 1948
Title: Breaking One Engagement
   Cast: Harold Peary (Gildersleeve), John Wald, Mary Lee Robb (Marjorie), Walter Tetley (Leroy), Earle Ross (Hooker), Lillian Randolph (Birdie), Shirley Mitchell (Leila), Richard LeGrand (Peavey), Una Merkel (Adeline), Hal March (Barney Caldwell)
   Summary: Acting upon a suggestion by Hooker, Gildersleeve attempts to interest Leila in a banker so she will break her engagement to him.
   Writers: Jack Robinson, Gene Stone
   Comments: Peavey sings a bit of "Just Because." The audience has to be

in agreement with Leroy's "Ha!" after Gildersleeve claims to be the cautious type who "hasn't made many mistakes where women are concerned." The peek into the future with Leila is prescient in its portrayal of old movies dominating TV programming, but the lengthy Truman presidency would not be possible after the 22nd amendment was ratified in 1951.

Date: November 24, 1948
Title: Helicopter Ride
   Cast: Harold Peary (Gildersleeve), John Wald, Mary Lee Robb (Marjorie), Walter Tetley (Leroy), Earle Ross (Hooker), Lillian Randolph (Birdie), Richard LeGrand (Peavey), Una Merkel (Adeline), Stan Farrar (Terwilliger)
   Summary: Gildersleeve is apprehensive about flying in a helicopter to open the storage reservoir.
   Writers: John Elliotte, Andy White
   Comments: Peavey sings "Off We Go into the Wild Blue Yonder." Throckmorton's answer to the bookish question "What color is your parachute?" would have been "Yellow" like the streak up his back.

Date: December 1, 1948
Title: Leroy Sells Newspapers
   Cast: Harold Peary (Gildersleeve), John Wald, Mary Lee Robb (Marjorie), Walter Tetley (Leroy), Earle Ross (Hooker), Lillian Randolph (Birdie), Richard LeGrand (Peavey), Arthur Q. Bryan (Floyd)
   Summary: Throckmorton, having second thoughts about Leroy's job peddling papers in the cold, runs into trouble when he takes the boy's place.
   Writers: Jack Robinson, Gene Stone

Comments: Meakin adds much to the flavor of this episode with "windy" and "dots and dashes" bridges. Gildersleeve's rash decision to call faithful friend Hooker derogatory names comes back to haunt him when he needs a reference.

Date: December 8, 1948
Title: Disappearing Gifts
   Cast: Harold Peary (Gildersleeve), John Wald, Mary Lee Robb (Marjorie), Walter Tetley (Leroy), Earle Ross (Hooker), Lillian Randolph (Birdie), Richard LeGrand (Peavey), Ken Christy (Gates), Una Merkel (Adeline)
   Summary: Throckmorton, suspecting that a burglar has taken Christmas gifts and his watch, calls in Chief Gates to help him solve the mystery.
   Writers: John Elliotte, Andy White
   Comments: Birdie sings "Jingle Bells." Meakin slows down "Up on the Rooftop" to accompany Gildy's furtive hiding of gifts. The writers provide an early clue to the mystery when the baby grabs Throckmorton's tie clasp while they are playing on the floor. The winning name for the little roamer is announced as Romerry.

Date: December 15, 1948
Title: Cutting Back on Gifts
   Cast: Harold Peary (Gildersleeve), John Wald, Mary Lee Robb (Marjorie), Walter Tetley (Leroy), Earle Ross (Hooker), Lillian Randolph (Birdie), Richard LeGrand (Peavey), Una Merkel (Adeline), Arthur Q. Bryan (Floyd)
   Summary: Gildersleeve finds it tough sledding when he tries to reduce spending on Christmas presents for family and friends this year.

Writers: Jack Robinson, Gene Stone

Comments: Gildersleeve sings "Santa Claus Is Coming to Town" and "Who's Afraid of the Big Bad Wolf?" The chorus sings "O Little Town of Bethlehem." Leroy has learned from Craig how to turn the flood of tears on and off to suit his purposes. Mr. Bentley responds with such an ebullient "Yes" that it sounds like the part was modeled after the obnoxious characters played by Frank Nelson on *The Jack Benny Program*.

Date: December 22, 1948
Title: Family Christmas

　Cast: Harold Peary (Gildersleeve), John Wald, Mary Lee Robb (Marjorie), Walter Tetley (Leroy), Earle Ross (Hooker), Lillian Randolph (Birdie), Richard LeGrand (Peavey), Una Merkel (Adeline), Arthur Q. Bryan (Floyd), Ken Christy (Gates)

　Summary: Throckmorton's plans for having a private Christmas at home are dashed when he begins inviting all his friends.

　Writers: John Elliotte, Andy White

　Comments: Birdie sings "Coventry Carol." Everyone joins in singing "Deck the Halls" and "Joy to the World." Gildersleeve's first reaction to hearing Bob's confession is a selfish thought that "he can't take her from me" until he probably faces the fact that the child was never legally his anyway.

Date: December 29, 1948
Title: Wedding Imminent

　Cast: Harold Peary (Gildersleeve), John Wald, Mary Lee Robb (Marjorie), Walter Tetley (Leroy), Earle Ross (Hooker), Lillian Randolph (Birdie),

Richard LeGrand (Peavey), Una Merkel (Adeline), Arthur Q. Bryan (Floyd), Ken Christy (Gates)

　Summary: Throckmorton and Adeline, both reluctant to go through with the wedding, find it difficult to say the words that will call it off.

　Writers: Jack Robinson, Gene Stone

　Comments: Hooker sings a bit of "Bells Are Ringing" and Peavey does the same with "There'll Be a Hot Time in the Old Town Tonight." The Jolly Boys sing "Love You Like I Never Loved Before" and "For He's a Jolly Good Fellow." Marjorie's reflection "Sometimes I wonder about Unkie" is her more genteel version of Leroy's "What a character!" That Gildy is only after the sensual pleasures women provide rather than the virtues which are necessary to sustain a meaningful, long-term relationship is particularly obvious in the line that since "we're not going to be married, how about a little kiss?" For the first time each member of the cast gets to say his or her name in the credits.

Date: January 5, 1949
Title: Takes Up Writing

　Cast: Harold Peary (Gildersleeve), John Wald, Mary Lee Robb (Marjorie), Walter Tetley (Leroy), Earle Ross (Hooker), Lillian Randolph (Birdie), Richard LeGrand (Peavey), Bea Benaderet (Eve), Arthur Q. Bryan (Floyd), Eleanor Audley (Mrs. Pettibone)

　Summary: Concerned with Christmas bills and attracted by the promise of easy money in magazine ads, Gildersleeve decides to earn cash by writing.

　Writers: John Elliotte, Andy White

Allusion: John Wald quotes from Plato's *Republic*: "Necessity is the mother of invention."

Comments: Throckmorton, as usual, goes off the deep end, imagining a life of wealth in books when his total output is a chapter number and his name. Bea Benaderet again sounds exactly right as Eve, the voice of calm reason, and Peary does his part, too, as rash Gildy who hears but not does not heed the sage advice she gives.

Date: January 12, 1949
Title: Good Neighbor
  Cast: Harold Peary (Gildersleeve), John Wald, Mary Lee Robb (Marjorie), Walter Tetley (Leroy), Earle Ross (Hooker), Lillian Randolph (Birdie), Richard LeGrand (Peavey), Gale Gordon (Rumson Bullard), Tommy Bernard (Craig)
  Summary: Gildersleeve's resolution to act amicably toward the Bullards is put to the test when Rumson causes property damage and Craig hits Leroy with a snowball.
  Writers: John Elliotte, Andy White
  Allusion: Hooker quotes from *Macbeth* by William Shakespeare: "The milk of human kindness."
  Comments: Gildersleeve sings "Love Thy Neighbor." Meakin contributes "Praise the Lord and Pass the Ammunition" and windy music to reinforce both the frigid weather and the icy relationships. Craig and Rumson make such an odious pair one gets the feeling they were the only ones in the audience giggling along with Tommy Udo when he pushed the lady in the wheelchair down the stairs in *Kiss of Death*.

Date: January 19, 1949
Title: Leroy's Toothache
  Cast: Harold Peary (Gildersleeve), John Wald, Mary Lee Robb (Marjorie), Walter Tetley (Leroy), Earle Ross (Hooker), Lillian Randolph (Birdie), Richard LeGrand (Peavey), Una Merkel (Adeline), Gloria Holliday (Bessie)
  Summary: Leroy, who doesn't want to have his bad tooth pulled, finds that his uncle is just as reluctant to go to the dentist as he is.
  Writers: John Elliotte, Andy White
  Comments: Birdie again comes to Leroy's defense when confronting Gildersleeve, having to shame her boss into altering his decision. Cowardly Throckmorton, who is unable to pull someone else's tooth, does not follow Dr. Cobb's advice at the end for he chooses to see his dentist just twice a decade.

Date: January 26, 1949
Title: Training Younger Man
  Cast: Harold Peary (Gildersleeve), John Wald, Mary Lee Robb (Marjorie), Walter Tetley (Leroy), Earle Ross (Hooker), Lillian Randolph (Birdie), Richard LeGrand (Peavey), Arthur Q. Bryan (Floyd), Stan Farrar (Terwilliger), Donald Woods (Charles Alexander)
  Summary: When he is instructed to show a young man how the water department works, Gildersleeve assumes that he is grooming his replacement.
  Writers: Jack Robinson, Gene Stone
  Comments: Floyd and Gildersleeve sing "While Strolling Through the Park One Day." Gildy bites twice at Floyd's bait, first buying a bill of goods, then, when really desperate, grabbing at straws.

Date: February 2, 1949
Title: Hat Shop Proposed
  Cast: Harold Peary (Gildersleeve), John Wald, Mary Lee Robb (Marjorie), Walter Tetley (Leroy), Earle Ross (Hooker), Lillian Randolph (Birdie), Richard LeGrand (Peavey), Una Merkel (Adeline), Gale Gordon (Rumson Bullard), Arthur Q. Bryan (Floyd)
  Summary: Throckmorton, about to start a petition against Adeline opening a millinery business in her house, becomes a partner with her after he learns he can make a quick profit in the endeavor.
  Writers: John Elliotte, Andy White
  Comments: Gildersleeve sings "Easter Parade." Dilatory Gildy has yet to get around to finishing his four-year-old copy of *A Tree Grows in Brooklyn*. Spendthrift Throcky buys expensive cigars before he has even recouped a dollar on his investment.

Date: February 9, 1949
Title: Hat Shop Opening
  Cast: Harold Peary (Gildersleeve), John Wald, Mary Lee Robb (Marjorie), Walter Tetley (Leroy), Earle Ross (Hooker), Lillian Randolph (Birdie), Richard LeGrand (Peavey), Una Merkel (Adeline), Arthur Q. Bryan (Floyd), Eleanor Audley (Mrs. Pettibone)
  Summary: A dispute between Adeline and the influential Mrs. Pettibone threatens to disrupt the opening of the hat shop.
  Writers: Jack Robinson, Gene Stone
  Comments: Meakin adds a bit of "La Marseillaise" and "Dixie" to the geography of this episode. Floyd, like Peavey, has become a counselor to Gilder-

sleeve, although much of his advice is of the unsolicited variety.

Date: February 16, 1949
Title: Leila May Close Shop
  Cast: Harold Peary (Gildersleeve), John Wald, Mary Lee Robb (Marjorie), Walter Tetley (Leroy), Earle Ross (Hooker), Lillian Randolph (Birdie), Shirley Mitchell (Leila), Richard LeGrand (Peavey), Una Merkel (Adeline)
  Summary: Gildersleeve plans to sweet-talk Leila out of her stated intention to shut down the hat shop operating in her house.
  Writers: John Elliotte, Andy White
  Comments: Gildersleeve sings "On a Slow Boat to China." Sometimes the ironies pour out of the great man's mouth with scarcely a beat in between, viz., his criticizing Leroy because "all he thinks about is money" followed immediately by "Let's open the mail and see how many checks came in."

Date: February 23, 1949
Title: Takes Singing Lessons
  Cast: Harold Peary (Gildersleeve), John Wald, Mary Lee Robb (Marjorie), Walter Tetley (Leroy), Earle Ross (Hooker), Lillian Randolph (Birdie), Richard LeGrand (Peavey), Arthur Q. Bryan (Floyd), Ken Christy (Gates), Hope Emerson (Madame Kimmel)
  Summary: When Gildersleeve decides to study for a career in the opera, he alienates his friends by declining to sing with the Jolly Boys.
  Writers: Jack Robinson, Gene Stone
  Comments: Gildersleeve sings "Indian Love Call" and "The Toreador Song." Madame Kimmel sings bits from

Carmen, La Bohème, and *Siegfried.* The Jolly Boys sing "Love You Like I Never Loved Before" and "When Good Fellows Get Together." Throckmorton calls the druggist "Richard Q. Peavey." (The middle name will not be revealed until the February 28, 1951 episode.) Hope Emerson would soon establish her redoubtable "she who must be obeyed" image in *Caged* and other films.

Date: March 2, 1949
Title: Leroy Treats Brenda
  Cast: Harold Peary (Gildersleeve), John Wald, Mary Lee Robb (Marjorie), Walter Tetley (Leroy), Lillian Randolph (Birdie), Richard LeGrand (Peavey), Arthur Q. Bryan (Floyd), Gale Gordon (Rumson Bullard), Martha Scott (Helen Knickerbocker), Barbara Whiting (Brenda Knickerbocker)
  Summary: Soon after warning his nephew about letting new friend Brenda take advantage of him, Gildersleeve finds himself in a similar situation with the girl's mother.
  Writers: John Elliotte, Andy White
  Comments: Floyd and Gildersleeve sing "I've Got My Love to Keep Me Warm." Barbara Whiting was starring in *Junior Miss* on Saturdays at this time with Gale Gordon playing her father. This is one episode in which the "like nephew, like uncle" theme is explicitly promoted. It appears that Peavey does not finish the list of ingredients that make up the confection he places before the children, but what would come on top of the tutti-frutti ice cream, chocolate syrup, pistachio ice cream, and strawberry syrup would just prolong the agony.

Date: March 9, 1949
Title: Summerfield 1903
  Cast: Harold Peary (Gildersleeve), John Wald, Mary Lee Robb (Marjorie), Walter Tetley (Leroy), Earle Ross (Hooker), Lillian Randolph (Birdie), Richard LeGrand (Peavey), Arthur Q. Bryan (Floyd), Ken Christy (Gates)
  Summary: Looking at an old newspaper in the basement sends Gildersleeve back in a daydream to 1903.
  Writers: Jack Robinson, Gene Stone
  Comments: The Bachelor Boys sing "Daisy, Daisy," "Sweet Genevieve," and "Rosie, You Are My Posie." Gildersleeve sings "On Moonlight Bay." Meakin contributes to the old-time theme with sounds simulating locomotives and the venerable standard "Put on Your Old Grey Bonnet." The writers put Peary through some mirthful slapstick in the basement. The episode which received the bronze medal from *Advertising and Selling* aired on April 7, 1948. Charlie Cantor as Clifton Finnegan delivers a teaser for *Duffy's Tavern* in order to attract carryover listeners.

Date: March 16, 1949
Title: Leroy's Competition
  Cast: Harold Peary (Gildersleeve), John Wald, Mary Lee Robb (Marjorie), Walter Tetley (Leroy), Earle Ross (Hooker), Lillian Randolph (Birdie), Richard LeGrand (Peavey), Barbara Whiting (Brenda Knickerbocker), Arthur Q. Bryan (Floyd)
  Summary: Leroy's efforts to impress girlfriend Brenda are stymied by another boy who possesses a multitude of talents.
  Writers: John Elliotte, Andy White
  Allusion: Marjorie quotes from

Locksley Hall by Alfred, Lord Tennyson: "In the spring a young man's fancy lightly turns to thoughts of love."

Comments: Marjorie provides an early clue that will prove relevant later when she mentions Leroy's ability to wiggle his ears. Even though the reputation of Orson Welles had deteriorated since his wunderkind days, the actor-director-writer was still the personality people like Throcky looked to when they needed a renaissance man.

Date: March 23, 1949
Title: New Secretary Zelda
    Cast: Harold Peary (Gildersleeve), John Wald, Mary Lee Robb (Marjorie), Walter Tetley (Leroy), Earle Ross (Hooker), Lillian Randolph (Birdie), Richard LeGrand (Peavey), Gloria Holliday (Bessie), Jeanette Nolan (Zelda Lovejoy), John McIntire (employment agency manager), Samuel Morris
    Summary: Tired of Bessie's inefficiency, Gildersleeve replaces her with a secretary who is so capable she makes life at the office unbearable for him.
    Writers: Jack Robinson, Gene Stone
    Comments: Gildersleeve sings "Oh, What a Beautiful Morning." Later Hooker and Peavey do the same. John McIntire and Jeanette Nolan were husband and wife. The episode was specially written to coincide with the certificate of membership in the American Waterworks Association presented to Peary by Morris.

Date: March 30, 1949
Title: Acting Police Commissioner
    Cast: Harold Peary (Gildersleeve), John Wald, Mary Lee Robb (Marjorie), Walter Tetley (Leroy), Earle Ross

(Hooker), Lillian Randolph (Birdie), Richard LeGrand (Peavey), Ken Christy (Gates), Stan Farrar (Terwilliger), Gloria Holliday (Bessie), Gil Stratton Jr. (Armstrong)
    Summary: Throckmorton, temporarily in charge of the police department, is on the spot when the safe in the water department is robbed by the whistling bandit.
    Writers: John Elliotte, Andy White
    Comments: The reaction of the audience to Jolly's statements indicates they see through his plot unlike clueless Gildersleeve. Scorekeepers will note that butterfingers Gildy fumbles twice, loses them both times, and barely recovers his old field position in the water department.

Date: April 6, 1949
Title: Conflicting Party Engagements
    Cast: Harold Peary (Gildersleeve), John Wald, Mary Lee Robb (Marjorie), Walter Tetley (Leroy), Earle Ross (Hooker), Lillian Randolph (Birdie), Richard LeGrand (Peavey), Martha Scott (Ellen Knickerbocker)
    Summary: Gildersleeve has difficulty deciding whether to go to the country club with Ellen or attend a birthday party for Romerry.
    Writers: Jack Robinson, Gene Stone
    Comments: Gildersleeve sings "A Kiss in the Dark." Meakin alternates "Brahms's Lullaby" with "A Kiss in the Dark" to reinforce Throckmorton's divided sentiments. The exchange between Gildy and Peavey regarding the parrot is a comic gem. John Wald provides a rare teaser for the following week by promoting its circus theme.

Date: April 13, 1949
Title: Circus in Town
Cast: Harold Peary (Gildersleeve), John Wald, Mary Lee Robb (Marjorie), Walter Tetley (Leroy), Earle Ross (Hooker), Lillian Randolph (Birdie), Richard LeGrand (Peavey), Barbara Whiting (Brenda Knickerbocker), Eddie Marr (Captain Blackie Sparks), Peggy Knudsen (Beatrice Sample)
Summary: After Gildersleeve cures Leroy of his circus fever, he assumes the role of ringmaster and entertains thoughts of traveling with the troupe during the summer.
Writers: John Elliotte, Andy White
Comments: Gildersleeve sings "Far Away Places." Meakin creates a festive atmosphere with several different versions of peppy circus music. Birdie must be a wizard with a needle and thread if she can get a size 36 outfit to fit size 47 Gildy. In a tense moment with the lion Throckmorton indicates he was born in August which contradicts his earlier birthday celebration on October 22, 1947. Actress Peggy Knudsen was married to Jim Jordan Jr., son of the man known as radio's Fibber McGee.

Date: April 20, 1949
Title: Haunted House
Cast: Harold Peary (Gildersleeve), John Wald, Mary Lee Robb (Marjorie), Walter Tetley (Leroy), Earle Ross (Hooker), Lillian Randolph (Birdie), Richard LeGrand (Peavey), Arthur Q. Bryan (Floyd), Ken Christy (Gates)
Summary: Gildersleeve gets a chance to use his new detective kit when he investigates peculiar noises coming from a deserted house.

Writers: Jack Robinson, Gene Stone
Comments: The Jolly Boys sing "When Good Fellows Get Together." Meakin produces some novel derisive notes after Hooker insults Gildy in the second act. The mention of *Mr. District Attorney* is not accidental for it subtly promotes the NBC program airing an hour after *The Great Gildersleeve* on Wednesdays. Peary earns the biggest laugh of the night when he pauses to look for his gun permit before approaching his quarry.

Date: April 27, 1949
Title: Burglar
Cast: Harold Peary (Gildersleeve), John Wald, Mary Lee Robb (Marjorie), Walter Tetley (Leroy), Earle Ross (Hooker), Lillian Randolph (Birdie), Richard LeGrand (Peavey), Gale Gordon (Rumson Bullard), Martha Scott (Ellen Knickerbocker), Tommy Bernard (Craig), Eddie Marr (Harry)
Summary: After Throckmorton muffs his first chance to capture a burglar in the neighborhood, he designs a disguise and adopts an accent in order to trap the crook.
Writers: John Elliotte, Andy White
Comments: Peary can be heard chuckling over Lillian's fluff and her quick recovery. *Mr. District Attorney* gets another plug as does the star of *Duffy's Tavern* when Gildy says, "Eddie Gardner." The reaction of the audience suggests that Peary must have dressed the part of the gardener for his scene with Peavey. Gordon really explodes in his Mayor LaTrivia manner when he orders Throckmorton to "Get off the property!" For the first time since May 17,

1942, Gildersleeve claims Princeton as his alma mater.

Date: May 4, 1949
Title: Woman on the Bus
   Cast: Harold Peary (Gildersleeve), John Wald, Mary Lee Robb (Marjorie), Walter Tetley (Leroy), Earle Ross (Hooker), Lillian Randolph (Birdie), Richard LeGrand (Peavey), Gloria Holliday (Bessie)
   Summary: Gildersleeve imagines a woman he met on the bus is in danger and dreams of rescuing her.
   Writers: Jack Robinson, Gene Stone
   Allusion: Gildersleeve paraphrases from "The Day Is Done" by Henry Wadsworth Longfellow: "Then she folded her tents like the Arabs and silently stole away."
   Comments: Gildersleeve sings a bit of "Bell Bottom Trousers." Throckmorton's declaration of "Here I go again" after his second backwards fall could also apply to his frequent forward lunges after the nearest pretty face.

Date: May 11, 1949
Title: Millionaire Friend
   Cast: Harold Peary (Gildersleeve), John Wald, Mary Lee Robb (Marjorie), Walter Tetley (Leroy), Earle Ross (Hooker), Lillian Randolph (Birdie), Richard LeGrand (Peavey), Arthur Q. Bryan (Floyd), Martha Scott (Ellen Knickerbocker), Donald Woods (Benjamin Barton Clay)
   Summary: Gildersleeve is chagrined when Ellen takes a shine to his wealthy houseguest.
   Writers: John Elliotte, Andy White
   Comments: Peary reprises the "six burners" fluff at the very end. The au-dience gets a bang out of the exploding cigar gag even before the sound effect is heard.

Date: May 18, 1949
Title: Marjorie's Dance Invitation
   Cast: Harold Peary (Gildersleeve), John Wald, Mary Lee Robb (Marjorie), Walter Tetley (Leroy), Earle Ross (Hooker), Lillian Randolph (Birdie), Richard LeGrand (Peavey), Arthur Q. Bryan (Floyd), Richard Crenna (Rodney Zimmerman)
   Summary: After causing a misunderstanding between Marjorie and boyfriend Rodney, Gildersleeve rents a costume and hopes to escort his niece to the big dance.
   Writers: Jack Robinson, Gene Stone
   Comments: This plot is reminiscent of the one used on March 10, 1946, although Gildy never gets to the dance this time around. Gildy again emerges worse for wear in his sixth tangle with Peavey's phone booth. Richard Crenna, more effective as athlete than aesthete, will get a role more suited to his style the following season as Bronco Thompson.

Date: May 25, 1949
Title: Lawsuit against Bullard
   Cast: Harold Peary (Gildersleeve), John Wald, Mary Lee Robb (Marjorie), Walter Tetley (Leroy), Earle Ross (Hooker), Lillian Randolph (Birdie), Richard LeGrand (Peavey), Arthur Q. Bryan (Floyd), Gale Gordon (Rumson Bullard), Tommy Bernard (Craig), Kay Starr
   Summary: Tired of being insulted by the Bullards, Gildersleeve takes Rumson to court for defaming his character.

Writers: John Elliotte, Andy White

Comments: Gildersleeve sings "Cruising Down the River." Kay Starr sings "How It Lies." This show has a different sound to it with full versions of songs interrupting the action and an integrated commercial with the announcer appearing at the home of the main character a la Harlow Wilcox's weekly stop at 79 Wistful Vista to chat with the McGees.

Date: June 1, 1949
Title: Folk Dancing

Cast: Harold Peary (Gildersleeve), John Wald, Mary Lee Robb (Marjorie), Walter Tetley (Leroy), Earle Ross (Hooker), Lillian Randolph (Birdie), Richard LeGrand (Peavey), Gloria Holliday (Bessie), Kay Starr

Summary: After embarrassing himself before a dance teacher, Gildersleeve attempts to lose weight and get in better shape.

Writers: Jack Robinson, Gene Stone

Comments: Gildersleeve sings "Some Enchanted Evening." Kay Starr sings "Wabash Cannonball." Meakin contributes the apposite bridges "School Days" and "Let's Have Another Cup of Coffee." This week Wald conveniently meets Throckmorton on the street to deliver his Parkay pitch. *Archie Andrews* is the summer replacement series this year.

Date: September 21, 1949
Title: Songwriter

Cast: Harold Peary (Gildersleeve), Jay Stewart, Mary Lee Robb (Marjorie), Walter Tetley (Leroy), Earle Ross (Hooker), Lillian Randolph (Birdie), Richard LeGrand (Peavey), Arthur Q. Bryan (Floyd), Ken Christy (Gates), Gale Gordon (Rumson Bullard), Joseph Kearns (Henry Kraus)

Summary: After Gildersleeve resurrects an old ditty from a trunk, he makes plans for the Jolly Boys to sing it before a New York publisher who happens to be in town.

Writers: Paul West, John Elliotte, Andy White

Comments: Birdie sings a bit of "The Hut-Sut Song" and Gildersleeve does the same with "Don't Tell Lulu." Gildersleeve sings his song by himself and also with the Jolly Boys. Jay Stewart takes over from John Wald as announcer. Paul West, who was also doing scripts for *Father Knows Best* at this time, joins the writing team of Elliotte and White. Marjorie may not be any older according to the show's calendar, but she no longer is in high school as she prepares for her first year in junior college. An indication of how much contests and prizes had infiltrated the media in the late 1940s is that the songwriting competition pushes all direct advertising aside until the post-tag citing of Kraft's brand of mustard. Almost certainly the funniest line delivered by a bit player in the show's history is the acerbic question asked by the caller named Jones: "Are you branding cows down at your house?"

Date: September 28, 1949
Title: Meets Kathryn Milford

Cast: Harold Peary (Gildersleeve), Jay Stewart, Mary Lee Robb (Marjorie), Walter Tetley (Leroy), Earle Ross (Hooker), Lillian Randolph (Birdie), Richard LeGrand (Peavey), Gloria Holliday (Bessie), Cathy Lewis (Kathryn Milford), Jane Morgan (Mrs. Milford)

RADIO *Life*

8¢

FORTY PAGES

Hal Peary
Great as "Gildy"
Page 4

Actors' Hang-Out: Ham 'n' Eggs with Phil Harris PAGE 36

Takes Her Vacation In Front of a Mike! PAGE 35

On the air or on magazine covers, Gildersleeve was the life of the party who always gave people their money's worth.

(none)

Summary: A wrong number and a water service call lead Gildersleeve to an attractive nurse and her kindly mother.

Writers: Paul West, John Elliotte, Andy White

Comments: Gildersleeve sings his song. Cathy Lewis appears for the first time as Kathryn Milford. At this time Cathy Lewis was appearing as Jane Stacy on *My Friend Irma* Monday evenings. Sundays Jane Morgan could be heard as Margaret Davis on *Our Miss Brooks*. Throcky, the hopeless romantic, falls in love with a pleasant voice and starts pursuing her even though he does know if she is married, hideous, or an escaped felon. Peary promotes the vinyl record of his song which, in 1949, could be ordered for a quarter and a Parkay flap and now is considered a bargain buy at $15.

Date: October 5, 1949
Title: Double Date with Marjorie
Cast: Harold Peary (Gildersleeve), Jay Stewart, Mary Lee Robb (Marjorie), Walter Tetley (Leroy), Earle Ross (Hooker), Lillian Randolph (Birdie), Richard LeGrand (Peavey), Cathy Lewis (Kathryn Milford), Richard Crenna (Bronco Thompson)
Summary: In order to keep an eye on Marjorie, Gildersleeve talks his niece into sharing the experience of a drive to Grass Lake for a dance.
Writers: Paul West, John Elliotte, Andy White
Comments: Gildersleeve sings his song. Richard Crenna should have been right at home in a jalopy for a similar rambling wreck served as his mode of transportation when playing Walter Denton on *Our Miss Brooks*. Listeners may wonder why Throckmorton is concerned about Marjorie's safety going *to* the dance unchaperoned but is content to let her return *after* the affair accompanied only by her peers in a vehicle probably every bit as idiosyncratic as Bronco's hot rod.

Date: October 12, 1949
Title: Expectant Father
Cast: Harold Peary (Gildersleeve), Jay Stewart, Mary Lee Robb (Marjorie), Walter Tetley (Leroy), Earle Ross

(Hooker), Lillian Randolph (Birdie), Richard LeGrand (Peavey), Arthur Q. Bryan (Floyd), Cathy Lewis (Kathryn Milford)
Summary: Gildersleeve, staying with a worried first-time father in the maternity ward, is joined by his pals to partake in an all-night vigil until the baby arrives.
Writers: Paul West, John Elliotte, Andy White
Comments: Gildersleeve is joined by his nephew in singing his song. Meakin inserts "Pretty Baby" and "time passing" bridges at appropriate moments. Hooker, a health food advocate ahead of his time, indulges in a celery phosphate at Peavey's soda fountain. Gildy and Peavey, who know which side their bread is Parkayed on, stick to cheese sandwiches.

Date: October 19, 1949
Title: Tomcat
Cast: Harold Peary (Gildersleeve), Jay Stewart, Mary Lee Robb (Marjorie), Walter Tetley (Leroy), Earle Ross (Hooker), Lillian Randolph (Birdie), Richard LeGrand (Peavey), Arthur Q. Bryan (Floyd), Ken Christy (Gates), Cathy Lewis (Kathryn Milford), Jane Morgan (Mrs. Milford)
Summary: After trying unsuccessfully to unload a pesky cat with various acquaintances, Gildersleeve decides to release the unwanted pet out in the country.
Writers: Paul West, John Elliotte, Andy White
Comments: The Jolly Boys sing Gildersleeve's song. Meakin keeps things moving along with some "rolling wheels" music. Peavey is conveniently not with

the Jolly Boys to set up the drugstore scene in order to lengthen a short script.

Date: October 26, 1949
Title: Intern Is Rival
   Cast: Harold Peary (Gildersleeve), Jay Stewart, Mary Lee Robb (Marjorie), Walter Tetley (Leroy), Earle Ross (Hooker), Lillian Randolph (Birdie), Richard LeGrand (Peavey), Cathy Lewis (Kathryn Milford), Richard Crenna (Bronco), Gloria Holliday (Bessie)
   Summary: Pleased after his advice to act aloof pays off with Marjorie in her relationship to Bronco, Gildersleeve finds it hard to stay away from Kathryn and ends up in cold water as a result.
   Writers: Paul West, John Elliotte, Andy White
   Comments: Gildersleeve sings his song. Meakin melodies include "Shine On Harvest Moon" and "Three Little Fishes." Kathryn now lives on Elm Street, a change from the address of 527 West Maple given on September 28th. The lily pond scene is hilarious, although the writers, perhaps uncertain how to end it, resort to cutting away to the next day, leaving listeners wondering how Gildy got to dry land without being discovered.

Date: November 2, 1949
Title: Carnival
   Cast: Harold Peary (Gildersleeve), Jay Stewart, Mary Lee Robb (Marjorie), Earle Ross (Hooker), Lillian Randolph (Birdie), Richard LeGrand (Peavey), Cathy Lewis (Kathryn Milford), Jane Morgan (Mrs. Milford), Eddie Marr (carny), Stuffy Singer (Billy)
   Summary: Throckmorton does not fare well against Clarence at the carni-

val until a lost boy helps him win the day with Kathryn.
   Writers: Paul West, John Elliotte, Andy White
   Comments: Gildersleeve sings his song. The carnival is naturally located at Kraft Park. Tetley's absence is explained as due to Leroy's being ill in bed. A comparison to Sam Spade could safely be made with *The Adventures of Sam Spade* being heard on NBC this season.

Date: November 9, 1949
Title: Marjorie's Tea Party
   Cast: Harold Peary (Gildersleeve), Jay Stewart, Mary Lee Robb (Marjorie), Walter Tetley (Leroy), Earle Ross (Hooker), Lillian Randolph (Birdie), Richard LeGrand (Peavey), Gloria Holliday (Bessie), Arthur Q. Bryan (Floyd), Cathy Lewis (Kathryn Milford)
   Summary: Deciding that Marjorie needs a maternal influence, Gildersleeve arranges for a party for his niece that is almost a disaster until Kathryn saves the day.
   Writers: Paul West, John Elliotte, Andy White
   Comments: With the song contest drawing to a close, the full commercial messages resume their usual spots. Meakin inserts some appropriate chords of "Mother." Peary delivers J.L. Kraft's inspiring message of the season.

Date: November 16, 1949
Title: Job for Bronco
   Cast: Harold Peary (Gildersleeve), Jay Stewart, Mary Lee Robb (Marjorie), Walter Tetley (Leroy), Earle Ross (Hooker), Lillian Randolph (Birdie), Richard LeGrand (Peavey), Cathy Lewis

(Kathryn Milford), Stan Farrar (Terwilliger), Richard Crenna (Bronco), Gloria Holliday (Bessie)

Summary: Throckmorton finds it hard to deliver on his promise to get Bronco a job in the water department.

Writers: Paul West, John Elliotte, Andy White

Comments: Marjorie sometimes considers her brother a regular weasel and Gildy may regard his nephew a regular wise guy, but there is no doubt that the seven prunes Leroy eats every breakfast make him regular.

Date: November 23, 1949
Title: Jolly Boys Band

Cast: Harold Peary (Gildersleeve), Jay Stewart, Mary Lee Robb (Marjorie), Walter Tetley (Leroy), Earle Ross (Hooker), Lillian Randolph (Birdie), Richard LeGrand (Peavey), Arthur Q. Bryan (Floyd), Ken Christy (Gates)

Summary: Leroy's decision to take up the trombone spurs Gildersleeve into forming a band with the members of his club.

Writers: Paul West, John Elliotte, Andy White

Comments: Gildersleeve, Floyd, and the Jolly Boys sing "Dear Hearts and Gentle People." Meakin delivers a parody of Guy Lombardo's "Old Lang Syne" and both a straight and discordant version of "Waltz of the Flowers." Gildy unfolds a hitherto unknown aspect of his past when he indicates he attended military school. Peary closes with an earnest Thanksgiving message for his listeners.

Date: November 30, 1949
Title: New Neighbor

Cast: Harold Peary (Gildersleeve), Jay Stewart, Mary Lee Robb (Marjorie), Walter Tetley (Leroy), Earle Ross (Hooker), Lillian Randolph (Birdie), Richard LeGrand (Peavey), Herb Vigran (Oliver T.P. Pearson)

Summary: Throckmorton lends a welcoming hand to a new neighbor, who turns out to be a chronic borrower.

Writers: Paul West, John Elliotte, Andy White

Allusion: Gildersleeve paraphrases a line from "Home" by Edgar A. Guest: "It takes a heap o' water to make a house a home."

Comments: Hooker sings "Hi, Neighbor." Veteran character actor Herb Vigran, who appeared on dozens of radio shows, had a regular part on *Father Knows Best* and starred in his own short-lived series *The Sad Sack* in 1946. Because both Pearson and Gildersleeve use the word *up* in reference to Sioux Center and South Dakota, it is safe to assume that Summerfield is not located in any state adjoining Canada. For all the fuss about this new character, Pearson turns out to be a one-shot pest who is not heard from again.

Date: December 7, 1949
Title: Bronco Bows Out

Cast: Harold Peary (Gildersleeve), Jay Stewart, Mary Lee Robb (Marjorie), Walter Tetley (Leroy), Earle Ross (Hooker), Lillian Randolph (Birdie), Richard LeGrand (Peavey), Richard Crenna (Bronco), Gil Stratton Jr. (Marshall Bullard)

Summary: By bringing Marshall Bullard back into Marjorie's life, Gildersleeve upsets his niece when Bronco breaks off their courtship.

Writers: Paul West, John Elliotte, Andy White

Allusion: Gildersleeve quotes from *Don Quixote* by Miguel de Cervantes: "Faint heart ne'er won fair lady."

Comments: At least in Summerfield hot news is still being relayed via telegraph, the latest flash being that the contest-winning title for Gildersleeve's song is "Tug o' My Heart."

Date: December 14, 1949
Title: Christmas Spirit
   Cast: Harold Peary (Gildersleeve), Jay Stewart, Mary Lee Robb (Marjorie), Walter Tetley (Leroy), Earle Ross (Hooker), Lillian Randolph (Birdie), Richard LeGrand (Peavey), Cathy Lewis (Kathryn Milford), Anne Whitfield (girl), Stuffy Singer (Stuffy)

Summary: Gildersleeve's drive to outspend his rival for Kathryn's present takes a U-turn when he reads a story about self-sacrifice to children at the hospital.

Writers: Paul West, John Elliotte, Andy White

Comments: Gildersleeve sings "Deck the Halls." Birdie sings "Candy Kisses." "Why the Chimes Rang" by Raymond Macdonald Alden is read with consummate skill by Peary. Anne Whitfield also was performing at this time as Phyllis on *The Phil Harris-Alice Faye Show*. There is significant irony in the *Break the Bank* promo following the reading of this poignant tale.

Date: December 21, 1949
Title: Marjorie Engaged
   Cast: Harold Peary (Gildersleeve), Jay Stewart, Mary Lee Robb (Marjorie), Walter Tetley (Leroy), Earle Ross

(Hooker), Lillian Randolph (Birdie), Richard LeGrand (Peavey), Cathy Lewis (Kathryn Milford), Richard Crenna (Bronco)

Summary: Gildersleeve plans to give a special family heirloom to Marjorie, unaware that his niece and Bronco have a surprise for him.

Writers: Paul West, John Elliotte, Andy White

Comments: The transcribed "portions of the following program" are those of the Kraft Choral Club singing "It Came Upon a Midnight Clear," "Angels We Have Heard on High," and "Joy to the World." Birdie sings "Coventry Carol." Peary convincingly conveys the mixed emotions of heartbreak and happiness Gildersleeve feels as he loses a filly and gains a Bronco.

Date: December 28, 1949
Title: New Year's Eve Hayride
   Cast: Harold Peary (Gildersleeve), Jay Stewart, Mary Lee Robb (Marjorie), Walter Tetley (Leroy), Earle Ross (Hooker), Lillian Randolph (Birdie), Richard LeGrand (Peavey), Arthur Q. Bryan (Floyd), Gale Gordon (Rumson Bullard), Cathy Lewis (Kathryn Milford)

Summary: After Throckmorton plans a hayride to end 1949, he discovers that most his acquaintances are already committed to a party being hosted by the Bullards.

Writers: Paul West, John Elliotte, Andy White

Comments: Everyone joins in on "Auld Lang Syne." Meakin plays "Jingle Bells" and "I'm Gonna Wash That Man Right Outa My Hair" at appropriate times. Leroy and Throckmorton remain kindred kids at heart, one wailing to get his way and the other bewailing his fate when things don't go his way. Frank Pittman gets another plug for providing the plug Pearl. The horse isn't the only creature wearing blinders: Gildy has to look the other way when near the mantle where the obvious invitation rests and the three males mounting the wagon have to turn their backs on the full load of passengers behind them.

Date: January 4, 1950
Title: Meets Bronco's Parents
Cast: Harold Peary (Gildersleeve), Jay Stewart, Mary Lee Robb (Marjorie), Walter Tetley (Leroy), Earle Ross (Hooker), Lillian Randolph (Birdie), Richard LeGrand (Peavey), Richard Crenna (Bronco), Joseph Kearns (Edward Thompson), Jeanette Nolan (Martha Thompson)
Summary: After writing the engagement notice for the newspaper, Gildersleeve brushes up on famous painters so he can be conversant when he meets Bronco's father, an art connoisseur.
Writers: Paul West, John Elliotte, Andy White
Allusion: Edward Thompson quotes from *The Rime of the Ancient Mariner* by Samuel Taylor Coleridge: "Water, water, everywhere."
Comments: Bronco's real first name is Walter, a natural choice for the writers to assign to radio's Walter Denton. Because Eve Goodwin is no longer on the scene and there is no need to bring them together on matters related to education, Throckmorton is now a former member of the school board.

Date: January 11, 1950
Title: Displaced Person
Cast: Harold Peary (Gildersleeve), Jay Stewart, Walter Tetley (Leroy), Earle Ross (Hooker), Lillian Randolph (Birdie), Richard LeGrand (Peavey), Arthur Q. Bryan (Floyd), Cathy Lewis (Kathryn Milford), Jerry Farber (Jean Pierre Boucher)
Summary: The Jolly Boys prepare to greet and temporarily care for a French boy.
Writers: Paul West, John Elliotte, Andy White
Comments: The Jolly Boys play "Blue Danube" and "La Marseillaise." Meakin sets the scenes with "Down by the Old Mill Stream," "K-K-K-Katy," "La Marseillaise," "Mademoiselle from Armentières," and "Yankee Doodle Dandy." The idea of welcoming a French orphan had been used for two weeks the previous summer on *The Phil Harris-Alice Faye Show* with Farber also playing the youngster on that program.

Date: January 18, 1950
Title: Dinner with Kathryn
Cast: Harold Peary (Gildersleeve), Jay Stewart, Mary Lee Robb (Marjorie), Walter Tetley (Leroy), Earle Ross (Hooker), Lillian Randolph (Birdie), Richard LeGrand (Peavey), Cathy Lewis (Kathryn Milford)
Summary: Gildersleeve convinces Birdie to play sick so he can have a romantic evening at home with Kathryn doing the cooking.
Writers: Paul West, John Elliotte, Andy White
Comments: Gildersleeve sings "Younger Than Springtime." Meakin adds "K-K-K-Katy" and "Yes, We Have

No Bananas." The mention of Dr. Andrew White is an in-joke that probably amused West and Elliotte more than Andy White. This episode paints a good portrait in stages of Kathryn: peach complexion, red hair, brown eyes, and a keen nose for detecting ruses.

Date: January 25, 1950
Title: Bronco's Parents Visit
   Cast: Harold Peary (Gildersleeve), Jay Stewart, Mary Lee Robb (Marjorie), Walter Tetley (Leroy), Earle Ross (Hooker), Lillian Randolph (Birdie), Richard Crenna (Bronco), Jeanette Nolan (Martha Thompson), Joseph Kearns (Edward Thompson)
   Summary: Gildersleeve plays host to the Thompsons for a meal and then shows them home movies.
   Writers: Paul West, John Elliotte, Andy White
   Comments: Meakin music includes newsreel music and "Home! Sweet Home!" The frequency with which the name of Hopalong Cassidy crops up in Leroy's conversation is a reflection of the popularity of William Boyd at this time. Kearns steals the show as the distracted father who appears to be asleep even when his eyes are open.

Date: February 1, 1950
Title: Samba Lessons
   Cast: Harold Peary (Gildersleeve), Jay Stewart, Mary Lee Robb (Marjorie), Walter Tetley (Leroy), Lillian Randolph (Birdie), Richard LeGrand (Peavey), Cathy Lewis (Kathryn Milford)
   Summary: Fearing that Kathryn does not want to go dancing with him because he is behind the times, Gildersleeve learns to samba.

   Writers: Paul West, John Elliotte, Andy White
   Comments: Gildersleeve sings "Goodnight, Sweetheart," "K-K-K-Katy," and "A Kiss in the Dark." Meakin gets in the South American spirit with "Brazil." Early in the first act Throckmorton succinctly states his raison d'être: "I like women." Leroy, who earlier dreaded dancing like Dracula disdained sunshine, is suddenly a junior José Greco. Peavey's 1950 pronouncement of "I'm no fuddy-duddy" rings as true as the "I'm no crook" claim made by a president 23 years later.

Date: February 8, 1950
Title: Should Marjorie Work?
   Cast: Harold Peary (Gildersleeve), Jay Stewart, Mary Lee Robb (Marjorie), Walter Tetley (Leroy), Earle Ross (Hooker), Lillian Randolph (Birdie), Richard LeGrand (Peavey), Richard Crenna (Bronco), Cathy Lewis (Kathryn Milford)
   Summary: Gildersleeve tries to smooth over the disagreement between Bronco and Marjorie regarding wives working which threatens to break up their engagement.
   Writers: Paul West, John Elliotte, Andy White
   Allusion: Gildersleeve quotes from *Hamlet* by William Shakespeare: "Sweets to the sweet."
   Comments: It is probably not accidental that the food discussed at the table is rhubarb. The tent scene is inserted to promote the 40th anniversary of the Boy Scouts as well as Peary's upcoming show to commemorate that milestone.

Date: February 15, 1950
Title: Marjorie's Wedding Date Set
  Cast: Harold Peary (Gildersleeve), Jay Stewart, Mary Lee Robb (Marjorie), Walter Tetley (Leroy), Earle Ross (Hooker), Lillian Randolph (Birdie), Richard LeGrand (Peavey), Richard Crenna (Bronco), Jeanette Nolan (Martha Thompson), Joseph Kearns (Edward Thompson)
  Summary: While Throckmorton and Mrs. Thompson bicker over where to hold the wedding, Bronco and Marjorie pursue a course of action that leads Gildy to think the young lovers have eloped.
  Writers: Paul West, John Elliotte, Andy White
  Comments: Hooker sings a bit of "Oh, Promise Me." Meakin glides into the central commercial with "The Skater's Waltz." Kearns again proves what LeGrand had been demonstrating for years, that underplaying can be just as amusing as chewing the scenery.

Date: February 22, 1950
Title: Jolly Boys Election
  Cast: Harold Peary (Gildersleeve), Jay Stewart, Mary Lee Robb (Marjorie), Walter Tetley (Leroy), Earle Ross (Hooker), Lillian Randolph (Birdie), Richard LeGrand (Peavey), Arthur Q. Bryan (Floyd), Ken Christy (Gates), Gloria Holliday (Bessie)
  Summary: Gildersleeve curries favor with the Jolly Boys in hopes of getting elected president of the group and thereby earning a trip to Chicago.
  Writers: Paul West, John Elliotte, Andy White
  Comments: Hooker sings "Silver Threads among the Gold." Peavey sings "There Is a Tavern in the Town." The Jolly Boys sing "When You Were Sweet Sixteen" and "For He's a Jolly Good Fellow." Meakin seamlessly weaves "Hail to the Chief" and "There'll Be a Hot Time in the Old Town Tonight" into and out of the action. At the end, regardless of whether Throcky chooses to go downhill on skis or travel to Chicago, it is likely to cost him an arm and a leg.

Date: March 1, 1950
Title: Marjorie's Bridal Shower
  Cast: Harold Peary (Gildersleeve), Jay Stewart, Mary Lee Robb (Marjorie), Walter Tetley (Leroy), Earle Ross (Hooker), Lillian Randolph (Birdie), Richard LeGrand (Peavey), Cathy Lewis (Kathryn Milford), Jeanette Nolan (Martha Thompson), Joseph Kearns (Edward Thompson)
  Summary: Gildersleeve and friends accompany a lively Mr. Thompson around town while Mrs. Thompson is attending a shower for Marjorie.
  Writers: Paul West, John Elliotte, Andy White
  Comments: Birdie sings "April Showers." Meakin music includes "K-K-K-Katy" and "Silver Threads among the Gold." It is no shock when Peavey reveals the card game he plays with his wife because he has been flinching from her for over 20 years. Both Stewart and Peary provide teasers for the upcoming promotion.

Date: March 8, 1950
Title: Blade Invention
  Cast: Harold Peary (Gildersleeve), Jay Stewart, Walter Tetley (Leroy), Earle Ross (Hooker), Lillian Randolph

(Birdie), Richard LeGrand (Peavey), Cathy Lewis (Kathryn Milford), Eleanor Audley (woman)

Summary: After altering a knife belonging to Mrs. Milford, Gildersleeve seeks to find a replacement, unaware that he has created a multi-faceted utensil.

Writers: Paul West, John Elliotte, Andy White

Allusion: Gildersleeve quotes from *Marmion* by Sir Walter Scott: "Oh, what a tangled web we weave, / When first we practice to deceive!"

Comments: Leroy sings "The Cry of the Wild Goose" while in retreat. Long before "product placement" became a buzz word, Kraft and the writers place the product all over the place in this broadcast. For the first time Leroy says "What a character!" about his uncle with admiration in his voice. Gildy borrows "I dooed it" from Red Skelton.

Date: March 15, 1950
Title: Considers Marrying Kathryn

  Cast: Harold Peary (Gildersleeve), John Hiestand, Mary Lee Robb (Marjorie), Walter Tetley (Leroy), Earle Ross (Hooker), Lillian Randolph (Birdie), Richard LeGrand (Peavey), Cathy Lewis (Kathryn Milford), Richard Crenna (Bronco)

  Summary: Gildersleeve is encouraged by Birdie, Bronco, and Marjorie to get married.

  Writers: Paul West, John Elliotte, Andy White

  Comments: Gildersleeve sings "K-K-K-Katy." Gildersleeve and Bronco sing "There's No Tomorrow." Meakin leads out of Gildy's snooze with "I Had a Dream, Dear." John Hiestand appears

for the first time as announcer. The original marriage date of May 1st has been changed to May 10th.

Date: March 22, 1950
Title: Picnic with the Thompsons

  Cast: Harold Peary (Gildersleeve), John Hiestand, Mary Lee Robb (Marjorie), Walter Tetley (Leroy), Earle Ross (Hooker), Lillian Randolph (Birdie), Richard LeGrand (Peavey), Richard Crenna (Bronco), Joseph Kearns (Edward Thompson), Bea Benaderet (Martha Thompson)

  Summary: Gildersleeve attempts to mend fences with Mrs. Thompson during a picnic at Grass Lake.

  Writers: Paul West, John Elliotte, Andy White

  Comments: Gildersleeve sings "When It's Springtime in the Rockies" and "Cruising Down the River." Meakin adds to the nautical theme with the "Sailor Song." Bea Benaderet returns for a one-shot appearance as Bronco's mother. It is fitting that Grass Lake is the setting for Bea's return since her first meeting with Throckmorton on the August 29, 1943, show occurred at the same location.

Date: March 29, 1950
Title: Hooker as House Guest

  Cast: Harold Peary (Gildersleeve), Jay Stewart, Mary Lee Robb (Marjorie), Walter Tetley (Leroy), Earle Ross (Hooker), Lillian Randolph (Birdie), Richard LeGrand (Peavey), Cathy Lewis (Kathryn Milford), ? (Floyd)

  Summary: In order to impress Kathryn with his generosity, Throckmorton invites Horace to stay at his home while the judge's house is being fumigated.

Writers: Paul West, John Elliotte, Andy White

Allusion: Hooker quotes from "Youth and Age" by Samuel Taylor Coleridge: "Friendship is a sheltering tree; / Oh, the joys came down shower-like."

Comments: The Jolly Boys play "The Merry Widow." Hooker tries a bit of "Blues in the Night." Meakin plays out of the first act with "Row Row Row" and adds bits of "There's a Small Hotel" to the second act. Bryan is absent so an unidentified actor (perhaps John Hiestand who acted as well as announced during his career) takes the part of Floyd. Peary thanks residents of Upper Sandusky and Palm Desert for honorary awards.

Date: April 5, 1950
Title: Apartment Upstairs
    Cast: Harold Peary (Gildersleeve), Jay Stewart, Mary Lee Robb (Marjorie), Walter Tetley (Leroy), Earle Ross (Hooker), Lillian Randolph (Birdie), Richard LeGrand (Peavey), Richard Crenna (Bronco), Gloria Holliday (Bessie), Cliff Arquette (Charlie Anderson)
    Summary: In spite of Gildersleeve's offer to make an apartment for them at home, Marjorie and Bronco are determined to search for a place of their own.
    Writers: Paul West, John Elliotte, Andy White
    Allusion: Gildersleeve paraphrases from *Don Quixote* by Miguel de Cervantes: "Faint heart ne'er won fair apartment."
    Comments: Meakin music includes "Smiles," a "rolling wheel" bridge, and "Home! Sweet Home!" Cliff Arquette,

who was being heard as various characters on *Fibber McGee and Molly* at this time, makes his first appearance on *The Great Gildersleeve* as Charlie Anderson. Birdie's philosophy regarding Bronco and Marjorie resembles the fatalistic viewpoint later put to music by Porter Wagoner: "What is to be will be, what ain't to be just might happen."

Date: April 12, 1950
Title: Leroy Buys a Goat
    Cast: Harold Peary (Gildersleeve), Jay Stewart, Walter Tetley (Leroy), Earle Ross (Hooker), Lillian Randolph (Birdie), Richard LeGrand (Peavey), Cathy Lewis (Kathryn Milford), Gloria Holliday (Bessie)
    Summary: Gildersleeve's good advice to Leroy about business and making money turns into bad practice when a goat the boy purchases becomes a nuisance.
    Writers: Paul West, John Elliotte, Andy White
    Comments: Gildersleeve sings "K-K-K-Katy" and "Drink to Me Only with Thine Eyes." Meakin music includes "Old Macdonald Had a Farm" with a derisive goat chorus. It was about eight years ago (April 26, 1942) that Gildy and Leroy last tangled with a goat. Listeners are asked to believe the goat's sleeping in the back seat stifles both its bleating and its reeking.

Date: April 19, 1950
Title: Marjorie's Wedding Gown
    Cast: Harold Peary (Gildersleeve), Jay Stewart, Mary Lee Robb (Marjorie), Walter Tetley (Leroy), Earle Ross (Hooker), Lillian Randolph (Birdie), Richard LeGrand (Peavey), Richard

Crenna (Bronco), Jeanette Nolan (Martha Thompson)

Summary: When the wedding gown belonging to Marjorie's mother cannot be found, Gildersleeve considers buying a new dress or borrowing one from a friend.

Writers: Paul West, John Elliotte, Andy White

Comments: A little of the show's prehistory is uncovered in the attic when the father's name is revealed to be Charles Forrester. Throckmorton's "I'd've Baked a Cake" statement alludes to the title of the most popular song in the country at this time. The closing PSA on behalf of the American economic system probably would have earned the Ayn Rand seal of approval.

Date: April 26, 1950
Title: Jolly Boys Rent Trailer

Cast: Harold Peary (Gildersleeve), Jay Stewart, Mary Lee Robb (Marjorie), Walter Tetley (Leroy), Earle Ross (Hooker), Lillian Randolph (Birdie), Richard LeGrand (Peavey), Richard Crenna (Bronco), ? (Floyd), Ken Christy (Gates), John McIntire (Sam Horn)

Summary: To help the newlyweds travel and economize during their honeymoon, the Jolly Boys rent a trailer as a wedding gift for Bronco and Marjorie.

Writers: Paul West, John Elliotte, Andy White

Comments: Gildersleeve sings "Singin' in the Rain." The Jolly Boys sing "By the Light of the Silvery Moon." Meakin music includes "Mean to Me," a tom-tom beat, and "Whistle While You Work." Bryan is absent from the cast again. Gildy is really going around

in circles this time, not only in his dealings with trader Horn but he also starts and ends the show in hot water.

Date: May 3, 1950
Title: Bronco Disappears

Cast: Harold Peary (Gildersleeve), Jim Doyle, Mary Lee Robb (Marjorie), Walter Tetley (Leroy), Earle Ross (Hooker), Lillian Randolph (Birdie), Richard LeGrand (Peavey), Richard Crenna (Bronco)

Summary: Marjorie suspects that Bronco is infatuated with old friend Hazel McCoy who just happens to be a bathing beauty.

Writers: Paul West, John Elliotte, Andy White

Comments: Gildersleeve sings "Oh Promise Me." Jim Doyle makes his first appearance as announcer. The reference to photographers from *Look* covering the wedding is fact on this fictitious program as the photos appeared in the May 23rd issue of that magazine. The asafetida bag Hooker possesses was worn around the neck supposedly to ward off diseases like a wreath of garlic might keep vampires at bay. The audience reaction during the sprint scene opening the second act suggests that Peary was running in place. Gildersleeve tangles with Peavey's phone booth for the seventh time. Marjorie didn't need to worry about Bronco chasing Hazel in 1950 for it would be another seven years before Richard Crenna got interested in *The Real McCoys*.

Date: May 10, 1950
Title: Marjorie's Wedding

Cast: Harold Peary (Gildersleeve),

Jay Stewart, Mary Lee Robb (Marjorie), Walter Tetley (Leroy), Earle Ross (Hooker), Lillian Randolph (Birdie), Richard LeGrand (Peavey), Richard Crenna (Bronco), Jeanette Nolan (Martha Thompson), Joseph Kearns (Edward Thompson), Arthur Q. Bryan (Floyd)

Summary: Minor mishaps disrupt the flow of last-minute preparations on the big day, but the wedding proceeds on schedule and ends with a bang.

Writers: Paul West, John Elliotte, Andy White

Comments: Bronco sings "The Girl That I Marry." Birdie Sings "I Love You Truly." Bryan returns as mischievous Floyd and immediately plays pixie. The panic over Marjorie disappearing is a rather contrived way to get uncle and niece to share a few last moments together. The credits fittingly give Mary Lee Robb and Dick Crenna featured billing.

Date: May 17, 1950
Title: Fishing at Grass Lake
  Cast: Harold Peary (Gildersleeve), Jay Stewart, Walter Tetley (Leroy), Earle Ross (Hooker), Lillian Randolph (Birdie), Richard LeGrand (Peavey), Cathy Lewis (Kathryn Milford)

Summary: Gildersleeve, at first reluctant to go angling at Grass Lake with Leroy, changes his mind when he sees it as an opportunity to interrupt a tryst between Kathryn and Clarence.

Writers: Paul West, John Elliotte, Andy White

Comments: Gildersleeve sings "K-K-K-Katy" and "Pagan Love Song." Meakin music includes "Three Little

Fishes." For once, Throckmorton is unhappy with his good luck in the boat because catching fish is not as important as hauling in his latest sweetheart.

Date: May 24, 1950
Title: Bronco the Realtor
  Cast: Harold Peary (Gildersleeve), Jay Stewart, Mary Lee Robb (Marjorie), Walter Tetley (Leroy), Earle Ross (Hooker), Lillian Randolph (Birdie), Richard LeGrand (Peavey), Gale Gordon (Rumson Bullard), Richard Crenna (Bronco), Gloria Holliday (Bessie)

Summary: Trying to help Bronco get started in real estate, Gildersleeve lists his house with the young man and is soon dismayed when someone buys it.

Writers: Paul West, John Elliotte, Andy White

Comments: Meakin music cleverly echoes the derisive laughter of Gildersleeve at the end. This episode may remind listeners of the October 1, 1944 adventure when Gildy temporarily sold his home. Gordon seems to relish the part of obnoxious Bullard, delivering evil chuckles like the caped villain in old-time melodramas and even responding to Throckmorton's "You're a harrrrd man, Bullard" with "Thank you" as if he received such a harsh assessment of his character as a glowing compliment.

Date: May 31, 1950
Title: Sadie Hawkins Dance
  Cast: Harold Peary (Gildersleeve), Jay Stewart, Mary Lee Robb (Marjorie), Walter Tetley (Leroy), Earle Ross (Hooker), Lillian Randolph (Birdie), Richard LeGrand (Peavey), Cathy Lewis

(Kathryn Milford), Gloria Holliday
(Bessie)

Summary: Gildersleeve is preoccupied with the thought of being asked to a big dance by his favorite nurse.

Writers: Paul West, John Elliotte, Andy White

Comments: Gildersleeve sings "There's a Rainbow 'Round My Shoulder" and "Room Full of Roses." Meakin opens and closes the show with "Great Day." This is one time when Gildersleeve acts as daffy as Bessie in conversations with his secretary.

Date: June 7, 1950
Title: Houseboat Purchase
Cast: Harold Peary (Gildersleeve), Jay Stewart, Mary Lee Robb (Marjorie), Walter Tetley (Leroy), Earle Ross (Hooker), Lillian Randolph (Birdie), Richard LeGrand (Peavey), Arthur Q. Bryan (Floyd), Cathy Lewis (Kathryn Milford)

Summary: Throckmorton persuades the Jolly Boys to buy a houseboat from Bronco.

Writers: Paul West, John Elliotte, Andy White

Comments: Gildersleeve sings "On Moonlight Bay," "Cruising Down the River," and "I'd Love to Live in Loveland." The Jolly Boys fail to consider how impractical a houseboat is from November to April. The reference to John L. Lewis is a nod toward the powerful head of the United Mine Workers of America.

Date: June 14, 1950
Title: Houseboat Vacation
Cast: Harold Peary (Gildersleeve), Jay Stewart, Mary Lee Robb (Marjorie),

Walter Tetley (Leroy), Earle Ross (Hooker), Lillian Randolph (Birdie), Richard LeGrand (Peavey), Arthur Q. Bryan (Floyd), Ken Christy (Gates), Cathy Lewis (Kathryn Milford), Richard Crenna (Bronco)

Summary: When Gildersleeve gets his vacation early, he makes plans to take his family on the houseboat for two weeks.

Writers: Paul West, John Elliotte, Andy White

Comments: Hooker sings "I Dream of Jeannie." Gates sings "Asleep in the Deep." The Jolly Boys sing "On Moonlight Bay." Meakin pipes Gildersleeve aboard with the "Sailor Song" and also adds "In the Good Old Summertime." Though Peary says, "We hope to see all of you again in September," this is his final appearance as Gildersleeve. On September 17 he would begin his new CBS program, _Honest Harold. The Falcon_ is the summer replacement for _The Great Gildersleeve._

Date: September 6, 1950
Title: Marjorie Expecting
Cast: Willard Waterman (Gildersleeve), John Hiestand, Mary Lee Robb (Marjorie), Walter Tetley (Leroy), Earle Ross (Hooker), Lillian Randolph (Birdie), Richard LeGrand (Peavey), Richard Crenna (Bronco), Arthur Q. Bryan (Floyd)

Summary: After Marjorie entrusts Gildersleeve with the secret of her pregnancy, the proud uncle discovers that all his friends already know of her delicate condition.

Writers: Paul West, John Elliotte, Andy White

Comments: Willard Waterman

makes his first appearance as Throckmorton P. Gildersleeve. John Hiestand is the new regular announcer. Robert Armbruster takes over as musical director. (Jack Meakin left with Peary to work on *Honest Harold*.) Introductory teasers between Leroy and Birdie are a hallmark of the new season. Waterman as Gildy truthfully twice confesses "I'm a new man." Leroy, though, is still the same immature boy, crying when he hears what he views as bad news and also wanting to run away to avoid facing a new situation.

Date: September 13, 1950
Title: Bronco's Aunt Victoria
   Cast: Willard Waterman (Gildersleeve), John Hiestand, Mary Lee Robb (Marjorie), Walter Tetley (Leroy), Earle Ross (Hooker), Lillian Randolph (Birdie), Richard LeGrand (Peavey), Mary Jane Croft (Victoria Chase), Isabel Randolph (Martha Thompson), Joseph Kearns (Edward Thompson)
   Summary: At first reluctant to meet Mrs. Thompson's sister, Throckmorton quickly pursues the lady after hearing her pleasant voice and seeing her pretty face.
   Writers: Paul West, John Elliotte, Andy White
   Comments: Gildersleeve sings "Indian Love Call." Armbruster inserts some hunting music when Throcky gets the scent of a woman. Isabel Randolph's best-known radio role was as Abigail Uppington on *Fibber McGee and Molly*. It seems odd that Peavey is open on Sunday, perhaps leading listeners to wonder if the pharmacist ever takes a day off from work. The "new for 1950" Gildersleeve slips in and out of Peavey's

phone booth with less discomfort than his predecessor. Throcky's comment, "Gildersleeve, you have a way with women" would be more accurate if worded the other way around.

Date: September 20, 1950
Title: New Secretary Hazel
   Cast: Willard Waterman (Gildersleeve), John Hiestand, Mary Lee Robb (Marjorie), Walter Tetley (Leroy), Earle Ross (Hooker), Lillian Randolph (Birdie), Richard LeGrand (Peavey), Arthur Q. Bryan (Floyd), Ken Christy (Gates), Sandra Gould (Hazel)
   Summary: Each of the Jolly Boys shower Gildersleeve with favors in hopes the commissioner will accept his choice as a replacement for Bessie.
   Writers: Paul West, John Elliotte, Andy White
   Comments: Peavey sings a bit of "There Is a Tavern in the Town." The Jolly Boys sing "When You Were Sweet Sixteen." Marrying Bessie off is a convenient way to drop that character because Gloria Holliday left to work with husband Hal Peary on *Honest Harold*. Hazel may not have been efficient, but Sandra Gould was proficient at playing daffy characters such as Miss Duffy on *Duffy's Tavern* and Bernadine, a substitute for Effie Perrine, on *The Adventures of Sam Spade* in the summer of 1948.

Date: September 27, 1950
Title: Piano Pledge
   Cast: Willard Waterman (Gildersleeve), John Hiestand, Mary Lee Robb (Marjorie), Walter Tetley (Leroy), Earle Ross (Hooker), Lillian Randolph (Birdie), Richard LeGrand (Peavey),

Even in the 1950s Leroy (Walter Tetley) had mischief in his eyes, Gildersleeve (Willard Waterman) knew things were looking up, and Marjorie (Mary Lee Robb) had sweet words on her lips.

Cathy Lewis (Kathryn Milford), Richard Crenna (Bronco)

Summary: Procrastinating Gildy finds it difficult to live up to his promise to practice the piano with Leroy.

Writers: Paul West, John Elliotte, Andy White

Allusion: Gildersleeve quotes from "Isle of Beauty" by Thomas Haynes Bayly: "Absence makes the heart grow fonder."

Comments: Gildersleeve sings "K-K-K-Katy." Armbruster music includes "The Loveliest Night of the Year" and "Come to the Fair." Filtered voices suggest a dream sequence to send Gildy off to cloud nine. The answer to Leroy's question of "Was I ever like this?" is "No, but you will be if you hang around your uncle long enough."

Date: October 4, 1950
Title: Community Chest Football Game
Cast: Willard Waterman (Gildersleeve), John Hiestand, Mary Lee Robb (Marjorie), Walter Tetley (Leroy), Earle Ross (Hooker), Lillian Randolph (Birdie), Richard LeGrand (Peavey), Arthur Q. Bryan (Floyd), Barbara Whiting (Brenda Knickerbocker)
Summary: Gildersleeve, enthused when he learns Leroy will play in an important football game, becomes depressed when the boy quits the team.
Writers: Paul West, John Elliotte, Andy White
Comments: Peavey sings "Song of the Wild Goose." Armbruster music includes "You've Got to Be a Football Hero," "Song of the Wild Goose," and "On, Wisconsin."

That uncoordinated Leroy would suddenly become starting quarterback sounds like the 1950 version of fantasy football. The theme of Leroy's unselfish act providing the climax of a story harks back to the holiday puppy episode of December 24, 1947.

Date: October 11, 1950
Title: Bullard Runs for Mayor
Cast: Willard Waterman (Gildersleeve), John Hiestand, Mary Lee Robb (Marjorie), Walter Tetley (Leroy), Earle Ross (Hooker), Lillian Randolph (Birdie), Richard LeGrand (Peavey), Gale Gordon (Rumson Bullard), Stan Farrar (Terwilliger), Bud Stefan (Alvin Beaver)

Summary: Gildersleeve is concerned about his job security when Bronco and his Junior Thinkers organization throw their support to mayoral candidate Rumson Bullard.
Writers: Paul West, John Elliotte, Andy White
Comments: Bud Stefan had played Milton Spilk on *Fibber McGee and Molly* the previous two seasons. When Gildy confesses "Water is all I know," it is really an indictment of his life because he knows very little about how water works in the waterworks.

Date: October 18, 1950
Title: Weight Reduction Plan
Cast: Willard Waterman (Gildersleeve), John Hiestand, Mary Lee Robb (Marjorie), Walter Tetley (Leroy), Earle Ross (Hooker), Lillian Randolph (Birdie), Richard LeGrand (Peavey), Richard Crenna (Bronco)
Summary: Embarrassed because he is more flabby than fit, Throckmorton tries to lose weight by eating less and exercising more.
Writers: Paul West, John Elliotte, Andy White
Comments: Armbruster selects the appropriate "Row Row Row" to accompany the rowboat scene. Hooker might be the first armchair coxswain who cannot resist barking out course corrections to a dry-docked oarsman.

Date: October 25, 1950
Title: Sons of Summerfield
Cast: Willard Waterman (Gildersleeve), John Hiestand, Mary Lee Robb (Marjorie), Walter Tetley (Leroy), Earle Ross (Hooker), Lillian Randolph (Birdie), Richard LeGrand (Peavey),

Cathy Lewis (Kathryn Milford), Gale Gordon (Rumson Bullard), Richard Crenna (Bronco), Gil Stratton Jr. (intern)

Summary: Although he feels honored after being selected to join the prestigious Sons of Summerfield, Gildersleeve is apprehensive about the severity of the club's initiation ceremony.

Writers: Paul West, John Elliotte, Andy White

Comments: The Sons sing "For He's a Jolly Good Fellow." Conversations involving Birdie to start the program are dropped in favor of the conventional opening. The Sons of Summerfield were ahead of the curve by wearing coonskin caps years before thousands of youngsters donned that same headgear to emulate their hero, Davy Crockett.

Date: November 1, 1950
Title: Election Day for Bullard
Cast: Willard Waterman (Gildersleeve), John Hiestand, Mary Lee Robb (Marjorie), Walter Tetley (Leroy), Earle Ross (Hooker), Lillian Randolph (Birdie), Richard LeGrand (Peavey), Gale Gordon (Rumson Bullard), Stan Farrar (Terwilliger), Arthur Q. Bryan (Floyd)

Summary: Gildersleeve has second thoughts about voting for Bullard when he pictures how life would be with his affluent neighbor as mayor.

Writers: Paul West, John Elliotte, Andy White

Comments: The writers include some political satire with references to pork barrels and polishing apples to go along with the timely message of encouraging listeners to go to the polls

and vote for the candidate who earns their respect, not one who buys their favor.

Date: November 8, 1950
Title: Mountain Climbing
Cast: Willard Waterman (Gildersleeve), John Hiestand, Mary Lee Robb (Marjorie), Walter Tetley (Leroy), Earle Ross (Hooker), Lillian Randolph (Birdie), Richard LeGrand (Peavey), Gale Gordon (Rumson Bullard), Arthur Q. Bryan (Floyd)

Summary: After being humiliated by Bullard in football, Throckmorton tries to interest Rumson in hiking, only to end up scaling Old Stoneface with his neighbor who is an experienced climber.

Writers: Paul West, John Elliotte, Andy White

Comments: Armbruster inserts a bit of "Go Tell It on the Mountain" at an appropriate time in the climb. Hooker mentions "ozone in my T-Zone," a reference to the popular cigarette claims that promised to deliver to the T-Zone ("T for taste, T for throat").

Date: November 15, 1950
Title: Birdie to Train Voice
Cast: Willard Waterman (Gildersleeve), John Hiestand, Mary Lee Robb (Marjorie), Walter Tetley (Leroy), Earle Ross (Hooker), Lillian Randolph (Birdie), Richard LeGrand (Peavey), Arthur Q. Bryan (Floyd), Theodore von Eltz (Mr. Hoyland)

Summary: Gildersleeve and family are pleased that Birdie has an opportunity to train for a singing career in Kansas City but saddened that they will miss her cooking and guiding hand.

Writers: Paul West, John Elliotte, Andy White

Comments: Gildersleeve and Leroy sing "In the Land of Sky Blue Waters." Birdie sings "Goin' Home." This episode reveals the story of the founding of Summerfield, named after Captain Otto K. Summer in 1850. Lillian Randolph makes the most of her chance to shine as she lives up to Gildy's assessment of Birdie: "What a fine woman." Hiestand makes a small fluff at the end, crediting "Dick Ross" instead of "Earle Ross."

Date: November 22, 1950
Title: Water Department Calendar

Cast: Willard Waterman (Gildersleeve), John Hiestand, Mary Lee Robb (Marjorie), Walter Tetley (Leroy), Lillian Randolph (Birdie), Richard LeGrand (Peavey), Richard Crenna (Bronco), Shirley Mitchell (Victoria Chase), Cathy Lewis (Kathryn Milford)

Summary: Gildersleeve finds himself in a revolting development when Vicki entices him into promising to put her photograph on a calendar after he had already given that honor to Kathryn.

Writers: Paul West, John Elliotte, Andy White

Comments: Shirley Mitchell returns as Victoria Chase, an aptly-named minx every bit as devious as Leila Ransome. When Throcky calls himself a smoothie, he could be referring to the ease with which women level him out and effortlessly walk all over him. Peavey's phone booth is now just used as a prop, not as a wooden girdle for Gildersleeve to try on for discomfort.

Date: November 29, 1950
Title: Leroy's Date with Brenda

Cast: Willard Waterman (Gildersleeve), John Hiestand, Mary Lee Robb (Marjorie), Walter Tetley (Leroy), Earle Ross (Hooker), Lillian Randolph (Birdie), Richard LeGrand (Peavey), Richard Crenna (Bronco), Gale Gordon (Rumson Bullard), Barbara Whiting (Brenda Knickerbocker)

Summary: After Bullard and Gildersleeve's petty bickering cancels a date between Brenda and Leroy, the uncles are thrown into a panic when they think the two children have run away.

Writers: Paul West, John Elliotte, Andy White

Allusions: Bronco paraphrases from *Don Quixote* by Miguel de Cervantes: "Fair Heart ne'er won fair maiden." Hooker melodically quotes from *Locksley Hall* by Alfred, Lord Tennyson: "In the spring a young man's fancy lightly turns to thoughts of love."

Comments: Leroy sings "Don't Fence Me In." Gordon probably felt at home declaring that he wouldn't marry into Gildersleeve's family "if you owned the state of Texas," having played Mr. Judson, the wealthy oilman who gave the impression on his visits with George Burns and Gracie Allen that much of the Lone Star state was his property. The use of *Union Station* is necessary to trigger the misunderstanding and the wild-goose chase, but the grim film noir is hardly the family fare that Throckmorton seems to suggest it is at the end.

Date: December 6, 1950
Title: Leroy's Laundry Business

Cast: Willard Waterman (Gildersleeve), John Hiestand, Mary Lee Robb

(Marjorie), Walter Tetley (Leroy), Earle Ross (Hooker), Lillian Randolph (Birdie), Richard LeGrand (Peavey), Arthur Q. Bryan (Floyd), Stan Farrar (Terwilliger)

Summary: Leroy forms the Million Dollar Laundry which turns into a million headaches when he does not mark the shirts he washed.

Writers: Paul West, John Elliotte, Andy White

Comments: Throckmorton is being Krafty when he tells Leroy he should sell something everybody needs "like bread or cheese." For the first time the sound of electric hair clippers is heard in the barbershop. Gildersleeve, known for asking himself how he gets involved in perplexing situations, now wonders why he is compounding his misery: "How did I ever get back *into* this?" Confusing a package containing dry bread with one holding four shirts is a very unlikely occurrence but a necessary one in order to leave hapless Gildy holding the bag.

Date: December 13, 1950
Title: Gates May Lose Job
Cast: Willard Waterman (Gildersleeve), John Hiestand, Mary Lee Robb (Marjorie), Walter Tetley (Leroy), Earle Ross (Hooker), Lillian Randolph (Birdie), Richard LeGrand (Peavey), Arthur Q. Bryan (Floyd), Ken Christy (Gates), Stan Farrar (Terwilliger), Porter Hall (Rollie Jones)

Summary: Because Chief Gates is in danger of being fired due to his failure to make any arrests, Gildersleeve and Floyd use a very small-time crook to stage a break-in at Peavey's Pharmacy so Gates can make a pinch and save his job.

Writers: Paul West, John Elliotte, Andy White

Comments: Hooker sings "Ta-Ra-Ra-Boom-De-Ay." Peavey sings "There Is a Tavern in the Town." The Jolly Boys sing "When Good Fellows Get Together." The writers again supply Gildy early with words that will come back to haunt him, in this case "Honesty's the best policy." Veteran character actor Porter Hall, who somewhat resembled Waterman, steps away from the hissable weasels he frequently played in films to take on the role of easygoing Rollie.

Date: December 20, 1950
Title: Christmas Spirit (Repeat)
Cast: Willard Waterman (Gildersleeve), John Hiestand, Mary Lee Robb (Marjorie), Walter Tetley (Leroy), Earle Ross (Hooker), Lillian Randolph (Birdie), Richard LeGrand (Peavey), Cathy Lewis (Kathryn Milford), Anne Whitfield (girl), Stuffy Singer (Stuffy)

Summary: Gildersleeve's drive to outspend his rival for Kathryn's present takes a U-turn when he reads a story about self-sacrifice to children at the hospital.

Writers: Paul West, John Elliotte, Andy White

Comments: Gildersleeve sings "Deck the Halls." Birdie sings "Candy Kisses." This is a repeat of the script used on December 14, 1949 with the addition of transcribed carols "It Came Upon a Midnight Clear," "Angels We Have Heard on High," and "Joy to the World" sung by the Kraft Choral Club.

Date: December 27, 1950
Title: Double Date with Bullard
Cast: Willard Waterman (Gilder-

sleeve), John Hiestand, Mary Lee Robb (Marjorie), Walter Tetley (Leroy), Earle Ross (Hooker), Lillian Randolph (Birdie), Shirley Mitchell (Victoria Chase), Richard LeGrand (Peavey), Cathy Lewis (Kathryn Milford), Gale Gordon (Rumson Bullard), Richard Crenna (Bronco)

Summary: Gildersleeve pretends he is attracted to Vicki during a double date with Rumson Bullard so Rumson will be jealous enough to turn his attentions away from Kathryn.

Writers: Paul West, John Elliotte, Andy White

Comments: For the purposes of plot entanglements Bullard is now a widower. When Gildersleeve mutters sweet nothings, it is all for naught because his mumbling is unintelligible. In an unusual ending, Waterman announces the credits with each actor giving his or her character name followed by the three members of Gildy's household delivering personal messages about driving safety.

Date: January 3, 1951
Title: Marjorie Craves Sauerkraut

Cast: Willard Waterman (Gildersleeve), John Hiestand, Mary Lee Robb (Marjorie), Walter Tetley (Leroy), Earle Ross (Hooker), Lillian Randolph (Birdie), Richard LeGrand (Peavey), Richard Crenna (Bronco)

Summary: After Gildersleeve advises Bronco to give in to Marjorie's whims, he finds himself traipsing quixotically around town in the middle of the night to satisfy his niece's insatiable appetite for sauerkraut.

Writers: Paul West, John Elliotte, Andy White

Comments: This is one of the best episodes during the Waterman era. Although Crenna has more to say than usual on this broadcast, it is Tetley, Ross, and LeGrand who get the funny lines. The show concludes with a heartwarming scene of Throckmorton keeping a watchful eye on his brood as they slumber.

Date: January 10, 1951
Title: Sleepy from Dating

Cast: Willard Waterman (Gildersleeve), John Hiestand, Mary Lee Robb (Marjorie), Walter Tetley (Leroy), Earle Ross (Hooker), Lillian Randolph (Birdie), Richard LeGrand (Peavey), Cathy Lewis (Kathryn Milford), Gale Gordon (Rumson Bullard)

Summary: Throckmorton, worn down after too much nightlife, finds it difficult to rest up before an important date with Kathryn.

Writers: Paul West, John Elliotte, Andy White

Comments: Gildersleeve sings "Asleep in the Deep." The first glimpse of Gildy at the office since September 20, 1950, is a brief one, not even long enough for a catnap.

Date: January 17, 1951
Title: Bronco a Worrywart

Cast: Willard Waterman (Gildersleeve), John Hiestand, Mary Lee Robb (Marjorie), Walter Tetley (Leroy), Earle Ross (Hooker), Lillian Randolph (Birdie), Richard LeGrand (Peavey), Richard Crenna (Bronco), Arthur Q. Bryan (Floyd)

Summary: To get Bronco's mind off the arrival of the baby, Gildersleeve takes the nervous young man to join the Jolly Boys for one night.

Writers: Paul West, John Elliotte, Andy White

Comments: Peavey sings his customary one line of "There Is a Tavern in the Town." The Jolly Boys sing "Down by the Old Mill Stream." The audience gets a kick out of portly Bryan as Floyd claiming that he weighed 3½ pounds at birth. Fans of *The Dick Van Dyke Show* who hear this episode will find Bronco's behavior similar to that of Rob Petrie in the famous "Where Did I Come From?" episode.

Date: January 24, 1951 (Script)
Title: Meets Katie Lee

Cast: Willard Waterman (Gildersleeve), John Hiestand, Mary Lee Robb (Marjorie), Walter Tetley (Leroy), Earle Ross (Hooker), Lillian Randolph (Birdie), Cathy Lewis (Kathryn Milford), Arthur Q. Bryan (Floyd), Porter Hall (Gus), Katie Lee

Summary: Gildersleeve becomes enraptured with a singer who is only going to be in town one night.

Writers: Paul West, John Elliotte, Andy White

Comments: Katie Lee sings "The Girl in the Wood." Gildersleeve sings "I Only Have Eyes for You." This is another episode that reveals Gildersleeve's hypocrisy, for right after criticizing Hooker for raving about a widow the judge had recently talked with in a health-food store and vowing that no man should fall head over heels for a woman he has just met, Gildy goes gaga over Katie Lee the minute she walks in Floyd's shop to get out of the rain.

Date: January 31, 1951
Title: Marjorie's Baby Shower

Cast: Willard Waterman (Gildersleeve), John Hiestand, Mary Lee Robb (Marjorie), Walter Tetley (Leroy), Earle Ross (Hooker), Lillian Randolph (Birdie), Richard LeGrand (Peavey), Cathy Lewis (Kathryn Milford), Gale Gordon (Rumson Bullard), Barbara Whiting (Brenda Knickerbocker)

Summary: Throckmorton's plan to host a shower for Marjorie dries up when everyone he knows is already invited to a similar event being held at the Bullards.

Writers: Paul West, John Elliotte, Andy White

Comments: Again, Gildy's procrastination gets him into another predicament. Leroy appears to be growing up — until a new western movie comes Hoppying into town.

Date: February 7, 1951
Title: Peavey's Day Off

Cast: Willard Waterman (Gildersleeve), John Hiestand, Mary Lee Robb (Marjorie), Walter Tetley (Leroy), Earle Ross (Hooker), Lillian Randolph (Birdie), Richard LeGrand (Peavey), Richard Crenna (Bronco), Arthur Q. Bryan (Floyd)

Summary: To commemorate Peavey's 30 years of service to Summerfield residents, Gildersleeve gives the pharmacist a day off by taking over the drugstore for one day.

Writers: Paul West, John Elliotte, Andy White

Comments: Armbruster slips in a bit of "We're in the Money" after the customers pour into the store. Tetley delivers two in-character plugs, one for NBC's *Double or Nothing* and the other for Kraft's Miracle Whip. The script celebrating Peavey's 30 years on the job was specially written in connection with the salute to LeGrand's 50 years in show business, capped off with the presentation of a scroll signed by 60,000 pharmacists to honor "America's favorite neighborhood druggist."

Date: February 14, 1951
Title: Leroy Behaves Too Well
Cast: Willard Waterman (Gildersleeve), John Hiestand, Mary Lee Robb (Marjorie), Walter Tetley (Leroy), Earle Ross (Hooker), Lillian Randolph (Birdie), Richard LeGrand (Peavey), Richard Crenna (Bronco), Arthur Q. Bryan (Floyd)
Summary: Throckmorton is concerned when Leroy the rebel is behaving without a cause like a perfect gentleman.
Writers: Paul West, John Elliotte, Andy White
Comments: Ross rolls over his blooper of "snow shoveling" very smoothly. The title of the book about raising children, *Out of the Rompers and into the Teens*, is a parody of the title of Ernest Hemingway's novel *Across the River and into the Trees*. Leroy slips in another plug, this time for *The Falcon*, also sponsored by Kraft and heard over NBC on Sunday afternoons at this time in 1951.

Date: February 21, 1951
Title: Twins Born
Cast: Willard Waterman (Gildersleeve), John Hiestand, Mary Lee Robb (Marjorie), Walter Tetley (Leroy), Earle Ross (Hooker), Lillian Randolph (Birdie), Richard LeGrand (Peavey), Cathy Lewis (Kathryn Milford), Richard Crenna (Bronco)
Summary: Gildersleeve battles a defective tire on the day Marjorie goes to the hospital to become a mother of twins.
Writers: Paul West, John Elliotte, Andy White
Comments: Birdie and Leroy sing "Rock-a-Bye Baby." Peavey addresses his wife on the phone as "Mrs. Peavey." That Peavey uses the pay phone to make a call makes one wonder if he takes orders and prescription requests in the booth. Like the unravished bride of quietness who must not be seen until the moment before a wedding, the new mother is kept in the wings by the writers until she and the proud papa can have some precious moments together.

Date: February 28, 1951
Title: Searching for Baby Names
Cast: Willard Waterman (Gildersleeve), John Hiestand, Mary Lee Robb (Marjorie), Walter Tetley (Leroy), Earle Ross (Hooker), Lillian Randolph (Birdie), Richard LeGrand (Peavey), Richard Crenna (Bronco), Isabel Randolph (Martha Thompson), Herb Butterfield (Edward Thompson)
Summary: Gildersleeve and Mrs. Thompson sharply disagree on naming rights for the twins.
Writers: Paul West, John Elliotte, Andy White
Comments: Hooker sings "Oh, What a Beautiful Morning." Isabel Randolph plays Martha Thompson with less hoity than she did Abigail Uppington on *Fibber McGee and Molly* but with still a considerable amount of toity. Herb Butterfield tries earnestly, but he was more effective portraying authority figures than eccentrics like

Mr. Thompson. Peavey reveals that his middle name is *Quincy*. Any burglar attempting to crack Hooker's unsafe safe would find its contents not worth a fig.

Date: March 7, 1951
Title: Twins Come Home
  Cast: Willard Waterman (Gildersleeve), John Hiestand, Mary Lee Robb (Marjorie), Walter Tetley (Leroy), Earle Ross (Hooker), Lillian Randolph (Birdie), Richard LeGrand (Peavey), Richard Crenna (Bronco)
  Summary: Throckmorton and Leroy feel left out on the day the babies are brought home from the hospital.
  Writers: Paul West, John Elliotte, Andy White
  Comments: The audience is in a clap happy mood, applauding the exit lines of Ross, Tetley, and LeGrand. Just as the babies have taken over the household, so the contest to give them names takes over the commercial time.

Date: March 14, 1951
Title: Jolly Boys or Singer?
  Cast: Willard Waterman (Gildersleeve), John Hiestand, Mary Lee Robb (Marjorie), Walter Tetley (Leroy), Earle Ross (Hooker), Lillian Randolph (Birdie), Richard LeGrand (Peavey), Arthur Q. Bryan (Floyd), Richard Crenna (Bronco), Katie Lee
  Summary: Throckmorton regretfully cancels a Jolly Boys meeting so he can meet a songstress arriving by train for a short visit.
  Writers: Paul West, John Elliotte, Andy White
  Comments: Peavey sings a bit of his favorite song "There Is a Tavern in the Town." Katie Lee sings "I Know My

Love" and "The Girl in the Wood." Katie records in her book *Sandstone Seduction* how her friendship with Andy White got her written into the show. She indicates there were many letters requesting more appearances, but that Waterman did not want to share the limelight with someone who might prove more popular than the star of the program. In any case, her abrupt departure at the end of this episode could be described as "[sing a] hit and run."

Date: March 21, 1951
Title: Bronco in Charge
  Cast: Willard Waterman (Gildersleeve), John Hiestand, Mary Lee Robb (Marjorie), Walter Tetley (Leroy), Earle Ross (Hooker), Lillian Randolph (Birdie), Richard LeGrand (Peavey), Arthur Q. Bryan (Floyd), Richard Crenna (Bronco), Lee Keel (babies)
  Summary: Acting upon a suggestion from Floyd, Gildersleeve lets Bronco run the household for a week.
  Writers: Paul West, John Elliotte, Andy White
  Comments: Gildy's opinion of Bronco flutters like a weathervane in a high wind, changing in the tag in a matter of seconds. Lee Keel provides the crying and cooing in this series of episodes centering on the twins.

Date: March 28, 1951
Title: Babysitting the Twins
  Cast: Willard Waterman (Gildersleeve), John Hiestand, Mary Lee Robb (Marjorie), Walter Tetley (Leroy), Earle Ross (Hooker), Lillian Randolph (Birdie), Richard LeGrand (Peavey)
  Summary: Leroy and Gildersleeve have their hands full when they mind

the babies while Bronco and Marjorie go to a movie.

Writers: Paul West, John Elliotte, Andy White

Comments: Gildersleeve sings a bit of "It Might as Well Be Spring." Birdie sings a slumber lullaby. Hiestand barely hesitates after his fluff of "nest announcement." Leroy takes the concept of playing with the babies literally when he suggests "Let's toss them around." W.G. Paul of the Invest in America Movement honors Waterman for his efforts to promote the role of the individual in "building America at the community level."

Date: April 4, 1951
Title: Bullard's Boat Access
Cast: Willard Waterman (Gildersleeve), John Hiestand, Mary Lee Robb (Marjorie), Walter Tetley (Leroy), Earle Ross (Hooker), Lillian Randolph (Birdie), Richard LeGrand (Peavey), Arthur Q. Bryan (Floyd), Gale Gordon (Rumson Bullard), Bill Thompson (Sir Jasper Balup)
Summary: Bullard treats Gildersleeve kindly only because he needs the water commissioner's permission to launch his boat.
Writers: Paul West, John Elliotte, Andy White
Comments: Bill Thompson, who occasionally played fumfering Britishers like Sir Jasper on *Fibber McGee and Molly*, was better known on that program for giving voice to Wallace Wimple and the Old Timer. Gildy's closing comment of "Snookered again" is fitting because all through the episode he and his neighbor have been playing a game of artifice and blackmail.

Date: April 11, 1951
Title: New Parents May Leave
Cast: Willard Waterman (Gildersleeve), John Hiestand, Mary Lee Robb (Marjorie), Walter Tetley (Leroy), Earle Ross (Hooker), Lillian Randolph (Birdie), Richard LeGrand (Peavey), Arthur Q. Bryan (Floyd), Richard Crenna (Bronco), Lee Keel (babies)
Summary: Throckmorton pretends he has an active lifestyle so Bronco and Marjorie will not think he is lonely.
Writers: Paul West, John Elliotte, Andy White
Comments: Birdie sings a bit of "The St. Louis Blues." Hooker sings the melody to "The Skater's Waltz." It is indicative of Leroy's immaturity that he cries when he complains that "I was just getting used to the twins crying." Gildy makes the remark "It's hard for me to be two-faced," a line loaded with significance because playing Janus is one of his more prominent characteristics.

Date: April 18, 1951
Title: Leroy's Date with Marcelle
Cast: Willard Waterman (Gildersleeve), John Hiestand, Mary Lee Robb (Marjorie), Walter Tetley (Leroy), Earle Ross (Hooker), Lillian Randolph (Birdie), Richard LeGrand (Peavey), Richard Crenna (Bronco), Arthur Q. Bryan (Floyd), Ken Christy (Gates), Lois Kennison (Marcelle Tremaine)
Summary: Gildersleeve is almost convinced his nephew is growing up after Leroy announces he is going to a school party with a new girl he met.
Writers: Paul West, John Elliotte, Andy White
Comments: The snapshots of Leroy

as a two-year-old that Throckmorton recalls fondly were taken a decade before Gildy moved to Summerfield. Christy is heard for the first time since the December 13, 1950, show. When Gildersleeve tells Birdie "It just doesn't seem possible that Leroy is 12 years old," he could easily have added "still" because the boy has been locked at that age for a decade. Tetley is very credible as the nervous hobbledehoy, especially considering he was an adult of 35 at the time. Again, the similarity between uncle and nephew is apparent in Leroy's relief at not having to consummate the date just as Gildersleeve is overjoyed when he bails out of marital commitments to women.

Date: April 25, 1951
Title: Leroy's Pony
   Cast: Willard Waterman (Gildersleeve), John Hiestand, Mary Lee Robb (Marjorie), Walter Tetley (Leroy), Earle Ross (Hooker), Lillian Randolph (Birdie), Richard LeGrand (Peavey), Ken Christy (Gates), Gale Gordon (Rumson Bullard), Jeffrey Silver (Jimmy)
   Summary: Leroy's efforts to keep new pony Butch are stymied by Butch's wandering ways and Summerfield's ordinance against such animals.
   Writers: Paul West, John Elliotte, Andy White
   Comments: The rapid clip-clopping makes little Butch sound like Diablo carrying the Cisco Kid in hot pursuit of scofflaws. The solution to this horse opera is like that presented five years earlier on April 28, 1946, when Leroy had a similar yen to hit the saddle.

Date: May 2, 1951
Title: Cleaning Hooker's House
   Cast: Willard Waterman (Gildersleeve), John Hiestand, Mary Lee Robb (Marjorie), Walter Tetley (Leroy), Earle Ross (Hooker), Lillian Randolph (Birdie), Richard LeGrand (Peavey), Arthur Q. Bryan (Floyd), Ken Christy (Gates)
   Summary: Gildersleeve's inability to restrain his pride over convincing his pals to spruce up the judge's home forces him into recruiting Leroy and Birdie to help finish the job.
   Writers: Paul West, John Elliotte, Andy White
   Comments: Armbruster sets the tone with Mendelssohn's "Spring Song." Peavey chimes in with his favorite "There Is a Tavern in the Town," but the Jolly Boys prefer "When Good Fellows Get Together" and "By the Light of the Silvery Moon." LeGrand muffs "good deeds" by saying "good dudes." Waterman offers a timely PSA on behalf of the Civil Defense program.

Date: May 9, 1951
Title: First Wedding Anniversary
   Cast: Willard Waterman (Gildersleeve), John Hiestand, Mary Lee Robb (Marjorie), Walter Tetley (Leroy), Earle Ross (Hooker), Lillian Randolph (Birdie), Richard LeGrand (Peavey), Richard Crenna (Bronco), Lee Keel (babies), Joe Forte (Foley)
   Summary: Gildersleeve arranges for a big celebration to commemorate Marjorie and Bronco's first anniversary, much to the displeasure of the young couple who prefer a private observance of the occasion.

Writers: Paul West, John Elliotte, Andy White

Comments: Once again, Gildersleeve's time spent on the job is very brief as the writers employ the convenient excuse of having the water commissioner dismiss his secretary before the action begins to eliminate any need for an office scene with dialogue. This is only the third time he has even been seen in city hall this season. The idea of the couple eloping on their first anniversary may show them to be romantic lovers, but leaving the babies on their own without telling anyone of their plan does not earn them high marks as attentive parents.

Date: May 16, 1951
Title: Bullard's Boat Date

Cast: Willard Waterman (Gildersleeve), John Hiestand, Mary Lee Robb (Marjorie), Walter Tetley (Leroy), Earle Ross (Hooker), Lillian Randolph (Birdie), Richard LeGrand (Peavey), Cathy Lewis (Kathryn Milford), Gale Gordon (Rumson Bullard), Arthur Q. Bryan (Floyd)

Summary: Hoping to interrupt a boating date between Kathryn and Rumson, Throckmorton convinces Floyd to take a canoe out on Grass Lake.

Writers: Paul West, John Elliotte, Andy White

Comments: Gildersleeve sings "K-K-K-Katy." Throckmorton displays such a lack of courtesy in his prying pursuit of personal information and acts so deceitfully in his scheming to break up the date that, at least on this occasion, he accomplishes what most listeners must have considered impossible: he is more obnoxious than Bullard.

Date: May 23, 1951
Title: Bronco's Mother Visits

Cast: Willard Waterman (Gildersleeve), John Hiestand, Mary Lee Robb (Marjorie), Walter Tetley (Leroy), Earle Ross (Hooker), Lillian Randolph (Birdie), Richard LeGrand (Peavey), Richard Crenna (Bronco), Jeanette Nolan (Martha Thompson), Joe Forte (Edward Thompson), Lee Keel (babies)

Summary: Members of the Gildersleeve household suffer trying times when Mrs. Thompson imposes her will upon them during a prolonged stay.

Writers: Paul West, John Elliotte, Andy White

Comments: Gildersleeve, Leroy, and Bronco sing "The Camels Are Coming." Hooker and Armbruster whet their whistles on "The Whistler and His Dog." Based on the fruit mentioned in both acts, the whole family might be singing "Every morning, every evening, ain't we got prunes?" Both Kraft and Parkay get incidental plugs in the dialogue. Leroy obviously prefers *The Bat Woman* in the theater to the battleax in the house. The prize-winning names given to the twins are Ronald Lynn and Rhonda Linda.

Date: May 30, 1951
Title: Family Vacation Stalls

Cast: Willard Waterman (Gildersleeve), John Hiestand, Mary Lee Robb (Marjorie), Walter Tetley (Leroy), Earle Ross (Hooker), Lillian Randolph (Birdie), Richard LeGrand (Peavey), Richard Crenna (Bronco), Lee Keel (babies)

Summary: After seeing Birdie off on a train, Gildersleeve and his brood find it very difficult to get their vacation to Half Moon Lake started when there seems to be insufficient room in the car for humans and luggage.

Writers: Paul West, John Elliotte, Andy White

Comments: The whole family sings "Sailing, Sailing." The cigar excuse is one of the most contrived in the series, as if buying and puffing on a stogie purchased at the drugstore is going to resolve the pressing issue of getting on the road. *The Falcon* is the summer replacement series for *The Great Gildersleeve*.

Date: September 5, 1951
Title: Leroy's Old Car

    Cast: Willard Waterman (Gildersleeve), John Hiestand, Mary Lee Robb (Marjorie), Walter Tetley (Leroy), Earle Ross (Hooker), Lillian Randolph (Birdie), Richard LeGrand (Peavey), Ken Christy (Gates)

    Summary: After rashly promising to teach Leroy to drive at such a time when the boy buys his own car, Gildersleeve is on the spot when his nephew rolls a relic he purchased for $5.00 into the driveway.

    Writers: Paul West, John Elliotte, Andy White

    Comments: How a pre-teen could get a driver's permit is about as great a mystery as why Throckmorton does not tell his nephew that a boy who still cries at the least provocation is not mature enough to operate an automobile. Birdie interacts with the announcer in the main commercial as she did in the 1948-1949 season, this time employing

her "triple repeat and belly laugh" routine.

Date: September 12, 1951
Title: Friendly to Bullard

    Cast: Willard Waterman (Gildersleeve), John Hiestand, Mary Lee Robb (Marjorie), Walter Tetley (Leroy), Lillian Randolph (Birdie), Richard LeGrand (Peavey), Cathy Lewis (Kathryn Milford), Gale Gordon (Rumson Bullard)

    Summary: To teach Leroy how to get along with a boy he has been fighting with, Gildersleeve behaves friendly toward Rumson Bullard.

    Writers: John Elliotte, Andy White

    Comments: Gildersleeve sings "Come to the Fair." Paul West now moves more into the background, serving as editor of the scripts Elliotte and White create. The women assess nephew and uncle perceptively, Marjorie asking her brother "Why don't you grow up?" and Kathryn telling Gildy "You're just like a little boy."

Date: September 19, 1951
Title: Meets Paula Winthrop

    Cast: Willard Waterman (Gildersleeve), John Hiestand, Mary Lee Robb (Marjorie), Walter Tetley (Leroy), Earle Ross (Hooker), Lillian Randolph (Birdie), Richard LeGrand (Peavey), Gale Gordon (Rumson Bullard), Jeanne Bates (Paula Winthrop)

    Summary: Throckmorton likes what he sees of Rumson Bullard's sister but is put off somewhat by what he hears from the brusque lady.

    Writers: John Elliotte, Andy White

    Comments: The "partially transcribed" portions are the bridges as the music becomes more canned and less tailored to specific plot developments. Jack Meakin is credited for the musical compositions. Gordon unleashes "Well, bully for you!" and "Oh, no!" in his Osgood Conklin tone of indignation. Rumson would almost certainly earn his sister's disapproval if she knew he was revealing her age and weight to people who show up at his front door.

Date: September 26, 1951
Title: Marjorie as Secretary
  Cast: Willard Waterman (Gildersleeve), John Hiestand, Mary Lee Robb (Marjorie), Walter Tetley (Leroy), Earle Ross (Hooker), Lillian Randolph (Birdie), Richard LeGrand (Peavey), Richard Crenna (Bronco), Stan Farrar (Terwilliger), Lee Keel (babies)
  Summary: Gildersleeve's plan to cure Marjorie of her desire to work by giving her a heavy load of work as his temporary secretary misfires when she proves to be very efficient.
  Writers: John Elliotte, Andy White
  Comments: The writers twice employ the surefire device of having Leroy come in late on conversations and ask questions for which he gets no answers. This is the first extended scene of Gildersleeve on the job since Waterman assumed the role in September of 1950. It is hard to picture Peavey as a cheerleader during his college years for it seems that whatever cheer was suggested by others he would have countered with "Well, now, I wouldn't shout that."

Date: October 3, 1951
Title: Jolly Boys Speak Candidly
  Cast: Willard Waterman (Gildersleeve), John Hiestand, Mary Lee Robb (Marjorie), Walter Tetley (Leroy), Earle Ross (Hooker), Lillian Randolph (Birdie), Richard LeGrand (Peavey), Arthur Q. Bryan (Floyd), Ken Christy (Gates), Richard Crenna (Bronco)
  Summary: Hard feelings result after Throckmorton encourages the Jolly Boys to openly express their opinions of each other.
  Writers: John Elliotte, Andy White
  Comments: Peavey sings "There Is a Tavern in the Town." The Jolly Boys sing "By the Light of the Silvery Moon" and "For He's a Jolly Good Fellow." Gildy accusing Floyd of acting juvenile is a clear case of the pot calling the kettle black.

Date: October 10, 1951
Title: Leroy Stays with Hooker
  Cast: Willard Waterman (Gildersleeve), John Hiestand, Mary Lee Robb (Marjorie), Walter Tetley (Leroy), Earle Ross (Hooker), Lillian Randolph (Birdie), Richard LeGrand (Peavey)
  Summary: Gildersleeve is dismayed when Leroy seems to be truly enjoying himself during a prolonged stay at Judge Hooker's home.
  Writers: John Elliotte, Andy White
  Comments: Hooker and Leroy separately sing "My Darling Nellie Gray." Leroy is canny enough to know when to turn the volume up to get his way. The twins must be sound sleepers if they can slumber through Leroy's imitation of Gene Krupa on the drum kit.

Date: October 17, 1951
Title: Anniversary of First Date
  Cast: Willard Waterman (Gildersleeve), John Hiestand, Mary Lee Robb

(Marjorie), Walter Tetley (Leroy), Earle Ross (Hooker), Lillian Randolph (Birdie), Richard LeGrand (Peavey), Richard Crenna (Bronco), Lee Keel (babies)

Summary: Because Marjorie fears her husband has forgotten the day they first dated, Gildersleeve tries to head off a domestic squabble by reminding Bronco so the young man can buy her a suitable gift.

Writers: John Elliotte, Andy White

Comments: Hooker works a message about the Community Chest into the early dialogue. For all of Gildy's bragging about being a cagey operator and possessing both poise and good sense, he acts like a child who has not learned that days of the week do not fall on the same numerical date every month.

Date: October 24, 1951

Title: Babs Frustrates Romance

Cast: Willard Waterman (Gildersleeve), John Hiestand, Mary Lee Robb (Marjorie), Walter Tetley (Leroy), Earle Ross (Hooker), Lillian Randolph (Birdie), Richard LeGrand (Peavey), Barbara Whiting (Babs Winthrop), Elsie Holmes (Paula Winthrop)

Summary: Paula's mischievous daughter makes it difficult for her mother to be alone with Throckmorton.

Writers: John Elliotte, Andy White

Comments: Some of Gildersleeve's braggadocio rubs off on Peavey who vocalizes pride in his shrewdness. Why Gildy simply doesn't go home and change his wet suit for a dry one is not explained. The writers make certain Gildersleeve specifies that Babs is asleep

in one corner of the back seat and Leroy in the other lest any listener picture the pair "sleeping together."

Date: October 31, 1951

Title: Lost Boy on Halloween

Cast: Willard Waterman (Gildersleeve), John Hiestand, Mary Lee Robb (Marjorie), Walter Tetley (Leroy), Earle Ross (Hooker), Lillian Randolph (Birdie), Richard LeGrand (Peavey), Arthur Q. Bryan (Floyd), Tommy Readick (Mike Smith)

Summary: Plans for Gildersleeve's date with Paula and also a party sponsored by the Jolly Boys are shuttled when Throckmorton and his friends try to help a lost boy get back home.

Writers: John Elliotte, Andy White

Comments: This is one episode in which Peavey lives up to his name, becoming so peeved with Gildy that he emits his version of the Bronx cheer and drops the contraction in his standard response by enunciating clearly "Well, now, I would *not* say that." Waterman really puts an electrified tone in his "Leeeroy!" exclamations when reacting to the boy's low-voltage prank. This episode, designed to show Throckmorton's innate humanity, is reminiscent of the November 2, 1949, broadcast when he came to the aid of a lost boy at a carnival.

Date: November 7, 1951

Title: Couple Buying a Lot

Cast: Willard Waterman (Gildersleeve), John Hiestand, Mary Lee Robb (Marjorie), Walter Tetley (Leroy), Earle Ross (Hooker), Lillian Randolph (Birdie), Richard LeGrand (Peavey), Richard Crenna (Bronco), Jeanette

Nolan (Martha Thompson), Joseph Kearns (Edward Thompson)

Summary: Gildersleeve, after trying to get Marjorie and Bronco to purchase a lot nearby, is upset when he learns that Mrs. Thompson is urging the couple to build a house near her home.

Writers: John Elliotte, Andy White

Comments: It is surprising that realtor Bronco needs assistance in locating property information. The return of Joseph Kearns as Edward Thompson increases the potential for merriment on the program considerably.

Date: November 14, 1951
Title: Oak Tree Problem
Cast: Willard Waterman (Gildersleeve), John Hiestand, Mary Lee Robb (Marjorie), Walter Tetley (Leroy), Earle Ross (Hooker), Lillian Randolph (Birdie), Richard LeGrand (Peavey), Richard Crenna (Bronco), Gale Gordon (Rumson Bullard)

Summary: Throckmorton is in a fix when he accepts money from Bullard to cut down a tree on Bronco and Marjorie's lot and then learns the couple wants the venerable oak to remain on their property.

Writers: John Elliotte, Andy White

Allusion: Bronco quotes and sings from "Trees" by Joyce Kilmer: "The tree that may in summer wear / A nest of robins in her hair."

Comments: Waterman is starting to employ the "Zeek!" neologism that Peary sometimes used as his "Oops!" expression. When Gildy says, "Actually, I'm making more of a problem of this than it really is," he is uttering a statement that could be inserted in practically every episode in the series. The image of Throcky racing for home with an ax-wielding Bullard in hot pursuit is sure to cause more chuckles than shudders at the conclusion of this misadventure.

Date: November 21, 1951
Title: Inviting Guests for Thanksgiving
Cast: Willard Waterman (Gildersleeve), John Hiestand, Mary Lee Robb (Marjorie), Walter Tetley (Leroy), Earle Ross (Hooker), Lillian Randolph (Birdie), Richard LeGrand (Peavey), Gale Gordon (Rumson Bullard), Tommy Readick (Mike Smith)

Summary: With plenty of food and few people to enjoy it, Gildersleeve invites Mike Smith and Rumson Bullard to join him and Leroy for Thanksgiving dinner.

Writers: John Elliotte, Andy White

Comments: This touching episode demonstrates that even grouches like Bullard have a heart. Waterman's closing remarks about attending church with a friend also applies to this broadcast because anybody who has heard it is richer for the experience.

Date: November 28, 1951
Title: Leroy Studies with Babs
Cast: Willard Waterman (Gildersleeve), John Hiestand, Mary Lee Robb (Marjorie), Walter Tetley (Leroy), Earle Ross (Hooker), Lillian Randolph (Birdie), Richard LeGrand (Peavey), Barbara Whiting (Babs Winthrop), Gil Stratton Jr. (Tiger Davis)

Summary: Leroy, at first reluctant to follow his uncle's suggestion to study with Babs, warms up to the idea when he sees it as a mark of maturity.

Writers: John Elliotte, Andy White

Comments: When Babs mentions "ninth grade stuff," she seems to suggest that Leroy is now a freshman, a supposition supported by the fact that the two youngsters are studying algebra at the end. Stratton's delivery of "toast *marshmallows?*" and "the *piano?*" cannot be bettered for sheer adolescent skepticism.

Date: December 5, 1951

There is no extant recording of this episode. Scripts from September 5, 1951, through December 26, 1951, are absent from the microfilm reel at the Wisconsin State Historical Society.

Date: December 12, 1951

Title: Leroy Sells Trees

Cast: Willard Waterman (Gildersleeve), John Hiestand, Mary Lee Robb (Marjorie), Walter Tetley (Leroy), Earle Ross (Hooker), Lillian Randolph (Birdie), Richard LeGrand (Peavey), Arthur Q. Bryan (Floyd), Ken Christy (Gates), Barbara Whiting (Babs Winthrop)

Summary: Leroy's gross of Christmas trees sell poorly until the Jolly Boys come up with ideas to increase traffic flow in the neighborhood.

Writers: John Elliotte, Andy White

Comments: The Jolly Boys sing "Down by the Old Mill Stream" and "Deck the Halls." Birdie sings "Jingle Bells" and "O Christmas Tree." Marjorie sees through the bait Babs dangles in front of Gildersleeve better than her uncle when she offers a sotto voce comment worthy of Leroy: "What a little operator." This episode ends rather abruptly, leaving the audience wondering if Leroy disposes of his small forest of evergreens.

Date: December 19, 1951

Title: Christmas Spirit (Second Repeat)

Cast: Willard Waterman (Gildersleeve), John Hiestand, Mary Lee Robb (Marjorie), Walter Tetley (Leroy), Earle Ross (Hooker), Lillian Randolph (Birdie), Richard LeGrand (Peavey), Elsie Holmes (Paula Winthrop), Tommy Readick (Tommy)

Summary: Gildersleeve's drive to outspend his rival takes a U-turn when he reads a story to children at the children's home.

Writers: John Elliotte, Andy White

Comments: The Kraft Choral Club sings "It Came Upon a Midnight Clear," "Angels We Have Heard on High," and "Joy to the World." The writers adapt the scripts used on December 14, 1949, and December 20, 1950, with the principal changes being moving the object of Gildy's affection from Kathryn to Paula and the setting from the hospital to the children's home.

Date: December 26, 1951

Title: Expensive Christmas Presents

Cast: Willard Waterman (Gildersleeve), John Hiestand, Mary Lee Robb (Marjorie), Walter Tetley (Leroy), Earle Ross (Hooker), Lillian Randolph (Birdie), Richard LeGrand (Peavey), Richard Crenna (Bronco), Gale Gordon (Rumson Bullard), Barbara Whiting (Babs Winthrop)

Summary: Rumson and Throckmorton, upset that Babs and Leroy have purchased costly gifts for each other, demand that the children return them and get their money back.

Writers: John Elliotte, Andy White

Comments: While it may be true that Marjorie "never had a set of pearls like this," she was given a fine set of pearls by Hooker on April 7, 1946, the same evening the judge presented Leroy with a gold watch made by Tiffany. Like the end-of-year show in 1950, Waterman identifies the actors who then give the name of his or her character.

Date: January 2, 1952

Title: Seeks New Job

Cast: Willard Waterman (Gildersleeve), John Hiestand, Mary Lee Robb (Marjorie), Walter Tetley (Leroy), Earle Ross (Hooker), Lillian Randolph (Birdie), Richard LeGrand (Peavey), Richard Crenna (Bronco), Stan Farrar (Terwilliger), Joe Forte (Johnson)

Summary: Spurred by Bronco's new position and higher salary, Gildersleeve applies for a new job and writes a vitriolic letter of resignation addressed to the mayor.

Writers: John Elliotte, Andy White

Comments: Peavey sings "Pennies from Heaven." Hooker sings "Smiles." The previous week Bronco addressed his father-in-law as "Uncle Mort" instead of "Mr. Gildersleeve," and this week the writers have him use the nickname "Mort" to indicate the shift in power in the family. It is not long after Gildy says "I'm no fool" that he foolishly vents his feelings in an ill-advised letter.

Date: January 9, 1952

Title: Mysterious Disappearance

Cast: Willard Waterman (Gildersleeve), John Hiestand, Mary Lee Robb (Marjorie), Walter Tetley (Leroy), Earle Ross (Hooker), Lillian Randolph (Birdie), Richard LeGrand (Peavey), Arthur Q. Bryan (Floyd), Richard Crenna (Bronco)

Summary: Gildersleeve's family and friends are concerned when he does not come home, his whereabouts known only by Bronco, who has been sworn to secrecy.

Writers: John Elliotte, Andy White

Comments: The Jolly Boys sing "When You Were Sweet Sixteen" and "My Buddy." Waterman prerecorded his small part before the appendectomy. Bryan, who had a pleasing if not outstanding singing voice, purposely strikes some strident chords to amplify the fact that the Jolly Boys miss Gildy and Gates.

Date: January 16, 1952

Title: Malingers after Surgery

Cast: Willard Waterman (Gildersleeve), John Hiestand, Mary Lee Robb (Marjorie), Walter Tetley (Leroy), Earle Ross (Hooker), Lillian Randolph (Birdie), Richard LeGrand (Peavey), Jeanne Bates (Paula Winthrop), Barbara Whiting (Babs Winthrop)

Summary: Finding few people who want to hear the description of his operation, Gildersleeve feigns weakness and goes to bed in hopes that Paula will offer him comfort and listen to his tale of woe.

Writers: John Elliotte, Andy White

Comments: Gildy sets up the bedroom scene like the wolf he is, hoping to pounce on his own Red Riding Hood. The judge's concluding admonition to "stay here and take your medicine" has a double meaning. The worst dose of that medicine might be the "heavy gloom" setting in when Peavey reads from *Gladys Tubbs, Girl Cheerleader.*

Date: January 23, 1952
Title: Getting Paula Alone
  Cast: Willard Waterman (Gildersleeve), John Hiestand, Mary Lee Robb (Marjorie), Walter Tetley (Leroy), Earle Ross (Hooker), Lillian Randolph (Birdie), Richard LeGrand (Peavey), Jeanne Bates (Paula Winthrop), Barbara Whiting (Babs Winthrop)
  Summary: Babs, who has been continually interfering in Gildersleeve's courtship of her mother, suddenly encourages the relationship after Leroy offers her an irresistible challenge.
  Writers: John Elliotte, Andy White
  Comments: Peavey sings "I Never See Maggie Alone." Barbara grabs the big laugh of the night with her "big moose" line. The use of filtered voices effectively conveys the mental doubts of the reluctant romantics.

Date: January 30, 1952
Title: Meets Mona Buckley
  Cast: Willard Waterman (Gildersleeve), John Hiestand, Mary Lee Robb (Marjorie), Walter Tetley (Leroy), Earle Ross (Hooker), Lillian Randolph (Birdie), Richard LeGrand (Peavey), Arthur Q. Bryan (Floyd), Sarah Selby (Mona Buckley)
  Summary: Deciding that Mona Buckley is a gold digger who covets Hooker's home and money, Gildersleeve tries to capture her attention so her fickle behavior will be evident to everyone.
  Writers: John Elliotte, Andy White
  Comments: Gildy rides a baseless

assumption down an ill-chosen primrose path.

Date: February 6, 1952
Title: Lovey Munson Hired
  Cast: Willard Waterman (Gildersleeve), John Hiestand, Mary Lee Robb (Marjorie), Walter Tetley (Leroy), Lillian Randolph (Birdie), Richard LeGrand (Peavey), Arthur Q. Bryan (Floyd), Gail Bonney (Lovey Munson)
  Summary: Throckmorton regrets giving Floyd's wife a job in the office because of her incessant gabbing and presumptuous familiarity.
  Writers: John Elliotte, Andy White
  Comments: Gildy jokingly mutters under his breath that his middle initial stands for Pigeon. On the October 22, 1940, broadcast of *Fibber McGee and Molly* Gildersleeve revealed his middle name to be Philharmonic. The writers, who have recently turned Floyd into Mr. Malaprop, give him a number of grammatical bombs to drop in this episode including *deficient, idiocentipedes, iron institution,* and *typhoons.* Gail Bonney was quite a versatile actress, equally credible when playing haughty society matrons or overbearing chatterboxes.

Date: February 13, 1952
Title: Engagement Ring Confusion
  Cast: Willard Waterman (Gildersleeve), John Hiestand, Mary Lee Robb (Marjorie), Walter Tetley (Leroy), Earle Ross (Hooker), Lillian Randolph (Birdie), Richard LeGrand (Peavey), Gale Gordon (Rumson Bullard), Jeanne Bates (Paula Winthrop)
  Summary: Complications ensue when Bullard assumes Marjorie's en-

gagement ring is one Gildersleeve is going to present to Paula when Throckmorton proposes to her.

Writers: John Elliotte, Andy White

Comments: Gale Gordon makes the most of the opportunity Elliotte and White give him as the prime mover of this misadventure. From the hilarious scene of Gildy's fearful flight away from Rumson's ire and flowerpot like terror-stricken Ichabod Crane fleeing the wrath of the Headless Horseman to a display of Gale's ability to go from low-key to high dudgeon in mid-sentence ("I'll give you a push—RIGHT INTO YOUR RESERVOIR!") to the veiled threat implicit in his story of a hapless jilter who fell into a loom and was woven to death to the concluding scene when the outsmarted Bullard is left sputtering in apoplectic rage, this broadcast is a showcase for the splendid talents of radio comedy's MSVP (Most Valuable Supporting Player).

Date: February 20, 1952
Title: Civic Coordinator
  Cast: Willard Waterman (Gildersleeve), John Hiestand, Mary Lee Robb (Marjorie), Walter Tetley (Leroy), Earle Ross (Hooker), Lillian Randolph (Birdie), Richard LeGrand (Peavey), Stan Farrar (Terwilliger), Mary Jane Croft (Harriet Pickens)
  Summary: Gildersleeve, pleased that his suggestion of hiring an efficiency expert to oversee civic spending is accepted, is disappointed when the mayor appoints a woman for the position instead of himself.
  Writers: John Elliotte, Andy White
  Comments: Mary Jane Croft is a fine choice for the part of the coordinator

for on the air she excelled at playing no-nonsense professional women who could stand their ground with men just like Rosalind Russell did on the screen. Once again, the snifter valve, that linchpin of the waterworks, is mentioned, although its precise function will never be fully explained.

Date: February 27, 1952
Title: Leroy Gets Independence
  Cast: Willard Waterman (Gildersleeve), John Hiestand, Mary Lee Robb (Marjorie), Walter Tetley (Leroy), Earle Ross (Hooker), Lillian Randolph (Birdie), Richard LeGrand (Peavey), Gale Gordon (Rumson Bullard), Barbara Whiting (Babs Winthrop)
  Summary: After Gildersleeve allows Leroy freedom to make his own decisions for a week, Babs wants the same privilege from Rumson Bullard, prompting more fireworks between the two uncles.
  Writers: John Elliotte, Andy White
  Allusion: Rumson paraphrases from *Moral Essays* by Alexander Pope: "As the twig is bent so grows the tree."
  Comments: This is the first episode in which the term *teenager* is applied to Leroy as the boy has at last moved on from the tenacious 12 that has clung to him for years like Jack Benny hung on to 39. The oath "Oh, Gad!" that Gordon used frequently on *Our Miss Brooks* is toned down on this show to a lukewarm "Gadfrey."

Date: March 5, 1952
Title: Bullard as House Guest
  Cast: Willard Waterman (Gildersleeve), John Hiestand, Mary Lee Robb (Marjorie), Walter Tetley (Leroy), Earle

Ross (Hooker), Lillian Randolph (Birdie), Richard LeGrand (Peavey), Gale Gordon (Rumson Bullard)

Summary: In order to get Bullard into a good mood so he will loan money to Bronco and Marjorie, Gildersleeve invites his neighbor to stay at his house while Rumson's home is being painted.

Writers: John Elliotte, Andy White

Comments: Throckmorton indicates that "even Kefauver couldn't get anything out of that Bullard," a reference to Senator Estes Kefauver, known at this time for his inquiries into organized crime and later for being the vice-presidential nominee on the Democratic ticket in 1956. The fact that a convention fills all the hotels in town is another indication that, while the show is not set in a metropolitan area, neither could it be said that Summerfield is a hamlet or village.

Date: March 12, 1952
Title: Trip to Omaha

Cast: Willard Waterman (Gildersleeve), John Hiestand, Mary Lee Robb (Marjorie), Walter Tetley (Leroy), Earle Ross (Hooker), Lillian Randolph (Birdie), Richard LeGrand (Peavey)

Summary: Gildersleeve is mystified how Leroy knows he is going to a meeting of water commissioners in Omaha, unaware that he is responding to the boy's questions while he is asleep.

Writers: John Elliotte, Andy White

Comments: Gildy asking Hooker if he looks like Eisenhower is another political reference in this election year. The cities mentioned (Duluth, Omaha, Sheboygan) suggest that Summerfield is located somewhere in the Midwest. The trip that Gildersleeve supposedly

took in 1932 mentioned by Peavey predates the events of this program, although Throckmorton could have revealed details of that experience after he arrived in Summerfield in 1941.

Date: March 19, 1952
Title: Plants a Garden

Cast: Willard Waterman (Gildersleeve), John Hiestand, Mary Lee Robb (Marjorie), Walter Tetley (Leroy), Earle Ross (Hooker), Lillian Randolph (Birdie), Richard LeGrand (Peavey), Gale Gordon (Rumson Bullard), Will Wright (Nick)

Summary: Gildersleeve, green with envy over Bullard's skillful hand at raising plants, discovers that acquiring a green thumb is not so easy when he tries to fill his front yard with flowers.

Writers: John Elliotte, Andy White

Comments: Birdie's bellowing "I'll get it!" not only rattles the rafters; it penetrates the aching bones of the prone Throckmorton who admits that "I felt that." Gildy gets to turn the tables on Rumson as he sends Bullard running for home lest he be hit with a potted Rumsonola rose.

Date: March 26, 1952
Title: Television Comes to Summerfield

Cast: Willard Waterman (Gildersleeve), John Hiestand, Mary Lee Robb (Marjorie), Walter Tetley (Leroy), Earle Ross (Hooker), Lillian Randolph (Birdie), Richard LeGrand (Peavey)

Summary: After Throckmorton adamantly refuses to buy a TV, Leroy devises a stratagem to convince his uncle that a set in the house will keep him home nights and out of trouble.

Writers: John Elliotte, Andy White

Comments: This script spotlights the chief attractions of the tube in those early years: wrestling, puppets, cowboys, and old movies. Glamorous Gus is a takeoff on the name of vainglorious grappler Gorgeous George.

Date: April 2, 1952

Title: Wilbur Cosgrove Lookalike

Cast: Willard Waterman (Gildersleeve), John Hiestand, Mary Lee Robb (Marjorie), Walter Tetley (Leroy), Earle Ross (Hooker), Lillian Randolph (Birdie), Richard LeGrand (Peavey), Noreen Gammill (Sarah Cosgrove)

Summary: Gildersleeve is stalked by a woman who claims he is her long-lost husband.

Writers: John Elliotte, Andy White

Comments: Apparently Leroy is not the only one who has managed to halt time's wingèd chariot because Marjorie places her uncle's age at about 30 in 1941 which makes him in his early 40s in 1952 just as he was throughout the previous decade. Gildy sheds some light on his life before he showed up in Wistful Vista in 1939 by recalling his employment in Oshkosh as an elastic inspector in 1938. Throckmorton reacts to his nephew's practical joke in the tag with "What a family," his version of Leroy's "What a character!" The conflict in Korea is mentioned for the first time in the closing appeal for blood donations.

Date: April 9, 1952

Title: Easter Sunrise Service

Cast: Willard Waterman (Gildersleeve), John Hiestand, Mary Lee Robb (Marjorie), Walter Tetley (Leroy), Earle Ross (Hooker), Lillian Randolph (Birdie), Richard LeGrand (Peavey), Jeanne Bates (Paula Winthrop)

Summary: After changing his mind several times regarding attending the early Easter service, Gildersleeve decides to go when Paula wants to ride along with the family.

Writers: John Elliotte, Andy White

Comments: Birdie sings "Were You There When They Crucified My Lord?" Although it is the lure of women that twice attracts Throckmorton to commit to the sunrise service, he does find it a spiritually rewarding experience thanks to Birdie's inspirational song.

Date: April 16, 1952

Title: Leroy Keeps Bees

Cast: Willard Waterman (Gildersleeve), John Hiestand, Mary Lee Robb (Marjorie), Walter Tetley (Leroy), Earle Ross (Hooker), Lillian Randolph (Birdie), Richard LeGrand (Peavey), Jeanne Bates (Paula Winthrop)

Summary: When Leroy uses $5.00 his uncle gave him to keep a swarm of bees, Gildersleeve finds himself kept from going outside by the pesky little stingers.

Writers: John Elliotte, Andy White

Comments: Peavey reveals of a bit of his hidden past as he recalls his days as a catcher for the Apple River Paddy Whacks. (There is an Apple River in both Wisconsin and Illinois.) Not once is the matter of how Leroy hopes to make money off the bees addressed.

Date: April 23, 1952

Title: Diving into Reservoir

Cast: Willard Waterman (Gildersleeve), John Hiestand, Mary Lee Robb (Marjorie), Walter Tetley (Leroy), Earle

Ross (Hooker), Lillian Randolph (Birdie), Richard LeGrand (Peavey), Cliff Arquette (Charlie Anderson)

Summary: To become better known to Summerfield residents, Gildersleeve arranges a publicity stunt of diving into the reservoir.

Writers: John Elliotte, Andy White

Allusion: Gildersleeve paraphrases Matthew 5:15: "I've been hiding my light under a bushel."

Comments: Cliff Arquette brings some chortling humor to the role of cranky Charlie Anderson, sounding more than a little like his Charley Weaver character. Waterman's closing remarks suggest that the April 9 broadcast was warmly received by many listeners.

Date: April 30, 1952
Title: Leroy's Report Card

Cast: Willard Waterman (Gildersleeve), John Hiestand, Mary Lee Robb (Marjorie), Walter Tetley (Leroy), Earle Ross (Hooker), Lillian Randolph (Birdie), Richard LeGrand (Peavey)

Summary: Fearful that a poor report card will prohibit him from going to summer camp, Leroy employs diversionary tactics to forestall his uncle from making his final decision.

Writers: John Elliotte, Andy White

Comments: The E Leroy receives in English is a peculiar grade, perhaps a last resort before a D- turns into an F. Throckmorton would have been more accurate if he had changed his appraisal of Leroy from "You've got character" to "You are a character."

Date: May 7, 1952
Title: Cowboy Singer

Cast: Willard Waterman (Gildersleeve), John Hiestand, Mary Lee Robb (Marjorie), Walter Tetley (Leroy), Earle Ross (Hooker), Lillian Randolph (Birdie), Richard LeGrand (Peavey)

Summary: Gildersleeve attempts to discourage Leroy from pursuing a career as a singing western star.

Writers: John Elliotte, Andy White

Comments: Leroy sings "99 Years Is a Long Time." Birdie sings "Home! Sweet Home!" "That guy who cries when he sings" is Johnnie Ray, the Prince of Wails. Of all the questions Peavey asked Gildersleeve in the last decade the one he poses on this evening may be the strangest: "Did you ever shake hands with a baboon?"

Date: May 14, 1952
Title: Bronco Returns

Cast: Willard Waterman (Gildersleeve), John Hiestand, Mary Lee Robb (Marjorie), Walter Tetley (Leroy), Earle Ross (Hooker), Lillian Randolph (Birdie), Richard LeGrand (Peavey), Richard Crenna (Bronco)

Summary: Leroy and Gildersleeve delay a fishing trip so they can welcome Bronco home, displeasing the young husband and wife who want to be alone.

Writers: John Elliotte, Andy White

Comments: Richard Crenna returns after being absent since January 9th. Gildy is particularly thick-headed and thick-skinned on this occasion as hints and even direct entreaties bounce off him. Just as happened on May 9, 1951, when the couple eloped to celebrate their anniversary, the twins are not even given an afterthought at the end.

Date: May 21, 1952
Title: Moving Day
Cast: Willard Waterman (Gildersleeve), John Hiestand, Mary Lee Robb (Marjorie), Walter Tetley (Leroy), Earle Ross (Hooker), Lillian Randolph (Birdie), Richard LeGrand (Peavey), Richard Crenna (Bronco)
Summary: Throckmorton, thinking he has forced Marjorie and Bronco to move into their new house prematurely, tries to make amends by giving them furniture and accessories from his home.
Writers: John Elliotte, Andy White
Comments: Bronco sings the melody of "Vesti La Giubba." It is natural for Waterman, born in Madison, to specifically mention his Wisconsin badger toothbrush. Little Ronny seems to have a free hand in the house as he helps himself to toxic substances, applying shellac and turpentine on anything he can reach. Gildersleeve mentions that his birthday is in July, contradicting the information given on October 22, 1947, when his birthday was celebrated on that day.

Date: May 28, 1952
Title: Motor for Bike
Cast: Willard Waterman (Gildersleeve), John Hiestand, Mary Lee Robb (Marjorie), Walter Tetley (Leroy), Earle Ross (Hooker), Lillian Randolph (Birdie), Richard LeGrand (Peavey)
Summary: After Gildersleeve insists Leroy raise the money for a motor the boy wants, he is shocked when his nephew plans to get the cash by renting the vacant room upstairs.
Writers: John Elliotte, Andy White
Allusion: Leroy paraphrases from

Moral Essays by Alexander Pope: "As the twig is bent so grows the tree."
Comments: On the phone LeGrand speaks in the same Swedish dialect he was using Tuesday nights when playing Ole on *Fibber McGee and Molly*. Gildy outsmarts himself repeatedly in this episode, right up to the conclusion when he is last seen riding (and riding and riding) into the sunset.

Date: June 4, 1952
Title: Katie Lee Returns
Cast: Willard Waterman (Gildersleeve), John Hiestand, Mary Lee Robb (Marjorie), Walter Tetley (Leroy), Earle Ross (Hooker), Lillian Randolph (Birdie), Richard LeGrand (Peavey), Katie Lee
Summary: When Katie Lee comes back to Summerfield, Leroy plans to head off a romance between her and his uncle but changes his mind after getting a glimpse of Hooker's life as a bachelor.
Writers: John Elliotte, Andy White
Comments: Katie sings "The Girl in the Wood" and a wandering song. The writers continue to give Leroy a more assertive role in the series as this is the third time in recent weeks he has approached Hooker and Peavey for assistance or advice.

Date: June 11, 1952
Title: Wall between Houses
Cast: Willard Waterman (Gildersleeve), John Hiestand, Mary Lee Robb (Marjorie), Walter Tetley (Leroy), Earle Ross (Hooker), Lillian Randolph (Birdie), Richard LeGrand (Peavey), Richard Crenna (Bronco)
Summary: Gildersleeve tries to convince Bronco to build a wall so the

twins will not be raising havoc on Gildy's property.

Writers: John Elliotte, Andy White

Comments: Leroy's laughter after Throckmorton kicks the can is helped by Waterman's blooper of "That rock had a can in it." For 15-month-old toddlers the twins are truly mobile and enterprising scamps, capable of wielding paintbrushes, stacking cans in a driveway, carrying hoses across a lawn, and opening car doors. It never occurs to Gildersleeve as he is taking the chicken's way out that the situation might be resolved if *he* built the wall instead of Bronco.

Date: June 18, 1952
Title: Bean Contest

Cast: Willard Waterman (Gildersleeve), John Hiestand, Mary Lee Robb (Marjorie), Walter Tetley (Leroy), Earle Ross (Hooker), Lillian Randolph (Birdie), Richard LeGrand (Peavey)

Summary: Gildersleeve is determined to win a spinning wheel lamp in a "guess the number of beans" contest so he can present it to Marjorie as a housewarming gift.

Writers: John Elliotte, Andy White

Comments: Elliotte and White net good results with the "beans in a jar" concept just as the writers for *Fibber McGee and Molly* and *The Life of Riley* had done in the mid-forties. They also cleverly set up the denouement by inserting a key bit of information early in the script regarding Throckmorton inviting some of his acquaintances to the housewarming.

Date: June 25, 1952
Title: Meets Gloria McKinley

Cast: Willard Waterman (Gildersleeve), John Hiestand, Mary Lee Robb (Marjorie), Walter Tetley (Leroy), Earle Ross (Hooker), Lillian Randolph (Birdie), Richard LeGrand (Peavey), Gloria Blondell (Gloria McKinley)

Summary: Gildersleeve's complaint about the woman in the complaint department at Hogan Brothers is that she attends to business and will not take any of his romantic funny business.

Writers: John Elliotte, Andy White

Comments: Throckmorton vacillates between patting himself on the back ("Gildersleeve, you're sly") to slapping himself across the face ("Gildersleeve, you bungled it again"). Hiestand invites listeners to tune in to *The Great Gildersleeve* throughout the summer, making this the first year the cast did not take a vacation.

Date: July 2, 1952
Title: Fourth of July Speech

Cast: Willard Waterman (Gildersleeve), John Hiestand, Mary Lee Robb (Marjorie), Walter Tetley (Leroy), Earle Ross (Hooker), Lillian Randolph (Birdie), Richard LeGrand (Peavey), Gloria Blondell (Gloria McKinley)

Summary: Gildersleeve leads Miss McKinley to believe he will be giving an important speech which is actually scheduled to be delivered by Judge Hooker.

Writers: John Elliotte, Andy White

Comments: It is no surprise that the holiday celebration will be held at Kraft Park. Once again Birdie displays more common sense than her employer. The content of the formal speech regarding citizenship and freedom echoes the message of the PSA that closed the previous broadcast.

Date: July 9, 1952

No broadcast on this date. Notation in the scripts at the Wisconsin State Historical Society indicates that the script for this date was not heard on July 9 because of coverage of the Republican National Convention being held in Chicago. The script was used for the broadcast on July 23, 1952.

Date: July 16, 1952
Title: Camping in Backyard

Cast: Willard Waterman (Gildersleeve), John Hiestand, Mary Lee Robb (Marjorie), Walter Tetley (Leroy), Earle Ross (Hooker), Lillian Randolph (Birdie), Richard LeGrand (Peavey)

Summary: An adventure of roughing it in the backyard turns into a misadventure for Leroy and Gildersleeve after being locked out of the house.

Writers: John Elliotte, Andy White

Comments: Leroy and Gildersleeve sing "Home on the Range." The movie with Humphrey Bogart that Peavey refers to is *The African Queen*. The moment Throckmorton asks to be zipped up with his arms inside the sleeping bag listeners surely have the same collective "You'll be sorry" thought as when they heard Fibber announcing that he was going to open that closet door.

Date: July 23, 1952 (This episode, originally to be aired on July 9, was delayed two weeks due to the coverage of the Republican National Convention.)
Title: Fishing with Hooker and Leroy
Cast: Willard Waterman (Gilder-

sleeve), John Hiestand, Walter Tetley (Leroy), Earle Ross (Hooker), Lillian Randolph (Birdie), Richard LeGrand (Peavey), Gloria Blondell (Gloria McKinley), George Neise (Bert Huggins)

Summary: Gildersleeve, at first reluctant to go angling at Grass Lake, changes his mind when he sees it as an opportunity to interrupt a tryst between Bert Huggins and Gloria McKinley.

Writers: John Elliotte, Andy White

Comments: Gildersleeve sings "Pagan Love Song." This episode borrows much of the plot from the May 17, 1950, script including Gildy's good luck at catching fish and his romantic rival getting seasick. On May 14, 1944, Hooker's residence was given as three blocks away from Gildersleeve's; now the distance is ten blocks.

Date: July 30, 1952
Title: Bronco the Realtor (Repeat)

Cast: Willard Waterman (Gildersleeve), John Hiestand, Mary Lee Robb (Marjorie), Walter Tetley (Leroy), Earle Ross (Hooker), Lillian Randolph (Birdie), Richard LeGrand (Peavey), Richard Crenna (Bronco), Jim Backus (Rumson Bullard)

Summary: Trying to help Bronco in his real estate business, Gildersleeve lists his house with the young man and is soon shocked when someone buys it.

Writers: John Elliotte, Andy White

Comments: This is a slightly-altered version of the script used on May 24, 1950. The primary difference is that Jim Backus replaces Gale Gordon in the part of Bullard. In the earlier show Gordon delivered an evil chuckle when welcoming Bronco into his home whereas Backus unleashes his Mr. Magoo laugh at the same juncture in the production.

Date: August 6, 1952
Title: Leroy Behaves Too Well (Repeat)
   Cast: Willard Waterman (Gildersleeve), John Hiestand, Mary Lee Robb (Marjorie), Walter Tetley (Leroy), Earle Ross (Hooker), Lillian Randolph (Birdie), Richard LeGrand (Peavey), Richard Crenna (Bronco), Arthur Q. Bryan (Floyd)
   Summary: Gildersleeve is concerned when Leroy the rebel is behaving like a perfect gentleman without a cause.
   Writers: John Elliotte, Andy White
   Comments: This episode is very similar to the script used on February 14, 1951. The principal change is a seasonal one: the snowballs that chased Gildy into the barbershop in February have been replaced by beans propelled from bean shooters. Because Floyd sold his shop during the winter and Bryan has been off the program since February 6, 1952, Gildy reintroduces the character with "I see you got your shop open again."

Date: August 13, 1952
Title: Weight Reduction Plan (Repeat)
   Cast: Willard Waterman (Gildersleeve), John Hiestand, Mary Lee Robb (Marjorie), Walter Tetley (Leroy), Earle Ross (Hooker), Lillian Randolph (Birdie), Richard LeGrand (Peavey), Richard Crenna (Bronco)
   Summary: Embarrassed that he is more flabby than fit, Gildersleeve tries to lose weight by eating less and exercising more.
   Writers: John Elliotte, Andy White

   Comments: The script for this episode is virtually the same as the one used on October 18, 1950. The plot-related music in the earlier broadcast has been replaced by generic bridges. A pre-recorded PSA regarding preventing forest fires concludes the show.

Date: August 20, 1952
Title: Leroy's Laundry Business (Repeat)
   Cast: Willard Waterman (Gildersleeve), John Hiestand, Mary Lee Robb (Marjorie), Walter Tetley (Leroy), Earle Ross (Hooker), Lillian Randolph (Birdie), Richard LeGrand (Peavey), Arthur Q. Bryan (Floyd)
   Summary: Leroy forms the Million Dollar Laundry which turns into a million headaches when he does not mark the shirts he washed.
   Writers: John Elliotte, Andy White
   Comments: This script is adapted from the December 6, 1950, broadcast. The main difference is that Terwilliger does not appear in this episode.

Date: August 27, 1952
Title: Cousin Emily Visits
   Cast: Willard Waterman (Gildersleeve), John Hiestand, Mary Lee Robb (Marjorie), Walter Tetley (Leroy), Earle Ross (Hooker), Lillian Randolph (Birdie), Richard LeGrand (Peavey), Charlotte Lawrence (Emily Forrester)
   Summary: Visiting relative Emily impresses everyone she meets except Throckmorton, who remains suspicious of her motives until he eavesdrops on one of her conversations.
   Writers: John Elliotte, Andy White
   Comments: Emily's remark of "coming down from Milwaukee" suggests

that Summerfield is located south of (but not far from) Wisconsin. Peavey's statement that he has known Gildersleeve for over 20 years goes about a decade beyond the time Throckmorton has been in Summerfield. Leroy's "Ha!" and "What a character!" pack extra gusto on a night when Gildy's stubborn behavior certainly deserves criticism.

Date: September 3, 1952
Title: Competition with Emily
   Cast: Willard Waterman (Gildersleeve), John Hiestand, Mary Lee Robb (Marjorie), Walter Tetley (Leroy), Earle Ross (Hooker), Lillian Randolph (Birdie), Richard LeGrand (Peavey), Charlotte Lawrence (Emily Forrester), George Neise (Gibson)
   Summary: Acting on a suggestion from Peavey, Gildersleeve attempts to win Leroy's favor back from Emily by proposing robust activities that he hopes are out of her league.
   Writers: John Elliotte, Andy White
   Comments: Gildersleeve has regressed from the tolerance he displayed at the end of the last broadcast back to acting like a self-centered malcontent who might be better off heeding his own assessment of this situation: "I don't know why I'm fretting about nothing."

Date: September 10, 1952
Title: Cleaning Bullard's Rug
   Cast: Willard Waterman (Gildersleeve), John Hiestand, Mary Lee Robb (Marjorie), Walter Tetley (Leroy), Earle Ross (Hooker), Lillian Randolph (Birdie), Richard LeGrand (Peavey), Gloria Blondell (Gloria McKinley), Marvin Miller (Rumson Bullard)

Summary: After entering Bullard's home solely to turn on the refrigerator, Gildersleeve spills ink on a Persian rug which leads to one mishap after another.
   Writers: John Elliotte, Andy White
   Comments: Elliotte and White deserve credit for creating an escalating comedy of errors that takes a splash of Fibber McGee's penchant for creating messes, drops in a drawn-out footsteps gag worthy of the walking man (Jack Benny), and adds Leroy as Gildy's cohort so as things get progressively worse the situation resembles one of the indoor catastrophes orchestrated by Phil Harris and Frank Remley.

Date: September 17, 1952
Title: Driving Test
   Cast: Willard Waterman (Gildersleeve), John Hiestand, Mary Lee Robb (Marjorie), Walter Tetley (Leroy), Earle Ross (Hooker), Lillian Randolph (Birdie), Richard LeGrand (Peavey), Jeanne Bates (Paula Winthrop), Bob Bruce (Officer Dolan)
   Summary: Gildersleeve, accompanying Leroy as the boy gets his driving permit, discovers that his license has expired and therefore has to take both a written exam and a test behind the wheel.
   Writers: John Elliotte, Andy White
   Comments: The writers are being coy about Leroy's current age, using phrases like "within the age limit" to indicate his eligibility to drive. With an officer in the front seat next to him and a watchful judge in the back seat during the driving test, no matter which way Gildy turns he will be singing the lament "I fought the law and the law won."

Date: September 24, 1952
Title: Hooker-Peavey Feud
    Cast: Willard Waterman (Gildersleeve), John Hiestand, Mary Lee Robb (Marjorie), Walter Tetley (Leroy), Earle Ross (Hooker), Lillian Randolph (Birdie), Richard LeGrand (Peavey)
    Summary: Despite warnings to stay out of a dispute between Peavey and Hooker, Gildersleeve remains determined to bring his friends back together.
    Writers: John Elliotte, Andy White
    Comments: Gildersleeve sings "Smiles." This is one time when meddlesome Gildy really gets egg on his face. The writers top the first act conclusion by having Throckmorton's empty boasts go up in smoke at the end.

Date: October 1, 1952
Title: Economizing
    Cast: Willard Waterman (Gildersleeve), John Hiestand, Mary Lee Robb (Marjorie), Walter Tetley (Leroy), Earle Ross (Hooker), Lillian Randolph (Birdie), Richard LeGrand (Peavey), Jeanne Bates (Paula Winthrop)
    Summary: To prove to Birdie and Leroy that he is serious about cutting back on expenses, Gildersleeve takes Paula out on a date with only a dollar to spend.
    Writers: John Elliotte, Andy White
    Comments: Leroy's sassiness is heard not just in his observation of Gildersleeve's retrenching in the living room but also in his reaction to the doggerel in the main commercial. Even though the election is a month away, Waterman concludes the show with a reminder to vote.

Date: October 8, 1952
Title: Dating Two Women
    Cast: Willard Waterman (Gildersleeve), John Hiestand, Mary Lee Robb (Marjorie), Walter Tetley (Leroy), Earle Ross (Hooker), Lillian Randolph (Birdie), Richard LeGrand (Peavey), Jeanne Bates (Paula Winthrop), Veola Vonn (Gloria McKinley)
    Summary: Trying to juggle dates with Gloria and Paula gets Gildersleeve into trouble with both women.
    Writers: John Elliotte, Andy White
    Comments: The writers slyly set up the need for women to be wearing gloves in October by having Gildy comment on the cool weather at the beginning of the car scene. Throckmorton's boastful remark "It isn't like me to make mistakes" rings as true as the star of *The Jack Benny Program* declaring "I must stop throwing my money around."

Date: October 15, 1952
Title: Leroy Wants a Watch
    Cast: Willard Waterman (Gildersleeve), John Hiestand, Mary Lee Robb (Marjorie), Walter Tetley (Leroy), Lillian Randolph (Birdie), Richard LeGrand (Peavey), Jeanne Bates (Paula Winthrop), Stan Farrar (Terwilliger)
    Summary: To prove that Leroy does not need a new watch, Gildersleeve uses the boy's old timepiece on a day filled with appointments.
    Writers: John Elliotte, Andy White
    Comments: When Leroy is fooled on his second phone call, he delivers an "Ooh!" of dismay worthy of his uncle. Gildy's adamant admission that "I guess I'm about as brassy as they come" is proved in his insensitive treatment of Paula on her doorstep.

Date: October 22, 1952
Title: Athletic Sham
   Cast: Willard Waterman (Gildersleeve), John Hiestand, Walter Tetley (Leroy), Earle Ross (Hooker), Lillian Randolph (Birdie), Richard LeGrand (Peavey), Jeanne Bates (Paula Winthrop), Bud Stefan (Cooley)
   Summary: Gildersleeve's pretense of being a stellar athlete leads the out-of-shape four-flusher into a vigorous tennis match with Paula.
   Writers: John Elliotte, Andy White
   Comments: Birdie's alliterative endorsement of the egg man ("We can't get cool with Mr. Cooley") takes its cue from the 1924 campaign slogan "Keep Cool with Coolidge." It is surprising that Peavey stocks tennis balls, a commodity that even today is not available in many drugstores.

Date: October 29, 1952
   There is no extant recording for this episode. Scripts for October 29, November 5, and November 12 are absent from the microfilm reel at the Wisconsin State Historical Society.

Date: November 5, 1952
Title: Clinic Patient
   Cast: Willard Waterman (Gildersleeve), John Hiestand, Walter Tetley (Leroy), Richard LeGrand (Peavey), Paula Winslowe (Miss Hatfield), Elizabeth Patterson (Mrs. Potter), Norman Field (Dr. Culpepper), Bud Stefan (Cooley)
   Summary: While practicing for a round of golf, Gildersleeve gets a crick in his neck which sends him to a clinic where he gets little relief for his ailment.
   Writers: John Elliotte, Andy White

   Comments: Paula Winslowe, who had been busy in her role as Peg Riley on *The Life of Riley* until the show concluded its radio run in 1951, appears for the first time since September 12, 1943. Elizabeth Patterson, veteran character actress on radio and in movies, perhaps is best remembered as the harried housekeeper in *I Married a Witch*. Because Randolph, Robb, and Ross are absent this week, the writers craft a show around Gildy in a setting outside the home where he can experience the vagaries of medical bureaucracy.

Date: November 12, 1952
Title: Meets Grace Tuttle
   Cast: Willard Waterman (Gildersleeve), John Hiestand, Mary Lee Robb (Marjorie), Walter Tetley (Leroy), Earle Ross (Hooker), Lillian Randolph (Birdie), Richard LeGrand (Peavey), Mary Shipp (Grace Tuttle), Bud Stefan (Cooley)
   Summary: After making a bad impression with Leroy's teacher, Gildersleeve makes things worse by trying to sneak into school on Parent's Night.
   Writers: John Elliotte, Andy White
   Comments: Mary Shipp seems a natural choice for this role as she was currently playing Miss Spaulding, patient teacher of Luigi Basco and fellow immigrants on *Life with Luigi*. The closet sneeze is an old wheeze, used on *My Favorite Husband, Our Miss Brooks*, and numerous other sitcoms to expose the skulkers hidden therein. Waterman slips in a very late plug for the article about *The Great Gildersleeve* in *Radio-TV Mirror*.

Date: November 19, 1952
Title: Missing Cuff Links

Cast: Willard Waterman (Gildersleeve), John Hiestand, Mary Lee Robb (Marjorie), Walter Tetley (Leroy), Earle Ross (Hooker), Lillian Randolph (Birdie), Richard LeGrand (Peavey), Elizabeth Patterson (Mrs. Potter), Bud Stefan (Cooley)

Summary: Gildersleeve is hard-pressed by Leroy to produce a pair of cuff links the boy gave him as a birthday present.

Writers: John Elliotte, Andy White

Comments: Hooker mentions Dugan's Hill which, in the overlapping geography of radio programs, must not be far in the imaginations of listeners from Dugan's Lake, favorite fishing spot of Fibber McGee and his cronies. Attentive members of the audience probably connect the dots between the progress reports on the snowman and the repeated inquiries about the cuff links before Leroy makes the clinching announcement at the end.

Date: November 26, 1952
Title: Bird Watcher's Club

Cast: Willard Waterman (Gildersleeve), John Hiestand, Mary Lee Robb (Marjorie), Walter Tetley (Leroy), Earle Ross (Hooker), Lillian Randolph (Birdie), Richard LeGrand (Peavey), Mary Shipp (Grace Tuttle), Bud Stefan (Cooley)

Summary: Throckmorton is unsuccessful in recruiting members for a club of birdwatchers.

Writers: John Elliotte, Andy White

Comments: The writers borrow a page from the Skelton Scrapbook of Satire by having Leroy ask questions of his uncle that make it seem like he is interested in a project before the boy issues a definitive negative response.

The tag is a bit rushed and no end credits are given.

Date: December 3, 1952
Title: Duck Dinner

Cast: Willard Waterman (Gildersleeve), John Hiestand, Mary Lee Robb (Marjorie), Walter Tetley (Leroy), Lillian Randolph (Birdie), Richard LeGrand (Peavey), Elizabeth Patterson (Mrs. Potter), Bud Stefan (Cooley)

Summary: Gildersleeve invites Peavey and Mrs. Potter for a duck dinner to celebrate Mrs. Potter's birthday.

Writers: John Elliotte, Andy White

Comments: Peavey sings a bit of "Singin' in the Rain." Everyone sings "Happy Birthday" to Mrs. Potter. Birdie emits her call of the wild so automatically at the sound of a bell that she probably started her day by answering the call of her alarm clock with a thunderous "I'll get it!"

Date: December 10, 1952
Title: Leroy's Job on Commission

Cast: Willard Waterman (Gildersleeve), John Hiestand, Walter Tetley (Leroy), Lillian Randolph (Birdie), Richard LeGrand (Peavey), Mary Shipp (Grace Tuttle), Bud Stefan (Cooley)

Summary: After Leroy takes a job at Peavey's on a commission basis, he drums up business by encouraging acquaintances to buy presents for each other at the drugstore.

Writers: John Elliotte, Andy White

Comments: The Christmas Seals pitch which is woven into the conversation between Peavey and Leroy may garner as much money for the National Tuberculosis Association as a more direct appeal in a PSA. This episode gives a glimpse into 1952 prices: $3.99 for a fountain pen, $3.60 for a box of cigars (probably 50 of the noxious El Lobos), and perfume considered a costly extravagance at $25 an ounce. At the conclusion Tetley delivers his "Ooh!" with a spray of saliva in the Hal Peary manner.

Date: December 17, 1952
Title: Grace's Brother Sidney
   Cast: Willard Waterman (Gildersleeve), John Hiestand, Walter Tetley (Leroy), Lillian Randolph (Birdie), Richard LeGrand (Peavey), Mary Shipp (Grace Tuttle), George Neise (Sidney Tuttle)
   Summary: After warning Leroy about letting people take advantage of him, Gildersleeve loans money and his car to Grace's brother.
   Writers: John Elliotte, Andy White
   Comments: One week after declaring "I haven't been a kid for over a year" Leroy resorts to his old "I'm just a little kid" line to achieve his goal. Peavey sounds so agreeable to the notion of seeing invisible customers that he would probably serve some sodas to both Elwood Dowd *and* Harvey.

Date: December 24, 1952
Title: Alone on Christmas
   Cast: Willard Waterman (Gildersleeve), John Hiestand, Mary Lee Robb (Marjorie), Walter Tetley (Leroy), Lillian Randolph (Birdie), Richard LeGrand (Peavey), Bud Stefan (Cooley), Elizabeth Patterson (Mrs. Potter)
   Summary: Leroy and Gildersleeve suffer the pangs of loneliness as they trim the tree and buy last-minute gifts.
   Writers: John Elliotte, Andy White

Comments: Peavey sings "Jingle Bells." The Kraft Choristers sing "It Came Upon a Midnight Clear," "Ding Dong Bells," and "Joy to the World." No end credits are given. The actor playing Bronco's small part is definitely not Richard Crenna.

Date: December 31, 1952
Title: Remembering Old Flames
   Cast: Willard Waterman (Gildersleeve), John Hiestand, Walter Tetley (Leroy), Lillian Randolph (Birdie), Richard LeGrand (Peavey), Shirley Mitchell (Leila), Mary Shipp (Grace Tuttle), Katie Lee
   Summary: After his date with Grace is cancelled, Gildersleeve spends part of New Year's Eve thinking back about his past romances.
   Writers: John Elliotte, Andy White
   Comments: Katie Lee sings "The Girl in the Wood." The last two weeks Meakin has tailored the music to the season or the plot (e.g., "Auld Lang Syne," "When Good Fellows Get Together"). The comic rhythm of the show picks up considerably when Leila appears due to Shirley Mitchell's keen playing of the teasing temptress. The actress recreating the porch scene is not Cathy Lewis; Mary Shipp may also have taken that part. No end credits are given.

Date: January 7, 1953
Title: Leila Returns Yet Again
   Cast: Willard Waterman (Gildersleeve), John Hiestand, Walter Tetley (Leroy), Lillian Randolph (Birdie), Richard LeGrand (Peavey), Shirley Mitchell (Leila), Mary Shipp (Grace Tuttle), Byron Kane (Sidney Tuttle)

Summary: After Leila returns to Summerfield, Gildersleeve considers breaking off his relationship with Grace Tuttle.

Writers: John Elliotte, Andy White

Comments: Absence not only makes the heart grow fonder; it also makes the houses in Summerfield grow farther apart. In the 1940s Leila lived right next door to Throckmorton. In 1953 Leroy claims his uncle has not been down the street where Leila's house is located since she left town. Sidney's admission "I owe Throck a great deal" passes without even a sotto voce "I'll say he does" from Gildy.

Date: January 14, 1953
Title: Helping Leila Clean House
    Cast: Willard Waterman (Gildersleeve), John Hiestand, Walter Tetley (Leroy), Lillian Randolph (Birdie), Richard LeGrand (Peavey), Shirley Mitchell (Leila), Byron Kane (Sidney Tuttle)

Summary: Gildersleeve agrees to help spruce up Leila's house because he wants to keep a jealous eye on Sidney and Leila.

Writers: John Elliotte, Andy White

Comments: The idea of buying the fancy red car is dropped quickly which is probably just as well because payments of $92.46 a month might be a trifle difficult to meet for a man whose take-home pay is $80.67 a week. Even Leila's phone number of Hibiscus 901 has a southern aroma to it. The writers insert a tantalizing teaser in the tag, hoping listeners will tune in the following week to discover the nature of Bert's surprise gift from Canada.

Date: January 21, 1953
Title: Great Dane as Gift
    Cast: Willard Waterman (Gildersleeve), John Hiestand, Walter Tetley (Leroy), Lillian Randolph (Birdie), Richard LeGrand (Peavey), Shirley Mitchell (Leila), Pinto Colvig (dog)

Summary: Cousin Bert's surprise gift turns out to be a 140-pound Great Dane who creates havoc inside and outside the house.

Writers: John Elliotte, Andy White

Comments: Peavey provides two more references to the Midwest by mentioning chicken wire from Kenosha and a cousin living in Peoria. The writers again create an office scene with Gildy interacting only with a friend, not with any employee at the city hall. Pinto Colvig also played Great Danes or other big dogs on *Fibber McGee and Molly* and *Our Miss Brooks.*

Date: January 28, 1953
Title: Dating Leila and Grace
    Cast: Willard Waterman (Gildersleeve), John Hiestand, Walter Tetley (Leroy), Lillian Randolph (Birdie), Richard LeGrand (Peavey), Shirley Mitchell (Leila), Mary Shipp (Grace Tuttle), Byron Kane (Sidney Tuttle), Pinto Colvig (dog)

Summary: Throckmorton is again trying to balance conflicting engagements between two women, old flame Leila and new sweetheart Grace.

Writers: John Elliotte, Andy White

Comments: Sidney's conversation with Grace suggests that his relationship with Leila is a secret from his sister. Gildersleeve sets out for the library with noble intentions until the scent of a woman causes the wolf in him to hunt prey in another direction.

Date: February 4, 1953
Title: Leila and Grace Squabble

Cast: Willard Waterman (Gildersleeve), John Hiestand, Walter Tetley (Leroy), Lillian Randolph (Birdie), Richard LeGrand (Peavey), Shirley Mitchell (Leila), Mary Shipp (Grace Tuttle), Paula Winslowe (Mademoiselle Bouffant)

Summary: Gildersleeve, fearing Grace and Leila will share information about him, attends a fashion show with hopes of getting the two women to argue about other matters.

Writers: John Elliotte, Andy White

Comments: Leila's house continues to move around as now it is just half a block away. With Peavey serving as the only adult male companion of Gildy most weeks, the writers are giving the druggist a larger role, frequently bringing him into the action in both acts. Paula Winslowe, not often credited in dialect parts, does a fine job as the French couturier.

Date: February 11, 1953
Title: Two Dates for Party

Cast: Willard Waterman (Gildersleeve), John Hiestand, Walter Tetley (Leroy), Lillian Randolph (Birdie), Richard LeGrand (Peavey), Shirley Mitchell (Leila), Mary Shipp (Grace Tuttle), Stan Farrar (Terwilliger)

Summary: Gildersleeve again has two dates for the same event, this time being the Valentine's Day party hosted by Mayor Terwilliger.

Writers: John Elliotte, Andy White

Comments: Throckmorton demonstrates his uncanny ability to turn a bad situation into a disastrous one by following his statement of "This is the worst predicament I've ever been in" with a blatant act of deception in the presence of his employer. When Leila warns Gildy about making a faux pas, she is talking to the king of social blunders, a man who opens a phone call to the woman he plans to ask for a date with the tactless remark "I don't suppose anybody's asked you to a Valentine party."

Date: February 18, 1953
Title: Concert Date

Cast: Willard Waterman (Gildersleeve), John Hiestand, Walter Tetley (Leroy), Lillian Randolph (Birdie), Richard LeGrand (Peavey), Shirley Mitchell (Leila), Mary Shipp (Grace Tuttle), George Neise (Clarence Olson), Pinto Colvig (dog)

Summary: Gildersleeve thinks his troubles with two women may be solved when Clarence Olson takes Leila to a concert while he goes with Grace.

Writers: John Elliotte, Andy White

Comments: Olson is making progress with Leila but does not seem any closer to setting up his own practice because he has remained an intern for over three years. After dropping one shoe with "There goes one girl," Gildy lets the other one dangle for several minutes before releasing "There goes the other one."

Date: February 25, 1953
Title: Peavey-Gildersleeve Feud

Cast: Willard Waterman (Gildersleeve), John Hiestand, Walter Tetley (Leroy), Lillian Randolph (Birdie),

Richard LeGrand (Peavey), Arthur Q. Bryan (Floyd), Shirley Mitchell (Leila), Pinto Colvig (dog)

Summary: Harsh feelings arise between Gildersleeve and Peavey when their pets cause damage in the drugstore.

Writers: John Elliotte, Andy White

Comments: Gildersleeve, Leila, and Peavey sing "Smiles." The Jolly Boys sing "Down by the Old Mill Stream." Leila lets the boys play in their field of dreams; she has her own mantra for adult men: "When Leila calls, they come."

Date: March 4, 1953
Title: Office Help

Cast: Willard Waterman (Gildersleeve), John Hiestand, Walter Tetley (Leroy), Lillian Randolph (Birdie), Richard LeGrand (Peavey), Shirley Mitchell (Leila), Mary Shipp (Grace Tuttle), Stan Farrar (Terwilliger)

Summary: Under pressure to finish an overdue water report, Gildersleeve resorts to using Grace as an after-hours secretary.

Writers: John Elliotte, Andy White

Comments: The excuse for not having a secretary, that Bessie never returned after going out for a malt, is a bit lame thirty months after her last appearance. Even though Grace has only known Gildy a short time, she assesses his character quite perceptively, noting that for him dawdling and thinking are synonymous.

Date: March 11, 1953
Title: Leroy Moves Next Door

Cast: Willard Waterman (Gildersleeve), John Hiestand, Mary Lee Robb (Marjorie), Walter Tetley (Leroy), Lillian Randolph (Birdie), Richard LeGrand (Peavey), Jerry Farber (Stuart Watson)

Summary: After Leroy vacates his room to stay with his sister, Throckmorton gives it temporarily to another boy in hopes that his nephew will then want to return home.

Writers: John Elliotte, Andy White

Comments: Gildy delivers another one of his loaded boasts, "I'm just exercising my usual farsightedness," when he should be truthfully admitting "I'm just exhibiting my customary narrow-mindedness." When Leroy sets the ground rules during his brief ascendency to power near the end, he is merely demonstrating his normal craftiness.

Date: March 18, 1953
Title: Jam Session

Cast: Willard Waterman (Gildersleeve), John Hiestand, Walter Tetley (Leroy), Lillian Randolph (Birdie), Richard LeGrand (Peavey), Barbara Whiting (Babs Winthrop), Anne Whitfield (Clara Pettibone)

Summary: Gildersleeve attempts to get Leroy to associate with Clara Pettibone in hopes the boy will become interested in classical music instead of bebop.

Writers: John Elliotte, Andy White

Allusion: Gildersleeve paraphrases from *Moral Essays* by Alexander Pope: "As the twig is bent so grows the tree."

Comments: Barbara sings "Chattanooga Choo Choo." All of a sudden stolid Summerfield has become Hipsville as hot licks replace the voice of the turtle. Barbara displays a pleasant singing voice as she sometimes demonstrated when teaming with sister Margaret.

Date: March 25, 1953
Title: Rummage Sale
   Cast: Willard Waterman (Gildersleeve), John Hiestand, Mary Lee Robb (Marjorie), Walter Tetley (Leroy), Lillian Randolph (Birdie), Richard LeGrand (Peavey), Mary Shipp (Grace Tuttle), Herb Vigran (Jake)
   Summary: The family members reluctantly give up items no longer being used for a rummage sale to buy playground equipment.
   Writers: John Elliotte, Andy White
   Comments: Birdie sings a bit of her version of "Camptown Races." Hypocritical Gildy follows "Women are certainly vain" almost immediately with "I think I'll dress up this morning." The promotion of Easter Seals is smoothly worked into the drugstore scene with no apologies for the plug or for the use of the phrase "crippled children." Waterman invokes for the first time a version of the declaration of despair often uttered by Peary: "This is one of my bad days."

Date: April 1, 1953
Title: Easter Sunrise Service (Repeat)
   Cast: Willard Waterman (Gildersleeve), John Hiestand, Mary Lee Robb (Marjorie), Walter Tetley (Leroy), Lillian Randolph (Birdie), Earle Ross (Hooker), Richard LeGrand (Peavey), Mary Shipp (Grace Tuttle)
   Summary: After changing his mind several times regarding attending the early Easter service, Gildersleeve decides to go when Grace wants to ride along with the family.
   Writers: John Elliotte, Andy White
   Comments: Birdie sings "Were You There When They Crucified My Lord?" Earle Ross is heard for the first time since November 26, 1952. The script for this episode is very similar to the one used on April 9, 1952, with the Paula Winthrop character being replaced by Grace Tuttle.

Date: April 8, 1953
Title: Mayor's Son Is Rival
   Cast: Willard Waterman (Gildersleeve), John Hiestand, Walter Tetley (Leroy), Lillian Randolph (Birdie), Richard LeGrand (Peavey), Stan Farrar (Terwilliger), Barbara Whiting (Babs Winthrop), Tommy Bernard (Freddy Terwilliger)
   Summary: Gildersleeve is concerned when Leroy's jealousy of the budding romance between Babs and the mayor's son might erupt in fisticuffs that could jeopardize his job.
   Writers: John Elliotte, Andy White
   Comments: Tommy Bernard has moved on from his part as Craig, an obnoxious six-year-old, to that of Freddy, an obnoxious teenager. Perhaps to attract a younger audience this episode, like the one that aired on March 18, centers on the trials of teens and is filled with the slang of the hipsters (e.g., *zero, natch, fab, cute dish*). Leroy is almost matching his uncle for delivering contradictory statements in rapid-fire sequence, in this case following "I'm growing up" with his explanation of what he had just been doing: "Reading comic books."

Date: April 15, 1953
Title: Boys' Club
　Cast: Willard Waterman (Gildersleeve), John Hiestand, Walter Tetley (Leroy), Lillian Randolph (Birdie), Richard LeGrand (Peavey), Earle Ross (Hooker), Arthur Q. Bryan (Floyd), Ken Christy (Gates), Robert Easton (Stretch), Stuffy Singer (Piggy)
　Summary: Leroy's newly-formed club takes over the room above the barbershop, leaving the Jolly Boys feeling dispossessed.
　Writers: John Elliotte, Andy White
　Comments: Peavey sings his customary bit of "There Is a Tavern in the Town." The Jolly Boys sing "By the Light of the Silvery Moon" and "When Good Fellows Get Together." The concept of a place for Leroy and his pals to congregate comes full circle because it was their rejection of such a proposed meeting spot on October 8, 1944, that brought about the formation of the adult group known as the Jolly Boys. Robert Easton, late in life a well-respected dialect coach to the stars, would become a member of the *Fibber McGee and Molly* cast in February 1954 as easygoing neighbor Lester Nelson.

Date: April 22, 1953
Title: Marjorie's Spat with Bronco
　Cast: Willard Waterman (Gildersleeve), John Hiestand, Mary Lee Robb (Marjorie), Walter Tetley (Leroy), Lillian Randolph (Birdie), Richard LeGrand (Peavey), Shirley Mitchell (Leila), Richard Crenna (Bronco)
　Summary: Throckmorton tries to patch up a dispute between Bronco and Marjorie that causes her to move back home.

　Writers: John Elliotte, Andy White
　Comments: Richard Crenna is heard for the first time since August 13, 1952. The twins that accompany Marjorie on her move next door are *not* heard as they have fallen into the background of this series.

Date: April 29, 1953
Title: Bottled Water Proposal
　Cast: Willard Waterman (Gildersleeve), John Hiestand, Mary Lee Robb (Marjorie), Walter Tetley (Leroy), Lillian Randolph (Birdie), Richard LeGrand (Peavey), Richard Crenna (Bronco), Stan Farrar (Terwilliger), Shirley Mitchell (Leila)
　Summary: Gildersleeve is shocked when Bronco forms a bottled water company and surprised when friends and family buy shares in the new business.
　Writers: John Elliotte, Andy White
　Comments: Birdie sings "We're in the Money." The writers skillfully organize the later meeting between commissioner and entrepreneur by having Gildy approaching with hat in hand and Bronco issuing his denial of the request with the curt sendoff "I'll call you" and the implied "Don't call me." The tag serves a double purpose: recognizing *One Man's Family*'s 21 years on the air and also tantalizing listeners about the May 6 wedding anniversary episode

Date: May 6, 1953
Title: Anniversary Gift
　Cast: Willard Waterman (Gildersleeve), John Hiestand, Mary Lee Robb (Marjorie), Walter Tetley (Leroy), Lillian Randolph (Birdie), Richard LeGrand (Peavey), Earle Ross (Hooker), Richard Crenna (Bronco)

Summary: Rather than ask Marjorie what she would like for an anniversary gift, Throckmorton purchases a clock that he later discovers she does not want.

Writers: John Elliotte, Andy White

Comments: Hooker sings a bit of "Oh, Promise Me." Gildy provides a clue to the troubles ahead when he boasts "Let's not tell me how to run somebody else's affairs." Even as he stumbles from one blunder to the next he cannot resist puffing himself up with "You're pretty foxy." So said the foolish rabbit inside the pretty, well-fed fox.

Date: May 13, 1953

Title: European Vacation Plans

Cast: Willard Waterman (Gildersleeve), John Hiestand, Walter Tetley (Leroy), Lillian Randolph (Birdie), Richard LeGrand (Peavey), Isabel Randolph (Mrs. Pettibone), Jess Kirkpatrick (Harry), Veola Vonn (Mae Kelly), Stan Farrar (Terwilliger)

Summary: To impress Mrs. Pettibone, Gildersleeve leads her to believe he is planning a trip to Europe during the summer.

Writers: John Elliotte, Andy White

Comments: Isabel Randolph really gets on her high horse as Mrs. Pettibone, prancing in her best Abigail Uppington manner. Gildy yields to she who must be obeyed (Mrs. Pettibone) and the face that launched the cruise ship (Miss Kelly). For once mealy-mouthed Peavey lays his cards on the table and confronts Throckmorton with a four flush. The publicists who gave screen star Ann Sheridan her nickname could also have called Veola Vonn the "Oomph Girl" of the airwaves in recognition of the way she used her seductive voice and voluptuous figure on comedy shows like *The Jack Benny Program* and *The Adventures of Ozzie and Harriet*.

Date: May 20, 1953

Title: Leroy's Theme

Cast: Willard Waterman (Gildersleeve), John Hiestand, Walter Tetley (Leroy), Lillian Randolph (Birdie), Richard LeGrand (Peavey), Jeanne Bates (woman), Jess Kirkpatrick (Harry), Byron Kane (officer)

Summary: Leroy follows Gildersleeve around for a day, intent on writing a theme of 2,500 words about his uncle.

Writers: John Elliotte, Andy White

Comments: Birdie rarely spoke truer words than this assessment of her boss: "It's human to make mistakes and you're the most human man I know." Apparently taking notes in Gildersleeve's office leads to an insatiable desire for liquid refreshment for whether it is a secretary taking dictation or a boy working on a composition the only suitable course of action is to go out for a milk shake. In the tag Throckmorton and Peavey deliver a timely reminder about buying poppies to support the veterans.

Date: May 27, 1953

Title: Wedding Witness

Cast: Willard Waterman (Gildersleeve), John Hiestand, Walter Tetley (Leroy), Lillian Randolph (Birdie), Richard LeGrand (Peavey), Earle Ross (Hooker), Arthur Q. Bryan (Floyd), Tommy Cook (Tommy Clark), Anne Whitfield (Susan Taylor)

Summary: After being asked to be a witness at a private wedding, Gildersleeve takes it upon himself to invite friends and family to take part in the ceremony.

Writers: John Elliotte, Andy White

Comments: Birdie sings "I Went to Your Wedding" and "I Love You Truly." Anne Whitfield has grown up before the ears of listeners in just a few years, advancing from playing wisecracking Phyllis on *The Phil Harris-Alice Faye Show* to assuming the part of a bride on this program. In the tag Waterman issues a call for blood, a reminder that the Korean War has not yet ended. (The armistice would be signed exactly two months after the date of this broadcast.)

Date: June 3, 1953
Title: Birdie's Temporary Move

Cast: Willard Waterman (Gildersleeve), John Hiestand, Mary Lee Robb (Marjorie), Walter Tetley (Leroy), Lillian Randolph (Birdie), Richard LeGrand (Peavey)

Summary: Gildersleeve encourages Birdie to live with Marjorie, leaving him and Leroy to fend for themselves.

Writers: John Elliotte, Andy White

Comments: Gildy should remind himself of his stated belief regarding the opposite sex (i.e., "If a man puts his mind to it, he can get along without women") the next time he meets Leila. Or Paula. Or Gloria. Or Grace. Or _____ [fill in the blank]. Leroy is patently faking an illness, but he could hardly be blamed for feeling less than chipper after ingesting a chocolate soda, two cheeseburgers, an order of French fries, and a double banana split,

and then being subjected to smoke arising from an aborted dinner.

Date: June 10, 1953
Title: House Being Painted

Cast: Willard Waterman (Gildersleeve), John Hiestand, Mary Lee Robb (Marjorie), Walter Tetley (Leroy), Lillian Randolph (Birdie), Richard LeGrand (Peavey), Veola Vonn (Carlotta Dale), George Pirrone (clerk), Larry Harmon (steward)

Summary: Throckmorton plans to stay with friends while the house is being painted, but Leroy prefers that they travel by train to visit Aunt Hattie.

Writers: John Elliotte, Andy White

Comments: That a likely carrier of mumps would be allowed to mingle with people in a store, hotel, and aboard a train is almost as unlikely as a city official breaking into and attempting to enter the home of a municipal court judge.

Date: June 17, 1953
Title: Gift for Miss Tuttle

Cast: Willard Waterman (Gildersleeve), John Hiestand, Walter Tetley (Leroy), Lillian Randolph (Birdie), Richard LeGrand (Peavey), Mary Shipp (Grace Tuttle), Stuffy Singer (Marvin)

Summary: After Leroy leaves a traveling case as a gift on Miss Tuttle's doorstep, Gildersleeve leads Grace to believe the present is from him.

Writers: John Elliotte, Andy White

Allusion: Gildersleeve paraphrases Matthew 5:15: "Don't hide your light under a bushel."

Comments: The writers continue to be evasive about Leroy's age and his grade in school, having the boy interrupt Birdie precisely after the words "is promoted to —" emerge from her lips. Some feminists might bristle at Tuttle's willingness to trade a career for housewifery, although the denouement suggests Grace was suffering from end-of-year burnout and merely needed some time off to regain her zeal for teaching. At the end Leroy gets the kiss his uncle was denied on the date that started the show. Poultry farmers certainly had plenty to crow about because three prominent males in Summerfield have now declared their favorite dish: Gildy loves fried chicken, Leroy finds chicken and dumplings to his liking, and chicken fricassee keeps Hooker happy.

Date: June 24, 1953
Title: Swimming at Grass Lake
  Cast: Willard Waterman (Gildersleeve), John Hiestand, Walter Tetley (Leroy), Lillian Randolph (Birdie), Richard LeGrand (Peavey), Veola Vonn (Mae Kelly), Tommy Cook (Piggy), Stuffy Singer (Marvin)
  Summary: Gildersleeve, hoping for a day of rest at home, reluctantly takes Leroy and his pals to Grass Lake.
  Writers: John Elliotte, Andy White
  Comments: Tommy Cook, a veteran of juvenile roles such as Little Beaver on *Red Ryder,* Junior on *Life of Riley,* and Alexander on *Blondie,* was now at the age (22) when he could be credible as a young marine recruit as he demonstrated a month ago and also take on the part of whiny adolescents like Piggy. Marvin not only disproves Gildy's statement of "a nine-year-old can't match wits with me" but Stuffy Singer also steals almost every scene he is in from Waterman.

Date: July 1, 1953
Title: Generation Gap
  Cast: Willard Waterman (Gildersleeve), John Hiestand, Walter Tetley (Leroy), Lillian Randolph (Birdie), Richard LeGrand (Peavey), Veola Vonn (Mae Kelly), Barbara Whiting (Babs Winthrop)
  Summary: Fearing that Leroy is drifting away to be with his own crowd, Gildersleeve resolves to act more modern so he will fit in with the younger set.
  Writers: John Elliotte, Andy White
  Comments: Maybe it is best that the recorded voice of Leroy gets stuck on "I think he's a —" so listeners are free to fill in what the censor would have taken out. "Zorch me a Coke" is apt to earn someone as many perplexed expressions today as it did in 1953. Again in 1953 *The Great Gildersleeve* continued through the summer with no break.

Date: July 8, 1953 (Script)
Title: Meets Marvin's Aunt
  Cast: Willard Waterman (Gildersleeve), John Hiestand, Walter Tetley (Leroy), Earle Ross (Hooker), Lillian Randolph (Birdie), Richard LeGrand (Peavey), Stuffy Singer (Marvin), Carol Brewster (Lola Rush)
  Summary: After lecturing Leroy about currying favor with Marvin just so he can swim in his pool, Gildersleeve also tries to win points with the boy when he meets Marvin's attractive aunt.
  Writers: John Elliotte, Andy White
  Comments: Peavey reads from a letter sent from his wife that is nothing like one penned by Elizabeth Barrett Browning to her beloved husband: "Dear Mr. Peavey, Don't forget to feed

the parrot. Don't forget to water the flowers. Don't forget to bring in the milk. Respectfully, Mrs. Peavey." Marvin is a crafty operator who leads lustful Gildy into envisioning Lola in a bathing suit and extracts money for allowing Throckmorton to gain access to the pool while withholding the information that she went home the night before.

Date: July 15, 1953
Title: Spray Gun Problems
  Cast: Willard Waterman (Gildersleeve), John Hiestand, Mary Lee Robb (Marjorie), Walter Tetley (Leroy), Lillian Randolph (Birdie), Richard LeGrand (Peavey), Richard Crenna (Bronco)
  Summary: Throckmorton gets both Peavey and Bronco upset when he forces upon them the idea of sharing a spray gun.
  Writers: John Elliotte, Andy White
  Comments: Five weeks after vacating the house because the smell of paint made him ill Gildersleeve is spray painting a picket fence. Leave it to Gildy to dilly-dally by making musical riffs instead of quickly completing the job. A PSA regarding National Farm Safety Week closes the broadcast.

Date: July 22, 1953
Title: Mae Kelly Engaged
  Cast: Willard Waterman (Gildersleeve), John Hiestand, Walter Tetley (Leroy), Lillian Randolph (Birdie), Richard LeGrand (Peavey), Veola Vonn (Mae Kelly), George Neise (Stan Murray)
  Summary: Gildersleeve, elated at first when Mae Kelly returns from her

vacation, becomes depressed when he learns she is engaged.
  Writers: John Elliotte, Andy White
  Comments: Peavey now has a phone near the counter so Gildersleeve does not have to battle the phone booth when he wants to call someone from the drugstore. Leroy is perspicacious in his assessment of his uncle's romantic flings: "He didn't want her till the other fellow got her." The second the field is clear for him to move toward the altar with Mae or any other woman Gildy backs up like a car stuck in reverse.

Date: July 29, 1953
Title: Leroy Visits Aunt Hattie
  Cast: Willard Waterman (Gildersleeve), John Hiestand, Walter Tetley (Leroy), Lillian Randolph (Birdie), Richard LeGrand (Peavey), Tommy Cook (Piggy), Stuffy Singer (Marvin), Jess Kirkpatrick (bus driver)
  Summary: Throckmorton is lonely after Leroy leaves to spend a week with Aunt Hattie.
  Writers: John Elliotte, Andy White
  Comments: Gildy's penchant for second-guessing and changing his mind is in high gear both while standing at the bus stop and at home before the ink dries on the letter he has written. If Gildersleeve is still driving that pre-war Studebaker, the next stop after the current 85,000 mile checkup should be the 90,000 mile chuck out.

Date: August 5, 1953
Title: Fired (Repeat)
  Cast: Willard Waterman (Gildersleeve), John Wald, Walter Tetley (Leroy), Earle Ross (Hooker), Lillian Randolph (Birdie), Richard LeGrand

(Peavey), Arthur Q. Bryan (Floyd), Earle Ross (Hooker), Stan Farrar (Terwilliger), Veola Vonn (Mae Kelly)

Summary: After Throckmorton is fired for loafing on the job, the Jolly Boys attempt to get him restored as water commissioner.

Writers: John Elliotte, Andy White

Comments: Peavey sings a bit of "There Is a Tavern in the Town." This episode is similar to the script used on June 2, 1948. On this occasion Leroy replaces Bessie and Mae Kelly replaces Adeline Fairchild. Marjorie and Gates, heard in the early show, do not appear in this broadcast.

Date: August 12, 1953
Title: Cabin on Lake

Cast: Willard Waterman (Gildersleeve), John Hiestand, Mary Lee Robb (Marjorie), Walter Tetley (Leroy), Lillian Randolph (Birdie), Richard LeGrand (Peavey), Arthur Q. Bryan (Floyd), Tommy Cook (Bud Hinkle)

Summary: Gildersleeve has trouble making up his mind about which cabin and which lake to select for his vacation site.

Writers: Paul West, John Elliotte, Andy White

Comments: It is as if the uncle-nephew roles are reversed during this misadventure with Leroy being the sensible one demonstrating mature judgment and issuing sage advice through a parable meant to edify the hearer. Paul West is again credited as part of the writing team for this and the next two episodes.

Date: August 19, 1953
Title: Fishing with Leroy (Repeat)

Cast: Willard Waterman (Gildersleeve), John Hiestand, Walter Tetley (Leroy), Lillian Randolph (Birdie), Richard LeGrand (Peavey), Arthur Q. Bryan (Floyd), Earle Ross (Hooker), Ken Christy (Gates), Jess Kirkpatrick (George)

Summary: After Leroy hauls in a bunch of bass at Grass Lake, Gildersleeve leads friends to believe he caught them even though he does not have a fishing license.

Writers: Paul West, John Elliotte, Andy White

Comments: Peavey sings "Sonny Boy." The Jolly Boys sing "For He's a Jolly Good Fellow." The script used on May 5, 1948, was slightly altered for this broadcast. For purposes of the story Leroy slips back to being 12.

Date: August 26, 1953
Title: Self-Sufficiency

Cast: Willard Waterman (Gildersleeve), John Hiestand, Mary Lee Robb (Marjorie), Walter Tetley (Leroy), Lillian Randolph (Birdie), Richard LeGrand (Peavey), Tommy Cook (Diz)

Summary: Throckmorton does not know how to occupy his time after a picnic is cancelled.

Writers: Paul West, John Elliotte, Andy White

Comments: Birdie's description of Gildersleeve as the most dependent independent person she knows on June 3 is proven unequivocally on this occasion. Selling comic books to youngsters in the front yard, still considered a harmless activity in 1953, would be frowned upon the next year after Fredric Wertham's *Seduction of the In-*

nocent cast a pall over distribution of such material.

Date: September 2, 1953
Title: Leroy Likes Jo McCoy
  Cast: Willard Waterman (Gildersleeve), John Hiestand, Walter Tetley (Leroy), Lillian Randolph (Birdie), Richard LeGrand (Peavey), Stuffy Singer (Marvin), Marilyn Carroll (Josephine McCoy)
  Summary: Gildersleeve tries to find out more about Leroy's new girl, a tomboy whose toughness the boy admires.
  Writers: John Elliotte, Andy White
  Comments: Marilyn Carroll is convincing both as hoyden on the roof and deb at the door. In the tag Gildy proves that he is asking for it even when somebody else is asking for it.

Date: September 9, 1953
Title: Advice about Ronny
  Cast: Willard Waterman (Gildersleeve), John Hiestand, Mary Lee Robb (Marjorie), Walter Tetley (Leroy), Lillian Randolph (Birdie), Richard LeGrand (Peavey), Richard Crenna (Bronco), Richard Beals (Ronny)
  Summary: Throckmorton upsets both Marjorie and Bronco with his unsolicited advice on raising children.
  Writers: John Elliotte, Andy White
  Comments: Ronny is at the age when he asks "Why?" all the time while his (not so) great-uncle is at the age where his constant blundering causes him to repeatedly wonder "Why did I do that?" Richard Beals, known for his appearances on radio westerns *The Lone Ranger* and *Gunsmoke* and as the voice of Speedy Alka-Seltzer, tackles the

difficult task of sounding like a two-year-old at the age of 26. How many other radio programs could boast of having three actors with the same first name in the cast?

Date: September 16, 1953
Title: Cake for the Fair
  Cast: Willard Waterman (Gildersleeve), John Hiestand, Mary Lee Robb (Marjorie), Walter Tetley (Leroy), Lillian Randolph (Birdie), Richard LeGrand (Peavey), Arthur Q. Bryan (Floyd), Stuffy Singer (Marvin), Elizabeth Patterson (Mrs. Peavey's mother)
  Summary: Gildersleeve compounds his mistake of sampling a cake Birdie was going to enter at the county fair by giving away the recipe for the tasty dessert.
  Writers: John Elliotte, Andy White
  Comments: Gildy knows what it is like to have his cake and feel the heat too. Peavey is more directly involved in the unfolding of this plot than in any other episode of *The Great Gildersleeve*. This is probably the only time Bryan's middle initial is not given with his name in the credits on any program featuring the portly actor. The promise of a recipe and prizes in the tag is an appetizing teaser that will bring many listeners back to their radios the following Wednesday.

Date: September 23, 1953
Title: Babysitting Ronny
  Cast: Willard Waterman (Gildersleeve), John Hiestand (radio announcer), Mary Lee Robb (Marjorie), Walter Tetley (Leroy), Lillian Randolph (Birdie), Richard LeGrand (Peavey), Richard Beals (Ronny)

Summary: Even though Ronny prefers Leroy to stay with him, Gildersleeve muscles his way into babysitting with the tyke and eventually going to sleep on the job.

Writers: John Elliotte, Andy White

Comments: Birdie sings "Crying in the Chapel." Apparently Peavey's formality with his wife is reciprocated by her because he reports that she addresses him as "Mr. Peavey." Waterman quickly rolls over his muff of the line "He isn't old enough to know what he wants." The plot of the previous week's episode serves as a springboard for the "Name the Cake" contest. The answer to Gildy's question "I raised you and Leroy, didn't I?" is a qualified "No" because Marjorie and her brother were both past middle childhood when he assumed guardianship in 1941.

Date: September 30, 1953

Title: Flattery Failure

Cast: Willard Waterman (Gildersleeve), John Hiestand, Walter Tetley (Leroy), Lillian Randolph (Birdie), Richard LeGrand (Peavey), Cathy Lewis (Irene Henshaw), Patrick McGeehan (Baldwin Hogan), Margaret Brayton (Mrs. Pettibone)

Summary: Throckmorton's insincere praising wins temporary favor with Mrs. Pettibone but earns disapproval from Leroy's principal.

Writers: John Elliotte, Andy White

Comments: Radio veteran Pat McGeehan is probably best-known for his work on *The Red Skelton Show*. Cathy Lewis returns in a new role, playing Miss Henshaw with the same keen sensibility she exhibited as Kathryn Milford who also saw through Gildy's shams. Leroy indulges in overstatement of his own when he tells his uncle that "sometimes you go overboard, but you always set the right example" because it is precisely by setting the *wrong* example as Gildersleeve does nearly every week that practical lessons are learned.

Date: October 7, 1953

Title: Haircut at Home

Cast: Willard Waterman (Gildersleeve), John Hiestand, Walter Tetley (Leroy), Lillian Randolph (Birdie), Richard LeGrand (Peavey), Arthur Q. Bryan (Floyd), Stuffy Singer (Marvin), Mary Shipp (Grace Tuttle)

Summary: Gildersleeve gets a botched haircut from Floyd that is made worse at home when Leroy uses clippers purchased from Peavey.

Writers: John Elliotte, Andy White

Comments: The writers give Marvin some pithy nuggets (e.g., "Murder," "Not bad, Baldy") that Singer rings up like the little trouper he is. Grace's comment that Gildy is lurking in the hallway "like Friday waiting with his Dragnet" delivers an incidental plug for the NBC program, though she would have been more accurate describing him as looking like Yul Brynner in a hairnet.

Date: October 14, 1953

Title: Dating Principal and Teacher

Cast: Willard Waterman (Gildersleeve), John Hiestand, Walter Tetley (Leroy), Lillian Randolph (Birdie), Richard LeGrand (Peavey), Cathy Lewis (Irene Henshaw), Mary Shipp (Grace Tuttle), Joanne Jordan (Miss Parish)

Summary: Throckmorton finds that

juggling commitments made to Irene and Grace gets him into trouble with both women.

Writers: John Elliotte, Andy White

Comments: Leroy indicates Miss Tuttle teaches seventh grade and that he is still in her class so it appears that the report card he brought home on June 17 promoted him to take one step forward and two steps back. But no matter where Leroy is in the Summerfield school system he cannot escape good old Ethel Hammerschlag. Gildy's transparency is obvious to cagey Leroy ("He can read me like a book") and to observant Irene Henshaw who tells him plainly "I think we know each other."

Date: October 21, 1953
Title: Electrical Wizard
  Cast: Willard Waterman (Gildersleeve), John Hiestand, Walter Tetley (Leroy), Lillian Randolph (Birdie), Richard LeGrand (Peavey), Cathy Lewis (Irene Henshaw), Jess Kirkpatrick (Jensen)
  Summary: When Gildersleeve learns of mischief in the school bell system, he assumes Leroy is the culprit because the boy had been responsible for similar pranks at home.
  Writers: John Elliotte, Andy White
  Comments: Gildy's declaration to Leroy to "stop insisting you're innocent when I keep telling you you're guilty" is about as shortsighted and unreasonable as a parent or guardian can be. Actually, when Throckmorton sticks his nose into Jensen's business by fiddling with a dangling wire *he* is the one who causes a disruption at school, not his nephew.

Date: October 28, 1953
Title: Witness to Accident
  Cast: Willard Waterman (Gildersleeve), John Hiestand, Walter Tetley (Leroy), Lillian Randolph (Birdie), Richard LeGrand (Peavey), Stan Farrar (Terwilliger), Cathy Lewis (Irene Henshaw), Tommy Cook (Piggy), Frosty Fowler (subpoena server)
  Summary: Gildersleeve is caught in the middle between Peavey and Terwilliger who are at loggerheads over a fender bender.
  Writers: John Elliotte, Andy White
  Comments: Peavey has officially supplanted the virtually-forgotten Hooker as Throckmorton's best friend. Gildy compares his pursuer to Crazylegs Hirsch, former collegiate gridiron legend and then-current NFL player known for his speed and open field evasiveness. Cathy Lewis appears briefly but is omitted from the credits.

Date: November 4, 1953
Title: Individualist
  Cast: Willard Waterman (Gildersleeve), John Hiestand, Walter Tetley (Leroy), Lillian Randolph (Birdie), Richard LeGrand (Peavey), Cathy Lewis (Irene Henshaw), Veola Vonn (Mae Kelly), Howard McNear (justice of the peace)
  Summary: Throckmorton impetuously decides to live impulsively, setting his own schedule for work, meals, and romance.
  Writers: John Elliotte, Andy White
  Comments: Howard McNear is heard for the first time on this program, hanging out his shingle as J.P. in place of his usual M.D. as Doc Adams on *Gunsmoke*. At the office flighty Gilder-

sleeve lets scarcely a second elapse between "I can really concentrate" and "I wonder what Irene's doing." Gildy's startled reaction to hearing "Minnowville" at the end might lead listeners to think he is about to go into a "Slowly I turned" routine.

Date: November 11, 1953
Title: Authority over Leroy
  Cast: Willard Waterman (Gildersleeve), John Hiestand, Walter Tetley (Leroy), Lillian Randolph (Birdie), Richard LeGrand (Peavey), Mary Shipp (Grace Tuttle), Barbara Whiting (Babs Winthrop), Stuffy Singer (Marvin)
  Summary: Gildersleeve recruits Birdie, Peavey, and Marvin to attest to his sagacity so Leroy will heed his advice.
  Writers: John Elliotte, Andy White
  Comments: Babs establishes her age as 14 and the problems of teenagers are expressly addressed on this broadcast so it is safe to assume that Leroy is again twixt 12 and 20. Rather than acting like a real troublemaker in the neighborhood as Gildy claims, Marvin sounds like the juvenile version of what silky Sarah Vaughan later praised in song as a "smooth operator."

Date: November 18, 1953
Title: Competing for Irene
  Cast: Willard Waterman (Gildersleeve), John Hiestand, Walter Tetley (Leroy), Lillian Randolph (Birdie), Richard LeGrand (Peavey), Cathy Lewis (Irene Henshaw), Tommy Cook (Piggy), Peter Leeds (Clarence Olson)
  Summary: After being embarrassed on the football field when Piggy tackles him, Throckmorton attempts to prove

his competitive spirit by engaging in a badminton game with his romantic rival.
  Writers: John Elliotte, Andy White
  Comments: Peter Leeds also worked with Cathy Lewis on her own program, *On Stage*. Gildy's claim of being able to play a good game of tennis must have been long before he disgraced himself on the court with Paula on October 22, 1952.

Date: November 25, 1953
Title: Dinner with Three Guests
  Cast: Willard Waterman (Gildersleeve), John Hiestand, Walter Tetley (Leroy), Lillian Randolph (Birdie), Richard LeGrand (Peavey), Cathy Lewis (Irene Henshaw), Veola Vonn (Mae Kelly)
  Summary: When his dinner dates with Mae and Irene are cancelled, Throckmorton invites Peavey to join him instead.
  Writers: John Elliotte, Andy White
  Comments: Gildy's belief that Leroy is "growing up too fast" is not borne out by the boy's age progression of about 12 months every 12 years. He also misspeaks when he claims his chief problem is "I'm too big-hearted" when actually it is his oversized oral cavity that gets him into most of his predicaments. Mrs. Peavey's letter suggests that the parrot ranks higher in the henpecking order than her husband does.

Date: December 2, 1953
Title: Christmas Money
  Cast: Willard Waterman (Gildersleeve), John Hiestand, Walter Tetley (Leroy), Lillian Randolph (Birdie), Richard LeGrand (Peavey), Cathy Lewis

(Irene Henshaw), Gloria Holliday (Bessie), Frosty Fowler (Riley)

Summary: Gildersleeve tries to sell insurance to friends to raise extra money for Christmas presents.

Writers: John Elliotte, Andy White

Comments: Gloria Holliday, not heard since May 31, 1950, returns as Bessie. Gildy's effort to be subtle results in Irene's misinterpreting his sales pitch for a marriage proposal, and he makes matters worse when he muffs his apology.

Date: December 9, 1953
Title: Takes Bessie to Dance

Cast: Willard Waterman (Gildersleeve), John Hiestand, Walter Tetley (Leroy), Lillian Randolph (Birdie), Richard LeGrand (Peavey), Cathy Lewis (Irene Henshaw), Gloria Holliday (Bessie Barstow), George Neise (Clarence Olson)

Summary: Throckmorton cancels a date with an understanding Irene so he can take Bessie to a dance where he meets a miffed Irene.

Writers: John Elliotte, Andy White

Comments: The writers employ a change of pace by having Irene and Birdie serve as narrators to open the two acts. Bessie's last name is given for the first time. Two-timing seems to be the theme of this romantic roundabout. Waterman announces the winner of the "Name the Cake" contest.

Date: December 16, 1953
Title: Renews Friendship with Hooker

Cast: Willard Waterman (Gildersleeve), John Hiestand, Walter Tetley (Leroy), Lillian Randolph (Birdie), Richard LeGrand (Peavey), Earle Ross

(Hooker), Paul Maxey (W. Roxwell Logan), Dick Ryan (Albert)

Summary: Gildersleeve feuds with Hooker after observing the judge host a social function to which he was not invited.

Writers: John Elliotte, Andy White

Comments: Birdie sings "Jingle Bells." Hooker sings "Dear Old Pal of Mine." Birdie introduces the early action, Leroy sets up the second act. Gildy wonders when he last saw the judge; Hooker was last heard almost four months earlier, on August 19. Again Birdie demonstrates her wisdom by recognizing that Hooker is blameless in this situation and that Gildersleeve's stubbornness and imprudence are at the root of the disagreement.

Date: December 23, 1953
Title: Needy Children's Christmas

Cast: Willard Waterman (Gildersleeve), John Hiestand, Walter Tetley (Leroy), Lillian Randolph (Birdie), Richard LeGrand (Peavey), Ken Christy (Gates), Cathy Lewis (Irene Henshaw), George Neise (Clarence Olson)

Summary: Throckmorton loses sight of the spirit of Christmas when he takes over a project to raise money for gifts to be given to underprivileged children.

Writers: John Elliotte, Andy White

Comments: The Kraft Choristers sing "It Came Upon a Midnight Clear," "Ding Dong Bells," "Angels We Have Heard on High," and "Joy to the World." Leroy opens the action by setting the Christmas scene. Peavey lets it be known that he is president of the Jolly Boys.

Date: December 30, 1953
Title: New Year's Eve Reminiscing
Cast: Willard Waterman (Gildersleeve), John Hiestand, Mary Lee Robb (Marjorie), Walter Tetley (Leroy), Lillian Randolph (Birdie), Richard LeGrand (Peavey), Cathy Lewis (Irene Henshaw), Barbara Whiting (Babs Winthrop)
Summary: As Throckmorton prepares to welcome 1954 with Irene, he recalls some important days in the lives of Marjorie and Leroy.
Writers: John Elliotte, Andy White
Comments: Leroy sings "There'll Be a Hot Time in the Old Town Tonight." Birdie introduces both acts. The flashback episodes include the attic scene from April 19, 1950, Leroy's first date from November 29, 1950, and the teen scene with Leroy and Babs from November 28, 1951.

Date: January 6, 1954
Title: Meets Irene's Father
Cast: Willard Waterman (Gildersleeve), John Hiestand, Walter Tetley (Leroy), Lillian Randolph (Birdie), Richard LeGrand (Peavey), Cathy Lewis (Irene Henshaw), Will Wright (Mr. Henshaw)
Summary: Gildersleeve is convinced that Mr. Henshaw is intent on bringing his daughter and Gildy to the altar.
Writers: John Elliotte, Andy White
Comments: Irene sings "I'm in the Mood for Love." Leroy sings a travesty of the same song. Leroy opens act one, Birdie introduces act two. Cathy Lewis, who did not get many chances to sing on the air, demonstrates a pleasing voice. Throckmorton's classification of his relationship with Irene as being

"purely platonic" is laughable because it is physical desire, not spiritual attachment, which attracts him to every one of his sweethearts.

Date: January 13, 1954
Title: Locked in Basement
Cast: Willard Waterman (Gildersleeve), John Hiestand, Mary Lee Robb (Marjorie), Walter Tetley (Leroy), Lillian Randolph (Birdie), Richard LeGrand (Peavey), George Neise (Clarence Olson), Joanne Jordan (Irene Henshaw)
Summary: While trying to patch up a quarrel between Mr. and Mrs. Peavey, Gildersleeve gets locked in their basement and misses a date with Irene.
Writers: John Elliotte, Andy White
Comments: Irene opens both acts in a surly mood, and the ill-tempered tone even spreads to Peavey's Pharmacy. The food Gildy munches on while in captivity suits him well because he is in a major jam *and* a real pickle.

Date: January 20, 1954
Title: Leroy Likes Wendy
Cast: Willard Waterman (Gildersleeve), John Hiestand, Mary Lee Robb (Marjorie), Walter Tetley (Leroy), Lillian Randolph (Birdie), Richard LeGrand (Peavey), Luanna Patten (Wendy Howard)
Summary: Throckmorton gives Leroy permission to go with a new girl provided that he can act as chaperone.
Writers: John Elliotte, Andy White
Comments: Birdie introduces the opening scene, Leroy brings things up to date after the main commercial. Gildy takes a page from the Chester A. Riley book of parental intolerance with

this gem: "I'm not going to be unreasonable about it. I'm just going to forbid it." The hot rods in Summerfield must be more horse than auto because Dinky's delight has to be tied to a lamppost.

Date: January 27, 1954
Title: Bronco Resents Meddling
   Cast: Willard Waterman (Gildersleeve), John Hiestand, Mary Lee Robb (Marjorie), Walter Tetley (Leroy), Lillian Randolph (Birdie), Richard LeGrand (Peavey), Lee Millar (Bronco)
   Summary: Bronco is upset when Throckmorton interferes in his affairs.
   Writers: John Elliotte, Andy White
   Comments: Birdie leads into both acts as narrator. The writers deliver a zinger at the other medium with Peavey's comment about wanting to watch a movie on TV he had not seen for 20 years. It is precisely because, in Gildy's words, "I've got a hide like an elephant" that he frequently has to hide like a rabbit.

Date: February 3, 1954
Title: Concerned about Schoolwork
   Cast: Willard Waterman (Gildersleeve), John Hiestand, Walter Tetley (Leroy), Lillian Randolph (Birdie), Richard LeGrand (Peavey), Mary Shipp (Grace Tuttle), Barbara Whiting (Babs Winthrop), Carolyn Wadsworth (Susan)
   Summary: Convinced that Leroy's mind is more on girls than on academic matters, Gildersleeve is determined to show a good example by concentrating on his work and resisting Grace's efforts to charm him.
   Writers: John Elliotte, Andy White

Comments: Birdie opens act one, Peavey leads into the second act. Mary Shipp demonstrates some of the classroom demeanor she exhibited as Miss Spaulding on *Life with Luigi*. Another reminder of the Cold War is given in Waterman's PSA for Radio Free Europe.

Date: February 10, 1954
Title: Annual Dinner with Hooker
   Cast: Willard Waterman (Gildersleeve), John Hiestand, Mary Lee Robb (Marjorie), Walter Tetley (Leroy), Lillian Randolph (Birdie), Richard LeGrand (Peavey), Earle Ross (Hooker), Mary Shipp (Grace Tuttle)
   Summary: Gildersleeve makes a date with Grace, thinking that Horace has forgotten the dinner the judge hosts every year for him and the children.
   Writers: John Elliotte, Andy White
   Comments: Birdie opens the first act, Gildy summarizes Grace's icy reaction in the store to open act two. This episode borrows the idea of a traditional dinner with Hooker from April 7, 1946, although the event has not been mentioned since that occasion which was in the spring, not on February 12 as Hooker claims on this date. There is more second-hand news than usual which Gildy learns from Marjorie, Leroy, and Birdie. Observance of Boy Scout Week is worked into the tag so a parrot gag can close the program.

Date: February 17, 1954
Title: Considers Political Career
   Cast: Willard Waterman (Gildersleeve), John Hiestand, Walter Tetley (Leroy), Lillian Randolph (Birdie), Richard LeGrand (Peavey), Cathy Lewis (Irene Henshaw), Stan Farrar (Ter-

williger), Myra Marsh (Mrs. Ramsey Nicholson), Byron Kane (Higgins)

Summary: Throckmorton envisions a career in politics for himself that he hopes to kick off with an address to the Parent-Teacher Association.

Writers: John Elliotte, Andy White

Allusion: Gildersleeve quotes from *Julius Caesar* by William Shakespeare: "There is a tide in the affairs of men, / Which, taken at the flood, leads on to fortune."

Comments: Hiestand once more sets the initial scene, Peavey opens the second act with a brief recap. It is typical of Gildersleeve to let the "big head" he takes pride in get even larger by leaping from a compliment on his job about which he has little knowledge into a career in politics about which he knows even less. It is best that Leroy's suggestion about his uncle giving samples during his speech was not followed to avoid an indelicate headline in the *Indicator-Vindicator* such as "Gildersleeve Passes Water at PTA Meeting."

Date: February 24, 1954
Title: Resigns from Jolly Boys

Cast: Willard Waterman (Gildersleeve), John Hiestand, Walter Tetley (Leroy), Lillian Randolph (Birdie), Richard LeGrand (Peavey), Earle Ross (Hooker), Arthur Q. Bryan (Floyd), Ken Christy (Gates)

Summary: Gildersleeve temporarily resigns from the Jolly Boys after missing a photo opportunity, then returns to run for president of the club.

Writers: John Elliotte, Andy White

Comments: The Jolly Boys sing "By the Light of the Silvery Moon" and

"When You Were Sweet Sixteen." Peavey sings his usual line of "There Is a Tavern in the Town." Part of "Silvery Moon" precedes Hiestand's setting the opening scene, Birdie welcomes Gildy after the central commercial. Jack Meakin is specifically mentioned as part of the cast for his piano playing. Instead of comparing her husband to a fat Rudy Vallee, Lovey would have been more accurate if she had said he resembled Elmer Fudd, the cartoon character whose voice Bryan supplied.

Date: March 3, 1954
Title: Paula Winthrop Returns

Cast: Willard Waterman (Gildersleeve), John Hiestand, Walter Tetley (Leroy), Lillian Randolph (Birdie), Richard LeGrand (Peavey), Jeanne Bates (Paula Winthrop), Mary Shipp (Grace Tuttle), Byron Kane (gas station attendant)

Summary: Throckmorton breaks a date with Grace because he wants to step up in society with wealthy Paula Winthrop.

Writers: John Elliotte, Andy White

Comments: Birdie narrates both acts. The writers rework the idea of Gildy trying to squeak through a date with little cash from October 1, 1952, and also toss in a prolonged footsteps gag first employed on September 10, 1952. Mary Shipp's fine delivery of "Well, Tallahassee" deserves a "Well said, Sassy." Again, Gildy's lust gets the better of him as a photograph of Paula in a seductive dress sends him over the edge.

Date: March 10, 1954
Title: Behind the Times

Cast: Willard Waterman (Gildersleeve), John Hiestand, Walter Tetley (Leroy), Lillian Randolph (Birdie), Richard LeGrand (Peavey), Jeanne Bates (Paula Winthrop), Barbara Whiting (Babs Winthrop)

Summary: Gildersleeve is concerned that Babs and Leroy consider him old-fashioned.

Writers: John Elliotte, Andy White

Comments: Gildersleeve sings "Stout-Hearted Men." It is appropriate that Gildy brags "I'm just as up-to-date as the next fellow" while standing next to Peavey. Rondo Hatton must have been ahead of his time because he was doing The Creep a decade before this episode aired.

Date: March 17, 1954
Title: Meets Marie

Cast: Willard Waterman (Gildersleeve), John Hiestand, Walter Tetley (Leroy), Lillian Randolph (Birdie), Richard LeGrand (Peavey), Mary Shipp (Grace Tuttle), George Neise (Clarence Olson), Gladys Holland (Marie Olson)

Summary: To get revenge on Clarence for dating his sweethearts, Throckmorton plans to move in on an acquaintance of the intern named Marie.

Writers: John Elliotte, Andy White

Comments: Birdie sings "Painting the Clouds with Sunshine." Peavey sings "Marie." Clarence opens the action and throws down a gauntlet at the same time, Birdie picks the plot thread up after the central commercial. Employing an actress who could speak with a distinct French accent and keeping the last name of Clarence's companion a secret makes for a real surprise ending. A

PSA for the American Red Cross is worked into the tag.

Date: March 24, 1954
Title: Hobby Show

Cast: Willard Waterman (Gildersleeve), John Hiestand, Walter Tetley (Leroy), Lillian Randolph (Birdie), Richard LeGrand (Peavey), Marie Shipp (Grace Tuttle), George Neise (Clarence Olson)

Summary: Feeling left out because he does not have anything to exhibit at a hobby show, Gildersleeve tries to build a lamp in one day despite frequent interruptions.

Writers: John Elliotte, Andy White

Comments: Grace opens the story, Birdie brings listeners back into the action after the main commercial. Even though a small cast is involved in this episode, the mention of the hobbies and participation of Floyd, Gates, and Hooker gives listeners the impression that more of the old guard are on hand than are actually present. The tag includes a practical example of how buying Easter Seals can change lives.

Date: March 31, 1954
Title: Royal Treatment from Marie

Cast: Willard Waterman (Gildersleeve), John Hiestand, Walter Tetley (Leroy), Lillian Randolph (Birdie), Richard LeGrand (Peavey), Mary Shipp (Grace Tuttle), Gladys Holland (Marie Olson)

Summary: Marie's complete devotion and subservient behavior almost convinces Throckmorton that Grace and his other regular sweethearts treat him too lightly.

Writers: John Elliotte, Andy White

Comments: The four-month run of character narrations ends as Hiestand resumes the role of setting the scenes. "Cross Over the Bridge" refers to the Top Ten hit by Patti Page. Gildy doesn't seem pleased with the music Grace selects, yet "In the Mood" aptly captures his romantic temperament quite well.

Date: April 7, 1954
Title: Bronco Learns French
   Cast: Willard Waterman (Gildersleeve), John Hiestand, Mary Lee Robb (Marjorie), Walter Tetley (Leroy), Lillian Randolph (Birdie), Richard LeGrand (Peavey), Richard Crenna (Bronco), Gladys Holland (Marie Olson)
   Summary: Marjorie is jealous when Bronco takes French lessons from attractive Marie Olson.
   Writers: John Elliotte, Andy White
   Comments: Peavey sings "Mademoiselle from Armentières." The reference to Zsa Zsa Gabor recalls that time when she was still considered ooh la la and had not yet become the Queen of Outer Camp. Waterman concludes the show with a serious PSA on behalf of the American Cancer Society.

Date: April 14, 1954
Title: Bronco's Boss Dates Marie
   Cast: Willard Waterman (Gildersleeve), John Hiestand, Marie Lee Robb (Marjorie), Walter Tetley (Leroy), Lillian Randolph (Birdie), Richard LeGrand (Peavey), Richard Crenna (Bronco), Gladys Holland (Marie Olson), Parley Baer (Dudley Hammond)
   Summary: Gildersleeve is displeased when Bronco's bachelor boss begins courting Marie.

Writers: John Elliotte, Andy White
   Comments: Leroy sings "Asleep in the Deep." Parley Baer, heard weekly on *Gunsmoke* and irregularly on *Escape* and the fifteen-minute version of *Fibber McGee and Molly*, makes his first appearance on *The Great Gildersleeve*.

Date: April 21, 1954
Title: Leroy Suspicious of Marie
   Cast: Willard Waterman (Gildersleeve), John Hiestand, Walter Tetley (Leroy), Lillian Randolph (Birdie), Richard LeGrand (Peavey), Earle Ross (Hooker), Arthur Q. Bryan (Floyd), Gladys Holland (Marie Olson)
   Summary: After Marie convinces Throckmorton to delay his fishing trip with his nephew, Leroy recruits the Jolly Boys to throw Gildy off the romantic track.
   Writers: John Elliotte, Andy White
   Comments: This is one scheme of Leroy's that backfires when his conspirators fall for the charms of Marie. The sweet-talker even soft-soaps Leroy by comparing him to William Holden, who was right at his peak after winning the best actor Oscar for *Stalag 17* and breaking into the ranks of top ten box office stars for the first of five consecutive years.

Date: April 28, 1954
Title: Meets Thelma Scott
   Cast: Willard Waterman (Gildersleeve), John Hiestand, Walter Tetley (Leroy), Lillian Randolph (Birdie), Richard LeGrand (Peavey), Mary Shipp (Grace Tuttle), Julie Bennett (Thelma Scott)
   Summary: Gildersleeve plans to save money by giving up dating.

Writers: John Elliotte, Andy White

Comments: Birdie gives her weight as 182 pounds, providing listeners with a picture of a formidable body to go with that booming voice and commanding presence. Peavey's sly technique in the buggy proves that the horse knows the way. Throckmorton's recollection of the teacher's convention in Kenosha and his confession that "I almost went up there" again places Summerfield south of (but close to) Wisconsin.

Date: May 5, 1954 (Script)

Title: Student Newspaper Article

Cast: Willard Waterman (Gildersleeve), John Hiestand, Walter Tetley (Leroy), Lillian Randolph (Birdie), Richard LeGrand (Peavey), Mary Shipp (Grace Tuttle), Stuffy Singer (Marvin), Ralph Dumke (Homer Crum), Mimi Simpson (Ruthie)

Summary: After Marvin observes him asleep on the job and being kissed by a girl, Gildersleeve fears that the boy will reveal the embarrassing incidents in the school paper.

Writers: John Elliotte, Andy White

Comments: Homer Crum is a tamer neighbor than Rumson Bullard but just as belittling when discussing Throckmorton's lack of intelligence. Marvin again gets the last laugh after Gildy confesses all to Grace Tuttle by informing the commissioner that, rather than submit the article to the school paper, he is going to give it to the editor of the town's newspaper.

Date: May 12, 1954

Title: Dinner for Clarence

Cast: Willard Waterman (Gilder-

sleeve), John Hiestand, Walter Tetley (Leroy), Lillian Randolph (Birdie), Richard LeGrand (Peavey), Mary Shipp (Grace Tuttle), George Neise (Clarence Olson), Herb Butterfield (Doctor Mason)

Summary: After learning that Clarence is leaving town, Gildersleeve is so pleased his rival will be out of the picture that he hosts a testimonial dinner for the departing intern.

Writers: John Elliotte, Andy White

Comments: Throckmorton, as usual, cannot leave well enough alone and flatters his competitor insincerely. Deflated Gildy does get the last laugh by deflating some tires.

Date: May 19, 1954

Title: Running for Sheriff

Cast: Willard Waterman (Gildersleeve), John Hiestand, Walter Tetley (Leroy), Lillian Randolph (Birdie), Richard LeGrand (Peavey), Richard Crenna (Bronco), Cathy Lewis (Irene Henshaw), Gail Bonney (Mama Hubbard), Olan Soule (Joe)

Summary: Encouraged by Irene to seek the job of sheriff, Gildersleeve thinks all will be smooth sailing until a redoubtable female challenger enters the race.

Writers: John Elliotte, Andy White

Comments: It is totally like impetuous Throckmorton to let a little flattery whet his appetite to go after a position without checking into the job's qualifications or forming any opinions on what he plans to do if elected. Gildy borrows one of the Kingfish's favorite ejaculations when he exclaims "Mama!"

Date: May 26, 1954

Title: Aunt Hattie Back Again

Cast: Willard Waterman (Gildersleeve), John Hiestand, Walter Tetley (Leroy), Lillian Randolph (Birdie), Richard LeGrand (Peavey), Cathy Lewis (Irene Henshaw), Isabel Randolph (Hattie)

Summary: After Gildersleeve institutes a strict disciplinary policy for Leroy, the boy invites Aunt Hattie to stay so she can give his uncle a bitter taste of his own medicine.

Writers: John Elliotte, Andy White

Comments: Gildersleeve sings "Indian Love Call." On other visits Hattie made life miserable for everyone; now she picks on Throckmorton until Leroy reverts to form. The writers test the censor's boundaries with Birdie's "She gives you hail, Columbia" and Gildy's "Oh, poo."

Date: June 2, 1954

Title: Getting Hattie to Leave

Cast: Willard Waterman (Gildersleeve), John Hiestand, Walter Tetley (Leroy), Lillian Randolph (Birdie), Richard LeGrand (Peavey), Stan Farrar (Terwilliger), Noreen Gammill (Hattie), Johnny McGovern (Piggy)

Summary: Gildersleeve and Leroy invite noisy houseguests to make Aunt Hattie uncomfortable enough so she will return home.

Writers: John Elliotte, Andy White

Comments: Peavey sings his customary line of "There Is a Tavern in the Town." Hattie gives Gildy's weight as 220 pounds. Hattie is back in harness as crepe hanger, her sourness and dark chasing any sweetness and light out of the house. Her switch from harried harridan to persuasive advocate in the mayor's office is very abrupt but nec-essary so Throckmorton can make another of his intrusive blunders.

Radio schedules in *The New York Times, The Chicago Tribune* and other newspapers indicate *The Great Gildersleeve* was also heard on June 9, 16, 23, and 30. These may have been repeats of earlier episodes.

Date: October 20, 1955

Title: Floyd's Inheritance

Cast: Willard Waterman (Gildersleeve), Don Rickles, Walter Tetley (Leroy), Lillian Randolph (Birdie), Richard LeGrand (Peavey), Earle Ross (Hooker), Arthur Q. Bryan (Floyd), Ken Christy (Gates)

Summary: Floyd uses a $1,500 inheritance to buy a car and expensive presents for his friends.

Writers: John Elliotte, Andy White

Comments: The Jolly Boys sing "When Good Fellows Get Together" and "For He's a Jolly Good Fellow." This is the first episode of the 1955-1956 season. Don Rickles is the new announcer. Virgil Reimer is credited as director. There are no commercials, only PSAs for the Community Chest and nurse recruitment as well as a promo for NBC *Monitor.* There are no musical bridges and the Jolly Boys sing a cappella.

Date: 1955–1957

Title: Laughing Coyote Ranch

Cast: Willard Waterman (Gildersleeve), Walter Tetley (Leroy), Amanda Randolph (Birdie), Shirley Mitchell (Leila), Richard LeGrand (Peavey), Doye O'Dell

Summary: At a dude ranch Gildersleeve is outmaneuvered for the affections and attention of Leila by singing cowboy Doye O'Dell.

Writer: Unknown

Comments: Doye O'Dell sings "You're the Only Star in My Blue Heaven." The extant recording of this undated episode is a hodgepodge. The opening which credits Kraft and Peary has Peary's distinctive laugh, but the show is clearly from the 1950s with Waterman playing the lead role. Amanda Randolph takes over the part of Birdie from her sister. There are no transitions or commercials. The laughter is clearly canned. There are no closing credits.

Date: 1955–1957
Title: Water Shut Off

Cast: Willard Waterman (Gildersleeve), Don Rickles, Walter Tetley (Leroy), Amanda Randolph (Birdie), Richard LeGrand (Peavey), Jack Moyles (Charlie Anderson), Betty Lou Gerson (June Steadman)

Summary: Gildersleeve implores June to persuade Charlie Anderson to get the water running in Summerfield homes again.

Writer: Virginia Safford Lynne

Allusion: Leroy paraphrases from *Rime of the Ancient Mariner* by Samuel Taylor Coleridge: "Water, water everywhere and not a drop to drip."

Comments: The commercials or PSAs have been removed. Lynne also wrote scripts for *The First Nighter*. Gildersleeve is careful not to refer to the place where the sink is located as the water closet, thus avoiding the brouhaha that led to Jack Paar walking off his TV show. The snifter valve again

proves to be the source of the water problems.

Date: 1955–1957
Title: Winter Sports

Cast: Willard Waterman (Gildersleeve), Don Rickles, Walter Tetley (Leroy), Amanda Randolph (Birdie), Richard LeGrand (Peavey), Gloria Holliday (Bessie), Bob Jellison (Hector)

Summary: Mishaps are the rule when Bessie, Hector, Gildersleeve, Leroy, and Birdie engage in skiing, sledding, and skating at a mountain retreat.

Writer: Virginia Safford Lynne

Comments: This AFRS rebroadcast features announcements promoting the FBI and USAFI. Bessie becomes somewhat more assertive in this outing. Waterman plays over Amanda's "sky lift" blooper.

Date: 1955–1957
Title: Antique Vase

Cast: Willard Waterman (Gildersleeve), Don Rickles, Walter Tetley (Leroy), Amanda Randolph (Birdie), Richard LeGrand (Peavey), Shirley Mitchell (Leila), Ken Peters (Miller)

Summary: Gildersleeve thinks he is in a jam after turning one of Leila's heirlooms into a lamp.

Writer: Virginia Safford Lynne

Comments: This is another AFRS rebroadcast. Judging by the directions Leila gives Birdie as they leave the house, she is again living nearby. Throckmorton's claim that he is "just slightly perfect" needs to be qualified with "but also grossly fallible." Rickles uses the nickname "Gildy," a familiarity not employed by the other announcers.

Appendix A: Cast Members

The Two Gildersleeves

HAROLD PEARY (1908–1985)

Peary first played the part of Throckmorton P. Gildersleeve on the October 3, 1939, episode of *Fibber McGee and Molly*. His primary purpose was to provide an adversary for McGee. When gasbag Gildy met garrulous Fibber inside or outside 79 Wistful Vista, the fur flew and the fun flourished.

Hal took the Gildersleeve character to Summerfield for a nine-year run on NBC, from August 31, 1941, to June 14, 1950. During the 1950–1951 season Peary starred in *Honest Harold* on CBS.

Peary's deep baritone, heard frequently on both *The Great Gildersleeve* and *Honest Harold*, was an outgrowth of his early vocal training and experience in musical comedies and vaudeville. The native Californian found radio work around San Francisco before gravitating to Chicago to learn the ropes on *Lights Out* and other NBC programs, including small parts on *Fibber McGee and Molly* beginning in September 1937.

Once the boisterous character of Gildersleeve became established, it proved to be both blessing and bane for Peary: the voice became his calling card but also a straitjacket because audiences seemed reluctant to accept him in any other guise than Mr. Bluster.

Harold Peary. Gildersleeve for nine years, Gildy for the rest of his life.

Hal appeared as Mayor LaTrivia in the very brief TV run of *Fibber McGee and Molly*, played secondary roles in two other short-lived series, *Blondie* (1957) and *Willy* (1954–1955), and made guest appearances on popular programs such as *Perry Mason* and *The Dick Van Dyke Show*.

Sponsors picked his ripe, pear-shaped tones frequently in the 1960s and 1970s to promote their products. Peary became both the voice and face of Gibraltar Savings and Loan in radio and TV commercials.

Harold officially retired in 1981, five years after his third wife died. His second wife, Gloria Holliday, played addlepated Bessie on *The Great Gildersleeve* beginning in January 1946.

WILLARD WATERMAN (1914–1995)

Willard played Throckmorton P. Gildersleeve on radio from September 6, 1950, to the end of the series in 1957. He made two earlier appearances in 1947 on *The Great Gildersleeve* in supporting roles.

While attending the University of Wisconsin in his hometown of Madison, Willard's experience on the school's station got him interested in working in radio as a career that soon after took him over the state line to Chicago to appear in *Chandu, the Magician, Tom Mix, Bachelor's Children, First Nighter*, and other shows broadcasting from the Windy City. A leading role in the comedy *Those Websters* brought him to the West Coast where he became a busy actor, heard not only on that series but also guesting on *Damon Runyon Theater, Our Miss Brooks, Yours Truly, Johnny Dollar, The Halls of Ivy, Leave It to Joan*, and *Amos 'n' Andy*.

Willard starred in all 39 episodes of the syndicated TV series of *The Great Gildersleeve* (1955–1956). In the next two decades he appeared on Broadway and on tour in *Mame* and in touring productions of *The Pajama Game* and *How to Succeed in Business Without Really Trying*. His film credits included *Auntie Mame* and *The Apartment*.

Waterman enjoyed being invited to old-time radio conventions and taking part in recreations of *The Great Gildersleeve* which allowed him to take all of his listeners back to Summerfield in mind and spirit.

Waterman and Tetley each merited a card in the 1953 Bowman "Television and Radio Stars of NBC" series.

The Supporting Players

BEA BENADERET (1906–1968)

Bea appeared as Eve Goodwin from September 5, 1943, to January 5, 1949. Any reliable list of best supporting actresses on radio must have Bea's name near the top. Although often a provoker of laughter with her dialects on other shows, Bea played Eve quite straight as one might expect from a wise school administrator who saw through most of Throckmorton's ploys.

But she also delivered surefire chuckles all over the dial as Gloria on *The Adventures of Ozzie and Harriet*, snooty Millicent Carstairs on *Fibber McGee and Molly*, puzzled Blanche Morton on *Burns and Allen*, impatient Mrs. Anderson on *A Day in the Life of Dennis Day*, and wisecracking Gertrude Gearshift on *The Jack Benny Program*. In 1950 she had her only chance to star in a radio series on the short-lived *Granby's Green Acres*.

When Burns and Allen moved to television in 1950, Bea went along with George and Gracie, although her most memorable TV roles came later as Pearl Bodine on *The Beverly Hillbillies* and Kate Bradley on *Petticoat Junction*.

ARTHUR Q. BRYAN (1899–1959)

Arthur Q. Bryan handled the clippers as crafty barber Floyd Munson from December 20, 1942 to 1955. Bryan's most memorable radio part was as Doctor George Gamble who traded barbs with the Squire of Wistful Vista on *Fibber McGee and Molly* from 1943 to 1956. Bryan's lone starring role was the title character of one of radio's "lost" comedies, *Major Hoople*. Bryan had a soft spot in his pudgy heart for the part of the truth-stretching blowhard,

Bea Benaderet in a thoughtful pose appropriate for perceptive principal Eve Goodwin.

The Jolly Boys (Arthur Q. Bryan, Ken Christy, Hal Peary, Earle Ross, and Richard LeGrand) raising their voices in five-part harmony in this magazine advertisement.

sometimes signing autographed photos "Amos Hoople" above or below his signature.

Other radio roles included Mr. Fuddle on *Blondie*, Rawhide Rolinson on *Red Ryder*, and Walt Levinson on *Richard Diamond, Private Detective*. Arthur also sat in on *Nitwit Court* and *The Grouch Club*.

The Elmer Fudd voice he displayed in the Warner Brothers cartoons went under wrascally names like Wichard Woberts or Waymond Wadcliffe when Bryan dropped in to confuse Milton Berle and Jimmy Durante. Arthur stepped into the control booth in

the summer of 1945 to direct *G.I. Laffs.*

In 1948 Bryan appeared on *Movieland Quiz*, one of the first televised game shows. He also was in the cast of the 1950 sitcom *The Hank McCune Show* (one of the first TV programs to use a laugh track) with radio veterans Sara Berner and Frank Nelson.

If Bryan's name appeared at all in movie credits, it was usually far down the line. However, his bits were usually memorable, such as the seasick Mr. Stanton in *The Road to Rio* and as crabby Mr. McGinty in the Bela Lugosi cheapie, *The Devil Bat.*

KEN CARPENTER (1900–1984)

Most recognizable of the six principal announcers on the program, Carpenter brought Gildersleeve and company into millions of homes from November 8, 1942, to May 27, 1945. Possessor of perhaps the best pipes ever to plug a product, Ken proved to be the Kraftiest pitchman on the air, not only on Sundays from Summerfield during World War II but also on Thursdays from 1936 to 1949 welcoming listeners into *The Kraft Music Hall.* From the Depression to the Space Age the folksy camaraderie between Carpenter and Bing Crosby displayed on four separate programs and three different networks suggests that Ken bantered with Bing longer than the Groaner traveled on the road to laughter with Bob Hope. Sponsors of the popular programs *One Man's Family, The Charlie McCarthy Show,*

Ken Carpenter, best-known of the Gildersleeve announcers, also delivered amiable pitches for cheese on *The Kraft Music Hall* over NBC and for consoles on *Philco Radio Time* over ABC.

and *Lux Radio Theatre* also employed Carpenter's services, and it was his reassuring, familiar voice the men and women serving their country far from home wanted to hear bringing on the stars doing a *Command Performance.*

KEN CHRISTY (1894–1962)

Ken played Chief Gates from October 25, 1942, to 1955. No Jolly Boys song could be called perfect until Christy's resonant bass refrain put an exclamation point on the melody. The voice could be heard just about any time of the day: on daytime soap operas (*The Gallant Heart, Stepmother*), late afternoon or Saturday juvenile fare (*Smilin' Ed's Buster Brown Gang, Jack Armstrong, the All-American Boy*), and primetime comedy (*The Alan Young Show, Meet Mr. McNutley, The Sad Sack*) or drama (*On Stage, Tales of the Texas Rangers*).

Christy's deep voice even became his identifier on television. "Tune in" to the January 25, 1959, episode of *The Jack Benny Program* in which Jack and Ernie Kovacs imagine what the prison of the future will be like and listen rather than look at the warden in that sketch. One almost expects the warden to tell Benny and Kovacs "Now, fellas. Let's all be jolly boys."

RICHARD CRENNA (1926–2003)

Richard assumed the role of Walter "Bronco" Thompson from October 5, 1949, to 1954. If Louise Erickson was entitled to be called teen princess of the airwaves, Crenna should have been crowned adolescent prince along radio row because as Oggie Pringle on *A Date with Judy* and as Walter Denton on *Our*

Richard Crenna played Marjorie's conscientious husband, Bronco Thompson.

Miss Brooks his adenoidal giggles and ejaculations rang the gong of authenticity every week. Crenna turned that adolescent fervor off on Wednesdays by playing Bronco as a level-headed young father who often showed more maturity than Gildersleeve.

On television Crenna appeared in the comedies *Our Miss Brooks* and *The Real McCoys* as well as a serious drama, *Slattery's People*. His notable films included *The Sand Pebbles*, *Body Heat*, and *Wait Until Dark*.

LOUISE ERICKSON (1928–)

Meet Miss Bobby Sox, the title of Louise Erickson's 1944 Columbia film, is perhaps the best way to introduce an actress who excelled at portraying the angst and ardor of teenage girlhood. Louise stepped into the saddle shoes of Marjorie Forrester for four seasons from September 3, 1944 through June 2, 1948. Even before she broke into her teens Erickson was heard on *Dreams of Youth* which prepared her for her role as the star of *A Date with Judy* from 1943 to 1950. It is appropriate that both Louise and Janet Waldo (lead in *Meet Corliss Archer*) played the part of effervescent Emmy Lou on *The Adventures of Ozzie and Harriet* because Erickson and Waldo reigned during the 1940s as the most realistically delightful ingénues on the air. After being heard briefly on *The Alan Young Show* in 1949 and in the 1950 summer series *Granby's Green Acres*, Louise virtually left show business. Her first husband was actor Ben Gazzara.

Her flame burned brightest during her adolescence, but it will outlast the night. It still gives a lovely light.

GALE GORDON (1906–1995)

Gale played the part of Rumson Bullard from May 26, 1948, to March 19, 1952. Gildersleeve frequently referred to Bullard as "a hard man to like." Gordon played the snobbish neighbor perfectly as "the man audiences loved to hate."

Although Gordon let off steam occasionally by calling Gildy a nincompoop, he reserved his major blow-ups for arguments with McGee on his weekly visits as Mayor LaTrivia on *Fibber McGee and Molly*. On other evenings he could be heard as Mr. Judson on *Burns and Allen*, Harry Graves on *Junior Miss*, Clyde Scott on *The Phil Harris–Alice Faye Show*, Rudolph Atterbury on *My*

The part of Rumson Bullard, Gildersleeve's irascible neighbor, was a perfect fit for radio veteran Gale Gordon.

Favorite Husband, John Granby on *Granby's Green Acres*, and, most notably, as the tyrannical principal Osgood Conklin on *Our Miss Brooks*.

From 1953 to 1956 he carried the part of Conklin over to the televised version of *Our Miss Brooks*. Gale's work with Lucille Ball on *My Favorite Husband* blossomed into major roles on the popular *Here's Lucy* and *The Lucy Show*.

RICHARD LEGRAND (1882–1963)

Richard "Dick" LeGrand mouthed the equivocations of pharmacist Richard Q. Peavey from September 13, 1942, to 1957. Already in his sixties when he assumed the role, the part of a wishy-washy mossback seemed a natural for an actor who had seen it all, from the heyday of Lillian Russell to the peak years of Alice Faye. A veteran of vaudeville and stock companies, LeGrand worked his Swedish dialect into early radio appearances and later revived the routine for a continuing role as Ole on *Fibber McGee and Molly* from 1949 to 1953. Speaking in his regular voice, Dick appeared in some spine-tingling episodes of *I Love a Mystery* and *Lights Out*.

LeGrand had a major role in *Gildersleeve on Broadway* and also appeared in *Gildersleeve's Bad Day*, *Gildersleeve's Ghost*, and *Getting Gertie's Garter*.

CATHY LEWIS (1916–1968)

Cathy appeared as Kathryn Milford from September 28, 1949, to September 12, 1951, and as Irene Henshaw from September 29, 1953, to May 26, 1954. When playing nurse Milford and principal Henshaw on *The Great Gildersleeve* or patient Jane Stacy who had to put up with the problems of her roommate on *My Friend Irma*, Cathy left the impression that, even if the intent of the programs was to amuse, her character would not tolerate much funny business.

Although she could be heard on numerous mystery shows such as *Michael Shayne, Suspense, The Whistler, The Adventures of Sam Spade*, and *I Love a Mystery*, Lewis is also fondly remembered for some innovative dramatic shows such as *The Clock* and *On Stage* in which she appeared with husband Elliott Lewis.

Cathy Lewis played two of Gildy's sweethearts, nurse Kathryn Milford and principal Irene Henshaw.

On TV she appeared as Jane Stacy on *My Friend Irma* from 1952 to 1953 and as Molly on the very brief run of *Fibber McGee and Molly* in 1959.

SHIRLEY MITCHELL (1919–)

As southern belle Leila Ransome, Shirley popped in and out of Summerfield from September 20, 1942, to 1957. Her other regular role on radio came during World War II when as Alice Darling she played a bubbly and sometimes bubble-headed war worker rooming from 1943 to 1946 with Fibber McGee and Molly.

Other parts included that of devious Shirley Wirley on *Leave It to Joan* and impatient Honeybee Gillis on *The Life of Riley*, although she also caused some fireworks as Louella, the Rileys' flirtatious neighbor.

Mitchell was cast in regular roles in two TV comedies, *Bachelor Father* and *Please Don't Eat the Daisies*, and also appeared on *I Love Lucy* and occasionally as Clara Appleby on *The Red Skelton Show*. Other TV appearances included *Green Acres*, *Perry Mason*, *My Three Sons*, and *Petticoat Junction*.

LILLIAN RANDOLPH (1898–1980)

Lillian put as much distinctive flavor into the advice she gave as the dishes her character, cook Birdie Lee Coggins, put on the table from September 7, 1941, to 1955. That she participated in church choirs and sang professionally early in her career comes as no surprise to anyone who listens to her stirring renditions of Christmas carols and Easter hymns on *The Great Gildersleeve*. Only Harold Peary stood in the musical spotlight on the program more than the talented Miss Randolph.

In addition to appearing as Madame Queen on *Amos 'n' Andy*, Lillian appeared on *Baby Snooks* and *The Billie Burke Show*. She took over the role of Beulah after Hattie McDaniel left the program and before her sister, Amanda, assumed the part. (Amanda is heard as Birdie on extant *Great Gildersleeve* episodes after 1955.)

Lillian was the only radio cast member to join Willard Waterman on *The Great Gildersleeve* television series. She also played ebullient Madame Queen on the televised version of *Amos 'n'*

In addition to her role as Birdie, Lillian Randolph was heard for a short time as the star of *The Beulah Show.*

Andy. Other TV work included *The Bill Cosby Show*, *Roots*, and *The Jeffersons.*

Randolph had the distinction of being the only member of the regular cast to appear in all four Gildersleeve movies with Harold Peary. Among her other films are *It's a Wonderful Life*, *Up in Arms*, *At the Circus*, and *The Onion Field.*

MARY LEE ROBB (1926–2006)

Mary Lee played Marjorie Forrester after September 8, 1948, although she appeared infrequently after 1953. Having substituted for Louise Erickson on some earlier broadcasts, she seemed a natural replacement when Louise left

the program. Robb's other radio work included such shows as *Burns and Allen*, *Lum and Abner*, and *The Penny Singleton Show.*

EARLE ROSS (1888–1961)

As Judge Horace Hooker, Earle Ross bleated out his opinions from August 31, 1941, to 1954, sounding more like an old goat than a legal eagle. Ross deliberately sharpened his delivery as he developed a perverse cackle, one unmatched this side of *The Hermit's Cave* and *The Witch's Tale.* He could be heard using his normal voice on *Meet Millie*, *Lux Radio Theatre*, *The Mel Blanc Show*, *Point Sublime*, *Michael Shayne*, and *The Billie Burke Show.*

Ross also appeared on the televised version of *Meet Millie* and guested on *I Married Joan* and *Our Miss Brooks.* Even in his early fifties Ross was playing elderly folks on the big screen such as the part of Grandpa in *The Courageous Dr. Christian.* A skeleton in the Earle Ross closet is *A Japanese Pipe Dream*, a 1943 exploitation documentary about Japan's reputed plan to use morphine and heroin to undermine its enemies for which Ross supplied the narration. Perhaps on a dusty shelf in that closet, like a magnum of choice wine, sits a vintage bottle of Kalak Water, Horace Hooker's favorite beverage.

WALTER TETLEY (1915–1975)

Walter appeared as Leroy Forrester for the entire run of *The Great Gildersleeve.* Due to a glandular disorder, Tetley remained, like Leroy, perpetually locked in a preadolescent state of below average height with the vocal capabilities of immature youth. Walter turned

A 1947 caricature of Tetley and Peary by Sam Berman.

imitated Sir Harry Lauder and other Scotsmen with an uncanny ear for impersonation. As a native of New York City, he could affect a Brooklyn dialect as he usually did when confronting Frank Remley and Phil Harris on *The Phil Harris–Alice Faye Show*, sometimes leaving the perplexed pair with the Bronx cheer of "So long, suckers."

This sass master, who also passed muster as the voice of the cartoon character Sherman on *The Bullwinkle Show* (1961–1962), was relegated mainly to bit parts in motion pictures such as the thirsty bellhop who gets the better of Lou Costello's character in *Who Done It?* His only role in any of the Peary films came in *Gildersleeve on Broadway*, again as a bellhop. Just as Tetley's voice was his fortune, his body was his misfortune, particularly after being involved in an accident in 1971 while operating a motorcycle. He never fully recovered and spent his last days in a wheelchair.

Leroy's frequent comment about life's vicissitudes was "Those are the breaks, kid." That kid didn't get enough of the good ones.

LURENE TUTTLE (1907–1986)

Lurene played Marjorie Forrester from the inception of the program through June 25, 1944. When she left the show because she had out-aged

this unusual condition into a career asset as he became a master of playing the "wise beyond his years" smart aleck who could match wits with his elders even if he happened to be older than that actors playing opposite him.

Tetley moved on from ensemble work on children's shows such as *Let's Pretend* and *Coast-to-Coast on a Bus* to step out on his own on *Raising Junior* and *The Fred Allen Show*. Even before Peary assumed the part of McGee's noisy neighbor, Tetley caught his eye and ear on the February 7, 1937, episode of *Fibber McGee and Molly*. Walter's gift for mimicry and for packing lines with significance far exceeding what was in the script made him a natural choice to play the nephew on the audition of *The Great Gildersleeve* in May of 1941.

Although not often called upon to display his talent with dialects when playing Leroy, in his early years Tetley (rather than outgrown) the part, there was no shortage of parts for an actress who could handle comedy and drama with aplomb.

As one of the medium's most dependable performers, she made the rounds at all the usual suspects: *Maisie, Arch Oboler's Plays, Lum and Abner, The Saint, A Date with Judy, Rogue's Gallery, Blondie, CBS Radio Workshop, The Whistler, Big Town, One Man's Family, Night Beat, Dr. Christian, Suspense,* and *Glamour Manor.* Her most memorable role was as Effie Perrine, secretary and confidante to "the greatest detective of them all" on *The Adventures of Sam Spade.* The banter between Tuttle and Howard Duff on that program is one of the great treasures of post-war radio. Her other notable comedic roles included that of Harriet's telephoning mother in *The Adventures of Ozzie and Harriet* and playing Daisy June and Junior's mother on *The Red Skelton Show.* In real life she was wife of actor-announcer Melville Ruick and mother of actress Barbara Ruick.

On television she had continuing roles in *Life with Father, Father of the Bride,* and *Julia.* Her movies included *Ma Barker's Killer Brood* and the Orson Welles version of *Macbeth* in which Lurene played two parts with aplomb, that of gentlewoman and witch.

Appendix B: Gildersleeve in Film and on Television

The Great Gildersleeve in Film

Harold Peary appeared as Gildersleeve in two corn-fed comedies, *Comin' Round the Mountain* (1940) and *Country Fair* (1941), and a pair of movies that revolved around the actions of Edgar Bergen and Fibber McGee and Molly, *Look Who's Laughing* (1941) and *Here We Go Again* (1942). RKO then gave Peary four opportunities to put people in the seats as star: *The Great Gildersleeve, Gildersleeve's Bad Day, Gildersleeve on Broadway*, and *Gildersleeve's Ghost*. Lillian Randolph joined Peary in all four pictures as Birdie. Richard LeGrand, cast in support in three movies, did have a major role in *Gildersleeve on Broadway*, but his masquerade as Gildy's wife and a dress-raising scene out of bad burlesque makes one wonder if the penultimate entry in the series should have been called *Peavey's Bad Day*.

The Great Gildersleeve (1942)

Directed by Gordon Douglas. Screenplay by Jack Townley and Julien Josephson. 62 minutes.

Cast: Harold Peary (Gildersleeve), Jane Darwell (Aunt Emma Forrester), Nancy Gates (Margie), Charles Arnt (Judge Horace Hooker), Freddie Mercer (Leroy), Thurston Hall (Governor Jonathan Stafford), Lillian Randolph (Birdie), Mary Field (Amelia Hooker), George M. Carleton (Frank Powers), John Dilson (Mayor Appleton), George Chandler (Messenger), Syd Saylor (Phil), Herb Vigran (George), Bruce Edwards (Secretary), Fern Emmett (Abigail), Clark Morgan, William J. O'Brien, Broderick O'Farrell, Stanley Price (Country Club Members), Franklyn Farnum (Bystander), Eddie Hall (Motorist), Donald Kerr (Photographer), Anne O'Neal (Martha), Lee Phelps (Bailiff), Lorin Raker (clerk), Russell Wade (Chauffeur)

Gildersleeve runs for his bachelor life from Amelia Hooker, Horace's sister.

Gildersleeve's Bad Day (1943)

Directed by Gordon Douglas. Screenplay by Jack Townley. 62 minutes.

Cast: Harold Peary (Gildersleeve), Jane Darwell (Aunt Emma), Nancy Gates (Margie Forrester), Charles Arnt (Judge Horace Hooker), Freddie Mer-

Only Lillian Randolph (right) appeared in all four Gildersleeve films with Harold Peary.

cer (Leroy Forrester), Russell Wade (Jimmy), Lillian Randolph (Birdie), Frank Jenks (Al), Douglas Fowley (Louie Barton), Alan Carney (Toad), Grant Withers (Henry Potter), Richard LeGrand (J.W. Peavey), Dink Trout (Otis), Harold Landon (George Peabody), Charles Cane (Police Chief), Ken Christy (Bailiff), Joey Ray (Tom), Joan Barclay (Julie Potter), James Clemons Jr. (Peanuts), Morgan Brown, W.J. O'Brien, Ralph Robertson, Lou Davis, Broderick O'Farrell, Eddie Borden, Herbert Berman, Larry Wheat, Richard Bartell (Jurors), Warren Jackson (Joe), Earle Hodgins (Earle), Kernan Cripps (Mason) Fern Emmett (Mrs. Marvin), Lee Phelps (Ryan), Danny Jackson (Messenger Boy), Fred Trowbridge (Defense Attorney), Arthur Loft (Lucas), Jack Rice (Hotel Clerk), Edgar Sherrod (Minister), Ann Summers, Pattie Brill, Barbara Hale, Margie Stewart (Girls at party)

This effort combines crooks with some World War II patriotism. Raising funds for a Canteen sets the stage for Gildy being suspected of taking a bribe during a jury trial. Ken Christy has a bit as a bailiff.

Gildersleeve on Broadway (1943)

Directed by Gordon Douglas. Screenplay by Robert E. Kent. 65 minutes.

Cast: Harold Peary (Gildersleeve), Billie Burke (Mrs. Laura Chandler), Claire Carleton (Francine Gray), Richard LeGrand (Peavey), Freddie Mercer

The one-sheet poster for the final Gildersleeve movie, *Gildersleeve's Ghost* (1944).

(Leroy), Hobart Cavanaugh (Homer), Margaret Landry (Margie), Leonid Kinskey (Window Washer), Ann Doran (Matilda Brown), Lillian Randolph (Birdie), Michael Road (Jimmy Clark), Barbara Hale (Stocking Saleslady), Joseph Bernard (Underwood), Eugene Borden (Pierre), George Carleton (Hawkins), Ken Christy (Detective Delaney), Walter Tetley (Bellhop), Harry Clay (Eddie), Robert Anderson (Clerk), Robert Bice (Eddie), Frank Dawson

(Minister), Eddie Borden (Elevator Operator), Fred Essler (LeMaire), Herbert Evans (Butler), Teddy Infuhr (Stanley), Forrest Lewis (Carson), Charles Miller (Judge), Edmund Mortimer (Party Guest), Jack Norton (Dobrey), Lee Phelps (Clancy), Larry Steers (Pharmacist), Lawrence Tierney (Cab Driver), Larry Wheat (Conventioneer), Barbara Coleman, Rita Corday, Daun Kennedy, Rosemary LaPlanche, Dorothy Malone, Shirley O'Hara, Elaine Riley (Models)

Gildersleeve and Peavey attend a convention of druggists in an effort to save the pharmacist's drugstore in Summerfield. Some measure of the troubles resulting from Gildy's simultaneous romances on radio is conveyed in this picture when Throckmorton is torn between Matilda, Laura, and Francine (and "Jennifer," Peavey in drag). Spotting Christy and Tetley from the radio cast and Forrest Lewis from the TV series is fun as is noting the early appearances of Barbara Hale (future secretary to Perry Mason), Lawrence Tierney (tough guy of film noir), Dorothy Malone (Academy Award–winning actress), and Rosemary LaPlanche (1941 Miss America and minor 1940s movie star).

Gildersleeve's Ghost (1944)

Directed by Gordon Douglas. Screenplay by Robert E. Kent. 63 minutes.

Cast: Harold Peary (Gildersleeve/ Ghost of Jonathan Gildersleeve/Ghost of Randolph Gildersleeve), Marion Martin (Terry Vance), Richard LeGrand (Peavey), Amelita Ward (Marie), Freddie Mercer (Leroy), Margie Stewart (Margie), Marie Blake (Harriet Morgan), Emory Parnell (Police Commissioner Haley), Nicodemus Stewart (Chauncey), Frank Reicher (John Wells), Joseph Vitale (Henry Lennox), Lillian Randolph (Birdie), Dink Trout (Judge Horace Hooker), Charles Gemora (Gorilla), Tom Burton, Harry Clay, Chris Drake, Steve Winston (Reporters), Jack Norton (Drunk), Mary Halsey (Blonde at Rally)

This time Gildersleeve runs for police commissioner with the help of two spirits (also played by Peary). Somehow a gorilla and mad scientists intent on making a blonde invisible are worked into this mixture that is more weird than spooky.

The Great Gildersleeve on TV

The syndicated program starring Willard Waterman ran from September 1955 to September 1956. Unlike the four Gildersleeve films which were written by people who had nothing to do with the radio show, a fair number of the TV scripts were crafted by Andy White and John Elliotte, who had worked on *The Great Gildersleeve* on radio for years. Unfortunately, Randolph was the only member of the radio cast to support Waterman and the replacements did not satisfy like the actors who had originated the roles.

The expectant father episode, for example, that had played so well on October 12, 1949, fizzled on television six years later. The Jolly Boys as portrayed on the small screen acted more like a fraternal group with their "over the head" (and over the top) gesture of membership than friends who met informally to harmonize and enjoy a night out in each other's company. There is no shading of character between Munson (played by Hal Smith), Hooker (Harry Antrim), and Peavey (Forrest Lewis); they are just three figures to hang dialogue on in the drugstore and the hospital waiting room. Conspicuously absent from the video version are Arthur Q. Bryan's sly humor, Earle Ross's pungent wit, and Richard LeGrand's fence-straddling complacency.

Contrary to Waterman's opinion that it was a mistake to emphasize Gildersleeve's ogling on TV, chasing after women had been Throckmorton's modus operandi for years on radio. Gildersleeve loved not wisely but too often and too many at the same time.

Television Credits

Numerous episodes were directed by Charles Barton. Writers included John Elliotte, Andy White, Richard Baer, and Joseph Calvelli.

Cast: Willard Waterman (Gildersleeve), Stephanie Griffin (Marjorie), Ronald Keith (Leroy), Lillian Randolph (Birdie), Harry Antrim (Hooker), Forrest Lewis (Peavey), Hal Smith (Floyd Munson), Carole Mathews (Kathryn Milford), Willis Bouchey (Terwilliger), Robert Foulk (Charlie Anderson), Barbara Stuart (Bessie), Doris Singleton (Lois Kimball), Marion Carr (Amy Miller), Burt Mustin (Foley), Doris Packer (Mrs. Hogan), Raymond Bailey (Fred Fuller).

The 39 Episodes

"Gildy Goes Broke"— Gildy lectures his nephew about spending money on girls, then does the same thing.

"Practice What You Preach"— Throckmorton tries to win his girlfriend back from her other acquaintances.

"Circumstantial Evidence"— Gildy quits as Water Commissioner after being unjustly accused of bribery.

"Gildy Goes Diving"— Throckmorton hopes to impress a girl by diving into the reservoir as a publicity stunt.

"Gildy and the Con Men"— Two con men take advantage of Gildersleeve.

"Gildy Stews about a Cook"— Gildy gets serious about women so Birdie will not give up her marriage plans to take care of the family.

"Gildy, the Private Eye"— Throckmorton is jealous of a detective investigating a burglary of an attractive woman.

"Gildy's Juvenile Delinquent"— Leroy convinces his uncle that another boy was responsible for a prank Leroy pulled.

"Gildy, King of Hearts"— Gildy is engaged to two women.

"One Too Many Secretaries"— Throckmorton gets in trouble when he pretends a girlfriend is his secretary.

"The Raffle"— Blowhard Gildersleeve is in a jam when he fabricates stories about his wealth.

"Water Commissioner's Water Color"— Nosy Gildy investigates the background of Marjorie's boyfriend.

"The Nightmare"— Gildy finds that the fiction he is reading carries over into his dreams.

"Bard of Summerfield"— Gildy borrows verses from the immortals to impress a girlfriend.

"Gildy Goes Hollywood"— Gildersleeve has visions of becoming a star when a movie crew comes to town.

"Golf Ball Incident" — Gildy slices himself a hunk of trouble when an errant shot hits a politician.

"Command Performance" — Throckmorton promotes Leroy as a budding singing star.

"The Quiet One" — Gildersleeve has to keep his mouth shut to join a club.

"Orange Blossoms in Summerfield" — Gildy hopes to get out of a romance by antagonizing the woman's family.

"The Good Scout" — An aunt tries to break up Gildy's latest romance.

"Gildy and the Expectant Father" — Throckmorton and the Jolly Boys try to calm a first-time father.

"Gildy Tangles with Leroy's Teacher" — Gildy talks to Leroy's teacher after the boy complains of too much homework.

"Gildy Loves Well, But Unwisely" — Gildersleeve discovers that he, not Hooker, is the intended target of a vamp.

"Protective Parent" — Throckmorton tries to prevent Marjorie's elopement.

"Birdie's Golden Dream" — Birdie's dream has more significance that Gildersleeve realizes.

"Two Girls, One Birthday" — Gildy tries to spend part of his birthday with two different girls.

"The Whistling Bandit" — Gildersleeve unwittingly helps a bandit but still saves the day.

"Gildy's Dancing Lessons" — Throckmorton falls for Leroy's attractive dancing instructor.

"Marjorie's Apartment" — Marjorie moves into an apartment to get peace and gets chaos instead

"Gildy the Go-Between" — Mediating a domestic brouhaha causes trouble for Gildersleeve.

"Gildy Pulls the Switch" — Throckmorton is on the spot when the mayor blames him for a robbery.

"Gildy's All-American Boy" — Gildersleeve encourages Leroy to copy Huck Finn and build a raft.

"Prisoner of Love" — A widow puts Gildy in a spot where he must choose marriage or his job.

"Gildy Hires an Eager Beaver" — Adding one more person to his staff endangers Gildy's own job.

"The Political Plum" — Throckmorton learns that in order to get an important position he must get married.

"Gildy's Efficiency Kick" — Gildersleeve wants to head a committee to make the city hall more efficient.

"Calling Dr. Bergstrom" — The pretty doctor Gildersleeve falls for sends him to the hospital.

"The Deed" — A crook tries to convince Gildersleeve he, not the city, owns the reservoir.

"Beauties and the Beast" — Two girlfriends want Gildy to act as witness to an incident in a beauty shop.

Appendix C:
Alphabetical List of Episodes

"Acting Mayor"— February 4, 1948

"Acting Police Commissioner"— March 30, 1949

"Adeline Fairchild Arrives"— February 18, 1948

"Adopting an Orphan"— December 4, 1946

"Advice about Ronny"— September 9, 1953

"After School Activities"— October 3, 1943

"Alone on Christmas"— December 24, 1952

"Ancestry"— March 24, 1946

"Ann Tuttle Returns"— January 7, 1948

"Anniversary Gift"— May 6, 1953

"Anniversary of First Date"— October 17, 1951

"Announcing Engagement"— November 3, 1948

"Annual Dinner with Hooker"— February 10, 1954

"Anonymous Valentine"— February 13, 1944

"Antique Vase"—1955–1957

"Apartment Upstairs"— April 5, 1950

"Appointed Water Commissioner"— October 18, 1942

"Arbor Day Speaker"— April 23, 1944

"Athletic Sham"— October 22, 1952

"Aunt Hattie Arrives"— January 28, 1945

"Aunt Hattie Back Again"— May 26, 1954

"Aunt Hattie Becomes Stubborn"— February 4, 1945

"Aunt Hattie Stays On"— February 18, 1945

"Aunt Hattie Visits Again"— October 13, 1948

"Authority Over Leroy"— November 11, 1953

"Babs Frustrates Romance"— October 21, 1951

"Babysitting Ronny"— September 23, 1953

"Babysitting the Twins"— March 28, 1951

"Bachelor Dinner"— June 20, 1943

"Balancing Checkbook"— March 5, 1944

"Bank Robber"— April 14, 1946

"Barbara Ann Visits"— December 7, 1941

"Baseball Field"— April 7, 1948

"Bean Contest"— June 18, 1952

"Behaving Badly, Making Up"— September 10, 1947

"Behind the Times"— March 10, 1954

"Ben Returns from Navy"— January 6, 1946

"Ben Sells Insurance"— January 13, 1946

"Best Dressed Racket"— March 15, 1941

"Bird Watcher's Club"— November 26, 1952

"Birdie to Train Voice"— November 15, 1950

"Birdie Visits Relatives"— December 13, 1942

"Birdie Works for Judge Hooker"— November 9, 1941

"Competition from Hooker"— September 27, 1943

"Concerned About Schoolwork"— February 3, 1954

"Concert Date"— February 18, 1953

"Concert Pianist"— November 28, 1943

"Conflicting Party Engagements"— April 6, 1949

"Confronting Leroy's Teacher"— May 21, 1947

"Considers Marrying Kathryn"— March 15, 1950

"Considers Political Career"— February 17, 1954

"Considers Virtues of Marriage"— March 10, 1948

"Couple Buying a Lot"— November 7, 1951

"Courting Amelia Hooker"— June 28, 1942

"Cousin Emily Visits"— August 27, 1952

"Cowboy Singer"— May 7, 1952

"Craig's Birthday Party"— May 7, 1947

"Cuts Elm Tree"— April 12, 1942

"Cutting Back on Gifts"— December 15, 1948

"Dancing Class"— January 22, 1947

"Date with Dolores"— December 3, 1944

"Dating Leila and Grace"— January 28, 1953

"Dating Principal and Teacher"— October 14, 1953

"Dating Two Women"— October 8, 1952

"Defense Stamps in Book"— March 8, 1942

"Diet Bet"— January 4, 1942

"Dieting Again"— March 7, 1943

"Dinner for Clarence"— May 12, 1954

"Dinner for Eve's Mother"— June 11, 1944

"Dinner with Kathryn"— January 18, 1950

"Dinner with Miss Piper"— April 2, 1947

"Diplomat"— February 3, 1946

"Disappearing Gifts"— December 8, 1948

"Dismissing Bessie"— February 26, 1947

"Displaced Person"— January 11, 1950

"Diving into Reservoir"— April 23, 1952

"Double Date with Bullard"— December 27, 1950

"Double Date with Marjorie"— October 5, 1949

"Dreams of Trial"— January 7, 1945

"Drives Mercedes"— May 26, 1948

"Driving Test"— September 17, 1952

"Driving to Fairview"— January 11, 1942

"Duck Dinner"— December 3, 1952

"Early Snow"— October 11, 1942

"Easter Egg Hunt"— April 5, 1942

"Easter Rabbits"— April 25, 1943

"Easter Sunrise Service"— April 9, 1952

"Easter Sunrise Service" (Repeat)— April 1, 1953

"Economizing"— October 1, 1952

"Election Bet"— November 5, 1944

"Election Day"— June 25, 1944

"Election Day for Bullard"— November 1, 1950

"Electrical Wizard"— October 21, 1953

"Engaged to Eve"— April 30, 1944

"Engaged to Leila"— January 3, 1943

"Engaged to Two Women"— November 10, 1948

"Engagement Ring Confusion"— February 13, 1952

"Engagement Strategy"— January 14, 1945

"Estate Report"— April 7, 1946

"European Vacation Plans"— May 13, 1953

"Eve's Mother Arrives"— June 4, 1944

"Eve's Mother Stays On"— June 18, 1944

"Expectant Father"— October 12, 1949

"Expensive Christmas Presents"— December 26, 1951

"Facing Old Age"— January 27, 1946

"Family Christmas"— December 22, 1948

"Family Together Again"— September 3, 1944

"Family Vacation Stalls"— May 30, 1951

"Fire Engine Committee"— January 31, 1943

"Fired"— June 2, 1948

"Job for Bronco"— November 16, 1949
"Job Hunting"— October 15, 1944
"Jolly Boys Band"— November 23, 1949
"Jolly Boys Election"— February 22, 1950
"Jolly Boys Fall Out"— November 18, 1945
"Jolly Boys Formed"— October 8, 1944
"Jolly Boys Invaded"— March 24, 1948
"Jolly Boys or Singer?"— March 14, 1951
"Jolly Boys Picnic"— July 1, 1945
"Jolly Boys Picnic" (Repeat)— June 9, 1946
"Jolly Boys Rent Trailer"— April 26, 1950
"Jolly Boys Speak Candidly"— October 3, 1951
"Katie Lee Returns"— June 4, 1952
"Keystone Club"— February 21, 1943
"Kitchenware Salesman"— April 28, 1948
"Labor Day at Grass Lake"— September 2, 1945
"Laughing Coyote Ranch"—1955–1957
"Lawsuit against Bullard"— May 25, 1949
"Leaving Wistful Vista for Summerfield (Audition)"— May 16, 1941
"Leaving Wistful Vista for Summerfield"— August 31, 1941
"Leila and Grace Squabble"— February 4, 1953
"Leila as New Secretary"— June 3, 1945
"Leila Back Again"— January 8, 1947
"Leila Hears a Prowler"— March 18, 1945
"Leila Instead of P.T.A."— September 25, 1946
"Leila Leaves Summerfield"— October 9, 1946
"Leila May Close Shop"— February 16, 1949
"Leila Returns"— September 26, 1943
"Leila Returns Again"— September 23, 1945
"Leila Returns Yet Again"— January 7, 1953
"Leila's New Suitor"— May 12, 1946
"Leila's Party"— April 22, 1945
"Leila's Sister Visits"— February 7, 1943
"Leila's Wedding Invitation"— October 2, 1946
"Leroy Arrested"— March 17, 1946

"Leroy Arrested" (Revised Version)— March 12, 1947
"Leroy Behaves Too Well"— February 14, 1951
"Leroy Behaves Too Well" (Repeat)— August 6, 1952
"Leroy Breaks a Vase"— October 14, 1945
"Leroy Buys Goat"— April 12, 1950
"Leroy Gets Independence"— February 27, 1952
"Leroy Hosts Ethel"— May 19, 1946
"Leroy Intimidated by Bully"— December 11, 1946
"Leroy Is Sick"— February 17, 1946
"Leroy Jealous of Baby"— September 22, 1948
"Leroy Keeps Bees"— April 16, 1952
"Leroy Likes Jo McCoy"— September 2, 1953
"Leroy Likes Wendy"— January 20, 1954
"Leroy Makes Nitroglycerin"— December 27, 1942
"Leroy Moves Next Door"— March 11, 1953
"Leroy Runs Away"— February 1, 1942
"Leroy Shy with Girls"— March 3, 1948
"Leroy Sells Newspapers"— December 1, 1948
"Leroy Sells Trees"— December 12, 1951
"Leroy Stays with Hooker"— October 10, 1951
"Leroy Studies with Babs"— November 28, 1951
"Leroy Suspended from School"— September 16, 1945
"Leroy Suspicious of Marie"— April 21, 1954
"Leroy Treats Brenda"— March 2, 1949
"Leroy Visits Aunt Hattie"— July 29, 1953
"Leroy Wants a Horse"— April 28, 1946
"Leroy Wants a Scooter"— December 18, 1946
"Leroy Wants a Watch"— October 15, 1952
"Leroy's Big Dog"— December 18, 1941

"Meets Gloria McKinley"— June 25, 1952
"Meets Grace Tuttle"— November 12, 1952
"Meets Irene's Father"— January 6, 1954
"Meets Katie Lee"— January 24, 1951
"Meets Leila Ransome"— September 20, 1942
"Meets Kathryn Milford"— September 28, 1949
"Meets Marie"— March 17, 1954
"Meets Marvin's Aunt"— July 8, 1953
"Meets Miss Tuttle"— October 8, 1947
"Meets Mona Buckley"— January 30, 1952
"Meets Paula Winthrop"— September 19, 1951
"Meets Thelma Scott"— April 28, 1954
"Memories of Leila"— May 26, 1946
"Millionaire Friend"— May 11, 1949
"Minding the Baby"— November 2, 1941
"Missing Cuff Links"— November 19, 1952
"Money Woes"— October 23, 1946
"Moose Hunting"— November 21, 1943
"More Discipline"— September 11, 1946
"Motor for Bike"— May 28, 1952
"Mountain Climbing"— November 8, 1950
"Moving Day"— May 21, 1952
"Mysterious Disappearance"— January 9, 1952
"Mystery Baby"— September 8, 1948
"Mystery Singer"— May 10, 1942
"Naming the Baby"— September 29, 1948
"Nature Hike"— April 18, 1943
"Needy Children's Christmas"— December 23, 1953
"New Bed for Marjorie"— January 18, 1942
"New Car or College?"— February 10, 1946
"New Neighbor"— November 30, 1949
"New Neighbors"— March 22, 1942
"New Parents May Leave"— April 11, 1951
"New Piano Teacher"— March 26, 1947
"New School Principal"— September 5, 1943
"New Secretary Hazel"— September 20, 1950
"New Secretary Zelda"— March 23, 1949
"New Year, New Man"— January 2, 1944
"New Year's Eve"— December 31, 1944
"New Year's Eve at Home"— December 30, 1945
"New Year's Eve Ball"— January 1, 1947
"New Year's Eve Hayride"— December 28, 1949
"New Year's Eve Reminiscing"— December 30, 1953
"New Year's Eve with Hooker"— December 31, 1947
"Night at the Opera"— December 16, 1945
"Oak Tree Problem"— November 14, 1951
"Office Help"— March 4, 1953
"Old Flame Violet"— March 25, 1945
"Old High School Friend"— February 12, 1947
"Oliver Visits"— October 26, 1941
"Opera Committee Chairman"— December 9, 1945
"Opera Sponsor"— December 2, 1945
"Operetta Star in Town"— November 29, 1942
"Organizing Work"— September 17, 1947
"Pal to Leroy"— November 1, 1942
"Palm Reader a Fraud?"— January 20, 1946
"Paula Winthrop Returns"— March 3, 1954
"Peavey–Gildersleeve Feud"— February 25, 1953
"Peavey Missing"— May 14, 1947
"Peavey's Day Off"— February 7, 1951
"Petition"— April 21, 1946
"Phone Problems"— October 19, 1944
"Piano Pledge"— September 27, 1950
"Picnic with Joanne"— April 9, 1947
"Picnic with the Thompsons"— March 22, 1950
"Pig for a Pet"— April 8, 1945
"Pig in the House"— April 1, 1945
"Planning Political Platform"— April 2, 1944
"Planting a Tree"— October 4, 1942

"Study Habits"— November 20, 1946

"Studying for Advancement"— October 22, 1947

"Substitute Secretary"— February 19, 1947

"Sulking in Room"— December 17, 1947

"Summer Theater Play"— June 14, 1942

"Summerfield 1903"— March 9, 1949

"Swimming at Grass Lake"— June 24, 1953

"Takes Bessie to Dance"— December 9, 1953

"Takes Singing Lessons"— February 23, 1949

"Takes Up Writing"— January 5, 1949

"Tchaikovsky Love Story"— April 30, 1947

"Teaching Auto Mechanics"— February 8, 1942

"Television Comes to Summerfield"— March 26, 1952

"Testimonial Dinner for Hooker"— May 24, 1942

"Testing Political Waters"— March 12, 1944

"Thanksgiving Dinner"— November 22, 1942

"Three Dates for Dance"— May 24, 1942

"Tom Sawyer Raft"— November 26, 1947

"Toothache"— December 6, 1942

"Torn Between Leila and Eve"— May 14, 1944

"Training Younger Man"— January 26, 1949

"Treats Birdie with Kindness"— February 28, 1948

"Trip to Omaha"— March 12, 1952

"Turns Off Water"— September 18, 1946

"Twins Born"— February 21, 1951

"Twins Come Home"— March 7, 1951

"Two Dates for Hayride"— November 5, 1947

"Two Dates for Party"— February 11, 1953

"Unpaid Water Bill"— December 5, 1943

"Vacation at Grass Lake"— August 29, 1943

"Valentine Prank"— February 14, 1943

"Wall Between Houses"— June 14, 1952

"War Bond Drive"— September 12, 1943

"Water Commissioner Again"— October 29, 1944

"Water Department Calendar"— November 22, 1950

"Water Shut Off"—19557–1957

"Waterworks Breaks Down"— October 4, 1943

"Wedding Day"— June 27, 1943

"Wedding Imminent"— December 29, 1948

"Wedding List"— May 9, 1943

"Wedding Shower for Leila"— June 6, 1943

"Wedding Witness"— May 27, 1953

"Weight Reduction Plan"— October 18, 1950

"Weight Reduction Plan" (Repeat)— August 13, 1952

"Welfare Investigator"— October 6, 1948

"Whole Town Is Talking"— April 16, 1947

"Wilbur Cosgrove Lookalike"— April 2, 1952

"Windfall"— May 20, 1945

"Winning the War"— September 13, 1942

"Winter Sports"—1955–1957

"Witness to Accident"— October 28, 1953

"Woman on the Bus"— May 4, 1949

"Women's Club Speaker"— January 17, 1943

"Wooing Banker's Son"— September 24, 1944

"Worried about Duel"— March 17, 1948

"Wrapping Christmas Presents"— December 23, 1945

Appendix D: Notable Occurrences

First Appearances

CAST

Ben Alexander, August 30, 1942

Robert Armbruster as musical director, September 6, 1950

Jim Bannon as announcer, August 31, 1941

Bea Benaderet, August 29, 1943

Arthur Q. Bryan, December 7, 1941

Ken Carpenter as announcer, November 8, 1942

Ken Christy, September 28, 1941

Richard Crenna, January 21, 1945

Louise Erickson, September 3, 1944

Gale Gordon, November 12, 1947

John Hiestand as announcer, March 15, 1950

John Laing as announcer, September 2, 1945

Richard LeGrand, April 26, 1942

Cathy Lewis, September 28, 1949

Jack Meakin as musical director, September 2, 1945

Una Merkel, February 18, 1948

William Randolph Mills, aka Billy Mills, as musical director, August 31, 1941

Shirley Mitchell, September 21, 1941

Harold Peary, August 31, 1941

Lillian Randolph, September 7, 1941

Mary Lee Robb, September 8, 1948

Earle Ross, August 31, 1941

Verne Smith as announcer, June 3, 1945

Jay Stewart as announcer, September 21, 1949

Claude Sweeten as musical director, March 14, 1943

Walter Tetley, August 31, 1941

Lurene Tuttle, August 31, 1941

John Wald, December 16, 1945; as principal Kraft announcer, September 10, 1947

Willard Waterman, May 18, 1947

CHARACTERS

Bessie (played by Pauline Drake), January 17, 1943

Bessie (played by Gloria Holliday), January 13, 1946

Birdie Lee Coggins, September 7, 1941

Craig Bullard, May 13, 1945

Rumson Bullard, April 29, 1945

Rumson Bullard (played by Gale Gordon), May 26, 1948

Adeline Fairchild, February 18, 1948

Leroy Forrester, August 31, 1941

Marjorie Forrester (played by Lurene Tuttle), August 31, 1941

Marjorie Forrester (played by Louise
Erickson), September 3, 1944
Marjorie Forrester (played by Mary
Lee Robb), September 8, 1948
Chief Gates, October 25, 1942
Throckmorton P. Gildersleeve (played
by Harold Peary), August 31, 1941
Throckmorton P. Gildersleeve (played
by Willard Waterman), September 6,
1950
Eve Goodwin (played by Bea Bena-
deret), September 5, 1943
Irene Henshaw, September 30, 1953
Horace Hooker, August 31, 1941
Brenda Knickerbocker (played by
Barbara Whiting), March 2, 1949
Kathryn Milford, September 28, 1949
Floyd Munson, September 27, 1942
Floyd Munson (played by Arthur Q.
Bryan), December 20, 1942
Richard Peavey, September 13, 1942
Leila Ransome, September 20, 1942
Terwilliger (played by Stan Farrar),
October 1, 1947

A Kraft jar cover that promoted the show
even in the refrigerator.

Bronco Thompson, October 5, 1949
Ben Waterford, February 14, 1943

First Scripts by Writers

John Elliotte and Andy White, Septem-
ber 17, 1947
Leonard Levinson, August 31, 1941
Sam Moore as co-writer with John
Whedon, January 17, 1943
Jack Robinson and Gene Stone, Sep-
tember 10, 1947
Paul West, February 12, 1947
John Whedon, August 30, 1942

First Sayings

BY GILDERSLEEVE
"This is going to be one of my bad
days," February 22, 1942
"Leroy!" September 6, 1942

BY LEROY
"Are you kiddin'?" October 4, 1942
"Ha!" June 17, 1945; first full-blown
"Ha!" January 6, 1946
"Oh, for corn's Sake!" May 3, 1942
"What a character!" May 9, 1943

MISCELLANEA
First episode in which Peary's laugh
no longer opens the show, Sep-
tember 8, 1948
First Wednesday evening broadcast,
September 11, 1946
First time Gildersleeve sings, Octo-
ber 5, 1941
Formation of Jolly Boys, October 8,
1944
Only episode Peary missed due to
illness, December 17, 1947

Top: In 1949 listeners could get their own record of Gildersleeve's Song for 25 cents.
Bottom: The winning names in this 1951 contest were Ronald Lynn and Rhonda Linda.

Appendix E: Ratings and Rankings Summary

Season	Rating	Ranking
1941–1942	12.7	Not among top 20 shows
1942–1943	18.0	Not among top 20 shows
1943–1944	16.0	Not among top 20 shows
1944–1945	16.3	Not among top 20 shows
1945–1946	19.7	11th
1946–1947	16.9	Not among top 20 shows
1947–1948	16.4	Not among top 20 shows
1948–1949	14.9	Not among top 20 shows
1949–1950	15.3	Not among top 20 shows
1950–1951	10.3	Not among top 20 shows
1951–1952	8.1	Not among top 20 shows
1952–1953	7.6	13th
1953–1954	5.8	Not among top 20 shows
1954–1955	3.6	Not among top 20 shows
1955–1956	3.2	Not among top 20 shows

RATINGS OF CBS COMPETITOR

1941–1942	10.6	*Melody Ranch*
1942–1943	9.7	*Melody Ranch*
1943–1944	6.4	*America in the Air*
1944–1945	11.6	*Baby Snooks*
1945–1946	14.8	*Baby Snooks*
1946–1947	13.5	*Dr. Christian*
1947–1948	12.5	*Dr. Christian*
1948–1949	9.8	*Dr. Christian*
1949–1950	17.0	*Dr. Christian*
1950–1951	12.7	*Dr. Christian*
1951–1952	10.0	*Dr. Christian*

RATINGS OF CBS COMPETITOR *(continued)*

| 1952–1953 | 6.6 | *Dr. Christian* |
| 1953–1954 | No rating given | *21st Precinct* |

Rankings are Hooper through the 1948–1949 season, Nielsen beginning with the 1949–1950 season.

SOURCE: Summers, Harrison B., ed. *A Thirty-Year History of Programs Carried on National Radio Networks in the United States 1926–1956* (New York: Arno Press, 1971).

Bibliography

Bartlett, John. *Bartlett's Familiar Quotations.* 17th edition. Boston: Little, Brown, 2002.

Brooks, Elston. *I've Heard Those Songs Before.* New York: Morrow Quill, 1981.

DeLong, Thomas. *Radio Stars.* Jefferson, NC: McFarland, 1996.

Dunning, John. *On the Air: The Encyclopedia of Old-Time Radio.* New York: Oxford University Press, 1998.

Fetrow, Alan. *Feature Films, 1940–1949.* Jefferson, NC: McFarland, 1994.

Gaver, Jack, and Dave Stanley. *There's Laughter in the Air!* New York: Greenberg, 1945.

Gildy's Scrapbook. Boalsburg, PA: BearManor, 2003.

Great Gildersleeve scripts, 1942–1954. Microfilm Collection. Madison: Wisconsin State Historical Society, 1970.

"The Great Gildersleeve TV Series." http://www.imdb.com/title/tt0047735/.

Hickerson, Jay. *The 2nd Revised Ultimate History of Network Radio Programming and Guide to All Circulating Shows.* Hamden, CT: Hickerson, 2001.

Lee, Katie. *Sandstone Seduction.* Boulder, CO: Johnson Books, 2004.

New York Times "Radio Today" Listings, 1941–1957. http://www.jjonz.us/RadioLogs/.

"O-h-h, Leroy." *Tune In* (July 1943), 17–19.

Price, Michael H., and George E. Turner. *Forgotten Horrors 2.* Baltimore: Midnight Marquee Press, 2001.

Price, Michael H., John Wooley, and George E. Turner. *Forgotten Horrors 3.* Baltimore: Midnight Marquee Press, 2003.

Salomonson, Terry. *The Great Gildersleeve: A Radio Broadcast Log of the Comedy Program.* Howell, MI: Salomonson, 1997.

Schaden, Chuck. *Speaking of Radio.* Morton Grove, IL: Nostalgia Digest Press, 2003.

Schulz, Clair. "Brush Up Your Gildersleeve." *Old Time Radio Digest* (September/October 1997), 8–11.

_____. *Fibber McGee and Molly: On the Air 1935–1959.* Albany, GA: BearManor, 2008.

Sterling, Christopher, ed. *The Museum of Broadcast Communications Encyclopedia of Radio.* New York: Fitzroy Dearborn, 2004.

Stumpf, Charles, and Ben Ohmart. *The Great Gildersleeve.* Boalsburg, PA: BearManor, 2002.

Summers, Harrison B., ed. *A Thirty-Year History of Programs Carried on National Radio Networks in the United States 1926–1956.* New York: Arno Press, 1971.

"Tiresome Taxes Throw Throckmorton." *Radio Life* (March 14, 1948), 4–5.

Index

Numbers in **bold italics** indicate pages with photographs.